READING PUTNAM

Hilary Putnam is one of the world's leading philosophers. His highly original and often provocative ideas have set the agenda for a variety of debates in philosophy of science, philosophy of mind and philosophy of language. His now famous philosophical thought experiments, such as the 'Twin earth' and 'the brains in the vat' have become part of the established canon in philosophy and cognitive science.

Reading Putnam is an outstanding overview and assessment of Hilary Putnam's work by a team of international contributors, and includes replies by Putnam himself. Divided into clear sections, it contains chapters on key aspects of Putnam's large body of writing, including:

- scientific realism and the changes that Putnam's thought has undergone on this topic;
- analyticity and ontology, including the important interconnections between the views of Putnam and Quine;
- Putnam's arguments concerning externalist views of meaning and reference, questions of conceptual relativity, and his preoccupation with ethics through a denial of the fact–value dichotomy;
- Putnam's developing views on perception.

Offering an excellent survey of Putnam's work *Reading Putnam* is essential for those studying philosophy of mind, philosophy of language, and philosophy of science, as well as for anyone interested in contemporary philosophy.

Contributors: David Albert, Maria Baghramian, Ned Block, Richard Boyd, Tyler Burge, Stanley Cavell, Michael Devitt, Russell Goodman, David Macarthur, John McDowell, Axel Mueller, Charles Parsons, Ruth Anna Putnam, and Charles Travis.

Hilary Putnam is Cogan University Professor Emeritus at Harvard University, USA. He is the author of eighteen books and numerous articles. His work has been instrumental in furthering research in philosophy of mind, philosophy of language, philosophy of science and mathematics.

Maria Baghramian is currently the Head of the School of Philosophy at University College Dublin, Ireland and the editor of the *International Journal of Philosophical Studies*. She is a member of the Royal Irish Academy.

READING PUTNAM

Edited by
Maria Baghramian

Routledge
Taylor & Francis Group

LONDON AND NEW YORK

First published 2013
by Routledge
2 Park Square, Milton Park, Abingdon, Oxon, OX14 4RN

Simultaneously published in the USA and Canada
by Routledge
270 Madison Ave, New York, NY 10016

Routledge is an imprint of the Taylor & Francis Group, an informa business

© 2013 Maria Baghramian for selection and editorial matter; individual contributors for their contributions.

All rights reserved. No part of this book may be reprinted or reproduced or utilised in any form or by any electronic, mechanical, or other means, now known or hereafter invented, including photocopying and recording, or in any information storage or retrieval system, without permission in writing from the publishers.

Trademark notice: Product or corporate names may be trademarks or registered trademarks, and are used only for identification and explanation without intent to infringe.

British Library Cataloguing in Publication Data
A catalogue record for this book is available from the British Library

Library of Congress Cataloging-in-Publication Data
Reading Putnam / edited by Maria Baghramian.
  p.cm.
  Includes bibliographical rferences and index.
  1. Putnam, ilary. I. Baghramian, Maria.
  B945.P874R425 2012
  191–dc23
  2012001958

ISBN: 978-0-415-53006-4 (hbk)
ISBN: 978-0-415-53007-1 (pbk)
ISBN: 978-0-203-11709-5 (ebk)

Typeset in Goudy
by Taylor & Francis Books

Printed and bound in Great Britain by
CPI Group (UK) Ltd, Croydon, CR0 4YY

CONTENTS

List of figures	viii
Acknowledgements	ix
Contributors	x
Introduction: a life in philosophy MARIA BAGHRAMIAN	1

Prologue   17

From quantum mechanics to ethics and back again   19
HILARY PUTNAM

I   The enigma of realism   37

1   What of pragmatism with the world here?   39
RICHARD BOYD

Comments on Richard Boyd   95
HILARY PUTNAM

2   Hilary and me: tracking down Putnam on the realism issue   101
MICHAEL DEVITT

Comments on Michael Devitt   121
HILARY PUTNAM

3   Putnam and the philosophical appeal to common sense   127
DAVID MACARTHUR

Comments on David Macarthur   140
HILARY PUTNAM

II On what there is 143

4 Putnam versus Quine on revisability and the analytic–synthetic distinction 145
AXEL MUELLER

Comments on Axel Mueller 179
HILARY PUTNAM

5 Putnam on existence and ontology 182
CHARLES PARSONS

Comments on Charles Parsons 202
HILARY PUTNAM

6 Some sources of Putnam's pluralism 205
RUSSELL B. GOODMAN

Comments on Russell Goodman 219
HILARY PUTNAM

7 Physics and narrative 225
DAVID Z. ALBERT

Comments on David Albert 237
HILARY PUTNAM

8 Hilary Putnam's moral philosophy 240
RUTH ANNA PUTNAM

Comments on Ruth Anna Putnam 257
HILARY PUTNAM

III Perception 261

9 Some remarks on "externalisms" 263
TYLER BURGE

Comments on Tyler Burge 272
HILARY PUTNAM

10 Wittgenstein and qualia 275
NED BLOCK

Comments on Ned Block . . . 319
HILARY PUTNAM

11 Affording us the world . . . 322
CHARLES TRAVIS

12 Concepts in perceptual experience: Putnam and Travis . . . 341
JOHN MCDOWELL

Comments on Travis and McDowell . . . 347
HILARY PUTNAM

IV Epilogue . . . 359

13 On Nietzschean perfectionism . . . 361
STANLEY CAVELL

Index . . . 376

LIST OF FIGURES

10.1 *Question-begging inverted spectrum scenario.* The captions express the way things look to the subject at each stage in terms of the existence of ways of looking, R and G. R is the way the red tomato looks to the subject at Stage 1. G is the way the red tomato looks to the subject at Stages 2, 3, and 4   294
10.2 Version of the inverted spectrum scenario that is not question-begging, but which violates the Principle of Normality. The same events are depicted as in Figure 10.1, but described without explicit mention of the ways things look or of 'R' and 'G'. The focus is on the colors that things look to have.   297
10.3 Version of the inverted spectrum scenario in which ways are introduced at Stage 4   298
10.4 The phenomenal realist contrasted with the memory skeptic   304
10.5 The bottom two hypotheses from Figure 10.4 elaborated   305
10.6 The top figure is the same as in Figure 10.5. The bottom figure illustrates a different sort of memory skeptic   306
10.7 Early thermometer   310

ACKNOWLEDGEMENTS

A majority of the chapters in this volume were delivered at a conference marking Hilary Putnam's 80th birthday at University College Dublin in March 2007. The conference was made possible with grants from UCD Seed Funding, Mind Association, and the Analysis Trust. I was grateful to receive a Publications Scheme Grant from the National University of Ireland and a UCD President's Fellowship for this project. I would like to express my thanks to Helen Kenny whose hard work ensured the success of the conference. Graduate students in UCD School of Philosophy gave enthusiastic assistance throughout the event and Fionn Dempsey took on the extraordinarily difficult task of transcribing and editing large parts of the conference proceedings from recordings. I am extremely grateful. I also benefitted greatly from the comments of two anonymous referees on a much earlier draft. The contributors to the volume showed patience and forbearance in the lengthy process of realizing this publication project. It has been a pleasure and privilege to know Hilary and Ruth Anna Putnam. Above else, my thanks go to the late and much missed Garret FitzGerald who gave me the idea of marking Hilary Putnam's 80th birthday and as the Chancellor of the National University of Ireland gave support to the event. The book is dedicated to his memory with love and admiration.

CONTRIBUTORS

David Albert is Frederick E. Woodbridge Professor of Philosophy at Columbia University, USA

Maria Baghramian is Associate Professor and Head of the School of Philosophy at University College Dublin, Ireland

Ned Block is Silver Professor of Philosophy, Psychology and Neural Science at New York University, USA

Richard Boyd is Susan Linn Sage Professor of Philosophy at Cornell University, USA

Tyler Burge is Distinguished Professor of Philosophy at University of California Los Angeles, USA

Stanley Cavell is Emeritus Walter M. Cabot Professor of Aesthetics and the General Theory of Value at Harvard, USA

Michael Devitt is Distinguished Professor of Philosophy, The Graduate Center, The City University of New York, USA

Russell Goodman is Regent's Professor of Philosophy at the University of New Mexico, USA

David Macarthur is Senior Lecturer in Philosophy in the University of Sydney, Australia

John McDowell is University Professor of Philosophy at the University of Pittsburgh, USA

Axel Mueller is Senior Lecturer in Philosophy, Northwestern University, USA

Charles Parsons is Emeritus Edgar Pierce Professor of Philosophy at Harvard, USA

Ruth Anna Putnam is Emeritus Professor of Philosophy at Wellesley College, USA

Charles Travis is Professor of Philosophy at King's College London, UK

INTRODUCTION
A life in philosophy

Maria Baghramian

Hilary Putnam, without doubt, is one of the most innovative and influential philosophers of our time. However, the breadth and variety of his philosophical contributions have made the task of summarizing and evaluating the full span of his work difficult, if not impossible. The present volume brings together articles by Putnam and thirteen other philosophers, many of them former students and colleagues, on central themes from his work. The papers, with a few exceptions, were first delivered at a conference in University College Dublin in March 2007, marking Hilary Putnam's 80th birthday.[1] The volume reflects the prevailing atmosphere where participants acknowledged not just the importance of Putnam's work, but also his enormous impact, as a colleague and teacher, on stimulating and shaping the thinking of several generations of philosophers in America and elsewhere. Accordingly, the collection not only engages with the work of a great philosopher, providing an overview and analysis of his thinking over several decades, but it also offers original contributions to ongoing philosophical debates in a number of areas.

Putnam, almost uniquely among the philosophical greats, is willing to rethink his views continuously and to reengage with the issues that have preoccupied him for six decades. Yet, a number of prominent themes run through his philosophical life. The question of realism, an insistence on the essential role of objectivity in characterizing truth and knowledge, preoccupation with questions of intentionality, opposition to a variety of positions arising out of logical positivism, a continuous concern with questions of norms and values, and an aversion to dichotomized thinking are constant themes. The present volume sheds light on some of these issues in their various permutations. In doing so, it offers ways of reading and re-reading Putnam and his impact on philosophy, an exercise to which Putnam contributes fully, in the Prologue, by reassessing his own philosophical positions and their development, and through responses to the individual contributors to the book.

I. A life in philosophy[2]

Hilary Whitehall Putnam was born on July 31, 1926 in Chicago, Illinois. His father, Samuel Putnam, a prolific translator, literary editor, and reporter, is probably best known for his landmark translation of *Don Quixote* (1949). His mother, Riva Lillian Sampson, was born in Chicago in a Jewish family who had come from Lithuania to the United States, via Manchester, in the late nineteenth century. Early in 1927, when Hilary was six months old, the family moved to France and stayed until 1933 where Hilary completed the first two years of his primary schooling in French.[3]

In 1933, with the election of FDR and hopes for radical political and cultural change in the United States, Samuel Putnam, like many other American intellectual self-exiles, returned home. They eventually settled in Philadelphia in 1935 where Hilary continued to live until his graduation from the University of Pennsylvania in 1948.

At the University of Pennsylvania, Putnam took courses in Philosophy, German and the emerging field of 'Linguistic Analysis' taught by Zellig Harris. One of his fellow students was Noam Chomsky, who had also been with Putnam in Central High, Philadelphia's renowned academic high school. Their friendship, however, was to develop later when they were working in Princeton and continued as colleagues in MIT. Putnam graduated in 1948 and even though he had simultaneously majored in Philosophy, German and Linguistics, he decided to pursue philosophy as a career. To this end, he spent one year in Harvard (1948–49), where he was Morton White's assistant, took courses in mathematical logic with Quine, and for the first time attended formal lectures in mathematics. For financial reasons, Putnam, who was now married to his first wife Erna Diesendruck, abandoned his studies in Harvard and moved to UCLA in 1949 where he completed a PhD, under the supervision of Hans Reichenbach, in a record time of two years. The dissertation, *The Meaning of the Concept of Probability in Application to Finite Sequences* (1951), where he came up with a theorem about the frequency interpretation of probability, was his first engagement both with mathematics and with philosophy of science. Reichenbach's profound influence led to a lifelong preoccupation with philosophy of physics and mathematics; it also spurred an increasingly critical engagement with logical positivism.[4] Some years later Putnam found out that Reichenbach in his letters of recommendation had called his young student 'a genius', a comment that was instrumental in his obtaining a prestigious Rockefeller Fellowship in 1951 and helped to launch a stellar academic career.

After two years of peripatetic academic life, Putnam was offered a teaching position in Princeton in 1953, where he stayed for the next seven years, and was awarded full tenure by the Departments both of Philosophy and of Mathematics. The Princeton years played a central role in Putnam's developing philosophical vision; not least because of the range of intellectual associations and friendships it offered. Of crucial significance were weekly gatherings at Rudolf Carnap's house; all of Putnam's publications from 1954 to 1959, in one way or another, have the imprint of these encounters. Two discussion topics had a particularly formative influence: Putnam's very first publication, 'Synonymity, and the Analysis of Belief Sentences' (1954) and the piece that helped Putnam find his philosophical voice, 'The Analytic and the Synthetic' (1962a), where he separates his views from that of his mentors Reichenbach and Carnap, and begins a lifelong critique of logical positivism (see Axel Mueller in Chapter 4).

The second important development from these weekly discussions was the germination of Putnam's highly original ideas in philosophy of mind. Putnam dates his interest in the topic to a small conference held in Carnap's house in 1954. The invitees included Herbert Feigl, C.G. Hempel, Ernest Nagel, Paul Oppenheim, Wilfrid Sellars, and the much younger Michael Scriven and Hilary Putnam. Carnap posed the seminal questions: how could a mental state be identical with a brain process? And how could a physical process be referred to by a mentalistic term such as 'pain'? The ensuing discussion would eventually lead to Putnam's rejection of two major approaches to philosophy of mind, behaviorism and mind–brain identity theory, and his formulation of functionalism, a theory that became the dominant account of the mind-brain relationship (Putnam 1960, 1963, and 1964). Decades later, in *Representation and Reality* (1987a), Putnam would repudiate functionalism for reasons that are quite similar to his earlier rejection of behaviorism and mind–brain identity theory. In the same way that mental states cannot readily be correlated with behavioral or brain states, propositional attitudes, such as hoping, desiring, fearing cannot be mapped into or realized in software uniquely. In arguing against mind–brain identity theory, Putnam had maintained that mental states are multiply realizable because they are 'compositionally plastic'. He now believes that mental states, and the propositional attitudes used to express them, are also 'computationally plastic'.[5]

Two other encounters in Princeton led to important work on mathematics and its philosophy. Putnam sees the co-publication of a proof of Hilbert's Tenth Problem with the mathematician Martin Davis (Davis and Putnam 1958) as one of the most important intellectual events of his life. Also important was the emergence of a lifelong friendship with Paul Benacerraf, who shared Putnam's interest in questions about the nature of mathematical truths. Their jointly edited collection, *Philosophy of Mathematics: Selected Readings* (1964), was Putnam's first book-length publication and remains a major landmark to this day.

In 1961 Putnam was offered the Chair of Philosophy of Science in MIT to create a new Department of Philosophy. Noam Chomsky, who had been at MIT since 1955, was instrumental in arranging this move. Some of Putnam's most important papers in philosophy of physics, logic and mind, including 'An Examination of Grünbaum's Philosophy of Space and Time' (1963a),

'Brains and Behavior' (1963), '"Degree of Confirmation" and Inductive Logic' (1963), 'Robots: Machines or Artificially Created Life?' (1964), and 'A Philosopher Looks at Quantum Mechanics' (1965), date to that period. It was, however, Putnam's move to Harvard in 1965 that became a watershed in his academic life, for there he would develop his most influential ideas in philosophy of language and would also train a new generation of philosophers.

In the course of his 1967–68 Philosophy of Language lectures in Harvard, Putnam began evaluating the then prevailing Descriptivist views of reference, a process that ultimately led to the publication of arguably the most important single article of the past fifty years, 'The Meaning of "Meaning"' (1972). The 1970 'Is Semantics Possible?' already contained many of Putnam's new ideas about reference, but it was with the 1972 article, written after several years devoted almost exclusively to political activism, that Putnam, in parallel with Kripke's *Naming and Necessity*, wrought the most radical change of perspective in philosophy of language since Frege and Russell. Tyler Burge's contribution to this volume (Chapter 9) deals with this momentous philosophical development from the perspective of a first-hand participant.

Putnam's 'linguistic turn' led to further reflections on the relation between linguistic representations and reality. His thinking, or rethinking, of these issues eventually led to the bombshell that was his presidential address to the Eastern Division of the American Philosophical Association in December 1976. To the dismay of friends and colleagues present, Putnam used the occasion to repudiate his older views, what he began to call 'metaphysical realism', and to outline an alternative position he called 'internal realism' (more on this below). Putnam vividly describes the event in the prologue and, with the benefit of thirty years' hindsight, assesses the scope and significance of this philosophical rupture. Putnam's publications of that time (in particular Putnam 1981, 1983, 1987 and 1990) elaborate, explain and defend the approach that aimed to provide a compromise alternative to the realist/anti-realist dichotomy. Richard Boyd (Chapter 1) and Michael Devitt (Chapter 2) bemoan this rather unexpected move by their teacher and former philosophical ally.[6]

Throughout his philosophical career Putnam has frequently expressed his own philosophical positions by engaging with the work of other philosophers. The tendency has become more marked since the 1980s. Aristotle, Kant, James, Wittgenstein are a few of the figures whose writings have not only inspired Putnam but also elicited genuinely original reactions from him. This openness to the work of other philosophers is not restricted to the greats of yore but shows itself in the way Putnam interacts with his contemporaries.[7] While internal realism, at least in its inception, had a Kantian flavor and was influenced by Michael Dummett's semantic anti-realism, Putnam's work in the 1980s was influenced by readings of Wittgenstein, the

Pragmatists and J. L. Austin, facilitated by his colleague Stanley Cavell (Chapter 13, Epilogue). This increasingly historical perspective on philosophy had a major impact on the development of the third or latest period of Putnam's philosophical development.

Putnam used the 1990 Gifford lectures in St Andrews to announce a further major shift in his philosophical thinking. It was there that he expressed publically his deep misgivings with core aspects of internal realism, particularly with its verificationist take on truth as justification under ideal conditions. In the course of those lectures and subsequent writings, Putnam rejected both the early metaphysical realism and the epistemic view of truth and moved towards a position of Naïve Realism of direct, unencumbered, contact with the world (Putnam 1999: 10). The successor position has been variously called 'natural', 'pragmatic' or 'common sense realism' – so called, Putnam claims, because it reflects our common sense 'that "external" things, cabbages and kings, can be experienced directly, for we perceive the world itself, and not the sense data caused by that world' (Putnam 1999: 20).

Putnam's current work develops and modifies the various consequences of natural realism; including a theory of perception that would allow the unencumbered access to the world that natural realism demands (Putnam, 'A Response to Travis and McDowell'). He also has been publishing extensively on philosophy of mathematics and physics (Putnam 2012).

II. Themes from Putnam

The book focuses on three broad but central and interconnected themes from Putnam's work: First, there is the problem of realism and the question 'how does the mind connect with the world?', probably the most central of Putnam's philosophical preoccupation. The second section addresses questions about the make up of the real, or what there is. The third section is on perception – the connecting link between us and the world – for of late Putnam has come to the view that any account of the 'real' and our relationship with it also requires an account of the perceptual.

a. Realism

A preoccupation with what he calls the 'great question of realism' (Putnam 1994: 295) – the question: how language connects with the world – is probably the most prominent thread running though Putnam's long and productive philosophical career. Yet, as we saw, his thinking on this very question has undergone very significant changes. The early Putnam was a Realist (with a capital r) not only about the existence of material objects but also about mathematical objects and purely theoretical entities such as fields and physical magnitudes. Science, the argument is, attempts to capture what is out there and scientific theories are true in so far as they succeed in this goal. Mathematics is a handmaiden of science and equally central in modeling, representing or mapping this mind-independent reality.

Putnam's first official defense of scientific realism appears in his paper 'What Theories are not', delivered at the International Congress on Logic, Methodology and Philosophy of Science on August 27, 1960, in Stanford, California. The paper shows the profound impact Carnap had on his thinking. It also signals his official break from the logical positivist conception of science, or at least Carnap's version of it. The 'received view', as Putnam calls the then prevailing logical positivist thinking on science, was that theories are 'partially interpreted calculi'. Putnam provides three alternative accounts of what such a view could amount to and concludes that that there is no interpretation of the received view that could become an acceptable model for a scientific theory, nor could they suit Carnap's own aims in philosophy of science. But his best-known argument for scientific realism, what has variously become known as the Putnam–Boyd or 'the no miracle' argument, was published in 1975. As in the case of the indispensability argument for mathematical realism, the best explanation for the predictive and explanatory success of a scientific theory is its truth or approximation to truth. 'For if the theory was not true, then it would be a miracle that it was capable of generating successful predictions and enabling us to gain control over our environment' (Putnam 1978: 18–22). Putnam credits this formulation to his one-time student Richard Boyd whose contribution to this volume engages critically with Putnam's view that anti-reductionism is incompatible with metaphysical realism (Chapter 2). Boyd proceeds to defend realism in all domains, including ethics. He argues that, except for an early brief foray into the other camp, when it comes to non-mathematical sciences Putnam has been steadfastly an anti-reductionist, but as his views have changed over time there have also been shifts in the target of his anti-reductionism. In his earlier work he seemed to defend a realist and broadly materialist conception of empirical inquiry and its subject matters; indeed, Boyd thinks that Putnam deserves credit for helping to establish non-reductionist materialism as a credible position. With the turn to 'internal realism' or pragmatism he rejected the viability of a non-reductionist version of materialism, or indeed any other realist metaphysical position, for any genuinely metaphysical realist positions, he thinks, are inevitably (and mistakenly) reductionist and should be rejected in favor of a broadly pragmatist or Wittgensteinian approach. Boyd concludes this important and detailed paper by arguing that Putnam is mistaken in his target of criticism, for a properly developed realist materialism would entail, rather than undermine, a rejection of reductionism.

Putnam in responding to Boyd and elsewhere points out that he still considers himself a scientific realist and that he retains a core commitment to the view that physical theories aim at discovering the truth about physical reality. Crucially, the early Putnam did not distinguish between scientific realism and what he came to criticize as 'metaphysical realism'. Realism in that period was the view that our representations aim at capturing a mind-independent reality and that the correspondence theory of truth is the criterion for assessing the success of such attempts and the means for establishing what is true, for 'Whatever else realists say they typically say that they believe in a correspondence theory of truth' (Putnam 1978: 19–20). And it is this reliance on a representational view of the mind and the very notion of correspondence with facts which he rejected in his middle period. Now he is willing to allow that true empirical statements can be said to 'correspond to states of affairs that actually obtain' (p. 97). But he understands correspondence in a Fregean disquotational sense and not in terms of the more traditional correspondence theory.

In the internal realist or 'middle period', Putnam argued that metaphysical realism is committed to the absurd view that we could conceive of a world independent of any particular representation of it, that we can think and talk about things as they are, independently of our minds, and we can do this in virtue of a correspondence relation between the terms in our language and a mind-independent world. The Metaphysical Realist also is committed to the view that even an epistemically ideal theory, one that satisfies the best criteria of justification, could turn out to be false. Putnam finds these views unacceptable, not least because they presuppose the impossible 'God's Eye point of view' (Putnam 1981: 49).

Michael Devitt, a former student of Putnam, cites early Putnam and Quine as major influences on his work, so it's not surprising that the radical shift in Putnam's views came as a most unwelcome shock to him, as to many of his students from that period. Since then a thirty-year-old debate has been on-going between former mentor and pupil, which despite its occasionally vitriolic tone, has proved fruitful, at least for those sitting on the sidelines.

Devitt disagrees with Putnam's characterization of metaphysical realism because of the central role it places on the correspondence theory of truth. Devitt's maxim in defining realism is: there is only one way of knowing, the empirical way that is the basis of science. What he wants is a metaphysical account of realism, a metaphysics that is constructed in purely naturalistic terms. The middle Putnam had famously proclaimed: 'The mind and the world jointly make up the mind and the word' (Putnam 1981: xi) and had defended ontological relativity. Devitt thinks that this would lead to 'constructivism', a pernicious conjunction of relativism and idealism, to the effect that 'we make the known world with our conceptual schemes'. Putnam's response to Devitt insists on the inescapable role of semantics in any characterization of realism.

Although much of the criticism leveled at metaphysical realism has retained its cogency for Putnam, the suggested solution has not. In the 1980s, Putnam gradually came to the conclusion that internal realism, with its epistemic view of truth, faced problems similar to those besetting metaphysical realism. The metaphysical realist needs to explain how access to the external world is possible, how the human mind could reach out, so to speak, and epistemically touch the world. Putnam came to believe that there was a similar problem in explaining our 'referential access to "sufficiently good epistemic conditions"' (Putnam 2007: 155–67). In Putnam's earlier thinking 'the world was allowed to determine whether I am in a sufficiently good epistemic situation or only seem to myself to be in one – thus retaining an essential idea from commonsense realism – but the conception of our epistemic situation was the traditional "Cartesian" one, on which our sensations are an interface "between" us and the "external objects"' (Putnam in Chapter 1 of this book, p. 25). By the early 1990s, Putnam had found this option unworkable – a realization that set the scene for the gradual emergence of his third response to the 'big question of realism'.

David Macarthur (Chapter 3) explores these later developments in Putnam's thinking. He examines the role Putnam ascribes to common sense in this conception of realism and his contention that 'progress in philosophy requires a recovery of the natural realism of the common man' (p. 127 in this book). There are two conceptions of the common sense in Putnam's recent writing, Macarthur argues. The positive conception sees common sense as a set of beliefs held by 'the common man'. The negative conception, on the other hand, is more Wittgensteinian in its orientation, where common sense is identified with a 'certain kind of quietist move that attempts to undermine a false metaphysical picture' (p. 133). MacArthur exhorts Putnam to give up the positive, more robust version of common sense, and to embrace the Wittgensteinian negative version. Putnam in his response confesses to a change of attitude towards Wittgenstein and attempts to step away from the philosophical quietism that followers of Wittgenstein advocate.

B. On what there is

Putnam's quest for a satisfactory conception of realism and the mind–world relationship is inseparable from his dealings with questions about what there is – the furniture of the world, so to speak – and how to characterize it. The articles in this section range over a number of topics, including analyticity, conceptual relativity, and the role of ethics. They help us understand better the philosophical and ontological commitments that Putnam is willing to undertake in his long search for an acceptable version of realism. Putnam's thinking about these issues was to a large part shaped by his reaction to Quine's. The first two chapters of this section take a close look at the relationship between Putnam and Quine on questions of necessity and ontology.

INTRODUCTION

As we saw, against Carnap, Putnam agreed with Quine that we should give up the talk of the apriori but this should not lead to the rejection of the useful, but more flexible, category of conceptual truths. Conceptual truths, unlike the apriori, are open to revision, could be modified or even abandoned – a fact demonstrated by our willingness to revise our long-held beliefs concerning the laws of Euclidean geometry. Unlike Quine, Putnam believes that there are such things as analytic sentences of natural languages, but that such sentences are few and far between. According to him, most so-called 'necessary sentences' are at best necessary relative to a body of current knowledge and consequently they are always open to revision (Putnam 1962 and 1975b).

Axel Mueller's article (Chapter 4) compares Putnam's criticism of the analytic–synthetic distinction with Quine's seminal attack on analyticity in the 'Two Dogmas of Empiricism' (Quine 1951) and examines the role of methodological constraints, such as fallibilism and holism, in his approach. Mueller argues that the work of Carnap, Quine and Putnam shows that fallibilism-cum-holism is equally compatible with defending, rejecting, or modifying the analytic–synthetic distinction, hence it cannot provide us with the rationale that Quine was seeking. Mueller also offers a useful discussion of the perplexing fact that Putnam, in spite of sharing much of Quine's presuppositions and a critical attitude towards the Carnapian view of analyticity, increasingly distanced himself from materialism. Putnam largely agrees with Mueller's analysis but thinks that more could have been said in Quine's favor.

Charles Parsons (Chapter 5) extends Mueller's comparisons of Quine and Putnam to an important but neglected area of disagreement between them. Quine, more than any other contemporary philosopher, was responsible for a revival of interest in questions of ontology (starting with Quine 1948). Carnap was deeply suspicious of the move and viewed questions about the ontological commitment to empirical observation statements as 'pseudo-questions'. Putnam sides more closely with Carnap than with Quine on this point. Parsons shows that Putnam's suspicion of the whole idea of ontology is not a recent development restricted to his *Ethics without Ontology* (2004) but goes back to his earliest writing in philosophy of mathematics where he questioned the significance of looking for ontological commitments in mathematical realism. Parsons argues that despite Putnam's protestations, at least on some matters, his views on ontology are either Quine's or quite close to them.

Realists, whether scientific or metaphysical, assume that successful theories 'carve nature at its joints' (to use Plato's metaphor from *Phaedrus*). But is there only one right way of such carvings or a plurality? Furthermore, when all is said and done, would there be room for value judgements in our successful account of what there is? These questions are addressed in the next three papers of this section.

In his internal realist period Putnam had denied that

> [T]here is a fact of the matter as to which of the conceptual schemes that serve us so well – the conceptual scheme of commonsense objects, with their vague identity conditions and their dispositional and counterfactual properties, or the scientific-philosophical scheme of fundamental particles and their "aggregations" (that is, their mereological sums) – is "really true." Each of these schemes contains, in its present form, bits that will turn out to be "wrong" in one way or another – bits that are right and wrong by the standards appropriate to the scheme itself – but the question "which kind of 'true' is really Truth" is one that internal realism rejects.
> (Putnam 1990: 96)

He concluded that that there is no single right way of classifying and characterizing objects and their properties because there could be equivalent descriptions of the same situation. Metaphysical realism embraces the idea that 'there is a totality of Forms, or Universals, or "properties", fixed once and for all' (Putnam 1999: 6). As we saw, Devitt believes that Putnam's conceptual relativity is a form of Constructivism, with all its relativistic consequence. But it is not clear if Putnam ever intended anything so radical. More recently he has clarified his position by distinguishing between conceptual relativity and conceptual pluralism. He believes that conceptual relativity is a limited phenomenon, applicable to science, or more specifically to physics only. Conceptual pluralism, on the other hand, is the more mundane claim that different levels of description may not be fully inter-translatable or reducible to each other.

Russell Goodman (Chapter 6) explores the historic roots of the idea of pluralism. He argues that pluralism may be seen as an alternative version of American pragmatism and both doctrines should be analyzed within the context of their intellectual tradition. Putnam's brand of pluralism, he argues, would be better understood once it is linked with the family of pluralistic views we can find in William James, Nelson Goodman and Ludwig Wittgenstein.

Putnam's response clarifies the ways in which his recent thinking has departed from Pragmatists' views of truth, Nelson Goodman's irrealism and Wittgenstein's quietism. As in the case of Boyd and others in this book, Putnam argues that Goodman's observations are applicable to the internal realist Putnam (1975–90) rather than his more recent views.

From his days as a student of Reichenbach at UCLA, Putnam was deeply immersed in the technical and philosophical questions of quantum physics. David Albert's chapter (Chapter 7) is a new and unexpected departure on a topic that he and Putnam have been discussing for several decades. The chapter offers a new theorem which suggests that the physical world has a family of foliation-dependent histories and not a unique one and therefore the history of the evolution of the world is not completely capturable by a single 'narrative', although there are other possible interpretations. Putnam's reaction is to advise that only time will show; the ultimate evaluation of Albert's results, and much else in this arena, will have to wait for a satisfactory interpretation of quantum mechanics. However, it is useful to remind ourselves that for Putnam theoretical physics is one area where conceptual relativity applies.

Ethical questions and the need for moral commitments have always been central to Putnam's life and thought. They motivated his political activism and more recently his gravitation towards Judaism (Putnam 2008). But despite a genuine concern with the ethical from the outset of his philosophical career (see Prologue, p. 19), this topic has come to prominence in his published work only recently. Putnam's first publication relevant to moral philosophy was his famous argument against the fact/value dichotomy (1976, published in Putnam 1981) where he questions the intelligibility of the empiricist belief in a sharp division between factual statements and normative judgements. Two recent books, *The Collapse of the Fact/Value Dichotomy* (2002) and *Ethics without Ontology* (2004) and a number of articles (Putnam 2012), deal in detail with some of the themes Putnam had explored earlier, demonstrating the centrality of ethics to Putnam's thinking. Ruth Anna Putnam's important contribution to this volume (Chapter 8) explores this frequently ignored area of Putnam's work. She charts Putnam's attempt to dispel the illusion that moral values, unlike the factual statements of science, are purely subjective and links his views to classical Pragmatists – William James and John Dewey in particular. She also points out that while Hilary Putnam's early arguments against the fact–value dichotomy were located in philosophy of language and philosophy of science, his recent work moves from the spectator to the agent point of view, a step that she finds crucial for avoiding the endless and futile conversation between skeptics and anti-skeptics.

Hilary Putnam reacts to Ruth Anna Putnam's chapter by confessing that, her rational reconstruction of his views on the centrality of the 'moral images of the world' in life is not just a restatement of what he has written, but a statement of what he should have written.

III. Perception

Putnam's natural or pragmatic realism addresses the old question of how the mind connects with the world in a novel way. He argues that the impasse between the realists and anti-realists is in large part the result of the false Cartesian assumption that we cannot perceive the world directly. He confesses that the guiding assumption, through his earlier work, was the neo-Cartesian view that

> [W]hen we see or hear events in the world, what actually happens is that certain visual or auditory sense data are produced in our minds/brains. ... .The relation between the tables and chairs we perceive and the sense data is, on this picture, simply a matter of causal impacts on the retina and on the eardrum, and of causal signals from the retina and the eardrum to processors in the brain; we have no direct cognitive relation to the objects of perception. Our sense data are, as it were, the interface between our cognitive processes and the world.
>
> (Putnam 2007: 196–97)

However, until quite recently, even in his philosophy of mind, Putnam had not focused on perception. As we saw, things began to change and, starting in the 1990s, a direct perception became the anchor for natural realism. What we are immediately aware of, at least in veridical cases of perception, Putnam argued, is the genuine properties of things in the world and not their representations in our brain, but as we'll see, in the essay written in response to McDowell and Travis, his views on this topic are becoming increasingly nuanced.

Tyler Burge's contribution to this volume (Chapter 9) addresses primarily the so-called 'externalist' approach to meaning and reference but also forges interesting connections with the topic of perception. He singles out aspects of Putnam's views for particular praise: the methodology of the twin-earth thought experiment for instance was a major breakthrough for testing our intuitions about meaning and the 'anti-individualism' of Putnam's semantic externalism opened the way for Burge's own influential version of anti-individualism about mental states. He also poses specific questions that Putnam addresses in his response. But Burge is also critical of the narrow focus on language, adopted by Putnam and Kripke, and their failure to follow reference back to its roots in perception. Elementary linguistic reference, Burge thinks, is to a large extent grounded in perception, for 'in many paradigmatic cases, the association of a name with its bearer, or of a natural kind term with the relevant kind, depends ultimately on perception' (Burge in this volume, p. 267). Burge's emphasis on perception is in line with Putnam's current thinking on the centrality of the role of perceptual experiences as the backdrop to a correct account of realism. But Burge also criticizes the absence of any engagement with empirical research on perception in Putnam's approach. The criticism is also directed at Travis and McDowell (Chapters 11 and 12).

The chapter by Ned Block (Chapter 10), while dealing with the issue of perception, takes a route that is more in line with Burge's approach. Block discusses the perennial problem of qualia, a topic that has also increasingly occupied Putnam. According to Block, Wittgenstein endorsed an 'innocuous' inverted spectrum hypothesis and rejected a 'dangerous' kind.

INTRODUCTION

The dangerous kind provides an argument for qualia – or the content of experiential states – which cannot be fully captured in public language. Block argues for the possibility and the coherence of the dangerous scenario, and tries to show that some standard arguments against qualia are ineffective against the version of the dangerous scenario he is advocating. Qualia, in Block's account, are the ways things look red or feel, for instance a sound or a smell. If things can look red in more than one way, Block argues, then 'looks red' would not fully capture the content of the state. Talk of qualia in a public shared language cannot capture the individuating particularity of the way that different people may experience a particular quale.

Block's article, apart from its intrinsic interest and originality, throws a welcome light on an important debate on the nature of perception between McDowell, Travis and Putnam. As Putnam points out in his response to McDowell and Travis, he now takes a similar view to Block's on qualia and, contrary to strong forms of naïve realism, he thinks that the phenomenal quality of our perceptual experiences are not exhausted by the objective appearance-properties of what is experienced. In other words, describing what we perceive in objective terms does not exhaust the phenomenology of perceptual experiences. Moreover, Putnam is now prepared to go with Block's suggestion that qualia are indeed brain events.

The last two papers of this section, by Travis and McDowell, and Putnam's response to them form one more leg of a not yet completed philosophical journey by these philosophers on the topic of perception. As we saw, starting with his Dewey lectures, Putnam has argued against the view that minds relate to the world outside only at the interface of sensory receptors. Putnam, with Travis and McDowell, also rejects the representational or 'intentional' theories of mind and perception, the view that the objects of perceptual experience are representations of external objects which may be experienced even in the absence of the relevant external objects. They favor instead direct theories of perception advocated by the so called 'Naïve Realists' according to whom external objects are constitutive of perceptual experiences and so called 'qualia' are indeed intrinsic properties of the common objects of experience.

However, Travis and McDowell disagree on the correct characterization of the way objects in the external world become objects of experience. McDowell follows the Kantian path of emphasizing the conceptual components of our experiences, while Travis advocates the Fregean notion of modes of experience. For McDowell, experience is conceptually, but no longer propositionally, structured. Travis, on the other hand, relies on the Fregean distinction between extra-conceptual and conceptual items and argues that only extra-conceptual items can be perceived. He attempts to show, through examples, that conceptual items possess a kind of generality that items of perceptions do not. Putnam's response is to reject both approaches. McDowell's mistake, he argues, is not to distinguish between 'impressions' and apperceptions, i.e. fully conscious perception. While Travis's mistake is to assimilate apperception to reflection and to leave impressions completely out of consideration, Putnam finds both assimilations misguided.

Epilogue

The last word in this book is left to a unique voice in contemporary English-language philosophy, Stanley Cavell. Cavell and Putnam first met at UCLA in their student days, but their philosophical paths began to converge in Harvard in the 1970s where Cavell's reading of Wittgenstein had a profound impact on Putnam's own philosophical reorientations. Due to illness, Stanley Cavell was unable to attend the Dublin conference, an absence that was keenly felt, not least by Putnam. From the outset Cavell had expressed a wish to contribute to any volume that might result from this gathering. The paper appearing here (Chapter 13) deals not with Putnam but with Nietzsche and Austin, but, as Cavell writes, it is distinctly relevant to Putnam's work in its concern with the relation of philosophy and religion, something that Cavell had never thematized before.[8]

The chapter is indeed significantly a new departure for Cavell. It draws together, in a manner unique to him, strands from Nietzsche and Austin as part of the never-ending process of philosophy 'as education for grown ups' and makes them a part of 'that unending confrontation of myself and my powers of intuition that constitutes a continuing of my education' (p. 364). The paper bears a dedication to Putnam also because Cavell sees it as an opportunity for a new philosophical conversation with an old friend. To read Cavell as he should be read, Putnam says, 'is to enter into a conversation with him, one in which your entire sensibility and his are involved, and not only your mind and his mind'. This is a task which Hilary has welcomed and I know would exhort his readers to follow as well.

Notes

1 The article by Devitt was written after the conference specifically for this volume. Because of ill health, Stanley Cavell was unable to travel to Dublin but was happy to contribute a piece dedicated to Putnam as a mark of their enduring friendship and high regard.
2 This philosophical biography draws on Putnam 1997, 'A Philosophical Autobiography', in the Putnam volume of the Library of Living Philosophers (forthcoming), and interviews I had with Hilary Putnam in Cambridge, Massachusetts in 2001 and in Santiago de Compostela, Spain, in 2004.
3 In his autobiography, *Paris was our Mistress* (1947), Samuel Putnam gives a fascinating account of their lives in Paris – among émigré artists such as James Joyce, Ford Madox Ford, and Pirandello – and his work as the editor of the literary magazine *The New Review*, with Ezra Pound as the associate editor and Henry Miller among its contributors.

4 Although Reichenbach collaborated closely with Carnap and was the co-editor of *Erkenntnis*, the official organ of logical positivism, Putnam insists that he should not be classified as a logical positivist but, at best, a logical empiricist.
5 Putnam still believes that some brain processes can be described in computational terms, but he wishes to avoid the reduction of the intentional level to either the neuronal or the computational levels.
6 During extended conversations on his philosophical development, Putnam has stated that the radical revision in his political beliefs in the early 1970s had an unintended impact on the way he interpreted and assessed the concurrent changes in his philosophical position. He subsequently has come to see that the shift in his views on realism was not as revisionary as he had believed them to be at that time.
7 See for example his *Renewing Philosophy* (1992a) for a clear example of this philosophical strategy.
8 From personal correspondence with Stanley Cavell.

Bibliography

Baghramian, M. (2009) 'Putnam's Long Journey', *Philosophical Topics* 35: 17–35.
Davis, M., Putnam, H., and Robinson, J. (1961) 'The Decision Problem for Exponential Diophantine Equations', *Annals of Mathematics* 74:3, 425–36.
Davis, M, and Putnam, H. (1958) Reductions of Hilbert's tenth problem. *Journal of Symbolic Logic* 23(2): 183–87.
Putnam, Hilary (1951/1990) *The Meaning of the Concept of Probability in Application to Finite Sequences*. Ph.D. dissertation, University of California, Los Angeles, 1951. New York: Garland.
——(1954) 'Synonymity, and the Analysis of Belief Sentences', *Analysis* 41: 114–22.
——(1960) 'Minds and Machines', in Sidney Hook (ed.), *Dimensions of Mind*, New York University Press.
——(1962a) 'It Ain't Necessarily So', *Journal of Philosophy* 59(22): 658–71.
——(1962b) 'The Analytic and the Synthetic', *Scientific Explanation, Space, and Time. Minnesota Studies in the Philosophy of Science*, vol. 3, ed. Herbert Feigl and Grover Maxwell, Minneapolis: University of Minnesota Press, 358-97.
——(1963) 'Brains and behavior', in Ronald J. Butler (ed.), *Analytical Philosophy: Second Series*, Oxford: Blackwell.
——(1963) 'An Examination of Grünbaum's Philosophy of Space and Time', *Philosophy of Science. The Delaware Seminar vol. 2, 1962-1963*, ed. Bernard Baumrin, New York: Interscience/John Wiley, 205-55.
——(1964) 'Robots: Machines or Artificially Created Life?', *Journal of Philosophy* 61(21): 668–91.
——(1965) 'A Philosopher Looks at Quantum Mechanics', in *Beyond the Edge of Certainty: Essays in Contemporary Science and Philosophy*, ed. Robert G. Colodny, Englewood Cliffs, N.J.: Prentice-Hall 75–101, in *Mathematics, Matter and Method* (1975), 130–58.
——(1975) *Mathematics, Matter and Method*, Cambridge, MA: Harvard University Press.
——(1975a) 'What is Mathematical Truth?', *Historia Mathematica* 2, 529–43.
——(1975b) 'The Analytic Synthetic?', *Mind, Language and Reality*, Cambridge University Press, 33–69.
——(1975c) *Mind, Language and Reality*, Cambridge, MA: Harvard University Press.

—— (1976) 'What Is "Realism?"', *Proceedings of the Aristotelian Society*, New Series, vol. 76: 177–94.
—— (1977) 'Realism and Reason', *Proceedings and Addresses of the American Philosophical Association* 50(6) 483–98.
—— (1978) *Meaning and the Moral Sciences*, Boston: Routledge & Kegan Paul; Cambridge University Press, 1983.
—— (1981) *Reason, Truth, and History*, Cambridge University Press.
—— (1982) 'A Defense of Internal Realism', in James Conant (ed.), *Realism with a Human Face*, Cambridge, MA: Harvard University Press, 30–42.
—— (1982a) 'Three Kinds of Scientific Realism', *Philosophical Quarterly*, 32: 195–200.
—— (1983) *Realism and Reason. Philosophical Papers*, vol. 3, Cambridge University Press.
—— (1987) *The Many Faces of Realism*, Chicago and La Salle, IL: Open Court.
—— (1987a) *Representation and Reality*, Cambridge, MA: MIT Press.
—— (1990) *Realism with a Human Face*, Cambridge, MA: Harvard University Press.
—— (1992) *Pragmatism. An Open Question*, Oxford: Blackwell.
—— (1992a) *Renewing Philosophy*, Cambridge, MA: Harvard University Press.
—— (1994) *Words and Life*, Cambridge, MA: Harvard University Press.
—— (1997) 'A Half Century of Philosophy, Viewed from within', *Daedalus*, vol. 126, no. 1, Cambridge, MA: MIT Press, 175–208.
—— (1999) *The Threefold Cord*, New York: Columbia University Press.
—— (2002) *The Collapse of the Fact/Value Dichotomy and Other Essays*, Cambridge, MA: Harvard University Press.
—— (2004) *Ethics Without Ontology*, Cambridge, MA: Harvard University Press.
—— (2007) 'Between Scylla and Charybdis: Does Dummett Have a Way Through?', in Randall E. Auxier and Lewis Edwin Hahn (eds.), *The Philosophy of Michael Dummett*, Chicago and La Salle, IL: Open Court, 155–67.
—— (2008) *Jewish Philosophy as a Guide to Life: Rosenzweig, Buber, Levinas, Wittgenstein*, Bloomington: Indiana University Press.
—— (2012) *Philosophy in an Age of Science: Physics, Mathematics, and Skepticism*, Cambridge, MA: Harvard University Press.
—— (forthcoming) 'A Philosophical Autobiography', in *The Philosophy of Hilary Putnam*, The Library of Living Philosophers, La Salle, IL: Open Court Press
Putnam, H. and Benacerraf, P. (1964) *Philosophy of Mathematics: Selected Readings*, Englewood Cliffs, NJ: Prentice-Hall; 2nd edn. Cambridge University Press.
Putnam, Samuel (1947) *Paris was our Mistress: The memoirs of a lost and found generation*, New York: The Viking Press.
—— (1951) 'Two Dogmas of Empiricism', *Philosophical Review* 60(1): 20–43.
Quine, W. V. (1948) 'On what there is', *Review of Metaphysics* 2: 21–38.

PROLOGUE

FROM QUANTUM MECHANICS TO ETHICS AND BACK AGAIN[1]

Hilary Putnam

As you will doubtless have guessed from the title of this chapter, I am going to talk about my philosophical career as a whole (up to the ninth decade, anyway). The "Back Again," by the way, does not mean I have abandoned my interest in ethics! Not at all. Rather it refers to the fact that in December 2005 I published a paper titled "A Philosopher Looks at Quantum Mechanics (Again)" (Putnam 2005). I could also have titled these reflections, "From Philosophy of Mathematics to Ethics and Back Again," since I recently delivered a lecture titled "Indispensability Arguments in the Philosophy of Mathematics."[2]

My reason for pointing this out is that I am tired of being described as a philosopher who was interested only in philosophy of science until the late 1970s, and who then turned to "soft" philosophy. A simultaneous interest in *both* science and ethics has characterized my thinking for decades; in fact, I gave a seminar on Metaethics in 1964, when I was Professor of Philosophy of Science at MIT (a seminar that Richard Boyd well remembers), although my first real published writing on the subject did not appear until 1981 (Putnam 1981). But I have also *never* stopped thinking about and writing about philosophy of physics and philosophy of mathematics.

In the introduction (dated "September 1974") to *Mathematics, Matter and Method*, the first volume of my first collection of papers, I wrote:

> It will be obvious that I take science seriously and that I regard science as an important part of man's knowledge of reality; but there is a tradition with which I would not wish to be identified, which would say that scientific knowledge is all of man's knowledge. I do not believe that ethical statements are expressions of scientific knowledge; but neither do I agree that they are not knowledge at all. The idea that the concepts of truth, falsity, explanation, and even understanding are all concepts which belong exclusively to science seems to me to be a perversion. That Adolf Hitler was a

monster seems to me to be a true statement (and even a 'description' in any ordinary sense of 'description'), but the term 'monster' is neither reducible to nor eliminable in favor of 'scientific' vocabulary. (This is not something discussed in the present volume. It is a subject on which I hope to write in the future.)

If the importance of science does not lie in its constituting the *whole* of human knowledge, even less does it lie, in my view, in its technological applications. Science at its best is a way of coming to know, and hopefully a way of acquiring some reverence for, the wonders of nature. The philosophical study of science, at the best, has always been a way of coming to understand both some of the nature and some of the limitations of human reason. These seem to me to be sufficient grounds for taking science and philosophy of science seriously; they do not justify science worship

(Putnam 1975: xiii–xiv)

I still stand by every one of those words.

Although the misdescription of the evolution of my thinking I just referred to usually comes from people who regret my interest in ethics, in American Pragmatism, and in Wittgenstein – people who think that, as Quine famously put it, "philosophy of science is philosophy enough" – there is a related but more subtle misunderstanding that I find even in the writings of some philosophers who are certainly sympathetic to the attitude expressed in those words I wrote in 1974. Today I often find myself divided into three "Putnams" (somewhat like "early, middle, and late Wittgenstein"). "Early Putnam" is said to have been a staunch scientific realist; "interim Putnam" is said to have repudiated scientific realism in favor of internal realism, and more recent Putnam is often described as defending "common sense realism" (which is not usually described in any detail at all). But that account is confused (although the confusion is partly my own fault, as I shall explain in a moment). To explain why it is confused, I need to say something about scientific realism.

Realism: scientific, metaphysical, and internal

The so called "interim" period in my career, that is, the period from 1976 to 1989 during which I espoused what I described as the "picture" of truth as "idealized rational acceptability," or verification under ideal conditions, opened with my reading an address titled "Realism and Reason" to the American Philosophical Association (Eastern Division) in December of 1976 (Putnam 1978: 123–38). That address was, in a way, the manifesto of what I called "internal realism." Yet the opening lines of that "manifesto" contained an unfortunate slip that was the cause of much of the confusion in subsequent years as to just what I meant to be defending. In my own mind, the purpose of those opening lines was to make it clear that I was *not* repudiating *scientific* realism. If you will forgive me for quoting from my previous self one more time, I should like to read part of those lines to you:

> In one way of conceiving it, realism is an empirical theory. One of the facts that this theory explains is the fact that scientific theories tend to 'converge' in the sense that earlier theories are very often limiting cases of later theories (which is why it is possible to regard theoretical terms as preserving their reference across most changes of theory). Another of the facts it explains is the more mundane fact that language-using contributes to getting our goals, achieving satisfaction, or what have you.
>
> The realist explanation, in a nutshell, is not that language mirrors the world but that *speakers* mirror the world – i.e. their environment – in the sense of *constructing a symbolic representation* of their environment. ... let me refer to realism in this sense – acceptance of this sort of scientific picture of the relation of speakers to their environment, and of the role of language – as *internal* realism. [N.B. I should have written "scientific realism". That was the slip.]
>
> *Metaphysical* realism, on the other hand, is less an empirical theory than a model ... It is, or purports to be, a model of the relations of *any* correct theory to all or parts of THE WORLD. I have come to the conclusion that this model is incoherent.
>
> (Putnam 1978: 123–38)

The slip might not have been important if I had continued to use "internal realism" as I explained it in this paragraph (although "scientific realism," would have been better), but later in that same lecture I gave it a very different sense. In a section titled "Why all this doesn't refute internal realism," I identified "internal realism" with the view that whether a theory has a unique intended interpretation "has no absolute sense." At that point it is clear that "internal realism" was *now* a name for the view I had developed in the lecture as a whole, a view on which truth and idealized verifiability were supposed to coincide, and *not* a name for the view described in the opening paragraphs that I just read you, the view according to which *both* metaphysical realists *and* holders of the anti-realist view I now advanced were supposed to be able to agree.

Although I have been aware for many years that I used "internal realism" in these two inconsistent ways in "Realism and Reason," it was only upon reading Maximilian de Gaynesford's book about the evolution of my views that I appreciated how much confusion that inconsistency had occasioned (de Gaynesford 2006). For in that book, a book with much of which I agree, and many of whose philosophical attitudes I share, "scientific realism," the term I had used repeatedly in my *Philosophical Papers* published by

Cambridge University Press in 1975, is identified with what I called "metaphysical realism" in "Realism and Reason," with the result that that lecture, and in fact everything written by "interim Putnam," is seen as a repudiation of almost everything that I had written in the papers collected in those retrospective volumes. The truth is that over the years I have only changed my mind with respect to *three* of the nineteen papers in *Mathematics, Matter and Method*, namely chapter 2 (which defended a Russellian "if-thenist" position in philosophy of mathematics) and chapters 9 and 10 (which dealt with quantum logic). Similarly, I have only changed my mind with respect to *four* of the twenty-two papers in *Mind, Language and Reality*, namely chapter 3 (which is one of the few places in those two volumes where I defended metaphysical realism) and chapters 18, 20 and 21 (which proposed "functionalism" in the philosophy of mind). Of course there are individual arguments in those papers I would now improve, and formulations I regard as needing qualification, but at no time did I regard myself as repudiating them. And yet those volumes are now supposed to represent a "metaphysical realist" period in my development! Although a confusion of this kind never seems to disappear from the literature, let me nevertheless repeat and emphasize: I have *always* regarded myself as a scientific realist, though of course not *only* a scientific realist, as the introduction to the first of those volumes made clear.

One more bit of history. I still owe you an explanation of *why* I called scientific realism "internal realism" in those opening paragraphs of "Realism and Reason." The reason has to do with a conversation I had in the late 1970s with my sorely missed and much admired friend and one-time colleague Rogers Albritton. At that time I defended – as I still do, to the disgust of some of my friends and former students – the claim that scientific realism is the only philosophy of science that doesn't make the success of science a miracle. As an argument against a sophisticated antirealism such as Michael Dummett's, or Crispin Wright's, or my own former "internal realism," this was not a good argument – indeed, as I pointed out in the paragraphs I quoted above, an "internal realist" will agree that "scientific theories tend to "converge" in the sense that earlier theories are very often limiting cases of later theories (which is why it is possible to regard theoretical terms as preserving their reference across most changes of theory)."[3] "Antirealism" as a *theory of truth* needs to be rebutted in other ways, as I tried to do with my own "internal realism" in my 1994 Dewey Lectures (Putnam 1994/1999). But as an argument against such positions as logical positivism and van Fraassen's "constructive empiricism," I still believe it.

Anyway, Rogers and I were discussing this, and he said "Well of course, scientific realism is *science's* philosophy of science." Coming from other lips, I would probably have heard that as praising scientific realism. But with the particular intonation that Rogers gave to those words, I understood at once that he meant something else. What he meant was that if "scientific realism" was, as Boyd and I claimed, "an empirical theory," then it could only be shown to be incompatible with antirealism if it could be shown that an antirealist had to reject at least some empirical theories. To just assume *that* was to beg the case against antirealism. In short, one could accept scientific realism as a *part* of science, as something *internal* to science, while adopting an antirealist view of language as a whole including scientific language (e.g. one could accept Dummett's view, or the view I went on to develop in *Reason, Truth and History*). And that is what I did, which is how I could refer to scientific realism as "internal realism," meaning in that sentence "the realism internal to science."

Conceptual relativity

The idea of "conceptual relativity" has been a controversial feature of my work. Indeed, this idea has often been seen as in itself an antirealist one, which is another reason that many commentators continue to describe me as an "internal realist", although I rejected the "verificationist semantics" which was the essential idea of my so-called "internal realism" in 1990.[4] In the next section I shall try to clear up that confusion by explaining why I believe conceptual relativity is fully compatible with realism in metaphysics. But first I want to briefly review what conceptual relativity amounts to.

First, a story. I taught for a quarter at the University of Washington in 2002, and one day when I stopped for a cup of coffee at one of the little cafeterias on the campus I struck up a conversation with Matt Strassler, a physicist who was there to give a lecture. We started talking about quantum mechanics, and I became quite excited as I realized that he was describing a phenomenon I had written about for a long time under the name "conceptual relativity." Of course, he did not call it that (physicists call it "duality"), nor did he know of my writing, and I did not know the papers he referred to, although he was kind enough to send me a list. In brief, what he told me is that what an analytic philosopher would probably call the "ontology" of a conceptual scheme (specifically, a quantum mechanical theory of a particular system) is not regarded as, so to speak, the load-bearing aspect of the scheme, because such a scheme has many different "representations" (Strassler's term), which are regarded as perfectly equivalent. For example, these representations may differ in how many dimensions they treat space (or spacetime) as having, and over whether the particles in the system are or are not bosons!

My own notion of "conceptual relativity" (which I originally called "cognitive equivalence") is beautifully illustrated by the case Strassler described. The different "representations" are perfectly intertranslatable; it is just that the translations don't preserve "ontology." What do they preserve? Well, they don't merely preserve macro-observables. They also preserve *explanations*. An explanation of a phenomenon goes over into another perfectly good explanation of the same phenomenon under these translations.

But who's to say what is a phenomenon? And who's to say what is a perfectly good explanation? My answer has always been: *physicists* are not linguists and not philosophers.

Of course, in my writing I have sought for simple examples, and the simplest, one which is now well known, involves mereological sums. The question, "are there really mereological sums," is, in my view, a pseudo-question. Although it is obvious that we could not do with only particles (in, for example, classical physics), it does not follow that we have to accept all the axioms/theorems of mereology, including the statement that for every X and Y there is a smallest object having both X and Y as parts. We can perfectly well do classical physics using sets rather than mereological sums, and we need the axioms of set theory anyway. Given that *all* scientific and non-scientific discourse can be formulated perfectly successfully with and without the "assumption" of mereological sums, their "existence" is, in my view, best regarded as a matter of convention. The positivists got that one right (although for the wrong reasons).

Similarly, I regard the question as to whether *points* (in space or in spacetime) are real "individuals" or simply logical constructs as a pseudo-question.

I spoke of the existence of mereological sums as a matter of convention. To be more precise: saying that there are seven objects on a certain table, namely three billiard balls and four additional mereological sums of billiard balls, is a matter of fact *as opposed to saying* that there are three such objects (the second statement is true if there are two billiard balls on the table), while saying that there are seven mereological sums that can be formed of the objects on that table *as opposed to saying* that there are three individual objects on the table and eight *sets* of those objects (N.B. mereological sums are not sets, and there is an empty set but no empty object) is a matter of convention. The fact that we say X rather than Y may be a matter of convention, in whole or in part, while the fact that we say X rather than Z is not at all conventional.

What this all has to do with realism

Since I criticized Maximilian de Gaynesford for portraying me (or at least "interim" me) as renouncing scientific realism, let me balance the account with some sincere praise: he rightly sees that the problem of intentionality has been a lifelong preoccupation of mine, and that various changes in my position were occasioned by the realization that one or another assumption about the nature of reference led to deep difficulties. As de Gaynesford rightly explains, I had to give up "functionalism," for example, that is, the doctrine that our mental states are just our *computational* states (as implicitly defined by a "program" that our brains are hard-wired to "run"), because that view is incompatible with the semantic externalism that years of thinking about the topic of reference had eventually led me to develop. If, as I said in "The Meaning of 'Meaning'," our intentional mental states aren't in our heads, but are rather to be thought of as *world-involving abilities*, abilities identified by the sorts of transactions with our environment that they facilitate, then they aren't identified simply by the "software" of the brain.[5] (A further reason for giving up computational functionalism was that mental states are not only compositionally plastic, that is, capable in principle of being realized in different sorts of hardware, but *computationally plastic*, that is, capable of being realized in different sorts of software. But I shall not go into further detail about my philosophy of mind today.)

Since at least one participant at the "PutnamFest" expressed regret that I gave up the slogan (that "the mind and the world together make up the mind and the world"), led me say how reflections on reference led me into and then out of that idea. (De Gaynesford is excellent on the first, how I was led into the position, but I would have liked him to say more about how I was led out of it.)

The heart of internal realism was what I called "verificationist semantics" (I even tentatively endorsed Michael Dummett's idea that we should adopt intuitionist logic in one of my publications (Putnam 1983)). In my version of that semantics, truth was identified with verifiability under epistemically ideal conditions. But I did not, as some mistakenly took me to be doing, adopt the Peircean view that such conditions involve infinitely prolonged scientific inquiry, or the corollary that truth about the past is determined by what we can or will find out in the future. I also recognized that it is possible that for a variety of empirical reasons we may be unable to attain epistemically ideal conditions with respect to some of our inquiries; thus the truth may outrun what we can as a matter of fact verify. But this recognition reinstated the very problem of "access" that internal realism was designed to block! If there is a problem as to how, without postulating "noetic rays," we can have access to external things, there is an equal problem as to how we can have referential access to "sufficiently good epistemic conditions" (Putnam 2007). On my "internal realist" picture, which differed in this respect from Dummett's "antirealist" one, the world was allowed to determine whether I am in a sufficiently good epistemic situation or only seem to myself to be in one – thus retaining an essential idea from commonsense realism – but the conception of our epistemic situation was the traditional "Cartesian" one, on which our sensations are an interface "between" us and the "external objects." By the time of the Gifford Conference on my philosophy at St. Andrews in 1990, I had decided that this just wouldn't do.

The alternative was to return to the Cartesian predicament itself and see if it could be avoided. I had accepted that predicament, because I had rejected Austin's criticisms of "sense-data" talk. I believed, as I wrote in "Models and Reality" that

> Although the philosopher John Austin and the psychologist Fred Skinner both tried to drive sense data out of existence, most

philosophers and psychologists think that there are such things as *sensations* or *qualia*. They may not be objects of perception, as was once thought (it is becoming increasingly fashionable to view them as states or conditions of the sentient subject as Reichenbach long ago urged we should); we may not have incorrigible knowledge concerning them; they may be somewhat ill-defined entities rather than the perfectly sharp particulars they were once taken to be; but it seems reasonable to hold that they are part of the legitimate subject matter of cognitive psychology and philosophy, and not mere pseudo-entities invented by bad psychology and bad philosophy.

(Putnam 1980, 1983: 15)

By 1990, however, I had begun to think that Austin's attack on the conception of our experiences as "sense-data" which somehow are directly perceived, while the "external objects" are only "indirectly perceived" was right. In addition, I had begun to read William James, and was impressed by his insistence that what he called "natural realism" (James 1976) could be defended (Putnam 1990). In sum, I began to think that the problem of "access" to external objects that I had elaborated with the aid of devices from mathematical logic (model theory) was a replay of the older problem of epistemological dualism, even if the dualism was no longer a dualism of mental substance and physical substance, but one of brain states and everything outside the head. I concluded, and still conclude, that "natural realism" with respect to perception can indeed be defended, and that with natural realism with respect to perception back in place the fear (or the bugaboo) that we may have no "access" to reality outside our heads can be dismissed as a bad dream.

I can now respond to the regret that I gave up the slogan "The mind and the world together make up the mind and the world." I called that slogan a "metaphor" (Putnam 1981: xi), and what it came to was this: we make up conceptual schemes, and those schemes, and the sentences in them that can be confirmed and disconfirmed, are the only "world" of which we can speak. No wonder Rorty was fond of my writing in that period! Not that he missed the realist elements in *Reason, Truth and History*, but that he regarded them as vestiges that he hoped to talk me out of. (Later he despaired of that hope.)

In sum, on the "internal realist" picture it is not only our experiences (conceived of as "sense data") that are an interface *between* us and the world; our "conceptual schemes" were likewise conceived of as an interface. And the two "interfaces" were related: our ways of conceptualizing, our language games, were seen by me as controlled by "operational constraints" which ultimately reduce to our sense data. And to give up "internal realism" and return to "natural realism," or to a reasoned philosophical defense of natural realism, involves giving up thinking of either experiences *or* concepts as "between" us and external realities. Or so I argued in my Dewey Lectures, and so I still believe.

For John McDowell's benefit, let me add that the problem with *Reason, Truth and History* isn't that I failed to realize that experiences are *conceptualized*. On the contrary, even then, in 1981, I emphasized that they are conceptualized (Putnam 1981: 54). It was that I failed to see that one could think of both experiences and concepts as forms – to use what I think is McDowell's own language – of *openness to the world*. I should not have seen us as "making up" the world (not even with the world's help); I should have seen us as *open* to the world, as interacting with the world in ways that permit aspects of it to reveal themselves to us. Of course we need to invent concepts to do that. There is plenty of constructive activity here. But we don't construct reality itself.

In "Realism and Reason" (the lecture I described as an internal realist "manifesto") and subsequently I also used the term "metaphysical realism." I now think that that was a mistake. The mistake was not a simple slip, like using "internal realism" to mean two different things, as I recounted above. But it *was* a mistake nonetheless.

It was a mistake because, although I repeatedly explained what I meant by the term, there is a natural understanding of the phrase "metaphysical realism" in which it refers to a broad family of positions, and not just to the *one* position I used it to refer to. Although I was often impatient with critics who said "But you haven't refuted *my* form of metaphysical realism," when "their" form wasn't the one I was talking about, I now sympathize with them. In effect I *was* saying that by refuting the one philosophical view I called by that name I was *ipso facto* refuting anything that deserved to be called "metaphysical realism," and that was not something I had shown.

As I explained "metaphysical realism" (Putnam 1990a) what it came to was precisely the denial of conceptual relativity. My "metaphysical realist" believed that a given thing or system of things can be described in exactly one way, if the description is complete and correct, and that way is supposed to fix exactly one "ontology" and one "ideology" in Quine's sense of those words, that is, exactly one domain of individuals and one domain of predicates of those individuals. Thus it cannot be a matter of convention, as I have argued that it is, whether there are such individuals as mereological sums; either the "true" ontology includes mereological sums or it doesn't. And it cannot be a matter of convention, as I have argued that it is, whether spacetime points are individuals or mere limits, etc., etc.

To be sure, this is *one form* that metaphysical realism can take. But if we understand "metaphysical realist" more broadly, as applying to all philosophers who reject all forms of verificationism and all talk of our "making" the world, then I believe it is perfectly possible to be a metaphysical realist in *that* sense and to accept the phenomenon I am calling "conceptual relativity."

The compatibility of conceptual relativity with realism

One of the many contributions of both John Austin and Ludwig Wittgenstein was to stress how many different sorts of things we do with language. A further insight, which they shared with the earlier American pragmatists, was that these uses and speech-acts are not simply discrete and separate (something that the metaphor of a "toolbox" that Josiah Royce used in *The Problem of Christianity* does not bring out) but interdependent. John McDowell has written about the impossibility of "disentangling" factual description and evaluation, and Quine famously spoke of the impossibility of disentangling fact and convention. I shall say more about the importance that the triple entanglement of fact, value and convention has had in my philosophy in a few moments. For the moment, however, let us focus on descriptions, though without forgetting that description can both depend upon and determine evaluations and conventions, or that descriptions can be of many different kinds and serve many different interests.

So how *should* realists who recognize the existence of cases of genuine conceptual relativity formulate their realism? Imagine a situation in which there are exactly three billiard balls on a certain table and no other objects (i.e. the atoms, etc., of which the billiard balls consist do not count as "objects" in that context). Consider the two descriptions, "There are only seven objects on that table: three billiard balls, and four mereological sums containing more than one billiard ball" and "There are only three objects on the table, but there are seven *sets* of individuals that can be formed of those objects." What it means to be a *realist who recognizes conceptual relativity* with respect to *this* case is to believe that there is an aspect of reality which is independent of what we think at the moment (although we could, of course, change it by adding or subtracting objects from the table), which is *correctly describable either way*.

The example is artificial because no one except a philosopher, to my knowledge, *ever* talks about "mereological sums." But in mathematical physics conceptual relativity is an ubiquitous phenomenon, and there the correct attitude is the same (or so I maintain). To take an example from a paper with the title "Bosonization as Duality" that appeared in *Nuclear Physics* B some years ago (Burgess and Quevedo 1994), there are quantum mechanical schemes some of whose representations depict the particles in a system as bosons while others depict them as fermions. As their use of the term "representations" indicates, real live physicists – not philosophers with any particular philosophical axe to grind – do not regard this as a case of ignorance. In their view, the "bosons" and "fermions" are simply artifacts of the representation used. But the system is mind-independently real, for all that, and each of its states is a mind-independently real condition, that can be represented in each of these different ways. And that is exactly the conclusion I advocate. (David Albert's paper in the present volume describes a much simpler case, one which needs no field theory, in which two different stories about the history of a two-particle EPR system are representations of the same reality, even though in one of them there is a period of time in which the spin of A in a certain direction is correlated with the spin of B in that same direction, rather than anti-correlated, and in the other "story" (frame-dependent history) there is no such period of time.)

To accept that these descriptions are both answerable to the very same aspect of reality, that they are "equivalent descriptions" in that sense, is to be a metaphysical realist without capital letters, a realist in one's "metaphysics," but not a "metaphysical realist" in the technical sense I gave to that phrase in "Realism and Reason" and related publications. And if I have long repented of having once said that "the mind and the world make up the mind and the world," that is because what we actually make up is not the world, but language games, concepts, uses, conceptual schemes. To confuse making up the *notion* of a boson, which is something the scientific community did over time, with making up real quantum mechanical systems is to slide into idealism, it seems to me. And that was a bad thing to slide into.

A caution

It is important not to confuse conceptual relativity with the very different phenomenon of conceptual pluralism. You may have noticed that all my examples of conceptual relativity come from science, which is where the phenomenon seems to occur. At one time, I confused it with simple conceptual pluralism, and that led me to mistakenly give the fact that I can (depending on my interests) describe the contents of a room *either* by saying that the room contains a table and two chairs *or* by saying it contains such-and-such fields and particles, as an example of conceptual relativity. I do indeed deny that the world can be completely described in the language game of theoretical physics; not because there are regions in which physics is *false*, but because, to use Aristotelian language, the world has many levels of form, and there is no realistic possibility of reducing them all to the level of fundamental physics. For example, it is a true description of one aspect of reality to say that Immanuel Kant wrote some passages in *The Critique of Pure Reason* that are difficult to interpret, but that statement cannot be "translated" into the language of physics in any reasonable sense of "translated." And it is a true description of another aspect of reality to say that Andrew Wiles and Richard Taylor gave a correct proof of Fermat's Last Theorem, and that statement too cannot be translated into the language of *physics*. And it is a true description of a third aspect of reality to say that the reason I took a certain route to Harvard Square on a certain day was that I mistakenly believed that it would be quicker. And both of the above descriptions of the room could well be correct. *But* the very fact that these descriptions do not belong to "schemes" which can be systematically translated into each other means that they are *not* "equivalent" in the technical sense of mutually relatively interpretable. That is why they illustrate *conceptual pluralism* but not conceptual relativity in my sense.[6]

Some objections

I have spoken of descriptions as answerable to "aspects of reality," and I know such talk will raise some hackles. Let me say a word about some of those "hackles."

One set of "hackles" I will not try to smooth down today (although they will be the subject of the paper I plan to start writing as soon as I get home to Massachusetts), are those of one sort of "Wittgensteinian." I say "one sort" because the Harvard Department of Philosophy was for years the scene of an intense disagreement about whether Wittgenstein was an "end of philosophy" philosopher. (My own view is that he was *sometimes* such a philosopher, but that isn't what made him a *great* philosopher.) On the "end of philosophy" view, my whole lifelong preoccupation with "realism" was a *mistake*. For example, my dear personal friend and strong philosophical opponent, Burton Dreben, used to call me a "Girondist" (as opposed to the true Wittgensteinians like himself, who were "Jacobins") (Dreben 1992: 315). According to him, realism and idealism are both nonsense, *period*.

Another dear personal friend and strong philosophical opponent who agrees with Dreben, although not for Wittgensteinian reasons, is Richard Rorty. In a paper[7] which will appear in the forthcoming volume on me in the Library of Living Philosophers, he even accuses me of being a throwback, not to the Girondists, but to Parmenides! According to him, talk of reality commits me to thinking of reality as a "superthing," and thereby as opening the pseudo-question, as he regards it, of the nature of reality.

Let me say for the record that I utterly and totally reject all versions of the "end of philosophy" story, whether they come from Wittgensteinians, Rortians, Heideggerians, Derridians, or whomever. My two favorite definitions of philosophy are Wilfrid Sellars' "How things, in the widest sense of the term, hang together, in the widest sense of the term,"[8] and Stanley Cavell's terse "education for grownups" (Cavell 1979: 125), and I think it vitally important that philosophy, in both of these senses, continue. Philosophy was not a mistake; not in Parmenides' time, not in Plato's time, not in Aristotle's or Descartes' or Hume's or Kant's times, and not in our time. As Etienne Gilson put it, "philosophy always buries its undertakers" (Gilson 1999/1937).

But let me turn to "hackles" whose lack of smoothness I take more seriously. Instead of speaking of "aspects of reality," I could obviously (if I hadn't wanted to raise the hackles I just said I won't discuss today) have said "states of affairs." And haven't Quine and Davidson convinced us, or at least convinced those of us who take them – as I certainly do – to have made great contributions to our subject, that such talk is useless and needs to be discarded?

For both of them, the objection stemmed partly from the belief that to quantify over so-called "abstract entities" such as states of affairs is to reify them, to be guilty of hypostatizing them. Even quantifying over *sets*, which Quine defended as necessary for science, was something that he accepted with explicit reluctance.[9] That is not an attitude that I share. But over and beyond that reason, Quine argued that there are no clear (i.e. no precise) criteria of *identity* and *nonidentity* in the case of states of affairs, propositions, and the like, and that *this* disqualified them from serious discourse (which Quine equated with *scientific* discourse).

However, as Quine himself recognized, to disqualify quantification over every sort of thing, in the widest sense of "thing," for which we lack precise criteria of identity has an enormous price. In particular, he observed (correctly) that there aren't precise criteria of identity for beliefs, for meanings (semantic contents) of words and sentences, for hopes, fears, and all the host of propositional attitudes. And Quine recognized that talk of all of these is indispensable in practice. At this point, however, he violated his own best pragmatic impulses by writing,

> Propositional and attributary attitudes belong to the daily discourse of hopes, fears, and purposes; causal science gets on well without them. ... a reasonable if less ambitious alternative [to attempting to make them "science worthy"] would be to keep a relatively simple and austere conceptual scheme, free of half-entities [sic], for official scientific business and then accommodate the half-entities in a second grade system.
>
> (Quine 1969: 24)

And he went on to tell us that only the first-grade system need be taken seriously in philosophy. Apparently the idea that there aren't really any such things as meaning, hopes, fears and purposes "gilt in der Philosophie aber in der Praxis nicht" [is valid in philosophy but not in practice] – an attitude that I find wrong both philosophically, because it frees philosophy from the control of relevance to practice, and practically, because it frees practice from the control of critical reflection.

In what was perhaps the first of my explicitly scientific realist papers – the paper I read to an international congress on logic, methodology, and philosophy of science on August 27, 1960, the day Ruth Anna and I met – I illustrated the indispensable scientific role of terms which are not "precise" when I wrote

> Usually a scientist introduces [a new technical term into the language] via some kind of paraphrase. For example, one might explain "mass"

as "that physical magnitude which determines how strongly a body resists being accelerated, e.g. if a body has twice the mass, it will be twice as hard to accelerate". (Instead of "physical magnitude" one might say in ordinary language "that property of the body" or "that *in* the body which ... ") Such "broad-spectrum" notions occur in every natural language and our present notion of a "physical magnitude" is already an extreme refinement.

(Putnam 1975b: 215–27)

I also counted "thing" as a "broad-spectrum notion." Well, I think "state of affairs" is also one of the "broad-spectrum notions" that we need in contexts in which we do not have a more precise notion available, and without which we could not intelligibly explain those more precise notions when we do introduce them. In short, I think we need to stop apologizing for talk of "states of affairs."

In addition to sharing Quine's worries, Davidson had an additional reason for shunning talk of states of affairs, namely that it might lead to the resurrection of the so-called "correspondence theory" of truth.

One problem with that "theory" is that it is hopelessly vague. As James and Kant both remarked, phrases like "agrees with reality" are if anything *less* clear than "true." But there are further problems as well, which I shall only mention briefly. Although there is a sense in which a true description "corresponds" to an aspect of reality, or to an actual state of affairs, or a way things actually happen to be (take your pick), not all true sentences are *descriptions*. My own view of truth ever since my Dewey lectures has been what I described as a "disquotational one," in a sense of that term I connected with Frege. *To make a statement is to assert something, and to say that that something is true is to assert the same thing*. But that does not commit me to inventing "states of affairs" to correspond to all the things that can be correctly asserted. And if one does invent such "states of affairs," then nothing is thereby added to the account of truth.

A further problem with "correspondence" talk, one also seen by Frege, I believe, and certainly seen by Wittgenstein, is that it makes it sound as if there is just *one* sort of correspondence, *one* single relation, that somehow stands behind all of our talk. But if one agrees with Wittgenstein that there are many uses even of so-called "descriptive" language, and further agrees with him in thinking of those uses as exercises of world-involving and context-sensitive abilities, then whether given words (even, say "the cat is on the mat") correspond to a particular state of affairs will depend on *which* world-involving ability to use those words is being exercised and in *what context* that ability is being exercised. One might say that when a true statement does "correspond" to an aspect of reality, what *sort* of "correspondence" is involved depends both on the meaning of the statement and the particular extra-linguistic context. It is certainly not a matter of mere "marks and noises" standing in a *fixed* relation R to something (to a state of affairs, the world as a whole, or ...).

To sum up: to say, as I do, that when we describe things, in Sellars' "widest sense of the term," we are *answerable* to those things, and that when we describe them correctly there is an aspect of reality that is as we assert it to be, is obviously to be a realist in one's view of "how things, in the widest sense of the term, hang together." My sort of realism is compatible with conceptual relativity (or the cognitive equivalence of some theories which are incompatible at the level of surface grammar), and it does *not* presuppose or require a "correspondence theory of truth" of the kind that Davidson feared.

Pragmatism

My first exposure to pragmatism occurred during my undergraduate years at the University of Pennsylvania. My first teacher in the philosophy of science, C. West Churchman, was a pragmatist (a student of E. A. Singer Jr., who was in turn a student of William James). And the idea of the triple entanglement of fact, theory, and convention that was to be so important to me when I finally turned to the topic of valuation was very much at the center of attention in Churchman's courses, although that early influence lay dormant in my mind for a long time, as I concentrated on work in mathematical logic, especially in the 1950s. (That work, together with my writing "The Analytic and the Synthetic" in 1957, resulted in my being awarded tenure in both the department of mathematics and the department of philosophy at Princeton in 1960.) In addition, I took a course with Abraham Kaplan, who was at that time strongly influenced by John Dewey, at U.C.L.A. in 1950, as well as a seminar on Dewey's *Logic* taught by Donald Piatt the following year. But my serious reading of William James only began forty years later.

Although I do not normally call myself a pragmatist, or any kind of "-ist" for that matter, I am not unhappy when I am so described, *except* when people assimilate my views to those of my aforementioned dear friend and philosophical opponent Richard Rorty. I do not share his reading of the classical pragmatists at all, nor do I know of any James or Dewey scholar who does. Nor do I share his desire to bring philosophy to an end, or his contempt for talk of experience, reality, and truth. But I don't wish to repeat myself.

I also want to stress the fact that my admiration for the classical pragmatists does *not* extend to any of the different theories of truth that Peirce, James, and Dewey advanced. But one can learn from any of the great philosophers without sharing all of their cherished beliefs. If that weren't the case, how could we still be learning, as I think we are and should be, from Aristotle or from Kant?

There are many things that I think we can learn from the pragmatists. I shall close by mentioning only the following two:

First of all, the realization that description and evaluation must not be regarded as two separate watertight boxes in which statements or uses of statements can be put. *All* description presupposes evaluation (although not necessarily *moral* evaluation) and *all* evaluation presupposes description. Although this idea of interdependence or mutual presupposition has been developed more carefully and extended by post-Quinean and post-Wittgensteinian philosophers, notably by Stanley Cavell, Philippa Foot, Iris Murdoch, John McDowell, Vivian Walsh, Morton White, and (beginning with *Reason, Truth and History*) myself, it was ubiquitous in the writing of James and Dewey (and even present in Peirce, although not ubiquitous).

Second, I heartily approve of the pragmatists' insistence that philosophy can and should matter to our moral and spiritual lives. Unfortunately, nowadays it is often claimed that analytic philosophy is a Good Thing precisely because it eschews thinking about that sort of stuff. If any philosophy that does not eschew the question of How to Live is not automatically convicted of being a Bad Thing, then at least it is shown to be Bad Philosophy, according to this point of view. (Although, fortunately, not all analytic philosophers agree! Paul Grice, for example, once devoted a highly analytic seminar to precisely that three-word question.) But reflection on our ways of living, and especially on what is wrong with those ways of living, has always been a vital function of philosophy. If philosophy abandons that aspiration, what is supposed to replace it? The aspiration that philosophy will become a cumulative body of knowledge? That is a pipedream.

The only argument that I have seen for rejecting the idea that such writers as Emerson, Kierkegaard, Sartre, Marx, and Thoreau *belong* in philosophy is that they do not give "arguments" (meaning: their writings don't look like logic texts). In addition, I have heard it said, there is the danger that such writings may convince someone by "irrational persuasion."

Well, *of course* there is that danger! And it *is* the responsibility of each reader to avoid irrationality – but not by relying on a "method." What the objection overlooks is that philosophy needn't have the sole function of establishing theses, pieces of propositional knowledge, via more or less rigorous argument. When that is the function, the standards of "analytic philosophy" are appropriate. But to read the writings of any of the philosophers I just listed isn't to encounter a series of theses; it is to encounter texts which anger, provoke, inspire, transform, repulse, or all of these at once; but such encounters are important because a life which does not encounter such issues and such reactions is not worth living.

What the pragmatists saw – and with this remark I shall close – is that philosophy can have both of these functions, and yet others besides. We don't need to erect firm boundaries around philosophy to keep the aliens out. We need their contribution. One of the things that was so enjoyable about teaching in the same department as Stanley Cavell all those decades ago is that he so thoroughly shares this "pragmatist" attitude, and has helped inculcate it in so many of his (and my) students.

Notes

1 This chapter originated as a closing lecture to the "PutnamFest" conference at University College Dublin, March 11–14, 2007.
2 This was delivered at the 40th Chapel Hill Colloquium in Philosophy, October 6–8, 2006.
3 When I wrote those words, I was thinking of "Terms in a mature science typically refer and theories accepted in a mature science are typically approximately true" – this was Richard Boyd's characterization of "scientific realism," which I still like, by the way.
4 I publicly renounced that idea in my reply to Simon Blackburn at the conference on my philosophy at the University of St. Andrews in November 1990 (Putnam 1994). The reasons I gave up my "antirealism" are stated in the first three of my replies in Putnam 1992, where I give a history of my use(s) of the unfortunate term "internal realism," and, at more length, in my Dewey Lectures (Putnam 1999). See also my exchange with Crispin Wright (Wright 2000) and Putnam 2001.
5 I still believe that our so-called "mental states" are best thought of as *capacities to function*, but not in the strongly reductionist sense that went with the model of those states as "the brain's software." They are, so to speak, "long-armed" functional states – their "arms" reach out to the environment, and, as Ruth Millikan has stressed, their identity depends on their evolutionary history.
6 The mistake was first pointed out to me by Jennifer Case (Case 2001). See Putnam (2006: 33–51) for a fuller discussion of conceptual relativity and conceptual pluralism.
7 Rorty's paper, which is still unpublished at this writing, is titled "Putnam, Pragmatism and Parmenides."
8 Sellars' definition is actually a definition of *metaphysics*, in the best sense, and not of philosophy as a whole. In the end, Cavell's is the more comprehensive.
9 "Here I have felt that if I must come to terms with Platonism, the least I can do is keep it extensional" (Quine 1990: 100).

Bibliography

Burgess, C.P. and Quevedo, F. (1994) "Bosonization as Duality," *Nuclear Physics* B421 373–90; e-Print Archive: hep-th/9401105; http://arxiv.org/abs/hep-th/9401105.
Case, Jennifer (2001) "The Heart of Putnam's Pluralistic Realism," *Revue Internationale de Philosophie* 55(4): 417–30.
Cavell, Stanley (1979) *The Claim of Reason*, Oxford: Oxford University Press.
de Gaynesford, Maximilian (2006) *Hilary Putnam*, Chesham: Acumen.
Dreben, Burton (1992) "Putnam, Quine – and the Facts," *Philosophical Topics* 20: 293–315.
Gilson, Etienne (1999/1937) *The Unity of Philosophical Experience*, Fort Collins, CO: Ignatius Press.
James, William (1976) "A World of Pure Experience," in *The Works of William James: Essays in Radical Empiricism*, ed. Frederick Burkhardt and Fredson Bowers, Cambridge, MA: Harvard University Press.

Putnam, Hilary (1975) *Philosophical Papers*, vol. 1, *Mathematics, Matter and Method*, Cambridge: Cambridge, University Press.
——(1975b) "What Theories are Not," *Philosophical Papers*, vol. 1, 215–27.
——(1978) *Meaning and the Moral Sciences*, London: Routledge and Kegan Paul.
——(1980, 1983) "Models and Reality," *Journal of Symbolic Logic* 45.3 (1980): 464–82. Collected in Putnam, *Philosophical Papers*, vol. 3.
——(1981) *Reason, Truth and History*, Cambridge: Cambridge University Press.
——(1983) *Philosophical Papers*, vol. 3, *Realism and Reason*, Cambridge: Cambridge University Press.
——(1990) "James's Theory of Perception," in *Realism with a Human Face*, Cambridge, MA: Harvard University Press, 232–51.
——(1990a) "A Defense of Internal Realism," in *Realism with a Human Face*, Cambridge, MA: Harvard University Press, 30–42.
——(1992) "Replies," *Philosophical Topics* 20 (1): 347–408.
——(1994) "Comments and Replies," in Peter Clark and Bob Hale (eds.), *Reading Putnam*, Oxford: Blackwell.
——(1994) "The Dewey Lectures 1994: Sense, Nonsense, and the Senses."
——(1999) "An Inquiry into the Powers of the Human Mind." Journal of Philosophy 91(9): 445–517. Reprinted in Putnam, *The Threefold Cord; Mind, Body and World*, New York: Columbia University Press, 1999, 3–70.
——(2001) "When 'Evidence Transcendence' is Not Malign," *Journal of Philosophy*, 98(11): 594–600.
——(2001a) "Reply to Jennifer Case," *Revue Internationale de Philosophie* 55(4): 431–38.
——(2005)"A Philosopher Looks at Quantum Mechanics (Again)," *British Journal for the Philosophy of Science* 56(4): 615–34.
——(2006) *Ethics Without Ontology*, Cambridge, MA: Harvard University Press.
——(2007) "Between Scylla and Charybdis: Does Dummett Have a Way Through?," in Randall E. Auxier and Lewis Edwin Hahn (eds.), *The Philosophy of Michael Dummett*,Chicago and LaSalle IL: Open Court, 155–67.
Quine, W. V. (1969) *Ontological Relativity and Other Essays*, New York: Columbia University Press.
——(1990) *Theories and Things*, Cambridge, MA: Harvard University Press.
Wright, Crispin (2000) "Truth as Sort of Epistemic: Putnam's Peregrinations," *Journal of Philosophy* 97(6): 335–64.

Part I
THE ENIGMA OF REALISM

1
WHAT OF PRAGMATISM WITH THE WORLD HERE?[1]

Richard Boyd

Putnam on "metaphysical realism" and "ontology"

Putnam as an anti-reductionist

Except for an early brief foray into the other camp (Oppenheim and Putnam 1958) Hilary Putnam has been pretty steadfastly an anti-reductionist at least in so far as the non-mathematical sciences are concerned. As his views have changed over time, however, there has been a shift in the target of his anti-reductionism. In his earlier work (prior to his adoption of an "internal realist" or "pragmatist" perspective) he seemed prepared to defend a realist and broadly materialist (but anti-reductionist) conception of empirical inquiry and its subject matters. With the turn to internal realism or pragmatism he appears to have rejected the viability of a genuinely non-reductionist version of metaphysical materialism, or indeed of any realist metaphysical position. At least as early as "Why there isn't a Ready Made World" (Putnam 1983b) and as recently as *Ethics Without Ontology* (Putnam 2004) Putnam appears to maintain that genuinely metaphysical realist positions are inevitably (and mistakenly) reductionist and are to be rejected in favor of a broadly pragmatist or Wittgensteinian conception. It is with this and related antirealist claims that I propose to take issue here.

Putnam on metaphysical realism

Putnam's characterization of the sort of metaphysical realism he opposes is interesting, in part because it includes features which one might not (I'll argue should not) think of as being at all closely related to the sorts of realism (about, e.g., scientific, psychological and moral theories and conceptions) to which many later twentieth-century philosophers – many of them following Putnam's early lead (in, e.g., Putnam 1972, 1975a, 1975b) – have devoted their attention. To a good first approximation, the later Putnam understands metaphysical realism regarding a domain of discourse as constituted by (or at least as entailing) six important doctrines.

(i) (CT) Truth is "correspondence truth"

This is the main target of Putnam's criticisms of "metaphysical realism." His criticisms rest on the association of this basic doctrine with five others, as follows.

(ii) (OTT) There is One True Theory with One True (reductive) Ontology

It seems to be the key metaphysical commitment of "metaphysical realism" that, within the relevant domain, there's a single true theory (presumably up to analytic translational equivalence or something like that) and that all legitimate concepts and theories are formulable in its vocabulary. Here's the crucial characterization of this component of metaphysical realism.

> The world consists of some fixed totality of mind-independent objects. There is exactly one true and complete description of 'the way the world is.' Truth involves some sort of correspondence relation between words or thought signs and external things and sets of things.
>
> (Putnam 1981: 49)

Strictly speaking, someone who accepted the doctrine that there is one true theory would not have to be a reductionist since she might adopt the eliminativist position that the only legitimate concepts are those of the theory in question so that there's nothing to reduce, but it's clear (in e.g. Putnam 1983b) that Putnam anticipates that the main targets of his critique will be versions of (allegedly) non-reductionist materialism.

(iii) (MI) The objects of that ontology are mind-independent

Related – in ways we'll discuss – to OTT is the doctrine that *both* the objects in the relevant ontology *and* (as these quotations indicate) *their status as appropriate objects* are mind-independent.

> 'Objects' do not exist independently of conceptual schemes. *We* cut up the world into objects when we introduce one or another scheme of description (1981: 52). If, as I maintain, 'objects' themselves are *as much made as discovered*, as much products of our conceptual *invention* as of the 'objective' factor in experience, the factor independent of our will, then of course objects intrinsically

belong under certain labels because those labels are just the *tools we use to construct a version* of the world with such objects in the first place.

(1981: 54 italics his)

> (iv) *(TRNE) Truth (and other semantic notions) are radically non-epistemic*

and

> (v) *(RPC) Reference is determined by purely causal*, non-conceptual, non-intentional *relations between term use and features of the world*

These two doctrines are very closely related. A central component of "metaphysical realism" according to Putnam (see e.g. Putnam 1978) is the doctrine that truth for the domain in question is a radically non-epistemic notion. The idea is that, according to the metaphysical realist, our best confirmed theories could turn out to be false, so that truth is a sort of epistemically inaccessible "standard" with respect to which our beliefs could turn out to fail. The intended contrast is provided by conceptions of truth in the verificationist or pragmatist traditions according to which truth is, or is very closely related to, idealized confirmation or by some even thinner conceptions according to which truth isn't a real property at all but according to which uses of "true" are guided by epistemically noncommittal deployment of something like Tarski's T-schema. These, in contrast to a radically non-epistemic conception, would avoid the skeptical consequences of treating truth as an epistemically inaccessible standard.

There is an important additional rationale in Putnam's anti-(metaphysical) realist project for assigning both TRNE and RCP to the metaphysical realist. In his internal realist/pragmatist writings Putnam seems consistently to follow Field (1973) in thinking that the (metaphysical) realist semantic project – at least in its "naturalistic" versions – entails offering a *physicalistic* reduction of semantic notions like reference and truth, so that they are ultimately explicable in non-intentional, non-semantic, non-conceptual, non-normative terms. Since epistemic notions are both normative and semantic, this constraint would rule out epistemic accounts of truth and, of course, it would rule out conceptions of reference which irreducibly appeal to conceptual or intentional factors.

It's important in understanding these doctrines to realize that, while Putnam's explicit characterizations of metaphysical realism don't include a commitment to naturalism or to materialism, it's clear (and explicit in Putnam 1983b) that it's with naturalist or materialist versions of metaphysical realism that he's been mainly concerned. Recognizing this focus on materialist or naturalist realism helps us to resolve an interpretive puzzle about the ways in which Putnam characterizes metaphysical realism.

"Officially," as it were, his characterization of metaphysical realism (and his critiques) should apply not just to materialist or naturalist realism but, for example, to objective idealist versions of metaphysical realism including, e.g., the view that all real phenomena are aspects of representations in the mind of god. Such a position would surely count as metaphysical and realist if anything would, and it could certainly incorporate a correspondence conception of truth as something sometimes epistemically inaccessible to us. But, it's hard to see how it could portray truth, reference or any other semantic phenomena as independent of matters conceptual or intentional: after all according to it *every* phenomenon is conceptual or intentional. So, it wouldn't satisfy either TRNE or RPC and wouldn't satisfy key features of Putnam's characterization of metaphysical realism.

If we think of Putnam's characterization "unofficially" as applying just to materialist or naturalist metaphysical realism, however, the puzzle is resolved. I'll argue later that this is the most perspicuous interpretation for purposes of the present chapter.

There is an additional consideration which is almost certainly operative in Putnam's assignment to metaphysical realism of TRNE and RPC to metaphysical realism. If we think of philosophical definitions (whether physicalistic or not) of truth, reference and other semantic notions as *introducing* definitions then – since conceptual and intentional relations are *already* semantic relations – deploying conceptual or intentional resources in defining reference (or any other semantic notions) would run a very serious risk of circularity. So a causal theory of reference, understood as introducing a definition of "reference," would have to be formulated in non-concept-or-intention-involving terms.

> *(vi) (BIV) Bivalence holds for all sentences in the relevant ontologically privileged vocabulary.*

The basic idea seems to be that, on the assumption that there is an ontological reality with respect to which realistically understood (correspondence-wise) truth values are determined, well-formulated statements will always have determinate truth values since, even though (insufficiently well-formulated) language use might be "vague," "reality" won't be. Here the influence of concerns from the philosophy of mathematics can be felt, since the intuitionist's reservations about positing mind-independent mathematical objects are systematically connected with rejection of the law of the excluded middle. I've chosen to explicitly formulate Putnam's notion of metaphysical realism as concerning metaphysical realism *regarding a domain of discourse* (which he does not do) precisely to draw attention to the fact that the plausibility of "metaphysical realism" as an account of (ordinary, everyday) philosophical realism may vary across domains. In particular, the idea that ordinary philosophical realism regarding, e.g., the theory of real analysis or set theory entails bivalence has a certain initial (and perhaps more than just initial) plausibility. One has (or at least I have) difficulty in imagining what a vague mathematical object (as opposed to a mathematical representation of vagueness) might be. As we shall see, it's much easier to understand how a natural phenomenon, like a biological species, might have "vague" boundaries without thereby being disqualified as part of a correspondence-wise truth-making condition.

Sorting out the reductionist components: physicalism and mind-independence

Four of the doctrines which Putnam attributes to "metaphysical realism" (all but CT and BIV) have an explicitly reductionist character. It appears that the attribution of these reductionist elements to metaphysical realism has two distinct sources.

"Metaphysical realism" versus non-reductionist materialism

Most of the time when Putnam discusses the commitment of metaphysical realists to One True Theory with its associated ontology, he has it in mind that the metaphysical realist will take that theory to be some fundamental physical theory. He's aware, of course, that there are philosophers who defend a putatively realist and materialist but non-reductionist conception of both scientific and semantic matters as part of a generally non-reductionist materialist metaphysics. Indeed, they seem to be the primary targets of his anti-(metaphysical) realist critique. In particular, in his critique of metaphysical realism in "Why there isn't a Ready Made World" (1983b), he explicitly argues against the viability of non-reductionist materialism. So he thinks that metaphysical materialism collapses to reductionist physicalism.

If we think of Putnam's primary targets and his conception of the dialectical situation in this way, then there is a unifying theme to OTT, MI, TRNE and RPC. Suppose, as Putnam does, that non-reductionist materialism isn't viable. Then a materialist metaphysical realist could countenance mental or psychological entities only if reference to them were reducible to the concepts of fundamental physics. Since Putnam and his non-reductionist metaphysical materialist targets agree that no such reduction is possible, it would follow that a consistent metaphysical materialist could not countenance minds or mind-dependent phenomena: hence MI. "Metaphysical realists" of whatever stripe are realists about correspondence truth and other semantic matters, so materialist metaphysical realists must be. If they are disbarred from countenancing mind-dependent phenomena, then they are disbarred from holding that truth, reference or other semantic matters have epistemic, intentional, or other mental features: hence TRNE and RPC. So reductionism about semantic matters would emerge for the materialist metaphysical realist as a special case of reductionist physicalism about matters metaphysical.

Reductionism and the reality of things

The fact that Putnam's main targets are defenders of non-reductionist materialism makes understanding the issue of mind-independence a complicated one. Two different sorts of mind-independence are at issue. On the one hand, there are phenomena which are *prima facie* mind-dependent because they straightforwardly involve minds: minds, for example, and mental states, but also human social structures and social artifacts, semantic phenomena, and the like. Putnam appears to hold that, for the fully consistent materialist metaphysical realist, such phenomena – and the concepts and language that refer to them – must be reducible to the phenomena and concepts of physics.

The other sort of mind-dependence concerns the ontological status of members of the "fixed totality of mind-independent objects." Recall that a central theme of Putnam's work both before and after his critiques of metaphysical realism is that natural kinds, like water, have essences (or defining properties or whatever) which are not provided by analytic definitions of the terms referring to them but which are discoverable by *a posteriori* investigations instead. Thus water = H_2O even though "water = H_2O" isn't analytically true. A central claim of many non-reductionist materialists is, roughly, that the naturalness of a natural object (a natural kind, relation, magnitude, thing, etc.) is discipline-specific. Thus, for example, pains might form a natural kind in psychology but (perhaps because of multiple realizability, perhaps for other reasons) not in physics. Since disciplines are mind-dependent, the non-reductionist materialist realist must maintain that the naturalness – and thus, I assume, the ontological standing – of natural objects is mind-dependent.

The obvious (and, I shall later argue, the correct) way to understand this claim is to see it as maintaining that natural objects *qua* natural objects are, in some important sense, partly constituted by the relevant disciplinary practices. The status of pain *as a natural kind in psychology*, for example, would be partly a matter of (the appropriateness of) the methodological role of the concept of pain in that discipline. Putnam agrees and he takes the recognition of this sort of constitution to be incompatible with the mind-independence requirement. So, for example, he offers the following as considerations *against* metaphysical realism.

> 'Objects' do not exist independently of conceptual schemes. We cut up the world into objects when we introduce one or another scheme of description.
>
> (Putnam 1981: 52)

> If, as I maintain, 'objects' themselves are *as much made as discovered*, as much products of our conceptual *invention* as of the 'objective' factor in experience, the factor independent of our will, then of course objects intrinsically belong under certain labels because those labels are just the *tools we use to construct a version* of the world with such objects in the first place.
>
> (Putnam 1981: 54, italics his)

Putnam maintains that the fully consistent materialist metaphysical realist must deny both sorts of mind-dependence. It's not entirely clear how these two issues are supposed to be related. For the metaphysical realist who is a materialist, they seem closely related. According to Putnam such a realist would have to be a physicalistic reductionist regarding each of the members of the "fixed totality of mind-independent objects" to which she was committed. Surely, too, she should be a physicalistic reductionist about whatever property qualifies objects for membership in that august category, so she could not appeal to, e.g., disciplines and social practices unless she could offer a physicalistic reduction of such notions. Even for materialist metaphysical realists, however, the strictures against the two sorts of mind-dependence are not logically equivalent. Some object (say a natural kind) might be physicalistically definable, so that its inclusion in the "fixed totality of mind-independent objects" would be compatible with the first stricture against mind-dependence, but its membership in that category still might not be explicable in physicalistic terms. Thus in evaluating Putnam's critiques of metaphysical realism we'll need to take account of both aspects of mind-dependence.

Putnam against metaphysical realism

I've already indicated that Putnam sees the metaphysical realist's commitment to a radically non-epistemic conception of truth and of related semantic notions as leading to an unacceptable skepticism. Regarding the pure (i.e. non-conceptual, non-intentional, ...) causal conception of reference, to the obvious implausibility of the claim that purely causal relations in this sense are able to establish determinate reference relations Putnam adds the famous "model theoretic arguments" against the determinateness of such relations (see Putnam 1980; 1981; for discussions see, e.g., Koethe 1979, Lewis 1984, Merrill 1980). Against the reductionism implied by the "one true theory/ontology" conception Putnam relies on widely accepted anti-reductionist considerations. He thus relies on the sort of ontological pluralism to which his indented targets (anti-reductionist realists) also subscribe.

There is an additional dimension to Putnam's ontological pluralism: he defends at various times (see, e.g., Putnam 1981, 2004) versions of "conceptual relativity" regarding ontological and existence claims: the idea that questions about the reality or the existence of things, kinds, magnitudes, etc., have determinate answers only relative to a choice of language, language game, conceptual scheme, research paradigm or some such thing. The proper interpretation of Putnam's views (and of Quine's and Carnap's closely related "ontological relativity") may be elusive (see, e.g., Eklund 2008, McGrath 2006), but it's clear that the appeal to conceptual relativity is intended to underwrite the defense of ontological pluralism by denying at the outset the cogency of distinctly metaphysical questions of ontology.

The moral sciences and doing without ontology

At least since *Meaning and the Moral Sciences* (1978) it's been clear that Putnam's rejection of "metaphysical realism" is closely connected with his concern to reject scientistic, reductionist approaches to the moral sciences, broadly understood, and this concern is manifest with respect to ethics (presumably *the* moral science) in *Ethics Without Ontology* (2004).

The relationship between metaphysical (or anti-metaphysical) issues and issues of methodology (in the sciences, the moral sciences or everyday life) is complex. If we take metaphysically realist materialism to be defined by Putnam's presentation of it, any *fully consistent* defender of genuinely metaphysical materialism would have to be a reductionist (or an eliminativist) about not just the moral sciences but, e.g., about chemistry and biology as well. On the all-but-consensus conception that reductionism fails as a way of understanding the study of (even slightly) complex systems, it follows that a consistent (genuinely) metaphysical materialist *who consistently practiced what she preached* would be committed to a profoundly flawed methodological approach to any questions outside (at most) fundamental particle physics. Of course, the main target in the philosophy of science of Putnam's anti-(metaphysical-)materialist arguments are philosophers who defend non-reductionist materialism. For the most part, Putnam does not seem to maintain that defenders of materialist metaphysical materialism in the philosophy of science are at risk of profound methodological errors in their own work (if any) in the physical and biological sciences, or in the methodological recommendations they would make to working scientists. So, it would seem, he recognizes that they favor genuinely anti-reductionist research strategies even though, according to him, this reflects an – I assume admirable – departure from what their (realist, materialist) metaphysical views would dictate.

By contrast there is the strong suggestion in Putnam's work (especially, of course, in *Ethics Without Ontology*) that someone who adopts a genuinely *metaphysical* concern with matters ontological *will* run the risk of methodological error in the moral sciences. In particular, Putnam suggests in *Ethics Without Ontology* that an ontological approach to ethics will lead to a reductive methodology which ignores the complexity of moral phenomena, especially the diversity of factors which contribute to moral value.

This situation is similar to that which obtained in the debate between logical empiricist verificationists and scientific realists (whether "metaphysical" or not, assuming that there's a distinction) over whether or not knowledge of unobservables is possible. Realists, and the later empiricists whose work led to the realist critique of verificationist instrumentalism (e.g., Feigl 1956, Maxwell 1962a, Boyd 1982, 1983, 1985a, 1985b; Byerly and Lazara 1973; Lipton 1993; Miller 1987; McMullin 1984; Psillos 1999; Putnam 1972, 1975a, 1975b) argued that it's impossible to rationalize methodologically central scientific practices without acknowledging knowledge of unobservables. It follows from this claim that a verificationist *whose practice consistently honored her own epistemological principles* would have a bankrupt scientific methodology. Nevertheless no defender of scientific realism suggested that, in practice, a philosophical commitment to verificationism subjected physicists and chemists to any substantial risk of methodological error. Practices in these disciplines are so well entrenched that they are largely insensitive to differences in scientists' (or philosophers') positions in the philosophy of science.

By contrast, many philosophers (and psychologists) have suggested that the widespread acceptance of logical empiricist conceptions of science, in particular its denial of knowledge of "unobservables," did in fact adversely influence the practice of psychologists, disposing them to accept behaviorism. Indeed this was a central theme in many early critiques of behaviorism (see, e.g., Fodor 1968, Chomsky 1955/1975; as a story about the *origin* of behaviorism, the influence of logical empiricism has been challenged by, e.g., Amundson 1983, 1986 and Smith 1986).

So, we can distinguish two different questions regarding logical empiricism – "Is it an adequate conception of scientific knowledge?" and "Does its acceptance have a positive or negative effect on scientific practice?" – And we can see that the answer to the latter question might be discipline-specific even if the answer to the former is "no."

Exactly the same situation obtains with respect to various formulations of metaphysical realism. One can ask about such a formulation whether or not it gets the metaphysics, semantics and epistemology of the relevant discipline or practice right; one can ask whether accepting it makes a positive or negative (or neutral) contribution to actual practice; and the latter question might turn out to have different answers with respect to different disciplines or practices, as Putnam's practice indicates.

Similarly, one could coherently maintain (as I do in Boyd 1999b) about contemporary scientific realism *both* that it gets the metaphysics, epistemology and semantics of science basically right *and* that acceptance of it has had an adverse effect in certain disciplines, ones in which realist assumptions have been deeply associated with misleading metaphysical presuppositions. This flexibility, however, comes with a price. One can cogently ask about *almost any* philosophical doctrine whether, or to what extent, it gets things right about matters metaphysical (or anti-metaphysical), epistemological or semantic.

One can cogently ask about the respects in which acceptance of a philosophical position contributes to or detracts from the reliability of actual practices *only if* there is some significant number of people who accept it. This consideration has important implications regarding the interpretation of Putnam's critiques of metaphysical realism.

Interpreting Putnam on "metaphysical realism"

There are two obvious strategies for understanding the target(s) of Putnam's critiques of metaphysical realism. One is to treat "metaphysical realism" as a technical or fused term taking the explicit characterizations he offered early on in his project (roughly the features outlined above (p. 48ff)) as definitive. The other is to treat the expression "metaphysical realism" as having ordinary compositional semantics, so that *metaphysical* realism regarding a domain is whatever sort of realism regarding it is genuinely *metaphysical*. The first of these options has the advantage of being pretty straightforward; the second requires that one have some appropriate analysis both of realism and of what it is for a realist position to be genuinely metaphysical. Nevertheless, faithfulness to Putnam's project requires that we adopt the second approach. Here's why.

Metaphysical realism is supposed to have methodological consequences in practice

In the first place, Putnam plainly does intend to be criticizing, as "metaphysical realist," approaches he thinks are genuinely methodologically misleading *because of their commitment to metaphysical realism*, at least as regards the moral sciences. As we have seen such a criticism would be inappropriate unless some people actually accept those approaches. Almost certainly no one accepts a philosophical approach incorporating anything like the points described above (p. 43ff). With respect to the empirical sciences (physical, biological or social) almost all realists, of whatever stripe, adopt an antireductionist approach, as Putnam recognizes in "Why There Isn't a Ready Made World" (1983b).

Perhaps the issue is a bit more complicated with respect to ethics. If there are any real utilitarians left, then perhaps they subscribe to conceptions which would count as reductionist, but most contemporary realist ethical naturalists deny the sort of simplistic reductive accounts that appear to be the target of *Ethics Without Ontology* (see, e.g., Boyd 1988; Brink 1984, 1989; Sturgeon 1985, 2006a, 2006b). With respect to the other major class of ontological approaches to ethics – theological ones – we need to distinguish between simple formulations of ethical doctrines and reductive or simple characterizations of moral properties or categories. A divine command theory (e.g., "Goodness is obedience to God's commands") or a theological

Platonism like, e.g., that of Adams (1999) ("Goodness is appropriate resemblance to God") may offer a simple ontological formula as a characterization of the good, but – unless it is accompanied by an implausibly simplistic account of the relevant commands, or of the relevant respects of resemblance – it will not (not explicitly, at any rate) imply (or even implicate) any simplistic or reductionist conception of ethical facts or any failure to recognize the complexities of moral life. So with respect to ethics, too, there does not seem to be a large body of philosophers or others who actually subscribe to the sort of reductionist conceptions which conform to Putnam's characterizations of metaphysical realism.

The upshot, I suggest, is that Putnam's critiques of the effects of commitments to metaphysical realism (and to ethics with ontology) on practice are best understood if we think of "metaphysical realism" as having ordinary compositional semantics. That way there will be some people who actually subscribe to versions of it so that the question of the effects of their metaphysical commitments on their practice will be cogent.

Of course this approach requires a different interpretation of Putnam's arguments against metaphysical realism. If his arguments are not, in the first instance, directed against something like the points explicated in his explicit characterization, they need to be understood as embodying two (distinct) interesting and important philosophical claims.

First, the sorts of allegedly non-reductionist, allegedly realist positions to which materialist philosophers and others *do* subscribe are philosophically unstable: under scrutiny they collapse either into reductionist conceptions that do fit his explicit characterization or into (perhaps correct) positions which, though perhaps realist, are no longer genuinely metaphysical. Second, perhaps for this reason, the acceptance of metaphysical realist conceptions does in practice leave thinkers vulnerable to reductionist errors in some domains of inquiry, especially in the moral sciences. As we've already seen, these are logically independent doctrines; in particular, the second can be defended independently of any defense of the first.

Putnam explicitly argues against the stability of non-reductionist metaphysical realism

We've already seen that Putnam's critiques of metaphysical realism are especially focused on materialist or naturalist versions. In this context he clearly thinks that a materialistically acceptable causal theory of reference would have to be physicalistically reductionist, as would the resulting "one true theory/ontology" metaphysical conception. It's important to see that these reductionist components of his explicit characterization of metaphysical realism (in its materialist versions) are not presented simply as *stipulations* about how "metaphysical realism" is to be understood. Instead, Putnam not only acknowledges that there are philosophers who defend a non-reductionist materialist metaphysics, he argues explicitly against the viability of their position. In "Why there isn't a Ready Made World" (1983b), for example, he argues that non-reductionist materialism is not a viable philosophical position. Putnam there considers responses to his reductionist conception of "metaphysical realism" including the suggestion of Boyd (1980, 1988, 1989) that the relation between the phenomena studied in the special sciences and the phenomena studied in fundamental physics is *causal realization* rather than reduction of concepts or vocabularies. According to such an account, an acceptable materialist position would not have to entail the conceptual or linguistic reducibility of the special sciences to physics, but would only need to affirm that the phenomena they study are realized by unexceptional operation of ordinary microphysical causal processes.

In response Putnam denies that there is any metaphysically respectable notion of cause *simpliciter*, or of "total cause," in terms of which the relevant sort of causal realization could be defined. Instead, the notion of cause is somehow derivative from the context-or-discipline-specific notion of *explanation*, so that any conception of realization by microphysical causal processes must in the end entail the reducibility of the relevant disciplines to microphysics. Any non-reductive position must abandon materialist metaphysics.

Putnam's argument that non-reductionist materialist realism must collapse to a reductionist position explains, of course, why he understands materialist metaphysical realism as a reductionist position. It's important to see that it also explains an otherwise puzzling feature of his account of causal theories of reference. In his famous early (pre-"internal realism") papers defending causal conceptions of reference (1975a, 1975b) Putnam showed no inclination towards the view that the relevant causal relations need be characterizable without reference to conceptual or intentional factors. Why, then, should reference to such factors be ruled out for consistent "metaphysical realists"? At least for the special case of metaphysical realists who intended to offer a materialist or naturalist metaphysics (the main foci of Putnam's critiques), the answer may be provided by his general critique of non-reductionist materialism. If the consistent metaphysical materialist must be a reductionist about all the special sciences, she must be a reductionist about semantic theory; so, in particular her account of reference cannot make irreducible reference to conceptual or intentional phenomena.

In the light of these considerations I propose to adopt the more complicated compositional semantics strategy for understanding "metaphysical materialism." It's to this task that we now turn.

Metaphysical realism

The approach I propose is not to try to say quite generally what it is for a position to be both genuinely realist and genuinely metaphysical. Consider an objective idealist theory according to which all aspects of reality are aspects of the mind of God. Surely it's a metaphysical position. But is it realist with respect to, say, the domain of atomic physics? On the one hand, it says that talk about atoms reduces somehow to talk about God's ideas, so it has affinities with phenomenalist treatments of, e.g., trees – *prima facie* an anti-realist approach to botany. On the other hand, what could be more real than an idea in the mind of God, if there is (just) one? Or, how about a version of occasionalism which accepts all of the findings of the physical, and biological, and social sciences more or less at (apparently unreduced) face value, as a scientific realist would, but adds that each occasion in which, according to a pre-philosophical understanding, one event causes another is really a case in which all the causing is done by the current operation of God's will. Is such a conception a realist conception of physics and the special sciences?

I'm not sure how to answer these questions; or, rather, I'm sure that they don't have determinate answers. What does, I think, make sense is to identify features which would qualify a *materialist* realism about natural and social phenomena as genuinely metaphysical. So, here are some features which are surely jointly sufficient to qualify a materialist realism, R, as genuinely metaphysical. I propose that R is surely a materialist, metaphysical realist position if according to R,

1. Reference is a real relation holding because of relevant causal interactions between language users and the features of the world to which their terms refer. The same is true for reference-like phenomena like partial denotation (*sensu* Field 1973).
2. Truth, approximate truth (and related semantic properties like, e.g., insightfulness or whatever) are genuine properties involving causally explanatory correspondence relations between sentences or other representational devices and features of the world.
3. The features of the world to which terms in the relevant domain refer (or to which they bear reference-like relations like partial denotation) are mind-independent in the sense that neither they, nor their status as real features of the world, depend in any philosophically problematical or controversial way on our concepts, theories, beliefs, etc.
4. Because of this sort of mind-independence nothing about the nature of truth or of other semantic phenomena guarantees that we cannot be very seriously wrong even "in the limit of inquiry" (whatever that means) about some features of the phenomena we study, but no generally skeptical conclusion follows.
5. All causally efficacious phenomena are materialistically acceptable. In particular, semantic, intentional and mental phenomena are real and causally efficacious, and are not counterexamples to materialism.

Advertisement: non-reductionist, materialist metaphysical realism

In response to Putnam's critiques of metaphysical realism I propose to defend here a non-reductionist materialist position which fully meets the criteria for being genuinely metaphysical. I'll explore its implications for the central issues about reductionism, reference, truth and the moral sciences raised by Putnam and I'll argue that it satisfies all of the anti-skeptical and anti-reductionist desiderata favored by Putnam without abandoning genuine realism. In particular I'll explore its implications with respect to the question of doing ethics (or whatever discipline) without ontology. The conclusions I'll reach are these.

Reference and accommodation

In the domain of the natural and social sciences (and daily life) linguistic reference is a matter of causally mediated *accommodation* between linguistic practices and relevant causal features of the world: accommodation of the sort that contributes to inductive, explanatory and practical achievements. Accommodation of practices to relevant causal structures is the basic phenomenon of representation, linguistic or otherwise.

Semantic properties and epistemology

Reference and (derivatively) truth, and other semantic phenomena are thus (as Putnam says, but not in the ways his pragmatist/verificationist remarks would suggest) epistemic phenomena. Reference, truth, etc. are epistemic phenomena which figure in explaining our epistemic successes (such as they are) in both theoretical and practical endeavors.

Kinds (etc.) and reference as social constructions

Natural kinds (magnitudes, relations, objects) to which natural kind (etc.) terms refer are discipline-relative social constructions, just as the suggestion that pains might form a natural kind in psychology but not in physics would suggest. Natural kinds are artifacts of certain discipline-specific patterns of language use.

Ontological pluralism

Ontological questions about the "reality" of kinds are best understood as questions about the contributions, if any, which the use of the relevant kind (etc.) terms makes to achieving discipline relevant accommodation. So, there is a sort of relativity of "reality" to disciplinary practices.

Determinateness of reference

Because natural kinds are themselves artifacts of actual language use, reference and kind definitions (and "reality") are aspects of a single phenomenon. Indeed the establishment of a natural kind and the establishment of reference to it by a natural kind term are basically the same phenomenon. Thus the problems of determinateness of reference raised by Putnam's "model theoretic" arguments do not arise. As the phenomenon of partial denotation indicates, reference is not always fully determinate but there is no problem about how to explain such determinateness as actually obtains.

"Causal" theories of reference

The apparent distinction between "causal" theories of reference for natural kinds and "descriptive" or "causal descriptive" theories is fundamentally misleading. Reference is *exactly* a matter of certain causal relations between actual language use and relevant causal structures; there is no one here but us causal theorists. Nevertheless the relevant causal relations obtain because (among other things) of the ways in which language users engage in descriptive practices and the ways in which they deploy their intentional and conceptual resources, etc. Descriptive (and other cognitive/intentional) factors thus play a *causal* role in establishing kinds and reference.

Complexity and non-reductionism

The definition of a natural kind is provided by families of relevant properties, but these need not form a set. Instead, many natural kinds (homeostatic property cluster kinds) are defined by an historically individuated homeostatic clustering of properties, and the properties involved in the defining cluster may sometimes vary across space and time. So natural kinds need not have simple reductionistic definitions provided by sets of necessary and sufficient conditions. "Water = H_2O" is in that respect a quite misleading example of the real definition of a natural kind.

Bivalence failure

Homeostatic property cluster (henceforth: HPC) kinds have irreducibly indeterminate boundaries: they cannot be precisified without undermining their naturalness – their accommodation to relevant causal structure. Thus bivalence fails for some sentences about such kinds.

"One should do X without ontology" is itself a metaphysical *proposal*

As Putnam suggests, it is sometimes, in some disciplinary domains, a good idea to investigate the relevant questions without recourse to distinctly metaphysical hypotheses. The fact that this is so does not, however, count in favor of some general critique of metaphysics or of metaphysical realism. Indeed the hypothesis that one should, at a given time, study X "without ontology" is itself best understood as reflecting a metaphysical hypothesis about how the conceptual resources of X at that time are and are not accommodated to the relevant causal structures. Importantly, this hypothesis can be (indeed, has been) false even when the relevant metaphysical hypotheses are for the most part profoundly mistaken.

Strategy

I've developed resources appropriate for defending these points in several papers (Boyd 1988, 1989,1990b, 1991, 1993, 1999a, 1999b, 2001b). What I propose to do in the rest of this essay is to sketch out in broad outline an argument for a non-reductionist, fully metaphysical realism, referring the reader to those earlier papers for details.

Natural kinds

Slogans

I've been trying to find memorable but informative slogans to capture an accommodationist conception of natural kinds for years, but I can't come close to matching Ruth Millikan's (Millikan 1997) suggestion that natural kinds are those "answered in nature by supporting ground of induction." I want to supplement it by putting forward some other slogans, rejecting some and accepting others. I propose that we can distinguish three different (natural) kinds of theories of kinds and reference by focusing on slogans reflecting what the three sorts of theories have to say about "linguistic legislation."

1 Unicameral theories (empiricist): We define kinds by "nominal essences."
2 Unicameral theories ("metaphysical realism," *sensu* Putnam?): The world sorts itself into kinds; we refer to them by something like pointing or describing.
3 Bicameral theories: We and the world jointly make natural kinds.

What will make the bicameral theory proposed here an unproblematically realist one is that it honors the Realist proviso:

TRUE: We and the world jointly make natural kinds;

BUT (IN THE RELEVANT SENSE) FALSE: We and the world jointly make the facts.

This proviso will be spelled out in detail, but its gist is provided by my all-time favorite slogan regarding kinds (despite its unicameralist origins).

Locke's dictum

I would not here be thought to forget, much less to deny, that Nature, in the production of things, makes several of them alike: there is nothing more obvious, especially in the race of animals, and all things propagated by seed. But yet I think we may say, the sorting of them under names is the workmanship of the understanding, taking occasion, from the similitude it observes amongst them, to make abstract general ideas, and set them up in the mind, with names annexed to them, as patterns or forms, (for, in that sense, the word form has a very proper signification,) to which as particular things existing are found to agree, so they come to be of that species, have that denomination, or are put into that classis.
(Locke 1689/1975: III.iii.13; see also III. vi, 36–38)

The key accommodationist idea

The key idea behind the accommodationist conception of natural kinds is that successful inductive/explanatory practice requires *accommodation* between linguistic, conceptual, taxonomic resources and relevant causal factors. Locke (1689/1975) suggests at several places (e.g., IV, iii, 25) that when kinds of substances are defined by purely conventional "nominal essences," as he thinks they must be, it will be impossible to have a general science of, say, chemistry. Nominal essences define kinds of substance in terms of sensible properties, but the factors which govern the behavior of substances are the fundamental properties of their insensible corpuscles. Since there is no reason to suppose that our conventional nominal essences correspond to uniformities in microstructure, there is no reason to believe that kinds defined by nominal essences will be apt for the formulation of general knowledge of substances. Only if we are able to sort substances according to their hidden real essences will systematic general knowledge of them be possible. Mill (1843), more optimistic about the possibility of induction, held that it's important for us to frame inductive inferences in terms of "natural kinds," which are to be distinguished from other kinds by the fact that their members are loci of a large number of scientifically relevant properties.

Scientific realists agree that certain kinds are especially relevant for induction and explanation. Terms in inductively successful scientific disciplines must be defined by *a posteriori* (often "unobservable") real essences, just as Locke thought, but *contra* Locke knowledge of real essences is possible (Putnam 1972, 1975a, 1975b; Boyd 1983, 1985a, 1985b, 1989, 1999a).

Accommodation and reliable induction

The philosophical theory of *natural* kinds thus addresses the question of how classificatory schemes contribute to the epistemic reliability of inductive and explanatory practices. The *naturalness* of natural kinds consists in their aptness for induction and explanation, and their definitions reflect the properties of their members which contribute to that aptness. According to the *accommodation thesis* what establishes the reliability of inferential practices – what reference to natural kinds makes possible – is the accommodation of inferential practices to relevant causal structures.

An example from kitchen chemistry illustrates this point. Suppose that you have been baking biscuits for a long time, adding sour cream and baking soda to the batter. Whenever you have done this before, the biscuits have risen and become fluffy when baked. You conclude that whenever you make batter with this recipe and bake it under ordinary kitchen conditions the biscuits will rise. You are right and your inductive success is not an accident; it is, in part, a reflection of the fact that the categories *sour cream* and *baking soda* are natural categories in kitchen chemistry.

There are indefinitely many false generalizations which equally well fit all your data. You discerned the true one because your inductive practices, including reference to these culinarily natural categories, allowed you to identify a generalization which was appropriately related to the causal structures of the relevant phenomena: sour cream contains lactic acid and baking soda is sodium bicarbonate. They react to form carbon dioxide gas under ordinary baking conditions and the gas bubbles cause the biscuits to rise. What distinguishes the generalization you accepted from the others, and what makes your inductive success non-accidental, is that in any situation in which its antecedent is true, the state of affairs described by the antecedent will (in the relevant environment) *cause* the effect described by its consequent.

In deploying the categories *sour cream* and *baking soda* you were relying on the culturally transmitted insights of millions of cooks and thousands of cook book writers who developed conceptual and classificatory resources which, in kitchen practices, facilitate the formulation of reliable recipes: ones that underwrite reproducible results. The cultural achievement reflected in the establishment of these culinary categories has a *forward-looking* feature (*sensu* Shoemaker 1980, 2003): typically when a recipe formulated in the culturally standard categories works with consistent success on some few occasions, it will prove successful on most subsequent occasions.

Consider a recipe with instructions, R, and form the conditional "If R are implemented then P," where P describes the production of the relevant foodstuff. We may put the points just made about culturally ratified culinary categories this way: when R and P are formulated in terms of those categories *as they are ordinarily employed in cooking and recipe writing*, and when, on some few occasions of cooking, the generalization has always (or almost always) proved to be true, then it will probably prove true on (almost) all subsequent trials. The categories deployed in describing R and P are natural kinds in kitchen chemistry because of their role in facilitating reliable culinary inductions. Our practice of deploying such culinary natural kinds in formulating recipes allows us to identify *causally sustained* generalizations about foodstuffs.

Other instances of inductive success are more complicated, but, in general, we can reliably identify true (or approximately true) generalizations just to the extent that we can identify generalizations which are sustained by relevant causal structures. In order to frame such generalizations at all we require a vocabulary, with terms like "sour cream" and "baking soda," which is itself accommodated to those structures (Boyd 1990a, 1990b, 1991, 1992, 1999a, 1999b).

In general, to explain the reliability of inductive methods in everyday or scientific disciplines one must posit a systematic *correspondence* between the use of natural kind terms, on the one hand, and causal structures, on the other. I propose that this correspondence is the reference relation upon which a correspondence conception of empirical truth should be grounded.

Disciplinary matrices and a sort of relativism

"Flour," "baking soda" and "sour cream" all refer to natural kinds in kitchen chemistry – kinds reference to which underwrites successful explanation and prediction in simple matters culinary. They are not natural kinds in, e.g., physics, to the reliability of whose practices they are irrelevant, nor in biochemistry, where different bacterial compositions in sour cream would be inductively or explanatorily relevant. In general the naturalness of a natural kind depends on the inferential architecture within which representations of it are embedded.

There are two aspects to this dependence. Consider the kind *salt of sodium*. In the first place, it's a natural kind just because reference to it contributes to the accommodation of the inductive and explanatory practices of chemists and others to relevant causal structures; it's not a natural kind in kitchen chemistry, nor in, e.g., psychology or economics. So, its naturalness is a matter of its appropriateness for induction and explanation in chemistry and related areas, its irrelevance in other disciplines notwithstanding. Importantly, its status as a natural kind also depends on other kinds also being natural kinds. Classifying reagents accurately as sodium salts and referring to them by the term "sodium salt" would make no such contribution except in the context of a whole bunch of theory-dependent classificatory, experimental and inferential practices involving – among other things – reference to lots of other chemical kinds. Only in a context involving a distinctive discipline-or-project specific cognitive and inferential architecture – involving the deployment of lots of other natural kind terms – is the "naturalness" of a given natural kind manifested. In particular, the accommodation thesis commends to us the terminology of philosophers who speak, for example, of psychological states like pain being natural kinds "from the point of view of psychology" but not (owing to multiple realizability, for example) "from the point of view of basic physics." Accommodation of the inferential practices of psychology to relevant causal structures requires descriptive resources like the term "pain," whereas accommodation of such practices in basic physics does not.

Thus the fundamental notion in the theory of natural kinds is not the notion of such a kind, *simpliciter*, but instead the notion of a family of kinds being natural with respect to a particular *inferential architecture*. When we talk simply of a natural kind, or of natural kinds generally, there is either tacit reference to some inferential architecture or tacit quantification over some domain of them. At least in the case of natural kinds in the sciences and in everyday life, that inferential architecture can best be thought of as being provided by a *disciplinary matrix*: a family of inductive and explanatory aims and practices, together with the conceptual resources and vocabulary within which they are implemented. The naturalness of a scientific natural kind is relative to the role reference to it plays in a disciplinary matrix.

Reference and natural kind definitions, first approximation

Ignoring issues like partial denotation (Field 1973) to which we'll return later, I advocate the following *accommodationist* conception of natural kind terms and their referents.

Definition: accommodation demands

By the *accommodation demands* of a disciplinary matrix, M, I mean the "fit" or accommodation between M's conceptual, classificatory and methodological practices, on the one hand, and relevant causal structures, on the other, which would be required in order for the characteristic inductive, explanatory or practical aims of M to be achieved.

Explanatory definitions of terms, $t_1, \ldots t_n$, in M: Families $F_1, ., F_n$ of properties such that:

Epistemic access condition: There is a systematic tendency – established by the causal relations between practices in M and causal structures in the world – for what is predicated of t_i within M to be approximately true of things which have F_i,[2] $i = 1, \ldots, n$, and

Accommodation condition: This fact, together with the causal powers of things possessing $F_1,\ldots,F_n$, causally explains how the use of $t_1,.,t_n$ in M contributes to *whatever tendency there is* for the *accommodation demands* of M to be satisfied.

Note that although the accommodation demands of a matrix are defined in terms of the aims, projects, etc. characteristic of its practices, the accommodation condition refers only to *whatever tendency there is* for those demands to be satisfied. So, if you hold that one of the central aims of Linnaean taxonomy as it was practiced in the eighteenth century was to reflect the design of the deity in the great chain of being, then you should hold that one of the accommodation demands of Linnaean practice was that it be aligned appropriately with features of the divine will. If you doubt that there is a divine will, you will understand the accommodation condition as requiring only that the assignment of explanatory definitions to Linnaean terms help to explain how eighteenth-century taxonomists *did* succeed with respect to some of their less august and ambitious aims.

Two complications and a better approximation

The preliminary accommodationist conception of reference and kind definitions is oversimplified in two respects – one concerning the nature of explanatory definitions, the other concerning partial denotation and the dynamic aspects of reference. When elaborated to take account of these complications it becomes, I think, an extremely good approximation to the truth about the semantics and the metaphysics of natural kind terms and the kinds to which they refer.

Homeostatic property cluster kinds: "vague" explanatory definitions

Some scientifically important natural kind terms (species' names, for example) exhibit a sort of indeterminacy. They have ineliminably vague extensions. That this can be so should be unsurprising. Suppose that a natural kind term, t, determinately denotes a natural kind, k. k will be defined by some family, F, of properties. F need not, however, be a *set* of properties which are necessary and sufficient for membership in the extension of t. Disciplinary practices in matrices in which complex phenomena are studied often take advantage of (imperfectly) homeostatically united clusters of properties in order to underwrite the employment of an explanatorily/inductively relevant natural kind term. The explanatory definition of the kind to which it refers (a *homeostatic property cluster*, or HPC, kind) is an (imperfectly) homeostatically united family of properties together with the homeostatic mechanisms which unite them. In the most general case, a HPC definition is a process-like historically individuated property cluster*ing*, so that the membership conditions it specifies may vary over space and time (for a fuller exposition see Boyd 1988, 1989, 1993, 1999a, 1999b; R. Wilson 1999a, 1999b).

All that is required for an HPC kind to be the referent of a natural kind term under such circumstances is that there be no kind, more "natural" (in the sense of explaining successful accommodation) in the relevant matrix, corresponding to a precisification of the homeostatic property cluster. Darwin saw that this was so with respect to species level taxa. The 'precision' that such a precisification would introduce fails to correspond to any biologically important causal phenomena, so reference to such a precisification would not contribute to accommodation. The accommodationist conception thus explains the ineliminable "vagueness" of HPC kinds like species.

Partial denotation, denotational refinement and Reference as a Dialectical Phenomenon

Field (1973) introduced the notions of partial denotation and denotational refinement. In the framework provided by the accommodationist conception we can say that a natural kind term, t, within a disciplinary matrix, M, partially denotes two different kinds[3] if there are two families, F_1 and F_2 of properties such that:

1. The satisfaction of the accommodation demands of M would be enhanced by the use of two terms, one with explanatory definition F_1 and one with explanatory definition F_2 (call these k_1 and k_2).
2. The epistemic access condition is satisfied to a significant extent by an assignment of kind terms to families of properties which assigns t to F_1 and by one which assigns t to F_2.
3. F_1 and F_2 are similar enough that the epistemic access which uses of t affords practitioners to k_1 and k_2 contributes to the epistemic reliability of practices in the disciplinary matrix, so that something like the accommodation condition is also satisfied by such assignments.

Denotational refinement takes place when 1–3 are recognized and separate terms come to be deployed to refer to k_1 and k_2 (ordinarily t will come to be used to denote one of those kinds). The paradigm cases of these phenomena involve the refinement of chemical terminology occasioned by the discovery of isotopes.

What the accommodation thesis indicates is that reference (at least for natural kind terms) is the relation between language use and the world which explains how the accommodation of language to relevant causal structures is achieved. I have argued elsewhere (Boyd 1993) that reference should thus be seen as the dialectical *process* of accommodation between the use of such terms and causal structures which is achieved by reliable inductive and explanatory practice. Both partial denotation *and denotational refinement* are aspects of the ongoing process of reference. The achievement of a referential situation in which a natural kind term enjoys a determinate explanatory definition is thus a *special case* of the phenomenon of reference.

When the referential situation of a natural kind term involves partial denotation, sentences containing that term will be, in a certain sense, ambiguous. They may be true on one reading and false on another. More importantly, each of the two readings may reflect a different aspect of approximation between scientific representations and actual causal structures, and denotational refinement will ordinarily be necessary in order to achieve more accurate approximate representations of them. Working with terms that are ambiguous in this way – and refining their use when the ambiguity is recognized – is central to reliable scientific (and everyday) practice. Any adequate conception of the growth of approximate knowledge in chemistry must, for example, say something very much like this with respect to uses of terms like "carbon" and "element" before and after the discovery of isotopes.

Reference and truth, properly understood, are thus no more determinate than the proposed accommodationist account of partial denotation and denotational refinement indicates. There is a metaphysically real referential *correspondence* between kind terms and the features of the world which underwrites our capacity to represent causal relations, but that correspondence has a dialectical complexity which attention to the special case of determinate reference renders obscure.

Materialist accommodationism

I've advertised the availability of a genuinely metaphysical *materialist* realist conception of reference and natural kinds. The accommodationist conception articulated thus far is not committed to materialism. Indeed, I think that something like it (perhaps exactly it) would be the appropriate conception of reference and natural kinds for a dualist. I'm even pretty sure that it, or a variation of it which supplements the notion of causation with a reference to whatever the way is in which the deity brings things about, would be the right choice for many theistic conceptions like, e.g., Adams' Platonist moral realism (see Adams 1999; Boyd 2003a, 2003b). I take it that the credibility of accommodationism is enhanced by its potential for broad applicability, but what I need at present of course is to defend a materialist version.

So, here's *materialist* accommodationism: (1) Accommodationism is true and (2) all natural phenomena and all phenomena causally or otherwise determinatively related to natural phenomena are physical (or "physicalistically acceptable," if you prefer). In particular, all the intentional, mental and purposive phenomena referred to in the specification of the epistemic access and accommodation conditions are physical. Of course some of Putnam's arguments suggest that this position is either incoherent or that it collapses into reductionist materialism, but that's an issue to which we'll soon turn.

Here are some key features of the accommodationist conception.

Kinds (and reference) are social constructions

Locke maintained that while Nature makes things similar and different, kinds are "the workmanship of men." The accommodationist conception ratifies this view without entailing nominalism. The theory of natural kinds *just is* (nothing but) the theory of how accommodation is (sometimes) achieved between our linguistic, classificatory and inferential practices and the causal structure of the world.[4] A natural kind *just is* the implementation, in language and in conceptual, experimental and inferential practice, of a (component of) a way of satisfying the accommodation demands of a disciplinary matrix. Natural kinds are features, not of the world outside our practice, but of the ways in which that practice engages with the rest of the world. Taxonomists sometimes speak of the "erection" of higher taxa, treating such taxa as, in a sense, human constructions. They are right – and the same thing is true of natural kinds in general.[5]

Kinds and reference are defined simultaneously rather than separately

The key Lockean idea which the accommodationist conception is supposed to articulate is that natural kinds are the workmanship of (women and) men established by (bicameral) *linguistic* legislation. They are not free-standing, language-independent phenomena[6] to which terms can become attached *via* some independent process of reference fixing (or reference sustaining, or whatever).

Kinds and reference are defined simultaneously for all of the terms used in a disciplinary matrix

What makes the accommodationist conception *accommodationist* is the idea that the theory of natural kinds is the theory of how the use of words facilitates the accommodation of the *inferential architecture* of a disciplinary matrix to the relevant causal structures in the world. The linguistic component of the inferential architecture of a disciplinary matrix doesn't somehow factor into a separate inferential architecture for each natural kind term. So, for example, the chemical term "acid" has as its definition the property of being an electron pair acceptor[7] because the epistemic access to electron pair acceptors which is associated with uses of the term "acid" in the relevant disciplinary matrix contributes to the explanation of inductive and explanatory successes of practices in that matrix *given the inferential practices which connect uses of "acid" with uses of* **other** *terms within that matrix* **and** *given the epistemic relations between the uses of those other term and relevant families of properties.*

Descriptive, conceptual and intentional factors are treated as causal factors

The accommodationist conception *entails* that descriptive, conceptual and intentional factors figure fundamentally in establishing reference to natural kinds *(and to establishing kind definitions, since these are the same phenomena according to accommodationism)*. Both the epistemic access and accommodation conditions make reference to such phenomena. According to accommodationism a tendency toward (approximately) truthful actual *predication* of natural kind terms, in service of (at least some of) the *aims and intentions* of participants in disciplinary matrices is fundamental to reference. So reference (and kind definition) are essentially concept, description and intention involving.

In the sciences (and, I believe, in other domains) there is a deeper respect in which the reference relation is underwritten by the acceptance in the relevant communities of approximately true statements involving the relevant natural kind terms. The methods of science are very highly theory-dependent, so that such epistemic reliability as scientists' practices within a disciplinary matrix at any given time may have with respect to the deployment of natural kind terms will always depend on the approximate truth of a great many of the generalizations they have already accepted at that time (the relevant "background theories").

No hybridization: reference is not a "causal-descriptive" phenomenon

Despite the deep involvement of descriptive and intentional factors in the accommodationist conception of reference, it would be highly misleading to describe it as a hybrid "causal descriptive" conception. The conceptual, descriptive and intentional factors which, according to accommodationism, figure in reference and in kind definition are all to be understood as causal factors in the relevant cognitive and social practices and in their engagement with the world. The accommodation condition, for example, refers to actual aims and intentions which play a causal role in disciplinary practices; the descriptive aspects of reference are a matter of the ways in which the actual deployment of descriptive resources in the relevant community and in the cognitive architecture of its members contribute (*causally*) to the epistemic reliability of practices; epistemic access is a matter of the extent to which the actual properties of things in the world causally regulate actual predications.

So, the accommodationist conception differs from other causal conceptions of reference not by adding *extra-causal* conceptual, descriptive or intentional factors to the characterization of reference (and kind definitions) but by emphasizing the causal role of actual conceptual, descriptive and intentional practices.

Defending (materialist, non-reductionist) metaphysical realism

Accommodationism and non-reductionist materialist metaphysical realism

I earlier advertised the availability of a viable non-reductionist materialist metaphysical realism which entails each of the following:

1 Reference is a real relation holding because of relevant causal interactions between language users and the features of the world to which their terms refer. The same is true for reference-like phenomena like partial denotation (*sensu* Field 1973).

2 Truth, approximate truth (and related semantic properties like, e.g., insightfulness or whatever) are genuine properties involving causally explanatory correspondence relations between sentences or other representational devices and features of the world.
3 The features of the world to which terms in the relevant domain refer (or to which they bear reference-like relations like partial denotation) are mind-independent in the sense that neither they nor their status as real features of the world depend in any philosophically problematical or controversial way on our concepts, theories, beliefs, etc.
4 Because of this sort of mind-independence nothing about the nature of truth or of other semantic phenomena guarantees that we cannot be very seriously wrong even "in the limit of inquiry" (whatever that means) about some features of the phenomena we study, but no generally skeptical conclusion follows.
5 All causally efficacious phenomena are materialistically acceptable. In particular, semantic, intentional and mental phenomena are real and causally efficacious, and are not counterexamples to materialism.

Of course, I now maintain that a materialist version of the accommodationist conception is a viable non-reductionist realist theory of kinds and reference satisfying 1–5. If it's viable, materialist accommodationism plainly satisfies 1, 2 and 5. Accommodationism just is a causal theory which (causally, of course) explains certain language-mediated epistemic achievements, so 1 is implied. Similarly accommodationism is non-reductionist by design: kind definitions and the naturalness of natural kinds are disciplinary matrix relative, so according to it there's no "one true (reducing) theory." And, of course, materialist accommodation implies materialism.

It remains to see about 3 and 4, and about the viability of *materialist* accommodationism. The distinctive feature which most clearly distinguishes materialist accommodationism from Putnam's characterization of "metaphysical realism" is that it cheerfully incorporates descriptive and intentional factors into the characterization both of reference and of natural kinds, which it treats as aspects of the same semantic phenomenon. Thus it provides neither a "pure causal" conception of reference nor a "mind-independent" characterization of natural kinds or of their naturalness. So we need to see whether these features compromise its claim to realism by compromising its claim to support 3 or 4, or compromise its claim to be genuinely materialist.

Mind-independence

Mind-independence and the casual powers of minds

Central to Putnam's critiques of metaphysical realism – whatever view we take that to be – is the idea that the metaphysical realist's commitment to the idea that natural kinds are mind-independent will commit her to an unacceptable reductionism. If there is to be more than one true theory – if natural kinds are discipline relative, for example – then mind-involving descriptive and intentional factors will have to be involved both in the metaphysics of the naturalness of natural kinds and also in the ways in which reference to them is achieved. Putnam apparently believes that acknowledging this sort of involvement is incompatible with maintaining, as metaphysical realism requires, that the phenomena we study (in particular the natural kinds we study) are appropriately mind-independent.

It's routine for philosophers and others in describing the commitments of realism to say that realism implies that the reality to which our terms and theories correspond, or the truth of the things we say, are "mind-independent," or "independent of our concepts and theories," or some such thing. Sometimes "independent" gets replaced by "largely independent." There's a reason for that replacement. Lots of things that realists harmlessly believe in, and that some people study, are mind-dependent: minds, for example, and social structures, meanings, industrial designs, laws (in the legislative sense), artifacts, etc.

Similarly, there are lots of statements and theories whose truth is not independent of our concepts and theories but which are such that this fact about them does not provide counterexamples to realism. Statements and theories which are straightforwardly about minds, for example, or (as before) about social structures, meanings, industrial designs, laws, artifacts, etc., depend for their truth values on what minds, social structures, etc., are actually like but this poses no problem for realism. Neither does a subtler form of dependence. Sometimes – indeed very often – whether or not the truth conditions of a statement obtain will depend on facts about certain mental or conceptual phenomena even when those phenomena are not part of the subject matter of the statement. This is so, for example, regarding statements about economic regularities, about patterns in the history of architecture, about patterns in the funding of scientific research. In such cases, whether or not the truth conditions of the statements obtain depends *causally* on mental and conceptual phenomena other than their subject matter.

It's even no problem for realism when the truth value of a statement depends in part on whether or not that very statement is accepted in some relevant community *provided that the explanation is an ordinary causal one*, as cases of self-fulfilling or self-undermining prophesies indicate. In general, if you're a realist about mental and conceptual phenomena then *prima facie* your commitment to realism is not compromised by your attributing to them the sorts of causal powers which ordinary scientific and everyday reasoning attributes to them, even when the manifestations of those causal powers *causally* influence mental, conceptual, semantic or representational phenomena.

Of course, the accommodationist conception of reference and natural kinds refers to mental, intentional and conceptual matters only in their roles as causal factors in human practices and in the relations between those practices and other causal features of the world. As we have seen above (pp. 62–3), when accommodationism takes account of intentions and purposes in identifying the accommodation demands of a disciplinary matrix it refers to just those intentional states that play a causal role in the relevant individual and social practices; when it acknowledges the roles of intentional, conceptual and descriptive elements in the epistemic access and accommodation conditions it acknowledges the roles of those elements as perfectly ordinary causal factors. So, there's no reason to take the "mind-dependence" of reference, kind definitions and naturalness acknowledged by accommodationism to undermine its claim to underwrite a metaphysical realist conception.

Conclusion so far: the accommodationist conception is fully compatible with the view that reference and natural kinds are "mind-independent" in whatever sense(s) are required for metaphysical realism. Strictly speaking, accommodationism doesn't imply the requisite sort of mind-independence – a neo-Kantian relativist idealist might be an accommodationist about reference and kinds – but materialist accommodationism does imply (the relevant sort of) mind-independence since it treats mental phenomena as ordinary physical phenomena. So, if materialist accommodationism is a coherent position it underwrites a *metaphysical realist* conception of reference and natural kinds.

Metaphysical innocence and fair play for humans

What we've just seen about realism and the mind-independence (*and dependence*) of reference and natural kinds is a special case of a more general result about what realism implies about the mind (in)dependence of phenomena generally. Realists must hold that human social practices are – in a certain sense – *metaphysically innocent*. The easy way to appreciate metaphysical innocence is to think about the neo-Kantian relativist position often attributed to Kuhn (1970), who apparently maintains in various places that scientists who work in different paradigms study different worlds or different phenomena. While this position is almost certainly best understood metaphorically, the arguments Kuhn gives for it (especially on pages 101–2) *appear* to commit him to the following pair of claims:

1 The laws of Newtonian mechanics constitute analytic definitions of the Newtonian magnitude terms; those of special relativity constitute analytic definitions of special relativistic magnitude terms.

2 Both sets of terms refer to sets of real physical magnitudes. The establishment of the Newtonian paradigm guarantees that there are such Newtonian magnitudes; the establishment of the Einsteinian paradigm guarantees that there are such relativistic magnitudes.

It's easy to see why this position (whether it was ever Kuhn's or not) was unacceptable to realists. Of course most realists reject the theory of reference which underwrites 1, but the real *metaphysical* (as opposed to semantic) issue between realists and fans of 1 and 2 (who were numerous in some of the social sciences and the literary humanities) concerned 2. It's not possible, realists believe, to create laws of nature just by establishing paradigms: the behavior of electrons, for example, doesn't depend on the curriculum prevailing in physics departments. Social practices, like establishing paradigms, can't determine the nature of physical phenomena in that way: they are, in that sense *metaphysically innocent*.

The conception that human social practices are metaphysically innocent represents the key realist conception of mind-independence, but articulating it requires some care. Some electron behavior *does* depend on the curricula in physics and engineering departments: absent such social constructions no electron ensembles would display the trajectories characteristic of electrons in cathode ray tubes, for example. I've examined the question of the relationship between mind-dependence and realism at some length elsewhere (Boyd 1989, 1990b, 1992, 1999a, 1999b, 2001b) and concluded that the appropriate realist version of the metaphysical innocence thesis is the *no non-causal contribution thesis* (henceforth: 2N2C): the thesis that human social practices make no *non-causal* contribution to causal properties and relations. What 2N2C denies is that, in addition to their ordinary causal impact, there is some further sort of contribution (logical, conceptual, socially constructive, or the like), explicable by distinctly philosophical rather than empirical theories, which the adoption of theories, conceptual frameworks and the like makes to the establishment of causal powers and relations.

Plainly the accommodationist conception does not undermine (and its materialist versions imply) 2N2C. It's puzzling that, e.g., the idea that the naturalness of natural kinds is discipline-specific (and thus interest and intention specific) should even *appear* to undermine metaphysical realism. It's puzzling in general why some philosophers, either on their own behalf or on behalf of realists, should think that mind-dependence or social construction is *prima facie* ontologically deflating. We seem to be the only animals for whom the fact that some entity is socially constructed by them is taken to undermine its ontological standing. Beaver (*Castor canadensis*) dams and beaver social structures are Castorian social constructions but no one thinks that this diminishes their reality. Beavers sometimes slap their tails on the water and when they do other beavers move into places inaccessible to predators. We cheerfully provide an explanation in terms of the evolutionary semantics of tail slaps: they signal the presence of predators. But, by "predators" here we mean, of course, predators on beavers, not, e.g., on fruit flies. No one thinks that this diminishes the cogency of the explanation or undermines its ontological standing even though the kind referred to by "predators" here is itself irreducibly Castorian.

It's true, of course, that philosophical and literary excursions into neo-Kantian relativist critiques of the reality of "social constructions" are often motivated by an admirable concern to defend tolerance and to rebut pernicious social ideology. These aims are in fact ill served by such excursions (Boyd 1992, 1999b; Sismondo 1993a, 1993b, 1996) and would be better served by a better (realist) metaphysics. We are just as real as beavers; the phenomena we construct are just as real as the ones they construct. Fair play for Humans! And for realists.

Accommodationism and non-reductionist materialism

So, materialist accommodationism – if it's a coherent position – would appear to be fully metaphysically realist. Is it coherent? Putnam's conception that it's not seems to rest on two distinct sorts of considerations, each connected with the idea that the metaphysical realist must hold that there is one true (reducing) theory. Considerations of the first sort are distinctly semantic. Putnam's conception of metaphysical realism entails that the metaphysical realist must account for reference and natural kinds in purely causal, non-conceptual, non-intentional terms. Pretty clearly no theory of reference to interest-dependent discipline-specific kinds will satisfy this conception, leaving the metaphysical realist with, at best, a one true reductive theory approach.

Of course, the metaphysical realist accommodationist conception on offer avoids this problem entirely, so if it's not incompatible with materialism for some other reason then non-reductionist materialist metaphysical realism is a viable philosophical position. Putnam's other arguments against the viability of such a position has nothing in particular to do with realism, semantics or natural kinds. In "Why There Isn't a Ready Made World" (1983b) Putnam argues against the one true theory conception in its materialist form but he recognizes that the typical materialist realist will subscribe to a non-reductionist conception apparently invulnerable to his argument. He responds that a non-reductionist version of materialism is unavailable, taking as his primary target the conception that the relationship between large-scale allegedly material phenomena and their material constituents is realization, not definability in some preferred physical language. Against this approach to understanding materialism he maintains that (a) a realization-based analysis of this sort would require that we have a viable notion of the "total cause" of a given event, that (b) we have no such notion, because (c) our only notions of cause arise from discipline- or interest-specific notions of explanation.

The position Putnam criticizes is one instance of a family of closely related approaches to understanding materialism which might be termed *compositional*. According to compositional approaches materialism affirms no particular relation between the concepts and terminology of basic physics and other concepts and terminology. Instead materialism about some domain is to be understood as the doctrine that all of the entities in that domain and all of their causal powers are composite from unproblematically physical entities and their causal powers. The relevant notions of composition are spelled out somewhat differently by different authors – in terms, e.g., of the *composition* of forces or of fundamental fields, the *contributions* of the causal powers of underlying states to the causal powers of aggregates, or of *realization* or *constitution* of macrophenomena by their microconstituents (see, e.g., Boyd 1980; Papineau 2001; Shoemaker 2003; Sturgeon 1985, 2006; Jessica Wilson 2002, 2006; Yablo 1992). What all of these approaches have in common is that they depart from the positivist tradition of "rationally reconstructing" materialism as a doctrine about the relation between terms and theories in favor of metaphysical formulations which accord much better with actual scientific thinking and practice.

What about Putnam's criticisms of such views? Several points are in order.

1. It's not clear that defenders of such conceptions require a concept of total cause or something like that, but if they do, we certainly have scientifically respectable concepts in the vicinity. How about the concept of the total force on an object? Or the Hamiltonian for a physical system (where forces correspond to gradients of the potential energy component)? Or the concept of the fields corresponding to the four (perhaps five) fundamental forces? Each of these concepts (or for that matter any concept of the total physical state of an approximately closed system) is a distinctly causal concept of the (allegedly) required level of generality.
2. What *is* required for a compositional conception of materialism to be viable is that there be scientifically respectable concepts corresponding to the basic idea of composition of entities and their causal powers. Of course, the concepts of addition of forces, or of the aggregate contributions of different fields to total potential energy of a system are examples, but the compositional conception seems to entail that less generic conceptions of composition are scientifically respectable. Of course they are. Molecular orbital theory studies how the available electron energy levels and electron densities of molecules are determined by the aggregation of the factors responsible for the orbital structures of constituent atoms. Systems ecology studies how aggregate population structures are realized by the interactions of constituent plant and animal populations. Economic theorists model the ways in which large-scale economic variables are determined by the aggregation of individual choices and transactions.

Perhaps the prestige of physics is such that only examples from physics are genuinely persuasive. OK, so there are two respectable disciplines in physics – condensed matter physics and solid state physics – which are concerned exactly with studying aspects of the ways in which macroscopic properties of physical systems arise from aggregations of the properties of their microconstituents.

3 It's true, as Putnam indicates, that our access to the concept of causation comes mainly from our discipline and interest-specific efforts to explain things. From an accommodationist point of view this is neither surprising nor worrisome. In the first place, it's widely recognized that evaluations of the explanatory power of theories is a crucial source of evidence for or against them, in large part because explanatory power is closely related to projectibility (see, e.g., Boyd 1985b, 1990b, 1999b; Kitcher 1981, 1993; Kitcher and Salmon 1989; Lipton 1991, 1993; McMullin 1984; Miller 1987; Salmon 1984, 1989). Thus the accommodationist should expect that efforts to explain things should figure centrally in the satisfaction of the epistemic access condition with respect to causal phenomena. It remains true, of course, that there is a discipline relativity to the sorts of causal factors which researchers count as explanatorily relevant, but this sort of relativity is just what the accommodation condition explains.

4 Finally, the arguments Putnam advances in "Why there isn't a Ready Made World" run afoul of extremely well-established science. If those arguments are successful against non-reductionist materialism regarding mental and conceptual phenomena then they're successful against non-reductionist materialism in any of the "special sciences," including even chemistry and solid-state physics as well as the biological sciences, where materialism has surely triumphed over vitalism. In these areas it's hard to deny that a non-reductionist materialist conception, far from being incoherent, is extremely well confirmed.

Scientific realism and metaphysical realism: a puzzle and a diagnosis

The last point above raises an interesting puzzle about Putnam's critiques of metaphysical realism. If anything is clear about Putnam's philosophical positions it is that, however much they have changed over time, he never meant to deny materialist scientific findings like the confirmation of a materialist rather than a vitalist conception of biological processes, nor of course did he (except perhaps in his very earliest papers) intend to defend a reductionist interpretation of such findings. How then can it be that the arguments he presented against metaphysical realism run afoul of materialist findings in the sciences? The answer, I believe, lies in an important aspect of Putnam's anti-(metaphysical) realist project, one shared with Arthur Fine's "Natural Ontological Attitude" (NOA) project (Fine 1984, 1986a, 1986b).

Both Putnam and Fine propose to rebut a certain sort of realism, but their intent is not to echo logical positivists' criticisms of scientific realism according to which realism fails because genuine knowledge of unobservables is impossible. According to "internal realism" and, I believe, according to all subsequent versions of Putnam's position, and according to NOA, the evidence for the atomic theory of matter provided by research in physics and chemistry is for all practical purposes conclusive. So, we know that there are atoms, and that ordinary matter is made up of them, even though they're too small to be observed by the unaided senses. Indeed, we even know that it's true that there are atoms. The problem with metaphysical versions of scientific realism, according to Putnam and Fine, is not that metaphysical scientific realists affirm knowledge of unobservables, but that they have too thick a conception of scientific truth. While we do know that it's true that there are atoms, the relevant notion of truth isn't some sort of metaphysical correspondence between linguistic entities and reality.

If the approach, common to Putnam and Fine, of saving some version of scientific realism from positivist criticisms while rejecting it as the foundation for metaphysics works, then we have no problem explaining Putnam's (1983b) position. The best scientific evidence strongly supports the conclusion that chemical, biological and mental phenomena are composed of the interactions of atoms and their associated fields, so we almost certainly know that materialist *scientific* conceptions are true even though we have good (scientific *and philosophical?*) reasons for rejecting conceptual reduction of the special sciences to fundamental physics. What we lack is any reason for accepting non-reductionist materialism (or any other position for that matter) as a metaphysical position reflecting the sort of correspondence with reality posited by metaphysical realists.

The problem for this reconstruction of Putnam's (1983b) position is that his arguments against the viability of non-reductionist materialist metaphysical realism appear to rest on a critique of non-reductionist materialism *considered as a scientific hypothesis*. He denies that we have a *scientific* conception of causation appropriate to a compositional conception of materialism. Almost certainly we do have such a conception, together with appropriate conceptions of the aggregation of things and their causal powers. So the case for distinguishing – as he and Fine want to do – between the legitimate anti-empiricist elements of scientific realism and the alleged metaphysical excesses involved in understanding realism in the light of a correspondence conception of truth has not been successfully made. *Prima facie*, scientific realism must be metaphysical scientific realism.

I have a speculation about how the tension between Putnam's commitment to something like pre-philosophical scientific realism ("internal realism," or whatever) and his critiques of metaphysical scientific realism arises. The deepest and most durable aspect of empiricist critiques of metaphysics generally and of scientific realism in particular, is the Humean critique of unreduced causal notions. All of the compositional conceptions of materialism seem committed to unreduced causal notions (forces or fields, or causal powers, ...) and a similarly unreduced notion of the aggregation (addition of forces, additive contributions of fields to potential energy, contributions of constituents to overall causal powers, ...). I suspect that Putnam's resistance to non-reductionist materialism (at least as of 1983b) may have reflected Humean concerns about such notions. If that's right, it's the topic for a quite different paper but I should indicate here that it's hard for me to see how one could accept (from a pre-philosophical scientific point of view) the idea that we know about electrons, protons and other charged particles and how they interact without thinking of the charge of a particle as something very, very much like a causal power.

Mind-independence and the possibility of error

Putnam (1978) argues that the metaphysical realist must treat truth as "radically non-epistemic," with the consequence that she cannot avoid skepticism. During this phase of his anti-(metaphysical) realism he proposed to think of truth along pragmatist lines as something like idealized rational acceptability in the limit of inquiry, so that it was a feature of his analysis that we couldn't (at least in the limit of inquiry) be radically mistaken. Of course according to accommodationism reference and, derivatively, truth and other semantic notions *are* epistemic notions, albeit not along the pragmatist/verificationist lines advocated in Putnam 1978. Plainly, unless there is a sound unrelated *a priori* argument for skepticism, accommodationist metaphysical realism does not entail a generally skeptical position. It is, in a pretty straightforward way, a non-reductionist, non-behaviorist updating of Quine's conception in "Natural Kinds" (1969b), so it relies on assumptions about our epistemic capacities which are (full blown skepticism aside) as unproblematic about us as are corresponding assumptions about a great many non-language using animals.

What about the possibility of radical error? Both the epistemic access condition and the accommodation condition imply that natural kind terms don't refer unless human social and linguistic practice underwrites some epistemically reliable access to fact about their referents. So, we couldn't be hopelessly wrong in every respect about the things that such terms refer to. But we could be – and indeed we have often been – fundamentally wrong in some important respects about natural kinds to which we referred. For most of the history of inquiry into natural history people have thought of species as in the first instance families of organisms, but for sexually reproducing species at least this is mistaken: conspecificity is, in the first instance, a relation between populations. Eighteenth-century biologists were extremely good at distinguishing between cases in which structures in two different species are homologous and cases in which they're analogous, and thus good at using the terms "analogy" and "homology" with their standard (contemporary) referents even though their conception of homology focused on questions of design rather than of common evolutionary origin. Newtonian conceptions of spatial and temporal intervals were fundamentally flawed but that doesn't mean that the basic magnitude terms used by Newtonian physicists failed to refer.

Indeed, isn't the whole point of having causal, causal-descriptive or otherwise "naturalistic" theories of reference (whatever the underlying metaphysical or anti-metaphysical conception one might have) to reflect the anti-empiricist insight that one can refer to phenomena about which one's conception is in some respects fundamentally mistaken?

What about fundamental errors "in the limit of inquiry," whatever that might mean? The idea of asking what results one would obtain in the ideal limit of inquiry as more and more data became available has its natural home in the context of a foundationalist conception of inductive inference. If there's an *a priori* justifiable, topic-and-possible-world-independent inductive logic or something like that, then (perhaps) it makes sense to ask what its output would converge toward in the limit as actual data became available over time. In that case the idealization involved in asking about convergence in the ideal limit of inquiry would involve ignoring human lifespan, memory capacity and information processing limitations.

The accommodationist conception of reference and natural kinds entails a profoundly non-foundational conception of inductive reasoning: reliable induction depends on historically contingent emergence of concepts and practices suitably accommodated to relevant (discipline dependent) causal structures together with an appropriate situation of inquiry in the relevant political and economic context (Boyd 1989, 1991, 1999b, 2001a, 2001b). Thus the idealization most congenial to "limit of inquiry" approaches is unavailable if the accommodationist conception is correct.

There are, however, two dimensions of idealization which might still be available. One we might think of as providing an idealization with respect to the *implementation* of historically contingent inductive strategies. We can abstract from limitations of human memory, diligence and data processing and ask, about a given historically situated inductive strategy, what conclusions if any its implementation would converge toward as actual data become available over time. Could inductive inferences idealized in this way converge toward significantly erroneous conclusions or toward none at all? In so far as this sort of counterfactual question has an answer (which I doubt) the accommodationist answer must be "yes." Unless the initial historically situated inductive practices happened to be very favorably accommodated to relevant causal structures there's no reason to suppose that significant errors could not be perpetuated indefinitely (on the political economy of *actual* error correcting see Boyd 1999b, 2001a).

Of course an idealization more closely modeled on the foundationalist approach would involve *epistemic* idealization: we could ask what conclusions would be reached in the limits of inquiry given the (or an) epistemically ideal inferential strategy, ideally implemented. If foundationalism is false in the way the accommodationist approach indicates, the only available epistemic parameter with respect to which the idealization could be defined would simply be truth conduciveness. Perhaps, again assuming that the counterfactual question at issue has an answer, it would follow that in the epistemically ideal limit of inquiry no radical errors would persist, but this would be a trivial result that tells us nothing about knowledge, reference, kinds or metaphysics.

I conclude that the accommodationist conception rejects skepticism, but not the possibility of fundamental error, and shows why pragmatist or verificationist appeals to epistemically idealized practices turn out to be misguided. Materialist accommodationism appears to satisfy the five proposed criteria and thus to underwrite a viable non-reductionist version of genuinely metaphysical materialist realism.

Other worries: referential determinateness and bivalence

It remains to see whether materialist accommodationism meets the two other challenges Putnam raises against metaphysical realism: that it is inappropriately committed to bivalence for sentences about natural kinds and that its reliance on a causal conception of reference makes it incapable of explaining how determinate reference relations are accomplished.

Bivalence

I've already indicated the basic accommodationist approach to bivalence. Some natural kinds (HPC kinds) are defined by natural and causally sustained clusterings of properties and by the mechanisms which underwrite them. Their naturalness – that is, their aptness for induction and explanation – depend on their being defined in this way, so that precisification of the terms or concepts that refer to them would, while underwriting bivalence, fail to meet the accommodation demands of the relevant disciplinary matrices and would thus fail to correspond to natural kinds.

So, accommodationist materialist realism is not committed to bivalence – indeed it's committed to bivalence failure for an important class of natural kinds. It's worth remarking on just why accommodationism is a realist position nonetheless. The reason why it's initially plausible to assign a universal commitment to bivalence to metaphysical realists is that it would certainly seem that realists are committed to there being (at a given time in a given reference frame) a determinate way the world is. I suppose that realists are so committed. Question: Would anti-metaphysical realists like Putnam feel comfortable denying that they are similarly committed? What's important is that the fact that bivalence fails for a sentence about an HPC at a time is perfectly compatible with there being a determinate state of the world at that time. When there is a failure of bivalence resulting from the predication of a homeostatic property cluster term the realist denies neither that there are facts of the matter regarding the homeostatic cluster property and the object of which it is predicated, nor that these facts are describable. What is important is that an appropriate description of the relevant facts regarding indeterminate or "borderline" cases of a homeostatic cluster kind consists not in the introduction of artificial precision in the definitions of the kind itself, but rather in a detailed description of the ways in which the indeterminate cases are like and unlike typical members of the kind. Suppose that some population, P, of animals has arisen from hybridization between two other populations, P_1 and P_2, such that P_1 and P_2 are unambiguously instances of two distinct species S_1 and S_2. It's compatible with the HPC conception that neither the sentence "P is in S_1" nor the sentence "P is in S_2" has a truth value. It would not follow that there is no fact of the matter about P's relation to S_1 and S_2. There would be all sorts of facts, describable in ecological, genetic, anatomical, physiological and developmental terms about the ways in which P participates in, and fails to participate in, the property clusterings which characterize S_1 and S_2. What would be true about these facts is that they're not adequately describable just using species names as predicates, but this is to be expected given the accommodationist conception. The deployment of species names contributes to accommodation in biology and related disciplines precisely because it aligns the vocabulary and concepts of biologists with certain very important loci of property clustering homeostatically sustained over many generations, but not all populations participate unambiguously in just one such clustering. Not all islands can be appropriately assigned to a continent either (though some can); this hardly undermines realism about either continents or islands.

Referential determinateness

In his famous (infamous?) model theoretic argument against metaphysical realism, Putnam argues that a causal theory of reference cannot account for the level of determinateness of reference which natural kind terms enjoy. It's easy to see why this is initially plausible. According to metaphysical realist causal theories, reference is a matter of epistemically relevant causal relations connecting uses of a natural kind term and instances of its referent. This suggests (but does not entail) a particular metaphysical picture: reference is a relation between linguistic entities and entirely *extra-linguistic* (and in that sense *independently existing*) natural kinds. Natural kinds are, somehow or other, in the world, and available for discovery and naming, independently of human practices. If that's the picture, then it's easy to see why determinateness of reference might be hard to come by. There are, presumably, lots of pretty similar natural kinds, and lots of epistemically relevant causal relations, so it's hard to see how determinate reference would obtain. The problem only gets worse if one thinks, as Putnam does, that the metaphysical realist must hold that the relevant causal relations don't reflect descriptive or intentional factors. It's worse yet if the metaphysical realist is a non-reductionist: there are even more natural kinds for those causal relations to distinguish between.

Finally (as Putnam 1983b indicates), reference to natural kinds is supposed to explain the inductive successes of scientific practice, so there must be some quite intimate connection between natural kinds and the conceptual machinery of the sciences. If one thinks of metaphysical realist theories as entailing that natural kinds are independent of that machinery, it is hard to see how the explanation could work unless it rested on some sort of *objective idealist* theory according to which natural kinds are somehow metaphysically (magically?) "fitted" for explanation and induction independently of the relevant practices.

The accommodationist conception avoids all these problems. It acknowledges the (causal!) role of (disciplinary matrix specific) descriptions and other conceptual factors in establishing reference, and it treats natural kinds, not as independent of human practices, but as artifacts of practices in particular disciplinary matrices. It *simultaneously* defines the reference relation, and the natural definitions and extensions of natural kind terms, in terms of the contributions which the deployment of those terms make to the satisfaction of accommodation demands of a particular matrix. For a natural kind term within a particular disciplinary matrix, there may be lots of kinds, natural *with respect to some disciplinary matrices or other*, which satisfy the epistemic access condition with respect to the term. The accommodation clause picks out the term's referent by identifying, as its defining properties, those which play the indicated role in explaining the satisfaction of the accommodation demands *of the particular disciplinary matrix*.

Of course, the epistemic access and accommodation conditions will not always pick out a unique referent even for a kind term fruitfully employed in a disciplinary matrix. Does this residual indeterminacy undermine a metaphysical realist correspondence conception of truth?

No. Whatever indeterminacy escapes the resources of these conditions is *really there*; reference (*understood as metaphysical correspondence*) is no more determinate than those conditions indicate.

As the treatment of partial denotation and denotational refinement above indicates (see p. 60), reference, in all its complexity, is really the dialectical *process* by which, within a disciplinary matrix, accommodation is achieved and maintained between the use of kind terms and relevant causal structures. Both partial denotation and denotational refinement are aspects of this ongoing process. The achievement of a referential situation in which a natural kind term enjoys a determinate natural definition is a *special case* of the phenomenon of reference (Boyd 1993). Thus, reference and truth, properly understood, really are no more determinate than the proposed realist accommodationist account of partial denotation and denotational refinement indicates. There is a metaphysically real referential *correspondence* between kind terms and the features of the world which underwrites our capacity to represent causal relations, but that correspondence has a dialectical complexity which attention to the formal apparatus of the Tarski definition renders obscure. It is a virtue, not a vice, of metaphysical realist causal *correspondence* conceptions of reference and truth that they can explain this dialectical element in reference.

Conclusion: non-reductionist materialist metaphysical realism and fair play for humans

Contrary to Putnam's critiques of metaphysical realism, non-reductionist materialist metaphysical realism is a viable philosophical position. There are three important keys to seeing this. First, one must understand the requirement that kinds and reference be "mind-independent" in such a way that appeals to the ordinary causal powers of minds and in such a way that social phenomena are not ruled out. Since this is in accord with the ways philosophers ordinarily understand mind-independence when evaluating idealist and relativist conceptions, no begging of the question against the anti-realist is involved. Second, one must recognize that no departure from realism, naturalism or materialism is implied if one acknowledges the role of descriptive, conceptual and intentional factors in determining reference to, and the definitions of, natural kinds provided that that role is understood in terms of the *causal* role of descriptive, conceptual and intentional practices. Finally, one must understand that the definition of natural kinds and the establishment of reference to them are aspects of the same ongoing dialectical process of the social construction of epistemically reliable discipline-specific concepts and classificatory practices.

For all of its simplistic associationist psychology, Quine's "Natural Kinds" (1969b) offered a useful beginning to our understanding of how evolutionarily important kinds could be "natural kinds" in the behavioral ecology of non-human animals. The kinds in question are evolutionary-role and species specific. Their recognition and representation involve the perceptual and cognitive capacities of the relevant animals. Although Quine doesn't develop this point, examples like bee dances and alarm calls in social mammals show that the relevant representational systems can be socially and communicatively mediated. No one thinks that this means that a behavioral ecology of (non-human) animal kind recognition and communication entails a non-realist conception either of the animals, or of their representational capacities, or of the kinds they recognize. If, ontologically speaking, we're as generous with ourselves as with our animal kin, there's no barrier to non-reductionist metaphysical realism.

Ethics (and other subjects) without ontology

One of Putnam's key concerns in *Ethics Without Ontology* (2004) is to deploy his critique of metaphysical realism as a foil against reductionist or simplistic conceptions in ethics. He favors a conception of ethics according to which there are lots of good-making features of things ideally held in an appropriate balance. His concern is that philosophers who seek a metaphysical foundation for ethics will end up subscribing to one or another reductionist conception, thereby denying the complexity of the subject matter. I'll here explore the implications of accommodationism for projects of doing ethics, and other subjects, without ontology.

Metaphysical realism and reductionism in ethics

In the preceding sections I've approached Putnam's arguments on the assumption that Putnam's real target is materialist metaphysical realism and that he argues that any consistently materialist metaphysical realism must be physicalistically reductionistic: that it must treat every discipline to which it applies as reducible to fundamental physics. Pretty clearly this approach won't work with respect to Putnam's concerns in *Ethics Without Ontology*. His concern there is not with the idea that ethics is reducible to the one true theory of fundamental physics. Instead he is concerned to reject the moral realist conception that there is one true *ethical* theory which identifies the metaphysical foundations of morals. His concern is not with mind-independence either. All of the plausible candidate ethical theories posit mind involving cognitive, affective, conceptual, social, or rational factors but Putnam doesn't rest his case on this consideration. So the arguments I've adduced thus far in defense of a non-reductionist materialist metaphysical realist understanding of accommodationism, except perhaps for the discussion of bivalence, don't address the central question Putnam is raising: Can a comprehensive metaphysical theory of the foundations of morals avoid a reductionist simplification of moral phenomena?

HPC consequentialist moral realism

You might say that the accommodationist conception of reference and kind definitions could have been designed precisely to answer "yes"; in fact it was designed largely for that purpose. In several papers (Boyd 1988, 1995, 2003a, 2003b) I deployed versions of the accommodationist conception of reference and kinds, and of the HPC conception of kind definitions, to defend a non-reductionist version of consequentialism, one according to which goodness is identified with contribution to human flourishing and flourishing is portrayed as a homeostatic unity of many different morally relevant factors. In fact, the conception of the metaphysics of the good which I defend in those papers is not very different from the conception Putnam defends in *Ethics Without Ontology*. If the arguments on pp. 54–63 above are right, then my HPC conception of the good, and Putnam's similar conception are examples of non-reductionist moral realism. The "one true" moral theory need not be reductionist or simplistic in order to qualify as metaphysically realist.

X without ontology: a proposal

The accommodationist conception implies that a precondition for the use of concepts and kind terms making a contribution to human accomplishments in some disciplinary matrix is that there be some appropriate accommodation in practice between the uses of those concepts and terms and relevant causal structures. At least for naturalistically inclined philosophers – and for lots of others as well – that sort of accommodation is an appropriate subject for metaphysical investigation, as the theory of natural kinds indicates. It does not follow that accomplishments in such a matrix will always be enhanced by systematic investigation of the underlying metaphysics.

For a matrix, X, and time, t, let WO(X,t) be the proposition that one can successfully do X at t without doing the metaphysics/ontology of X. WO(X,t) implies that the accommodation of practices in X at t to relevant causal structures would not be significantly increased by such metaphysical investigations as would be forthcoming at t. So, WO(X,t) is a (partly) metaphysical thesis: it's a thesis about what sorts of accommodation exist between the concepts and terminology of X and relevant causal structures and about the state of the art at t in metaphysical inquiry regarding X. If WO(X,t) is false, then at t we have a license, so to speak, to do metaphysics of X.

~WO(X,t)? Simple cases: misclassification and partial denotation

How might WO(X,t) be false? Several different but mutually compatible possibilities are important here, two of them obvious. First, it might happen that, at t, metaphysical investigations regarding X would result in relevantly more nearly accurate applications of the distinctive concepts and terminology associated with X. So, for example, metaphysical inquiry into the nature of species might result in greater accuracy in our theories about species in general, about speciation and about particular species. Similarly, such investigations might improve the accuracy of our representations in X by alerting us to cases in which some terms deployed in X partially denote and by guiding us in appropriate denotational refinement. If we think of nineteenth- and twentieth-century studies of the nature of atoms and of chemical elements as instances of empirical metaphysics (and why not?) then the drawing of the distinction between atomic mass and atomic number and the drawing of the associated distinction between elements and isotopes provide the paradigmatic example.

In cases like these WO(X,t) is false because of defects in the inferential architecture of X of sorts very familiar to philosophers of science and philosophers of language who advocate causal or naturalistic conceptions of reference and of natural kinds. After all, the idea that the most important prevailing standards for the application of a scientific term at a time might be in some respects defective was one of the central motivations for the adoption of such conceptions in the first place and the articulation of conceptions of partial denotation and denotational refinement by Field (1973) was one of the first important developments of those conceptions.

There are other, perhaps somewhat subtler, ways in which the inferential architecture of a disciplinary matrix may be defective, and thus other ways in which WO(X,t) may – under conditions favorable to the relevant metaphysics – be false. The other important possibilities are associated with the role of ideology in human inquiry – ideology both in the broad sense which encompasses widely held ideas and inferential practices, and in the pejorative political sense.

Epistemic access without (much) accommodation: concept-inferential strategy mismatch

One way in which prevailing ideology – prevailing conceptual and classificatory resources and prevailing inferential practices – can exhibit a defect which might be corrected by appropriate metaphysical inquiry involves cases in which a term or concept which corresponds to a genuine kind, natural with respect to one or more disciplinary matrices, is deployed in those matrices in such a way that it makes relatively little contribution (perhaps, on balance, a negative contribution) to epistemic successes within those matrices. The paradigm cases here are racial concepts and categories. Ordinary racial and ethnic categories certainly correspond to natural kinds in disciplinary matrices concerned with social structure, stratification and power: members of an ethnic or racial category in a particular culture often share (in the ways appropriate to an HPC conception) distinctive causal powers (including, of course, causal vulnerabilities) and recognition of these differences is crucial in relevant social sciences. Such inductive and explanatory successes as we have in studying such matters depend on our capacity to pretty reliably assign people to different ethnic or racial categories that correspond to different profiles of causal powers and vulnerabilities.

Nevertheless, it's notorious that the history of studies of race is full of inductive and explanatory failures (see, e.g., Gould 1981). It's standard, and correct, to say that one of the problems here is that researchers (and others) have got the *metaphysics* of races wrong. Of course, one way to make this claim has been to deny that ordinary racial categories are natural kinds, to insist that instead they are "social constructions," and, on those grounds, to deny that they are "real." A slightly more sophisticated formulation of such criticisms has been one according to which races are (something like) "natural kinds in sociology" (or whatever) but not "natural kinds in biology."[8]

What many important critics of our understanding of race and racism have done – successfully – is to address the *metaphysical* question, "What is the nature of race and races?" Their metaphysical investigations have made a positive contribution to social science studies of race and ethnicity. Over the past few decades, investigating the history, sociology and political economy of race and racism *without ontology* would have been a mistake. It's true, of course, that many important practitioners of ideology critique have formulated their accounts of the nature of race in relativist or anti-realist terms. Like Putnam, many of these scholars identify realist conceptions of kinds and categories with reductionist ones.

Nevertheless their insights can be perfectly accommodated (pun intended) by the realist account offered here. Races are natural kinds in the social sciences especially relevant to the explanation of how social stratification, inequality and exploitation are rationalized. They are HPC kinds. The key insight that so often receives relativist or anti-realist formulations is that, except for the role which superficial phenotypic traits play in facilitating racial classification, the different property clusters which underwrite race differences in causal powers and vulnerabilities are matters of social, political and economic factors rather than biological ones.

So the social study of race illustrates two important phenomena. First, it represents a case in which critical inquiry which was often framed in metaphysical terms ("the nature of race") made an important contribution to important research. Second, it shows that in order for metaphysical inquiry to contribute to epistemic success the metaphysical conclusions reached need not be exactly true: the distinct causal powers and vulnerabilities associated with membership in racial or ethnic groups *are* social constructions – that's the metaphysical insight – but (contrary to many antirealist formulations) that doesn't diminish the metaphysical reality of races. As in the rest of science and philosophy, in metaphysics relevantly good approximations will often do.

Distinctly philosophical metaphysical contributions to accommodation: non-reductionist conceptions in psychology and cognitive science

If one wants an example of a case in which X without ontology was floundering and in which philosophers doing metaphysics came to the aid of X, one need look no further than English-language experimental psychology during the 1950s and early 1960s. Return with us now to those thrilling days of yesteryear when the stranglehold of behaviorism was broken by a motley coalition of pioneer "artificial intelligence" types, neurophysiologists and philosophers who first defended a materialist but non-behaviorist conception of mind (think: Smart, Place) and then showed – along broadly functionalist lines – that a materialist conception could take an even less reductionist form (think: Fodor and, of course, Putnam). We need not decide just what materialist conception of mind is correct in order to recognize the genuine contribution which philosophical work on the nature of mind (which is surely metaphysics if anything is) made to the emergence of contemporary cognitive science. Psychology without ontology would have been a mistake in the 1960s (and probably would be now).

I'm inclined to think that there's another psychological research domain that's been doing without ontology – without sufficient attention to metaphysical analyses of competing conceptions of the implications of materialism – for too long. I have in mind the "discipline" of human sociobiology/ "evolutionary psychology." Central to this discipline is the idea that findings from evolutionary theory provide independent constraints on theories of human developmental psychology, so that some theoretical issues can, at least *prima facie*, be resolved by appeals to "predictions" from evolutionary theory. To a very good first approximation the central inferential patterns in human sociobiology involve advocating an evolutionary scenario, S, regarding selection for a behavior, B, in the environment of evolutionary adaptation and taking that scenario to "predict" that humans have an innate and relatively non-malleable unconscious motive with the same propositional content as the evolutionary function which S assigns to B.[9]

These inference patterns reflect deep confusions about broadly metaphysical issues regarding reduction, functional explanations, projectibility, philosophy of mind and heaven knows what else. Despite the efforts of philosophers like those just cited the credibility of sociobiological methods remains very high. Since the appropriate critiques deploy resources well within the mainstream of contemporary metaphysics and philosophy of science, this is another case in which doing X without ontology would not be a good idea.

I do not mean, of course, to suggest that WO(X,t) is always false. From the latter part of the eighteenth century biologists have been very, very good at distinguishing between homologous and analogous characteristics of organisms. Prior to the acceptance of evolutionary theory, insofar as biologists and philosophers examined the metaphysics of the distinction they understood homologies as manifestations of common elements of divine design. There's no reason to think that during the early nineteenth century the excellent work of anatomists in deploying the distinction would have been improved by increased metaphysical speculation.

Metaphysics and ideology critique, II: unwanted "achievements"

In the case of the metaphysics of race, the discovery that races are – in the relevant sense – social constructions rests on the recognition that appeals to racial categories and stereotypes play a crucial role in the maintenance of oppression and exploitation. Racial category terms refer to real kinds (in the theory of oppression and exploitation) precisely because of the ways in which racist practices, including ones which involve the deployment of terms for racial categories, rationalize and stabilize oppression and exploitation. Whatever contribution, limited but real, the use of terms for racial categories makes to our theoretical understanding of exploitation, the use of such terms also contributes to a different sort of non-epistemic "achievement": the stabilization of exploitative social relations for the benefit of a small ruling class.[10] So here we have a case in which getting the referential semantics of some terms right provides a clue to the broader ideological functions of the discourses in which they are involved.

Similar contributions to ideology critique can arise from other sorts of diagnoses regarding referential semantics. Terms involved in the celebration of allegedly distinctive ethnic or national virtues – "White Man's burden," "American individualism," "Russian genius," "French élan," … , take your pick – don't refer and, given suitable background information, this is a clue to their ideological function. Similar results obtain for some cases of partial denotation. Almost certainly the adjective "democratic" (analogously "democracy") partially denotes two importantly different properties which a system of governance might possess. On the one hand there is the property which such a system possesses if it has the formal hallmarks of "democracy": free elections, an officially uncensored press, no formal restriction, by gender, ethnicity or social class, on office holding, etc. Then there is the (much rarer) property which a system possesses if its institutions in practice provide all participants with the opportunity to have a genuine impact on policies that affect their lives. Once this partial denotation is diagnosed, it's easy to see what the ideological function is of passing the former off as the latter.

So, to illustrate these points here are some further speculations about referential semantics and ideology (in both senses of the term).

WO(X,t) probably true:

  Mid-eighteenth century biology
  Contemporary applied physics
  Birthday conference planning

WO(X,t) probably false:

  Mid-eighteenth century chemistry
  Biology for decades after Darwin
  Mid-twentieth century cognitive psychology
  Ordinary partial denotation
     "element" early twentieth century
     "meaning" mid-twentieth century (Putnam!)
     "fitness" mid-twentieth century evolutionary biology
  Partial denotation with unwanted "achievements"

"justice" (Think: Thrasymachus, Marx)
"objectivity" (Think: radical/feminist/postmodernist ideology critique)
"altruism" (Think: human sociobiology)
Denotation failure with unwanted "achievements"
"national interest"
"patriotic duty"
"manifest destiny"

Ethics without ontology?

Here I'm of two minds. I subscribe to a certain pluralist conception of the ontology of the good – a homeostatic property cluster conception (Boyd 1995, 1999a, 1999b) – which I take to be a very good first approximation to the pluralist conception that Putnam himself defends. The main difference, according to me, is that I recognize that pluralist positions of the sort we both accept are (metaphysical) realist, but non-reductionist, conceptions of ethics. In one mood I think that at the present moment articulation of the sorts of moral realist positions which (on my reading of the matter) Putnam and I defend is really important. My position – and his, however it is best interpreted – represent critiques of the sorts of moral relativism which dominate much thinking both in and outside the academy.

I'm inclined to think that the critique of relativism is morally important. In the first place, adopting a moral relativist stance tends, I think, to undermine the effectiveness of critics of morally defective social policies. Often, people who are concerned to criticize social evils feel compelled to adopt a moral relativist conception in order to justify their critiques of culturally chauvinist or bigoted intolerance. It's hard, however, to be an effective critic of, say, some form of bigotry if your "official" position, as it were, is that bigoted moral positions are on a par with their rivals. We need to equip ourselves with better ways of defending appropriate forms of tolerance, ones that don't impede our efforts to level serious moral criticisms when they're appropriate.

I'm inclined to think that this point is especially cogent when moral relativist conceptions are put into play in defense of tolerance of cultural differences. We must, of course, find ways to avoid and criticize the sorts of cultural chauvinism and racism which are the legacies of imperialism. Nevertheless, it's pretty clear that the main application of moral and cultural relativist conceptions in current debates about tolerance between cultures has been to dilute criticisms of cultural practices which involve the subjugation of women. We seem to need pretty urgently to work on non-relativist conceptions of how to reject racism and cultural chauvinism while licensing appropriate moral critiques of aspects of our own and others' cultures.

On the other hand, it often seems to me that the sorts of broadly metaphysical debates characteristic of contemporary ethical theory – whether they're debates in metaethics or debates about the relative merits of particular ethical theories – are morally beside the point. Consequentialists, Kantians, virtue theorists, theistic Platonists, divine command theorists, whatever, all agree that war, poverty, oppression, bigotry, are profoundly wrong. Even moral relativists, non-cognitivists, error theorists, etc., agree in practice. Our difficulties in eliminating these things don't stem mainly from our failure to get the right theories in ethics or metaethics. Instead, they seem to stem from the difficulties facing us when we ask certain difficult empirical questions in, roughly, political economy: What sorts of social, political and economic structures and practices explain the persistence of such social evils? What alternative structures and practices would be necessary to eliminate or attenuate these evils? What sorts of political and cultural work would be most effective in establishing those structures and practices?

Of course these are extremely difficult questions, but might it not be a better use of the time and research skills of moral philosophers if we focused mainly on them? The answer, of course, depends on how effective research on these questions would turn out to be. That's a topic beyond the scope of this essay.

But here's the crucial point: The issue only arises to the extent that a metaphysical hypothesis is true: that our inferential practices in moral inquiry are to some significant extent already aligned with the factors that non-reductively underwrite the good. I think that's true, and I think that Putnam thinks so too.

Final thoughts: apologies for realism

Ambiguity is a special case of partial denotation, so, in the spirit of our discussion of matters semantic, here are apologies for realism.

Apologia: success without correspondence truth

In the archaic sense this whole essay is an apology for metaphysical realism. I want to add one more (pragmatist!) point to that *apologia*. One theme in many pragmatist/Wittgensteinian/neo-Kantian critiques of correspondence theories of truth is that our philosophical focus should be on the *use* of language *rather than* on *correspondence truth*. In an important sense, the accommodationist conception of reference and natural kinds presented here represents a denial that the implied contrast is real: in order to explain how we successfully *use* language in explanation and induction one must adopt a realist conception of *reference, natural kinds* and *correspondence truth*.

It remains true, however, that sometimes we use language successfully, even in scientific settings, in contexts in which the usefulness of our concepts (and their linguistic manifestations) doesn't seem to be straightforwardly explained in terms of approximate truth. Many cases in which $WO(X,t)$

holds seem to be cases in which some broadly metaphysical conception contributes to the accommodation of inferential/explanatory practices to relevant causal structures even though the relevant terms don't refer and that conception isn't, on any plausible conception of approximation, approximately true. So, however much some notion of approximate (correspondence) truth might figure in characterizing the relevant inductive/explanatory achievements, we seem to have cases in which the contribution that the *use* of the relevant metaphysical concepts and language makes to accommodation cannot be explained in terms of *reference* or *truth*. For example, theistic (or deistic) conceptions of design plainly informed highly successful eighteenth- and early nineteenth-century efforts to distinguish between analogous and homologous traits even though it's really a stretch to say, e.g., that "design" referred to natural selection. Still, conceptions of design were *use*ful: they were, as we might say, onto something. Teleological/design conceptions contributed to the accommodation of eighteenth- and nineteenth-century practices to evolutionary factors without referring to anything, or at least so I'm inclined to say. If you're more generous than I am in positing reference, consider medical research on the effectiveness of acupuncture or on the therapeutic effects of religiously grounded meditation techniques. One would not want to hold the conclusion that these techniques are *onto something therapeutically* hostage to evidence that the terms in which they were traditionally described actually *refer*.

What I want to propose in response to cases like this is that we should think of the (approximate) truth of theories and of the reliability of methods as special cases of the broader phenomenon of accommodation of linguistic, conceptual and inferential practices to relevant causal structures. On such a conception approximate truth would be understood as a special case of accommodation approximately governed by Tarski-style compositional semantics and accomplished via referential (or partial denotational) use of natural kind terms. The epistemic reliability of particular inferential/ explanatory practices would be largely a matter of conduciveness to identification of approximate truths. There would, however, be recognized a broader representational function of, e.g., projectibility judgments, intuitions, research styles, hunches, conceptual schemes, etc., in terms of their causal contributions, via alignment with relevant causal structures, to the epistemic reliability of practices. In particular the positive representational function of a conceptual scheme or methodology – its contribution to the achievement of epistemically valuable alignment of practices with relevant causal structures – would not always have to be localized, as it were, to matters of the referential correspondence of particular terms to discrete features of the world. We would then have available a representational theory of insight – of *being onto something* – that does not always require that insights involve reference or approximate truth but that does explicate insight terms of the broader correspondence-involving notion of accommodation. An additional advantage of such a theory would be that it would provide a theoretical link between modes of representation peculiar (so far as we know) to human concepts and language and those modes of representation deployed by other organisms (see Boyd 2001b).

I haven't yet worked out the details of such a conception beyond the points just made but it seems to me that when further developed this sort of accommodationism would fully meet the requirement that it take seriously the use of language and concepts without any compromises regarding metaphysical realism. Insight, on the proposed interpretation, would still be a matter of bicameral linguistic/conceptual legislation.

Apology: too many concessions to logical empiricism

I've argued here that Putnam's critiques of metaphysical realism rest on a mistaken conception of what a genuinely metaphysical realist position must entail. The broadly reductionist conception Putnam attacks is not the conception that a consistently articulated metaphysical realism implies: quite the opposite. The fault, it must be acknowledged, does not lie largely with Putnam. Much realist thinking – both within professional philosophy and elsewhere in the academy – does seem to be influenced by the sorts of reductionist conception that Putnam is at pains to criticize. For example, many realists think of realism as entailing that the world has an interest-and-project independent natural kind structure (see, e.g., Psillos' excellent 1999). Similarly many, many metaphysical realists who are also non-reductive physicalists about mental phenomena continue to formulate physicalism by reference to notions like "the vocabulary of fundamental physics," thereby echoing the reductionist formulations of yore (for discussions see, e.g, Jessica Wilson 2002, 2005, 2006; Dowell 2006; Shoemaker 2003, Horgan 1993). Much realist work in the epistemology of science has focused on technical issues rather than on, e.g., the implications of the social embedding of scientific practice, and so on.

In large measure, these features of recent realist work can be attributed to the fact that contemporary scientific realism is, at least in English-language philosophy, largely an outgrowth of logical empiricism: a reflection of the ways in which logical empiricists themselves became critical of their own critiques of metaphysics.[11] While rejecting anti-metaphysical applications of verificationism the early defenders of scientific realism retained much of the legacy of logical empiricism: an algorithmic and foundationalist conception of methods, a reductionist conception of materialism, a conception of reference and of linguistic precision with deep roots in both empiricism and formal logic, and (with the important exception of an interest in the possibility of a physicalist theory of mind) an almost exclusive focus on physics (indeed on atomic and subatomic physics) as the paradigm science.

In the light of this history it's easy to see why much realist thinking has the sort of reductionist cast that it does. It hasn't helped matters either that much of the important academic work in the history, sociology and literary theory of science which thoroughly rebuts the reductionist and foundationalist conception of science has been associated with utterly relativist post-modernist slogans whose hostility to science is matched only by their incoherence. I've argued elsewhere (Boyd 1999b) that nevertheless almost all of these slogans capture important insights – insights which are compatible with, indeed entailed by, a properly developed (metaphysical) realism. Of course I think the same is true of Putnam's anti-reductionist insights.

On Putnam (himself)

When I was an undergraduate at MIT, I, and many of my friends, adopted a particular approach to Hilary's classes. Hilary would require only a long-term paper in his courses, thus encouraging undergraduates to try their hands at original philosophical work. What we'd do was to postpone decisions about our term-paper topics until Hilary said something in a lecture that we really, really disagreed with and then write papers attacking his positions. It's a measure of his greatness as a teacher that this was exactly the sort of project that he encouraged and rewarded. It's a measure of his greatness as a philosopher that these were very challenging projects indeed, requiring us to come to terms with truly deep philosophical issues. Nothing has changed.

Notes

1 I've benefited from help from lots of people in developing the view I present here, including participants in a decade worth of conversations and seminars in the Cornell philosophy department. I want especially to thank W. Christopher Boyd, Eric Hiddleston, Jessica Wilson, Matthew Haug, Howard Engelskirchen, Sydney Shoemaker and Nicholas Sturgeon.

  Regarding the title: many years ago I gave a philosophy of science talk at Pittsburgh. In the same series Nelson Goodman was scheduled to give a talk titled "What of Science with the World Gone." I wasn't able to attend his talk and I've been unable to locate a copy of his paper, but I thought the title raised issues about realism and anti-realism in a neat way, so I sort of borrowed the idea but with a twist.

2 I have it in mind here that when t_i is predicated of some thing, a, we should think of that predication as equivalent to predication of t_i that a falls under it. So the epistemic access clause will, for many terms, t_i, be satisfied in large measure because, often enough, t_i is applied to things just when they have (many of) the properties in F_i. In such cases something the association with t_i of (approximately) reliable detection procedures for F_i will be central to reference in ways suggested by Dretske 1981. I've employed the more convoluted terminology because there seem to be natural kind terms for which the relevant epistemic access is not mainly secured by reliable detection: "neutrino," "endosymbiosis," "speciation," "fitness," "reference," "natural kind." ... OK, the last two entries do reflect the particular position defended here.

3 This analysis generalizes in obvious ways to cases in which there are more than two partial denotata.

4 Actually, I agree with the suggestion, implicit in Quine 1969, that the theory of natural kinds can be thought of as extending as well to the ways in which accommodation is achieved in non-human inductive and inferential systems.

5 For simplicity, I've here ignored an obvious complication. There are, of course, natural kinds – species for example, or as yet unsynthesized chemical kinds – which have not yet been named. So a fully worked-out version of the accommodationist conception would have to refer both to kinds which correspond to possible extensions of the vocabulary of existing disciplinary matrices and to possible but not actual disciplinary matrices. There's a modal aspect to the claim that natural kinds are social constructions: when philosophers write about natural kinds they are writing about possible natural kinds. So, the claim that natural kinds are social constructions is analogous to the claim that computer programs are social constructions: it applies to possible as well as to actual examples.

6 Except in the modal sense indicated in the preceding footnote.

7 For simplicity, I here ignore the further complication that there's an important broader conception of acidity: Lewis acids are electron pair acceptors whether or not they're proton donors. So it's probably right to say that "acid" partially denotes Brønsted–Lowry acids (proton donors) and Lewis acids (see Stanford and Kitcher 2000).

8 For a useful discussion of the relevant science, including issues about whether or not some racial categories might be, as one might say, "natural kinds in medicine and pharmacology," see Social Science Research Council 2007. For much more sophisticated treatments look at the emerging literature in critical race studies; see, e.g., Crenshaw et al. 1996, Delgado 1995.

9 For an even better approximation add some inference patterns which trade on conflating the psychological use of "altruism" and "altruistic" with technical metaphorical uses of those terms in evolutionary theory. For an almost perfect approximation, add inferences from premises of the form "B has a biological/ genetic basis" to "B is innate and relatively nonmalleable." See Kitcher 1987, Buller 2005, Boyd 2001a.

10 I here adopt a Marxist, or at any rate internationalist, conception of the political and economic role of racism and racist divisions. Readers with a different political analysis will have in mind some other stratification-stabilizing role for racism.

11 To a remarkable extent one can get an overview of logical empiricists' internal criticisms of their own anti-metaphysical positions by reading Quine's *Ontological Relativity and Other Essays* (1969a) and the first three volumes of *Minnesota Studies in the Philosophy of Science* 1956–62; see especially Feigl 1956, 1958; Hempel 1958; Maxwell 1962a, 1962b; Putnam 1962.

Bibliography

Adams, Robert (1999) *Finite and Infinite Goods*, New York and Oxford: Oxford University Press.

Amundson, R. (1983) "E. C. Tolman and the Intervening Variable: A Study in the Epistemological History of Psychology," *Philosophy of Science* 50, 268–82.

——(1986) "The Unknown Epistemology of E. C. Tolman," *British Journal of Psychology* 77, 525–51.

Boyd, R. (1980) "Materialism Without Reductionism: What Physicalism Does Not Entail," in N. Block (ed.), *Readings In Philosophy of Psychology*, vol.1. Cambridge: Harvard University Press.

——(1982) "Scientific Realism and Naturalistic Epistemology," in P. D. Asquith and R. N. Giere (eds.), *PSA 1980. Volume Two*. E. Lansing: Philosophy of Science Association.

——(1983) "On the Current Status of the Issue of Scientific Realism," *Erkenntnis* 19: 45–90.

——(1985a) "Lex Orandi est Lex Credendi," in Churchland and Hooker (eds.), *Images of Science: Scientific Realism Versus Constructive Empiricism*, Chicago: University of Chicago Press.

——(1985b) "Observations, Explanatory Power, and Simplicity," in P Achinstein and O. Hannaway (eds.), *Observation, Experiment, and Hypothesis In Modern Physical Science*, Cambridge: MIT Press.

——(1985c) "The Logician's Dilemma," *Erkenntnis* 22: 197–252.

——(1988) "How to be a Moral Realistm," in G. Sayre McCord (ed.), *Moral Realism*, Ithaca: Cornell University Press.

——(1989) "What Realism Implies and What It Does Not," *Dialectica*.

——(1990a) "Realism, Approximate Truth and Philosophical Method," in Wade Savage (ed.), *Scientific Theories*, Minnesota Studies in the Philosophy of Science, vol. 14. Minneapolis: University of Minnesota Press

——(1990b) "Realism, Conventionality, and 'Realism About'," in Boolos (ed.), *Meaning and Method*, Cambridge: Cambridge University Press.

——(1991) "Realism, Anti-Foundationalism and the Enthusiasm for Natural Kinds," *Philosophical Studies* 61: 127–48.

——(1992) "Constructivism, Realism, and Philosophical Method," in John Earman (ed.), *Inference, and Other Philosophical Frustration*.

——(1993) "Metaphor and Theory Change," (second version), in A. Ortony (ed.) *Metaphor and Thought*, 2nd edn, New York: Cambridge University Press.

——(1995) "Postscript to 'How to be a Moral Realist'," in Paul K. Moser and J. D. Trout (eds.), *Contemporary Materialism: A Reader*, New York: Routledge.

——(1999a) "Homeostasis, Species, and Higher Taxa," in R. Wilson (ed.), *Species: New Interdisciplinary Essays*, Cambridge: MIT Press.

——(1999b) "Kinds as the 'Workmanship of Men': Realism, Constructivism, and Natural Kinds," in Julian Nida-Rümelin (ed.), *Rationalität, Realismus, Revision: Proceedings of the Third International Congress, Gesellschaft für Analytische Philosophie*, Berlin: de Gruyter.

——(2001a) "Reference, (In)commensurability, and Meanings: Some (Perhaps) Unanticipated Complexities," in Paul Hoyningen-Huene and Howard Sankey (eds.), *Incommensurability and Related Matters*, Dordrecht: Kluwer.

——(2001b) "Truth through Thick and Thin," in Richard Schantz, ed. *What is Truth?* Berlin and New York: Walter de Gruyter.

——(2003a) "Finite Beings, Finite Goods: The Semantics, Metaphysics and Ethics of Naturalist Consequentialism, Part I," *Philosophy and Phenomenological Research* 66(3): 505–53.

——(2003b) "Finite Beings, Finite Goods: The Semantics, Metaphysics and Ethics of Naturalist Consequentialism, Part II," *Philosophy and Phenomenological Research* 57(1): 24–47.

Brink, David O. (1984) "Moral Realism and the Skeptical Argument from Disagreement and Queerness," *Australasian Journal of Philosophy* 62: 111–25.

——(1989) *Moral Realism and the Foundations of Ethics*, Cambridge: Cambridge University Press.

Buller, David (2005) *Adapting Minds: Evolutionary Psychology and the Persistent Quest for Human Nature*, Cambridge, MA: MIT Press/Bradford Books.

Henry C. Byerly and Vincent A. Lazara (1973) "Realist Foundations of Measurement," Philosophy of Science 40 (1):10-28.

Chomsky, N. (1955/1975) *The Logical Structure of Linguistic Theory*, Chicago: University of Chicago Press. (Published by UCP in 1985. Originally appeared in unpublished manuscript form in 1955.)

Crenshaw, Kimberly, N. Gotanda, and K. Thomas (eds.) (1996). *Critical Race Theory: The Key Writings that Shaped the Movement*, New York: New Press.

Delgado, Richard (1995) *Critical Race Theory: The Cutting Edge*, Philadelphia: Temple University Press.

Dowell. J. L. (2006) "The Physical: Empirical not Metaphysical," *Philosophical Studies* 131: 25–60.

Dretske, F. (1981) *Knowledge and the Flow of Information*, Cambridge, MA: MIT Press.

Eklund, M. (2008) "Putnam on Ontology," To appear in "Putnam on Ontology", Maria Uxia Rivas Monroy, Concepcion Martinez Vidal, and Celeste Cancela (eds.), *Following Putnam's Trail: On Realism and Other Issues*, Amsterdam: Rodopi.

Feigl, H. (1956) "Some Major Issues and Developments in the Philosophy of Science of Logical Empiricism," in H. Feigl and M. Scriven (eds.), *Minnesota Studies in the Philosophy of Science*, vol. 1. Minneapolis: University of Minnesota Press.

Feigl, Herbert (1958) "The 'Mental' and the 'Physical'," in Herbert Feigl, Michael Scriven, and Grover Maxwell (eds.), *Concepts, Theories and the Mind-Body Problem*, Minnesota Studies in the Philosophy of Science, vol. 2. Minneapolis: University of Minnesota Press, 370–497.

Feigl, Herbert and Scriven, Michael (eds.) (1956) *Foundations of Science and the Concepts of Psychology and Psychoanalysis*, Minnesota Studies in the Philosophy of Science, vol. 1. Minneapolis: University of Minnesota Press.

Feigl, Herbert, Scriven, Michael, and Maxwell, Grover (eds.) (1958) *Concepts, Theories and the Mind–Body Problem*, Minnesota Studies in the Philosophy of Science, vol. 2., Minneapolis: University of Minnesota Press.

Feigl, Herbert and Maxwell, Grover (eds.) (1962) *Scientific Explanation, Space, and Time*, Minnesota Studies in the Philosophy of Science, vol. 3. Minneapolis: University of Minnesota Press.

Field, H. (1973) "Theory Change and the Indeterminacy of Reference," *Journal of Philosophy* 70: 462–81.

Fine, A. (1984) "The Natural Ontological Attitude," in J. Leplin (ed.) *Scientific Realism*, Berkeley: University of California Press.

——(1986a) *The Shaky Game*, Chicago: University of Chicago Press.

——(1986b) "Unnatural Attitudes: Realist and Instrumentalist Attachments to Science," *Mind* 95: 149–79.

Fodor, J. (1968) *Psychological Explanation*, New York: Random House.

Goodman, N. (1954) *Fact Fiction and Forecast*, Cambridge, MA: Harvard University Press.

Gould, Stephen Jay (1981) *The Mismeasure of Man*, New York: Norton.

Hempel, C. G. (1958) "The Theoritician's Dilemma," in Herbert Feigl, Michael Scriven, and Grover Maxwell (eds.), *Concepts, Theories and the Mind–Body Problem*, Minnesota Studies in the Philosophy of Science, vol. 2. Minneapolis: University of Minnesota Press, 37–98.

Horgan, Terence (1993) "From Supervenience to Superdupervenience: Meeting the demands of a material world," *Mind* 102: 555–86.

Kitcher, Philip (1981) "Explanatory Unificationm," *Philosophy of Science* 48: 507–31.
——(1987) *Vaulting Ambition: Sociobiology and the Quest for Human Nature*, Cambridge, MA: MIT Press.
——(1993) *The Advancement of Science*, New York: Oxford University Press.
Kitcher, Philip and Salmon, Wesley (eds.) (1989) *Scientific Explanation*, Minneapolis: University of Minnesota Press.
Koethe, J. (1979) "Putnam's Argument Against Realism," *Philosophical Review* 88: 92–99.
Kuhn, T. (1970) *The Structure of Scientific Revolutions*, 2nd edn. Chicago: University of Chicago Press.
Lewis, David (1984) "Putnam's paradox," *Australasian Journal of Philosophy* 62: 221–36.
Lipton, P. (1991) *Inference to the Best Explanation*, London: Routledge and Kegan Paul.
——(1993) "Is the Best Good Enough?," *Proceedings of the Aristotelian Society* 93/2: 89–104.
Locke, J. 1689/(1975) *An Essay Concerning Human Understanding*, Oxford: Oxford University Press.
Maxwell, Grover (1962a). "On the Ontological Status of Theoretical Entities," in Herbert Feigl and Grover Maxwell (eds.), *Scientific Explanation, Space, and Time*, Minnesota Studies in the Philosophy of Science, vol. 3. Minneapolis: University of Minnesota Press, 3–27.
——(1962b) "The Necessary and the Contingent," in Herbert Feigl and Grover Maxwell, (eds.), *Scientific Explanation, Space, and Time*, Minnesota Studies in the Philosophy of Science, vol. 3. Minneapolis: University of Minnesota Press, 398–404.
McGrath, Sarah (2006) "Review of H. Putnam, *Ethics without Ontology*". *Philosophical Review* 115(4): 533–35.
McMullin, E. (1984) "A Case for Scientific Realism," in J. Leplin (ed.), *Scientific Realism*, Berkeley: University of California Press.
——(1987) "Explanatory Successes and the Theory of Truth," in N. Rescher (ed.), *Scientific Inquiry in Philosophical Perspective*, Lanham: University Press of America.
——(1991) "Comment: Selective Anti-Realism," *Philosophical Studies* 61: 97–1080.
Merrill, G. H. (1980) "The Model Theoretic Argument against Realism," *Philosophy of Science* 47: 69–81.
Mill, J. S. (1843) "A System of Logic," in *Collected Works of John Stuart Mill*, ed. J. M. Robinson, Toronto: University of Toronto Press.
Miller, R. (1987) *Fact and Method*, Princeton: Princeton University Press.
Millikan, R. (1997) "Historical Kinds and the Special Sciences," *Philosophical Studies* 95(1–2): 45–65.
Oppenheim, P and Putnam, P. (1958) "Unity of science as a working hypothesis," in Herbert Feigl, Michael Scriven, and Grover Maxwell (eds.), *Concepts, Theories and the Mind–Body Problem*, Minnesota Studies in the Philosophy of Science, vol. 2. Minneapolis: University of Minnesota Press, 3–36.
Papineau, D. (2001) "The Rise of Physicalism," in Carl Gillett and Barry Loewer (eds.), *Physicalism and its Discontents*, Cambridge: Cambridge University Press, 3–36.
Psillos, S. (1999) *Scientific Realism: How Science Tracks Truth*, New York and London: Routledge.
Putnam, H. (1962) "The Analytic and the Synthetic," in Herbert Feigl and Grover Maxwell (eds.), *Scientific Explanation, Space, and Time*, Minnesota Studies in the Philosophy of Science, vol. 3. Minneapolis: University of Minnesota Press.

——(1972) "Explanation and Reference," in G. Pearce and P. Maynard (eds.), *Conceptual Change*, Dordrecht: Reidel.
——(1975a) "The Meaning of "Meaning'," in H. Putnam, *Mind, Language and Reality*, Cambridge: Cambridge University Press.
——(1975b) "Language and Reality," in H. Putnam, *Mind, Language and Reality*, Cambridge: Cambridge University Press.
——(1975c) "What Theories are Not," in H. Putnam, *Mathematics, Matter and Method*, Cambridge: Cambridge University Press.
——(1978) *Meaning and the Moral Sciences*, London: Routledge and Kegan Paul.
——(1980) "Models and Reality," The Journal of Symbolic Logic 45(3): 464–82.
——(1981) *Reason, Truth and History*, Cambridge: Cambridge University Press.
——(1983a) ""Vagueness and Alternative Logic," in H. Putnam, *Realism and Reason*, Cambridge: Cambridge University Press.
——(1983b) "Why There Isn't a Ready Made World," in H. Putnam, *Realism and Reason*, Cambridge: Cambridge University Press.
——(2004) *Ethics Without Ontology*, Cambridge: Harvard University Press.
Quine, W. V. (1969a) *Ontological Relativity and Other Essays*, New York: Columbia University Press.
——(1969b) ""Natural Kinds," in W. V. Quine, *Ontological Relativity and Other Essays*, New York: Columbia University Press.
Salmon, W. (1984) *Scientific Explanation and the Causal Structure of the World*, Princeton: Princeton University Press.
——(1989) *Four Decades of Scientific Explanation*, Minneapolis: University of Minnesota Press.
Shapere, D. (1964) "The Structure of Scientific Revolutions," *Philosophical Review* 73: 383–94.
Shoemaker, S. (1980) "Causality and Properties," in P. van Inwagen (ed.), *Time and Cause*, Dordrecht: D. Reidel.
——(2003) *Identity, Cause and Mind (Expanded Edition)*, New York and Oxford: Oxford University Press.
Sismondo, S. (1993a) "Some Social Constructions," *Social Studies of Science* 23: 515–53.
——(1993b) "Response to Knorr Cetina," *Social Studies of Science* 23: 563–69.
——(1996) *Science without Myth*, Albany: State University of New York Press.
Smith, L. D. (1986) *Behaviorism and Logical Positivism: A Reassessment of the Alliance*, Stanford: Stanford University Press.
Social Science Research Council (2007) "Is Race 'Real'?," http://raceandgenomics.ssrc.org/
Stanford, K. and Kitcher, P. (2000) "Refining the Causal Theory of Reference for Natural Kind Terms," *Philosophical Studies* 97: 99–129.
Sturgeon, N. (1985) "Moral Explanations," in David Copp and Zimmerman (eds.), *Morality, Reason, and Truth*, Rowman & Littlefield Publishers.
——2006a. "Moral Explanations Defended," in James Dreier (ed.), *Contemporary Debates in Moral Theory*, Oxford: Blackwell, 241–62.
Sturgeon, N. (2006b) "Ethical Naturalism," in David Copp (ed.), *The Oxford Handbook of Ethical Theory*, Oxford: Oxford University Press, 91–121.
Wilson, Jessica (2002) "Causal Powers, Forces, and Superdupervenience," *Grazer Philosophische Studien* 63: 53–78.

——(2005) "Supervenience-based formulations of physicalism," *Nous* 29(3): 426–59.
——(2006) "On Characterizing the Physical," *Philosophical Studies* 131: 61–99.
Wilson, R. (1999a) *Species: New Interdisciplinary*, Cambridge: MIT Press.
——(1999b) "Realism, Essence, and Kind: Resuscitating Species Essentialism," in R. Wilson (ed.), *Species: New Interdisciplinary Essays*, Cambridge: MIT Press.
Yablo, Stephen (1992) "Mental Causation," *The Philosophical Review* 101(2): 431–51.

COMMENTS ON RICHARD BOYD'S "WHAT OF PRAGMATISM WITH THE WORLD HERE?"

Hilary Putnam

I agree with many of the things Richard Boyd says. The extent of our agreement would be apparent from my chapter in this volume. What's more, I have agreed with those things for a long time, although I think Boyd missed this because he has been reading me in a systematically wrong way. Boyd was so upset by the things I wrote in my "internal realist" period that he has been projecting those views onto my publications ever since, and he shouldn't be doing that. But even in that period, as I have explained in "From Quantum Mechanics to Ethics and Back Again," I mistakenly believed that Boyd's sort of scientific realism (Putnam 1978: 20 ff) was *compatible* with my "verificationist semantics" (Putnam 1983).[1] That was the result of a conversation with Rogers Allbritton, which I have described in that paper. I know this will disappoint Axel Mueller, who has criticized me for accepting Boyd's principles, or the ones that I learned from Boyd, namely that *theories in the mature science are typically approximately true*, and *terms in the mature sciences typically refer*. I have long believed those principles (since the 1960s, anyway), and I am unrepentant in that respect (Putnam 2012).[2] However, I also think that those principles are not enough to refute the idea that the "right" semantics is verificationist semantics (whether of Dummett's kind, or of the kind I advocated in *Reason, Truth and History*), because the anti-realist can simply *reinterpret the whole language*, including all scientific hypotheses expressible in it, and if these principles represent a scientific hypothesis, in a very liberal sense of "scientific" (as we both claim), then the antirealist can reinterpret them too. And that was what I tried to do in my lecture titled "Realism and Reason" (Putnam 1977) and subsequently: accept scientific realism, *but reinterpret it to make it compatible with verificationist semantics*. I have always been a scientific realist, in spite of the misunderstanding, which is very widespread, that I renounced scientific realism – that's just wrong. And I've never accepted Nelson Goodman's idea that we "make" the world.

Moreover, I even repented, in my Dewey Lectures (Putnam 1999) of saying that "the mind and the world together make up the mind and the world" (Putnam 1981: xi). And I've written a lot about Pragmatism, and in every single paper I say that I don't think that the Pragmatist theories of truth – *any* of the Pragmatist theories of truth – Peirce's, James' or Dewey's – were right. (Fortunately, Dewey never really *depended* on the pragmatist theory of truth. He has one footnote in the *Logic*, saying that Peirce's theory is right, but what Dewey is concerned with is *warranted assertibility*, and that means that, fortunately, his belief that Peirce got the definition of truth right actually plays no real role in anything Dewey does. But in any case, one can learn from a philosopher without believing everything he says, or even believing everything he regards as tremendously important. John McDowell and I both believe we can learn a great deal from Kant, but that doesn't mean we don't reject certain ideas from the *First Critique* which Kant would have regarded as absolutely essential to his whole vision. It had better be the case that we can learn from dead philosophers, 'cause we're all gonna be dead!)

Now, with respect to Ethics Without Ontology: I did not mean to reject the idea of metaphysics with a small "m." Sometimes I describe what I do as metaphysics, but I know that very often, because of who my teachers were,[3] and perhaps because of the bad influence of a certain side of Wittgenstein, I do use the word "metaphysics" as a pejorative. But I am very well aware that I have metaphysical views. And the point of *Ethics Without Ontology was not* that one shouldn't have a metaphysical view – a *naturalist* metaphysical view – of the nature of ethical judgement and ethical practices. In fact, in *Ethics Without Ontology* I tried to present one, namely, I suggested that ethics rests on a certain set of human interests. I compared ethics to a table on many legs, and as you know, I said such a table wobbles a lot because the ground isn't even, but it is very hard to overturn. And I had something to say about what those interests are. Like Stanley Cavell (Putnam 2012a), I think that ethics isn't the only way, but it is far preferable to other ways of settling conflicts. It's not the only way of settling conflicts, Cavell says, but the other ways are often inaccessible or brutal. And I don't think that it should be a constraint on the semantics of ethical terms that anyone who repudiates ethics or rejects ethics is *irrational*. A lot of bad arguments for non-cognitivism assume that cognitivists think that something like that *is* a constraint on the semantics of ethical terms. They think that a cognitivist must make a certain traditional philosophical Platonist view come out right. But that isn't what I think.

But let me return to the subject of ontology, and to my dissatisfaction with Quine's criterion of ontological commitment, and the implicit assumption that goes with it, the assumption that "exist" is univocal.[4] I wish to draw a distinction here that is foreign to Quine's way of thinking: the distinction between saying that an expression has different *truth conditions* in two or more different circumstances, and saying it has "different meanings" in the sense that is connected with translation practice[5] (call it, "the usual linguistic sense"). In the latter sense, it is (roughly) true that "exist" has a constant meaning. I say that because, with Charles Travis, I think that a word may have the same meaning in different contexts even though the truth-evaluable content of what you say by using that word may vary with the context. ("There is a lot of coffee on the table" may be used to say either that there is coffee to drink, or that coffee has been spilled on the table; these uses go with different truth conditions, but it is not the case that the words have meanings other than those given in a good dictionary, and those meanings are the same in the two cases.) The truth-evaluable content of what we say using the word "exist" varies a great deal, and in some contexts it is perfectly right to say that mereological sums exist, and in other contexts it is right to say, there aren't really such things as mereological sums, that's "just one way of talking," and we can say what we want to say without it, for example by talking about sets. I'm sure Carnap would have said it's a matter of convention whether or not we say that there are such things as mereological sums, and my gut feeling is that that's got to be right. The view that somehow there is a deep problem as to whether mereological sums "really exist" seems absurd. I know that Gideon Rosen thinks that the problem is so hard that we'll never know whether there are really mereological sums or not. That seems to me crazy! And I would assume that Dick probably shares my intuition here. But it's this idea that there's just one correct way of using "exist" *and* that way determines a unique answer to the question, "are mereological sums included in the furniture of the universe or not?" – that I reject. That's the sort of "ontology" that I wrote an obituary for.[6]

My own vision is similar to Richard Boyd's in many respects, but there do remain a couple of deep issues about which we may disagree. I agree with Boyd that true empirical statements correspond to states of affairs that actually obtain. But I would not say that I have a "correspondence theory of truth." In *The Threefold Cord: Mind, Body, and World* I defended what I described as Fregean *disquotation* (not, please note, Fregean *deflation*). I believe that the disquotational property of "true" is an extremely important one, as Frege and Tarski both realized, whatever the differences between their theories, but neither thought that the disquotation property is all there is to say about truth, which is the characteristic thesis of what is called "deflation" (Horwich 1990). I think one problem with speaking of truth as defined in terms of a correspondence theory of truth is first that it's misleading. I believe that, in addition to the disquotation property, it is a property of the notion of truth that to call a statement of any kind – not only an empirical statement, but also a mathematical statement, a statement of logic (e.g., *such-and-such a schema is valid*), an ethical statement, etc., etc. – true is to say that it has the sort of correctness appropriate to the kind of statement it is. When we speak of "states of affairs"[7] what we normally think of are empirical states of affairs, ways the universe can be. And correspondence to such a state of affairs – one that actually obtains – is the standard of correctness for empirical statements. Here Boyd and I agree, I believe. When we confine attention to empirical statements, *both* correspondence and disquotation are features of truth. But even this statement is misleading.

It is misleading because said just like that it could be read as implying that there is one and the same kind of correspondence at stake no matter what the empirical statement is, and no matter what the occasion of its utterance may be. But that is not the case: "This piece of beef weighs one pound" may "correspond to reality" by the standard of correspondence appropriate to a butcher's shop, but be extremely wrong by the standard of laboratory science. And the kind and degree of correspondence changes again when the statement is "John is very neurotic," or ... The difficulty in giving a picture of our notion of truth (I doubt we can give anything that deserves the title of a "theory") is to do justice simultaneously both to the *unity* of the notion, and the *plurality* of the correctness-conditions that go with it and give it content.

Moreover, when it comes to mathematical statements and logical statements I am not sure I want to speak of their correctness conditions as "correspondence"; but I don't have time to unpack this remark here.[8] Suffice it to say, that if one must speak of correspondence, then let us recognize that *what sort of thing* (in what Sellars once called "the widest possible sense of thing") a statement has to correspond to in order to count as "true" varies from language game to language game. Nevertheless, the concept of truth does exhibit certain constant features; the disquotation schema describes one.

I would also like to say that "true" is a logical word like "and," "or," or "not." That is why it can apply to every kind of sentence, without being incompatible with the fact that different sorts of sentences have different sorts of truth-conditions. I can say a tautology is true without being forced to regard the tautology as "describing" something or "corresponding to a state of affairs," or inventing a "vacuous state of affairs" for tautologies to correspond to. Just as one can conjoin a descriptive sentence and an evaluation with an "and" or an "if – then," one can say that a descriptive sentence and an evaluation are both "true" without implying that they have the same sort of truth-conditions. And, by the way, my rejection of the fact/value *dichotomy* doesn't mean that there's no use for a *distinction* between descriptions and evaluations. A metaphysical dichotomy and a distinction are not the same thing. But if I say, for example, "If you'd practiced the piano an hour every day for the last year, you would have played better," I am putting an "if – then –" between an empirical statement and a judgment of aesthetic merit. And that's perfectly fine.

In closing, what I've said doesn't necessarily preclude correspondence-talk. But I fear that "correspond" tends to suggest that truth depends on a relation (moreover, one and the same relation) between whole statements and something (reality? parts of reality? what sort of parts?) no matter what sort of statement we are calling "true." So I would prefer to say that *descriptive* statements (note the restriction!) are connected to the world via the reference of the names and predicates that they contain, and *reference* is a relation to things (and sets of things, and sets of ordered pairs of things, etc.) in the world. This is a difficult metaphysical issue but I don't think it bears on whether one is a realist in Boyd's sense or not a realist in his sense.

Notes

1 I identified "internal realism" with the thesis that truth is "idealized rational acceptability" in Putnam (1981). I used the term "verificationist semantics" in Putnam (1983).
2 I explain why I am unrepentant in Putnam (2012).
3 Here I am thinking primarily of W. V. Quine and Hans Reichenbach.
4 There are deep tensions in Quine's thinking: for example between thinking of "exist" as univocal, and admitting that it admits of both "objectual" and "nonobjectual" interpretations. Moreover, even when Quine clearly thinks of "exist" as univocal, he equivocates (or, perhaps, he is torn) between thinking of the univocality of "exist" as something trivial (what better standard of univocality do we have, he asks in effect, than how something looks when properly "regimented"?) and thinking of it as involving a substantive claim, the claim that being committed to the existence of abstract entities (when quantification over them cannot be explained away as "nonobjectual") is doing something he calls "positing" intangible objects, objects whose existence has to be inferred from the contribution that positing their existence makes to the success of prediction, particularly in physics.
5 For more on these two senses, see my *Ethics Without Ontology* (Cambridge, MA: Harvard University Press, 2004).
6 Chapter 4 of *Ethics Without Ontology* is titled "'Ontology': An Obituary."
7 On the indispensability of such talk, see Prologue: "From Quantum Mechanics to Ethics and Back Again."
  For a useful discussion of the relevant science, including issues about whether or not some racial categories might be, as one might say, "natural kinds in medicine and pharmacology," see Social Science Research Council 2007. For much more sophisticated treatments look at the emerging literature in critical race studies; see, e.g., Crenshaw et al. 1996, Delgado 1995.
8 See chapter 3 of *Ethics Without Ontology* for an explanation of why I say this.

Bibliography

Horwich, Paul (1990) *Truth*, Oxford: Oxford University Press.
Putnam, H. (1977) "Realism and Reason," *Proceedings and Addresses of the American Philosophical Association* 50: 483–98. Reprinted in Meaning and the Moral Sciences (1983), 123–40.
——(1978) *Meaning and the Moral Sciences*, London: Routledge and Kegan Paul.
——(1981) *Reason, Truth, and History*, Cambridge: Cambridge University Press.
——(1983) "Computational Psychology and Interpretation Theory," in *Philosophical Papers*, vol. 3, *Realism and Reason*, Cambridge: Cambridge University Press, 139–54.

——(1999) "Sense, Nonsense, and the Senses: An Inquiry into the Powers of the Human Mind," *Journal of Philosophy* 91(9) in *The Threefold Cord: Mind, Body and World*, New York: Columbia University Press.
——(2004) *Ethics Without Ontology*, Cambridge, MA: Harvard University Press.
——(2012), "On Not Writing Off Scientific Realism," in *Philosophy in the Age of Science*, Cambridge, MA: Harvard University Press, 91–108.
——(2012a) "The Fact/Value Dichotomy and Its Critics," *Philosophy in the Age of Science*.

2

HILARY AND ME
Tracking down Putnam on the realism issue

Michael Devitt

Hilary Putnam's contribution to the Michael Dummett volume of the *Library of Living Philosophers*, "Between Scylla and Charybdis: Does Dummett Have a Way Out?" (2007), is on the realism issue. He concludes a brief defense of Dummett's anti-realism from my criticisms in *Realism and Truth* (1984/1991b) as follows: "Devitt's dismissive attitude is as unphilosophical as Samuel Johnson's stone-kicking" (2007: 159). Dummett responds with delight: "I very much enjoyed Hilary Putnam's criticism of Michael Devitt's attempted refutation of anti-realism, and thought it wholly to the point." Dummett concludes that my argument is "a severe case of *ignoratio elenchi*" (2007: 184).

My essay is a response to these harsh comments, against a background of my thirty-year struggle with Putnam's views on the realism issue.[1]

1. Introduction

The preface of the first edition of *Realism and Truth* begins: "I have always been a realist about the external world." But I immediately go on to list four major influences on "the present shape of my realism." The first of these "was Hilary Putnam in lectures at Harvard in the late sixties." I credit him, along with the writings of Quine, for "my view of philosophy and of the place of epistemology in it" (Devitt 1984: vii). Putnam features again, but in a less favorable light, in my account of what prompted me to write the book. For, the third and final prompt was Putnam's *Meaning and the Moral Sciences* (1978). The prompt was, on the one hand, "the shock of discovering that Putnam had joined the opposition" and, on the other hand,

> the baffling nature of the book. What, according to Putnam, was realism? What had it to do with truth? What had it to do with convergence? What had reference to do with truth? I found no clear answers in the book.
>
> (Devitt 1984: viii)

But struggling with them led me, I like to think, to a much clearer picture of the realism issue.

Putnam looms large in the preface to the second edition too. First, in noting the extent and chaos of the realism debate in recent years, I remark: "Hilary Putnam ingeniously derives anti-realism from just about everything" (Devitt 1991b: vii). Second, my own approach to the realism issue arises from the naturalism and physicalism I took from Quine and the early Putnam. This approach seems to be what Putnam is rejecting in saying that "scientism is ... one of the most dangerous contemporary intellectual tendencies" (Putnam 1983: 211). I do not take this criticism lying down: "I have a candidate for *the* most dangerous contemporary intellectual tendency. Sadly, it is a doctrine that Putnam himself embraces: 'constructivism'" (Devitt 1991b: viii). Finally, it is noteworthy that Putnam is the philosopher with the largest entry in the book's index. Clearly, I have been bothered by his views on the realism issue!

Why am I bothered? First, I have a very big problem with his view of the nature of realism, and in particular, with his conflation of metaphysical and semantic issues. In section 2, I shall set out my own view of what realism is. In section 3, I shall criticize Putnam's view. It is a consequence of my criticisms that Putnam's critique of "metaphysical realism," particularly the famous model-theoretic argument, are largely beside the metaphysical point.

If a metaphysical issue of realism is, as I argue, sharply distinct from any semantic one, including one about truth, which issue should have priority? My second problem is that Putnam gives priority to the semantic. This is related to his mistaken attribution to realists of the (delightfully named) "God's Eye View"; in section 4, I shall argue that we should "put metaphysics first."

Putnam's critique of realism leads him to a version of the sadly popular "constructivism": we make the known world with our conceptual schemes. I take a very dim view of this doctrine in section 5.

Finally, in section 6, I turn to the harsh responses of Putnam and Dummett to my criticisms of Dummett.

My discussion in sections 3–5 draws heavily on earlier works, particularly on *Realism and Truth* (1984/1991b) and "Aberrations of the Realism Debate" (1991a). (It should be noted that this discussion addresses only the views of Putnam's "interim period" of 1976 to 1989. I appreciate that some of his views have changed since then.)

2. The nature of realism

A striking aspect of the realism debate is that it contains almost as many doctrines under the name "realism" as it contains participants.[2] However, some common features can be discerned in this chaos. First, nearly all the doctrines are, or seem to be, partly semantic. Consider, for example, Jarrett

Leplin's editorial introduction to a collection of papers on scientific realism. He lists ten "characteristic realist claims" (1984b: 1-2). Nearly all of these are about the truth and reference of theories. Not one is straightforwardly metaphysical.³ However, second, amongst all the semantic talk, it is usually possible to discern a metaphysical doctrine, a doctrine about what there is and what it's like. Thus "realism" is now usually taken to refer to some combination of a metaphysical doctrine with a doctrine about truth, particularly with a correspondence doctrine. The doctrine that Putnam famously named "metaphysical realism" is a paradigm: "there has to *be* a determinate relation of *reference* between terms in L and pieces (or sets of pieces) of THE WORLD ... THE WORLD is ... *independent* of any particular representation we have of it ... *truth* is ... *radically non-epistemic*" (Putnam 1978: 125).⁴

The metaphysical doctrine, which is what I call *"Realism"* has two dimensions, an existence dimension and an independence dimension (Devitt 1984/1991b: ch. 2; 1997a: 302–4). The existence dimension commits the realist to the existence of such commonsense entities as stones, trees and cats, and such scientific entities as atoms, viruses and photons. Typically, idealists, the traditional opponents of realists, have not denied this dimension or, at least, have not straightforwardly denied it. What they have denied is the independence dimension. According to some idealists, the entities identified by the first dimension are made up of mental items: "ideas" or "sense data" and so are not external to the mind. In recent times another sort of idealist has been much more common. According to these idealists, the entities are not in a certain respect "objective": they depend for their existence and nature on the cognitive activities and capacities of our minds. Realists reject all such mind dependencies. Relations between minds and those entities are limited to familiar causal interactions long noted by folk theory: we throw stones, plant trees, see cats, and so on.

Though the focus of the debate has mostly been on the independence dimension, the existence dimension is important. First, it identifies the entities that are the subject of the dispute over independence. In particular, it distinguishes a realism worth fighting for from what I call "Fig-Leaf Realism": a commitment merely to there being *something* independent of us (Devitt 1984: 22; 1991b: 23). Second, in the discussion of unobservables – the debate about *scientific* realism – the main controversy has been over existence.

I capture the two dimensions in the following doctrine:

Realism: Tokens of most commonsense, and scientific, physical types objectively exist independently of the mental.

This doctrine covers both the observable and the unobservable worlds. Some philosophers, like van Fraassen, have adopted a different attitude to these two worlds. So, for the purpose of argument, we can split the doctrine in two: *Commonsense Realism* concerned with observables, and *Scientific Realism* concerned with unobservables.

In insisting on the objectivity of the world, realists are not saying that it is unknowable. They are saying that it is not *constituted by* our knowledge, by our epistemic values, by our capacity to refer to it, by the synthesizing power of the mind, nor by our imposition of concepts, theories, or languages; it is not limited by what we can believe or discover.[5] Many worlds lack this sort of objectivity and independence: Kant's "phenomenal" world; Dummett's verifiable world; the stars made by a Goodman "version"; the constructed world of Putnam's "internal realism"; Kuhn's world of theoretical ontologies;[6] the many worlds created by the "discourses" of structuralists and postmodernists.

Realism takes both the ontology of science and common sense, and the folk epistemological view that this ontology is objective and independent, pretty much for granted. Science and common sense are not, for the most part, to be "reinterpreted."[7] It is not just that our experiences are *as if* there are cats, there are cats. It is not just that the observable world is *as if* there are atoms, there are atoms. As Putnam once put it, *Realism* takes science at "face value" (1978: 37).

Realism is the minimal realist doctrine worth fighting for. Once it is established, the battle against anti-realism is won; all that remains are skirmishes. Furthermore, *Realism* provides the place to stand to solve the many other difficult problems that have become entangled with it.

Any semantic doctrine needs to be disentangled from *Realism* (1984/1991b: ch. 4; 1997a: 304–7). In particular, the correspondence theory of truth needs to be disentangled: it is in no way constitutive of *Realism* nor of any similarly metaphysical doctrine.

On the one hand, *Realism* does not entail any theory of truth or meaning at all, as is obvious from our definition. So it does not entail the correspondence theory. On the other hand, the correspondence theory does not entail *Realism*. The correspondence theory claims that a sentence (or thought) is true in virtue of its structure, its relations to reality, usually reference relations, and the nature of reality. *This is compatible with absolutely any metaphysics.* The theory is often taken to require the objective mind-independent existence of the reality which makes sentences true or false; for example, Putnam's metaphysical realism. This addition of *Realism*'s independence dimension does, of course, bring us closer to *Realism*. However, the addition seems like a gratuitous intrusion of metaphysics into semantics. And even with the addition, the correspondence theory is still distant from *Realism*, because it is silent on the existence dimension. It tells us what it is for a sentence to be true or false, but it does not tell us which ones *are* true and so *could* not tell us which particular entities exist.

Not only is *Realism* independent of any *doctrine* of truth, we do not even need to use "true" and its cognates to *state Realism*, as our definition shows.

This is not to say that there is anything "wrong" with using "true" for this purpose. Any predicate worthy of the name "truth" has a "disquotational" property captured by the "equivalence thesis." The thesis is that appropriate instances of

s is true if and only if p

hold, where an appropriate instance is obtained by substituting for "p" a sentence which is the same as (or a translation of) the sentence referred to by the term substituted for "s".[8] Because of this disquotational property, we can use "true" to talk about *anything* by referring to sentences. Thus we can talk about the whiteness of snow by saying "'Snow is white' is true." And we can redefine the metaphysical doctrine *Realism* as follows:

> Most common-sense, and scientific, physical existence statements are objectively and mind-independently true.

This redefinition does not make *Realism* semantic (else every doctrine could be made semantic); it does not change the subject matter at all. It does not involve commitment to the correspondence *theory* of truth, nor to any other theory. Indeed, it is compatible with a *deflationary* view of truth according to which, roughly, truth isn't anything.[9] This inessential redefinition *exhausts* the involvement of truth in constituting *Realism*.[10]

Realism is about the nature of reality in general; it is about the largely inanimate impersonal world. If correspondence truth has a place, it is in our theory of only a small part of that reality: it is in our theory of people and their language.[11]

Objection 1. "You are simply insisting that the *word* 'realism' be used metaphysically not semantically. That is a merely verbal point."

My main point is not verbal at all. I am insisting on a distinction between two doctrines, whatever they are called. I am insisting on carving theory at reality's joints.

On the verbal point, I claim that metaphysical doctrines like mine capture the only thing that is *distinctive* about views that have been called "realist" about the external world throughout the long debate. I have already indicated that correspondence truth is not distinctive. It would be rather perverse to use "realism" to refer to a doctrine that had no metaphysical intent.[12]

Objection 2. "Your realist doctrine is not what all the argument is about."

All the argument is not about this doctrine, but part of it certainly is. It is precisely because the doctrine is so often denied in philosophy that it is worth asserting. For examples of its denial one need only look to the history of idealism. And it is still being denied; see above. Either familiar ontic commitments are, explicitly or implicitly, paraphrased away, or, more frequently, the world is made strangely mind-dependent. It is because of these somewhat scandalous facts that the realist goes in for the "desk-thumping, foot-stamping shout of 'Really!'" that Arthur Fine likes to mock (Fine 1986a: 129).

The realism dispute arises from the age-old metaphysical question, "What ultimately is there, and what is it like?" I am sympathetic to the complaint that *Realism*, as part of an answer to this question, is rather boring. Certainly it brings no mystical glow. Nevertheless, it needs to be kept firmly at the front of the mind to avoid mistakes in theorizing about other, more interesting, epistemological and semantic matters where it makes a difference.

3. Putnam on the nature of realism

Why has metaphysics been conflated with semantics? I have made a few suggestions before (1991b: 48–50), one of which is particularly pertinent to my disagreement with Putnam. For Putnam is one of the most influential conflaters.

Though doctrines of truth are not in any way essential to *Realism*, they have traditionally played a very significant role in *the way the issue has been argued* and the degree to which it seems interesting and controversial. But, of course, arguments are one thing, their conclusions another.

The typical argument against realism has been along the following lines:

(1) If the realist's independent reality exists, then our thoughts/theories must mirror, picture, or represent, that reality.
(2) Our thoughts/theories cannot mirror, picture, or represent the realist's independent reality.
(3) So, the realist's independent reality does not exist.

The center of the debate about this argument has been on (2); that is to say, the center has been about the correspondence of our ideas or language to independent reality. Traditionally, the problem has come up in epistemology: "How could we know about such a reality?" More recently, the problem has come up in the theory of reference or intentionality: "How could our language or thought refer to such a reality?"

These questions have seemed metaphysically important only because (1) has been assumed, mostly without argument. Indeed (1) has seemed so irresistible that to deny a correspondence theory has often been seen as tantamount to denying realism. Consider, for example, this statement by Putnam:

> whatever authority [ontology and epistemology] had depended entirely on our conceiving of reality and sensations as, respectively,

the makers-true and the makers-justified of the sentences we produce – not the makers-true and the makers-justified from within the story, but the things outside the story that hook language onto something outside itself.

(Putnam 1985: 78; see also 1987: 15–16)[13]

Irresistible or not, (1) is false: "to question whether our theories aim at 'picturing' the world" is not "to question whether electrons 'really' exist" (Leeds 1978: 119). *Realism* may make the rejection of correspondence truth implausible, but it does not make it paradoxical or incoherent.

It follows from this discussion that a metaphysical doctrine like *Realism* cannot be attacked *simply* by arguing against certain semantic theories of truth or reference; for example, against correspondence truth. As a result, much contemporary anti-realist argument is largely beside the *Realist* point. Putnam's famous model-theoretic argument is an example (Putnam 1978: 125-7; 1983: 1-25).[14]

Putnam's argument is against "metaphysical realism" and in favor of "internal realism." Putnam starts by arguing that there cannot be determinate reference relations to a mind-independent reality. As a result, there is no way in which the "ideal" theory – one meeting all operational and theoretical constraints – could be false. So metaphysical realism is "incoherent." The argument has generated a storm of responses.[15]

Now whatever the rights and wrongs of this debate, the issue has no direct bearing on *Realism*.[16] It has to do with reference, with the theory of representation. Metaphysical realism, as noted, is a hybrid of something like *Realism* with something like correspondence truth. The only part of this hybrid that *may* be directly affected by Putnam's argument about reference is correspondence truth. Indeed, the challenge of Putnam's argument can be posed, and often seems to be posed, in a way that presupposes *Realism*: a representation is related by one causal relation to certain mind-independent entities and by another causal relation to other such entities. Which relation determines reference?

Putnam's critique of metaphysical realism proceeds by surrounding the metaphysical core of the doctrine, *Realism*, with a variety of other doctrines, none of which are essential to the core, and attacking those. The model-theoretic argument against correspondence truth is one example. Here are two others.

First, Putnam commits the metaphysical realist to the doctrine that "there is exactly one true and complete description of 'the way the world is'" (Putnam 1981: 49). One wonders what it is to be a "true and complete" description of the world. Whatever it is, there is no reason why a *Realist* has to be committed to there being just one.

Putnam alleges that the doctrine that there *is* just one, together with correspondence truth, requires "a *ready made* world ... : the world itself has to have a 'built-in' structure" (Putnam 1983: 211). Now, whatever we think of this doctrine, it follows from my argument that the *Realist* does not have to go down *this* route to it. Still, what attitude should the *Realist* take to the doctrine anyway?

The *Realist* commits himself to independent objects of kinds like *cat* and *atom*, picked out by words in common sense and science because these objects are the ones he can be precise about. He should allow that there are objects of indefinitely many other kinds, equally independent, that for one reason or another we have not picked out by words. In this respect, *Realism* is "modest" as Curtis Brown nicely puts it:

> when we develop a language we are not imposing an organization on the world, but selecting one of the world's organizations for our own use. On this view the world 'in itself' has *more* objects than we usually talk about, not fewer.
>
> (Brown 1988: 148)

The *Realist* agrees with Putnam's metaphysical realist that there is "a *ready made* world," but this is not a commitment to the world having *just one* "built-in structure."

Consider one of the kinds that we have so far overlooked: the kind of object that strains the credulity of tourists from Peoria. Let us introduce a name for this kind of object: "peorincred." Now, as a matter of fact, echidnas are peorincreds. But our linguistic decision did not make them so: they always were peorincreds and would have been even if we had never introduced the word "peorincred" nor any other word. Peorincreds are part of the independent ready-made world. Indeed, select any set of physical objects at random and name the kind consisting of those objects, "blah." Even blahs are part of the independent ready-made world.

To think clearly about realism issues it is vital to distinguish sharply two sorts of freedom, a freedom we have and a freedom we don't have. The freedom we *do* have is to choose to name any kind we like, whether for explanatory reasons, for frivolous reasons, or for no reason at all; naming kinds is a subjective matter. The freedom we *do not* have is to choose whether something is a member of a kind, whatever our reason for naming that kind in the first place; kind membership is an objective matter. We have chosen to name cats for very good explanatory reasons and peorincreds for no good reason at all. But peorincreds exist as objectively and mind-independently as cats. My naming them "peorincreds" didn't make them peorincreds any more than people naming cats "cats" made them cats. It is common to talk as if, in doing science, we impose our concepts to "carve up reality." But this is not literally so: we choose our concepts in an attempt to discover the causally significant features of a nature that is already "carved up." The importance of distinguishing theory making from world making could hardly be exaggerated.[17]

The *Realist* may be thought to deny the freedom we do have by holding that there is something special about the kinds *Realism* is committed to. The *Realist* need not hold this. Clearly, our choices about which kinds to name are guided by our interests: explanatory interests, practical interests, perhaps playful interests. A kind picked out by an explanatory interest may qualify as a "natural" one. I think that the kinds of objects that *Realism* is committed to *are* mostly natural ones and hence in that respect special. However, this opinion is not important because *Realism* does not involve any claim to that effect. *Realism* does not claim any special status for its kinds, except their independence. Whether there are any natural kinds, and if so, which they are, is another matter.[18]

Second, Putnam commits the metaphysical realist to a form of essentialism (1983: 205–28). The realist's belief in independent objects of various kinds is alleged to require that those objects be essentially members of those kinds. Putnam's criticism of this essentialism is "bluff and parody" as Nicholas Wolterstorff points out (1987: 251). More importantly, it is irrelevant to *Realism*. The *Realist* need not accept this sort of individual essentialism and, even if he does accept it, he will surely want to be committed to the independent existence of objects of kinds that are *accidental* to the objects (p. 252).

Even if Putnam's criticisms of these surrounding doctrines were correct, they would leave the *Realist* core largely untouched.

4. Putting metaphysics first

I have been emphasizing that the metaphysical issue of *Realism* is distinct from semantic ones. Similarly, it is distinct from epistemic ones. So, the question arises: Which issue should we start with? Traditionally, philosophers started with an epistemic issue and argued for anti-realism on the ground that the realist's world would be unknowable. Recently, philosophers have tended to start with a semantic issue and to argue for anti-realism from verificationism. (I gave the general form of such arguments in section 3.) But suppose that we start with the metaphysical issue. I have argued that we can then establish *Realism* (Devitt 1984/1991b: ch. 5; 2002; 2005c) and proceed by abduction to non-verificationism: the best explanation of language in a *Realist* world is one involving correspondence truth (1996a; 1997a: 320–30). Which starting place is better? We should start with *Realism*. We should, as I now like to say, "put metaphysics first" (1999, 2001a, 2002).

Consider the priority of *Realism* over semantics, for example. The argument for *Realism*, independent of semantics, is very strong. The argument for verificationism, independent of metaphysics, is very weak. Indeed, that argument seems to rest entirely on a priori reflections about linguistic competence. Why should we believe these claims about what meanings we could grasp and what concepts we could have, particularly since they threaten something as plausible as *Realism*? What is the *basis* of these claims?

Whence cometh this knowledge (Devitt 1984: 204–20; 1991b: 268–86)? (This bears on the discussion of Dummett in section 6.)

My view of where to start reflects my naturalism. I take the theory of language to be an empirical, conjectural, theory like all others. So there is no question of giving semantics an unearned privileged position in deciding what there is and what it is like. Perhaps naturalism is *needed* to justify my view of where to start. If so, so be it.[19]

Putnam has a different view of the priorities: we should start building a metaphysics from semantics. This mistake seems to be related to a certain caricature of realism. Realism requires "a transcendental match between our representation and the world in itself" (Putnam 1981: 134). It requires a "God's Eye View" (ibid.: 74; see also pp. 49, 73), "direct access to a ready made world" (ibid.: 146), the capacity to "say *how* THE WORLD is theory-independently" (Putnam 1978: 133; see also 1981: 49). Similar remarks are made about the realist's view of reference. "To pick out just *one* correspondence between words or mental signs and mind-independent things we would have already to have referential access to the mind-independent things" (Putnam 1981: 73; see also pp. 46–47, 51, 66, 211). There is "a puzzle how we could *learn to express*" what the realist wants to say (ibid.: 46).

Putnam's view is that realism requires our knowing the unknowable and speaking the unspeakable. Much the same view of realism can be found in many other places. Thus, according to Richard Rorty, the realist believes that we can "step out of our skins" (1982: xix; see also 1979: 293) to judge, without dependence on any concepts, whether theories are true of reality. Fine has a similar view (1986a: 131-2; 1986b: 151–52). But, of course, no sane person believes any of this. What realists believe is that we can judge whether theories are true of reality, *the nature of which* does not depend on any theories or concepts.

What lies behind these bizarre, and always undocumented, anti-realist fantasies?[20] I think that the answer is clear: the Cartesian picture.

According to this picture we start the quest for knowledge locked in our minds, contemplating our ideas, and asking the following questions: Is there a world out there causing this inner show? Does it resemble the show? How can our ideas reach out to this world? But the naturalist does not start from scratch with epistemic and semantic questions. Those questions arise when we already have wide-ranging, well-based opinions about the world, opinions derived from common sense and science. The questions arise when we focus on a small part of the world: people. We go on to seek empirical answers to those questions; we seek a naturalistic epistemology and semantics. The theories that result have no special status. Indeed, given our lack of confidence in these areas, the theories should have rather a lowly status. To suppose that we can derive the right metaphysics from epistemology or semantics is to put the cart before the horse.

From the naturalistic perspective, the relations between our minds and reality are not, in principle, any more inaccessible than any other relations. Without jumping out of our skins we can have well-based theories about the relations between, say, Barack and Hillary. Similarly, we can have such theories about our epistemic and semantic relations to Barack and Hillary.

5. Putnam's constructivism

Putnam's solution to the problem posed by his model-theoretic argument is a form of constructivism. He gives up the idea that reference is to a mind-independent world[21] and adopts "internal realism." Just as Kant closed the epistemic gap by bringing the world into the mind in some sense, so likewise, Putnam closes the referential gap. In what sense? Putnam offers "the metaphor" that "the mind and world jointly make up the mind and the world" (1981: xi). How is the metaphor to be cashed? "'Objects' do not exist independently of conceptual schemes. *We* cut up the world into objects when we introduce one or another scheme of description" (p. 52). This construction of objects is not from conceptually uncontaminated experiential inputs, for those inputs are "themselves to some extent shaped by our concepts."

Is there anything that is uncontaminated? Presumably there must be, to account for the constraints other than coherence on construction: that is, to account for the extent that inputs are *not* shaped by our concepts. Putnam does talk in a Kantian way, of the noumenal world and of things-in-themselves as constraints, thus implying that he is what I call a Fig-Leaf Realist (Devitt 1991b: 23). However, he seems ultimately to regard this talk as "nonsense" even if perhaps psychologically irresistible (Putnam 1981: 61–62, 83). I think the talk probably is nonsense (Devitt 1991b: 237–38). But if it is, there is nothing that Putnam can say about the constraints (except coherence). This avoids the "facile relativism" of "anything goes" (Putnam 1981: 54) by fiat: we simply are constrained, and that's that. Even if the talk is not nonsense, it lacks any explanatory power. To say that our construction is constrained by something beyond reach of knowledge or reference is whistling in the dark. We might as well settle for dogmatic anti-relativism.

Worse still, if that is possible, is the idea that Putnam shares with the most relativistic constructivist: we make the known world of stones, trees, cats, and the like with our concepts. How could dinosaurs and stars be dependent in any way on the activities of our minds? It would be crazy to claim that there were no dinosaurs or stars before there were people to think about them. Constructivists do not seem to claim this. But it is hardly any less crazy to claim that there *would not have been* dinosaurs or stars if there *had not been* people (or similar thinkers).[22] And this claim seems essential to Constructivism: unless it were so, dinosaurs and stars could not be dependent on us and our minds.

111

If it proves very difficult to naturalize reference, then perhaps we should seek a non-referential theory of mind and language. If we were *completely* desperate, perhaps we *might* contemplate giving up naturalism. What we should *never* countenance for a moment is constructivism. To accept that idea is not to rebuild the boat whilst staying afloat, it is to jump overboard.[23]

6. Putnam's and Dummett's responses

As noted at the beginning of this essay, according to Putnam my criticisms of Dummett are "as unphilosophical as Samuel Johnson's stone-kicking" (Putnam 2007: 159). Dummett is delighted, and adds insult to this injury by describing my argument as "a severe case of *ignoratio elenchi*" (Dummett 2007: 184). Both these responses to my argument are careless (to put it delicately).

Putnam starts by attributing to me the following view: "the realism issue is simply, 'Is there a mind-independent reality or not?' (*thump*) and *that* question has nothing to do with semantics" (Putnam 2007: 158). This is not precisely my view – see the definition of *Realism* in section 2 – but it captures the spirit of it well enough. After a short digression on Lenin, however, Putnam takes my realism to be a commitment to the view that "the behavior of the stars is independent of human sensation and thoughts and beliefs." I am alleged to portray anti-realists as denying this. What I actually, and quite plainly, portray anti-realists as denying is that *the existence and nature* of the stars are in various ways independent of our minds. But this misrepresentation pales into insignificance beside the following:

> Devitt's argument ... simply assumes – what anti-realists of course deny – that the anti-realist cannot *interpret* the sentence 'the behavior of the stars is independent of human sensation and thoughts and beliefs' in a 'justificationist' way, interpret it so that it is 'true' (in the anti-realist sense).
>
> (ibid. 158)

This claim is the full extent of Putnam's argument against my critique of Dummett. (There is an implicit "*thump*."). This is his sole basis for the stone-kicking charge.

So, according to Putnam, I make that mistaken assumption about interpretation and thus conclude that the Dummettian anti-realist cannot accept (something like) my *Realism*. Hence, presumably, Putnam thinks that I take my *Realism* to refute that anti-realist. This is preposterous! Putnam simply ignores the significance of the most prominent distinction in my discussion of realism, the distinction between *metaphysical* doctrines like my *Realism* and any *semantic* doctrine at all.[24] The distinction is, of course, crucial to my discussion of Dummett because Dummett *identifies* realism with a semantic doctrine: he identifies it with a commitment to sentences having "evidence-transcendent" truth conditions.[25] I have argued at great length against this identification; see section 2 and the items it cites. So, in my view, we have two distinct issues: the metaphysical issue over doctrines like my *Realism* and the semantic issue over doctrines like Dummett's anti-realism. It is then, of course, appropriate to probe the relations between these two issues. *Realism and Truth* does this extensively in discussions that Putnam seems to have missed.[26]

First, I do not "simply assume" but rather *argue* that an epistemic doctrine of truth like Dummett's, is *likely*, though not certain, to lead by abduction to the rejection of *Realism* (Devitt 1984: 39–40; 1991b: 44–46). It is very difficult for a *Realist* to find a plausible epistemology to accompany an epistemic doctrine of truth. But my most important point is that this way of proceeding – from semantics to metaphysics – is precisely the wrong way. Semantics is among the weakest places to start from. We should put metaphysics first; see section 4 above and the items it cites.

When we do put metaphysics first, we can present a powerful argument for *Realism* that makes no appeal to semantics (Devitt 1984/1991b: ch. 5; 2002; 2005c). Then we see what follows about semantics. I have labored mightily to come up with a good abduction from *Realism* to the semantic realism of a correspondence theory of truth. The first edition of *Realism and Truth* proposed one (Devitt 1984: 73–103; 110–12). I had scarcely sent that off when I had second thoughts. In time these led to the very different abduction in the second edition (Devitt 1991b: 83–107; 121–23). My confidence in this did not last long either and I proposed another abduction in the "Afterword" (Devitt 1997a: 320–30 based on Devitt 1996a). I still stand by that one. If it is right, then any epistemic doctrine of truth, including Dummett's semantic anti-realism, is wrong. So Dummett cannot "interpret" my statement of *Realism*, indeed any statement of anything, "in a 'justificationist' way."

In sum, I argued against Dummett's identification of the metaphysical issue of realism with a semantic issue. With the issues distinct, I argued that we should proceed from the metaphysics to the semantics. I presented a case for *Realism* and, from that basis, have given three different arguments for correspondence truth and against Dummettian semantic anti-realism. All in all, my critique of Dummett is about as far from dismissal by stone-kicking as one could get.

Putnam and Dummett wonder what I mean by "independent" and see a choice between *logical* and *causal* independence. I am quite explicit about what I mean and it is neither of these. I mean *constitutive* independence: thus, as I say above (section 2), the known world

> is not *constituted by* our knowledge, by our epistemic values, by our capacity to refer to it, by the synthesizing power of the mind, nor

by our imposition of concepts, theories, or languages; it is not limited by what we can believe or discover.

In contrast, Dummett decides, without apparently bothering to check, that I must mean causal independence. He responds: "Of course the behavior of the stars is causally independent of human sensations, desires and beliefs" (Dummett 2007: 184). So, he thinks, his anti-realism is untouched by my argument for *Realism*. The problem with this is that, with Putnam's help, he has simply invented the argument he attributes to me and ignored my actual one. So his response is "a severe case of *ignoratio elenchi*" if ever there was one. Versions of my actual argument have been available in several places for twenty-five years (Devitt 1983; 1984: ch. 12; 1991b: ch. 14). It would be interesting to know his response to those.

7. Conclusion

There is a metaphysical doctrine of realism about the external physical world. I have named that doctrine "*Realism.*" It has two dimensions, an existence dimension specifying the sorts of entities it is committed to, and an independence dimension claiming that those entities are, in almost all respects, independent of our minds. No doctrine of truth is part of this doctrine. Putnam's "metaphysical realism" entangles this metaphysical doctrine with a doctrine of correspondence truth. Even if his famous model-theoretic argument against metaphysical realism was good, it would strike at correspondence truth. It is largely beside the point of a metaphysical doctrine like *Realism*.

Given that the metaphysical issue of realism is sharply distinct from any semantic one, including one about truth, which issue should have priority? I have argued that we should put the metaphysical one first because we know much more about the metaphysics than we do about the semantics. Putnam has a different view, which is related to his attribution of the "God's Eye View" to realists. That attribution reflects the grip of the Cartesian picture. From a naturalistic perspective, that picture must be rejected.

Putnam's critique of realism leads him to a version of constructivism. This doctrine is *very* bad news. On the one hand, it leaves us with no possibility of explaining the constraints on our theorizing. On the other hand, the idea that we make the known world with our conceptual schemes is about as implausible as it gets.

Finally, I turned to the harsh responses of Putnam and Dummett to my criticisms of Dummett. Putnam accuses me of "stone-kicking" without apparently attending to any of my arguments. In particular, he ignores my argument that, contrary to what he suggests, it is very difficult to combine an epistemic notion of truth, hence Dummettian semantic anti-realism, with *Realism*. And he ignores my abduction from *Realism* to correspondence truth.

It is nicely ironic that Dummett should describe my argument as "a severe case of *ignoratio elenchi*." His own argument is a paradigm of that failing.

Notes

1 Maria Baghramian encouraged me to submit the essay for this volume but I do wonder whether she was right to do so. For, the volume arises out of the Dublin conference celebrating Hilary Putnam's 80th birthday and yet this essay is highly critical of Putnam's views. The paper I actually gave at the conference, "Resurrecting Biological Essentialism" (2008), was suitable for that celebratory event because it defended Putnam's position on biological essentialism (1975) from the consensus in the philosophy of biology. This consensus has led to some severe criticisms of Putnam. Michael Ruse, for example, places Putnam, along with Saul Kripke and David Wiggins, "somewhere to the right of Aristotle" on essentialism and talks of them showing "an almost proud ignorance of the organic world" (1987: 358n). John Dupré argues that the views of Putnam and Kripke are fatally divergent from "some actual biological facts and theories" (1981: 66). I argue that the consensus is quite wrong about essentialism and hence that these criticisms are misplaced. However, I could not contribute this paper to the present volume because the paper was to be published elsewhere. And I had nothing else suitable on that topic. Still, I very much wanted to contribute to a volume honoring my esteemed old teacher and friend. So I was persuaded by Maria to make the present critical contribution.
2 Susan Haack (1987) distinguishes *nine* "senses" of "realism"!
3 Some other examples: Hesse (1967: 407); Hooker (1974: 409); Papineau (1979: 126); Ellis (1979: 28); Boyd (1984: 41–2); R. Miller (1987); Fales (1988: 253–4); Jennings (1989: 240); Matheson (1989); Kitcher (1993); J. R. Brown (1994).
4 See also the account of realism by Arthur Fine (1986a: 115–16, 136–7).
5 For lots more on the independence dimension, including the independence of tools and social entities, see my (1991b: 246–58, 266).
6 For fairly accessible accounts of these worlds see, respectively: Kant (1783); Dummett (1978: preface and chs. 10 and 14); Goodman (1978); Putnam (1981); Kuhn (1962).
7 For the reasons for the qualification, see my 1991b: 18–19, 131–32. Brian Ellis demonstrates nicely some further reasons for qualification (1985: 52–8).
8 More needs to be said to allow for the paradoxes, ambiguity, indexicals, and truth-value gaps.
9 It is tempting to say that, according to deflationism, the equivalence thesis captures all there is to truth (Horwich 1990: 12; Devitt 1991c: 30; Richard 1997: 57). I have argued that this is a mistake (Devitt 2001b). According to deflationism properly conceived, the equivalence thesis explains the meaning of the truth term but *not* the nature of truth. Indeed, truth has no nature to explain. "Tarski's theory of truth" is not a theory of truth; it is a theory of some truth terms.
10 Some will object that we cannot assess *Realism* until we have *interpreted* it and this requires a semantic theory that talks of truth (S. Blackburn 1980: 354); (Fine 1986a: 138–9, 152; 1986b: 175–6). I have argued against this line of thought at length elsewhere (Devitt 1984: 40–46; 1991b: 50–59; 1996b; 1997a: 304–20).
11 My view that realism does not involve correspondence truth flies so much in the face of entrenched opinion that I went on to labor the point (1991b: 46–48).
12 For more on the verbal point, see my 1988: 160–1; 1991b: 40.
13 A similar view may lie behind Kim 1980: 596–97. See also Wright 1986: 1–2.
14 Three other examples are Laudan 1981, discussed in my 1991b, ch. 9 and 2005c; Rorty 1979, discussed in ch. 11; Dummett 1978, discussed in ch. 14.

15 Lewis (1984) is a particularly helpful one. My own response criticized Putnam's dismissal of the causal-theory solution: the point of the solution is not that the causal theory's use of "cause" determines reference but that causation itself does (1983; 1984: 188–91; 1991b: 225–29). Putnam was not impressed (1983: xi–xii, 295-6). I have responded (Devitt 1997a: 330–38; 1997b).

16 Cf., for example, three responses to Putnam: Heller 1988; Fales 1988; LePore and Loewer 1988. See also T. Blackburn 1988: 179.

17 It is easy even for staunch realists to slip into loose ways of talking that suggest world making. Thus Hilary Kornblith says that when we "group objects together under a single heading on the basis of a number of easily observable characteristics … we thereby create a nominal kind" (1993: 41). But we don't! We create a *concept* that picks out a kind that may or may not be "real" in Locke's terms but which has its members independently of our creation. And Richard Boyd, talking of kinds with nominal essences, says that their "boundaries" are "purely matters of convention" (1999: 142). But they aren't! Our naming a kind picked out by a certain set of descriptions is conventional but the boundary of the kind thus picked out is not. I think that Locke's distinction between nominal and real essences can lead to confusion here (Devitt 2008: 346, n. 4).

18 I am writing in an ontologically robust way about kinds. Nominalists might well object. I sympathize, for I have nominalist leanings. However, the talk is just a very convenient manner of speaking. The *Realist* insists that whether or not something is a cat or a peorincred is not a matter of our linguistic doing. Whether or not there are kinds *cat* and *peorincred* is another matter.

19 I have defended my naturalism elsewhere (Devitt 1998, 2005a, 2005b, 2011).

20 Bill Lycan has nicely mocked the fantasies with his name "Turtle Realism": antirealists should go all the way and accuse realists of believing that the earth sits on the back of a giant turtle (1988: 191). Australian realists believe that the turtle sits on the back of a giant crocodile: "Crocodile Realism."

21 It is not clear how this helps, as Curtis Brown points out (1988: 152).

22 Constructivism is so bizarre and mysterious that one is tempted to seek a charitable reinterpretation of constructivist talk. But, sadly, charity is out of place here (Devitt 1991b: 239–41).

23 For some helpful criticisms of the idea and what leads to it, see Aune 1987; Wolterstorff 1987; C. Brown 1988; McMichael 1988; and, most enjoyable, "Philosophy and Lunacy: Nelson Goodman and the Omnipotence of Words" in Stove 1991.

24 Putnam's Lenin scholarship is faulty too. He rightly supposes (2007: 166 n. 12) that the title of my early criticism, "Realism and the Renegade Putnam" (1983), was a play on the title of a famous article by Lenin. However, that title was not "Marxism and the Renegade Kautsky" but rather "The Proletarian Revolution and the Renegade Kautsky."

25 In *Realism and Truth* (1984: 198–200; 1991b: 261–63), I cite evidence that Dummett makes this identification. In the "Afterword" to that book (Devitt 1997a: 307), I find further evidence in Dummett's valedictory lecture in Oxford (1993: 468). Panu Raatikainen has drawn my attention to an earlier part of that lecture where Dummett seems, however, to accept that the metaphysical and semantic issues are distinct whilst finding the semantic one more interesting (p. 465). Indeed, as I noted in the book, "Dummett attaches no significance to the difference between these two views" of the issues (Devitt 1984: 199; 1991b: 262). The view that the semantic issue has a certain priority over the metaphysical one is certainly more reasonable than the identification of the issues, but a central tenet of my book is that the view is very wrong (except, perhaps, in the realm of Dummett's favorite example, mathematics (Devitt 1984: 200–204; 1991b: 263–67).

26 Curiously, Putnam is not alone in missing these discussions. (i) Alexander Miller (2003), who agrees with my rejection of what I call "the Metaphor Thesis" – metaphysics beyond meaning is mere metaphor (1991b: 264) – and of Dummett's identification of the realism issue with a semantic issue, thinks that I have "overlooked" (Miller 2003: 192) "that Dummett's arguments against semantic realism can be viewed as attempting to establish that common-sense realism cannot be conjoined with [the Truth-Conditional Conception of meaning and understanding]" (p. 207). (ii) Drew Khlentzos – whose 2004 is, according to Putnam, "a convincing criticism" of my response to Dummett (Putnam 2007: 166, n. 10) – includes me among philosophers who think that "all they need do to disarm the antirealist's challenge is show that the metaphysical issue of realism has nothing to do with disputes about the nature of truth" (16). In fact, to repeat, I consider the relationship between the metaphysical and semantic issues at some length (see also Devitt 1999: 93–98).

Another point to note in assessing Khlentzos' criticisms (2004: 31–35), is that my commitment to "evidence-transcendent" truth conditions is *only* a commitment to the view that

> statements have truth conditions that are not in any way constrained by our epistemic capacities (Maxim 5). So it is *possible* that a statement might be true and yet we might not be able to detect this (which is not to say that the truth of any true statement is *actually* undetectable; 3.5, 7.4).
>
> (Devitt 1991b: 260)

Bibliography

Aune, Bruce (1987) "Conceptual relativism," in Tomberlin 1987: 269–85.

Auxier, Randall E., and Lewis Edwin Hahn (eds.) (2007) *The Philosophy of Michael Dummett*, Chicago: Open Court Publishing Company.

Blackburn, Simon (1980) "Truth, Realism, and the Regulation of Theory," in French, Uehling and Wettstein 1980: 353–71.

Blackburn, Thomas (1988) "The Elusiveness of Reference," in French, Uehling, and Wettstein 1988: 179–94.

Boyd, Richard N. (1984) "The Current Status of Scientific Realism," in Leplin 1984a: 41–82.

——(1999) "Homeostasis, Species, and Higher Taxa," in Robert A. Wilson (ed.), *Species: New Interdisciplinary Essays*, Cambridge, MA: MIT Press: 141–85.

Brown, Curtis (1988) "Internal Realism: Transcendental Idealism?," in French, Uehling, and Wettstein 1988: 145–55.

Brown, James Robert (1994) *Smoke and Mirrors: How Science Reflects Reality*, New York: Routledge.

Devitt, Michael (1983) "Realism and the Renegade Putnam: A Critical Study of *Meaning and the Moral Sciences* by Hilary Putnam," *Noûs* 17: 291–301.

——(1984) *Realism and Truth*, 1st edn. Oxford: Blackwell.

——(1988) "Rorty's Mirrorless World," in French, Uehling, and Wettstein 1988: 157–77.

——(1991a) "Aberrations of the Realism Debate," *Philosophical Studies*, 61: 43–63. Reprinted in Devitt 2010.

——(1991b) *Realism and Truth*, 2nd edn. Oxford: Blackwell.

——(1991c.) "Minimalist Truth: A Critical Notice of Paul Horwich's *Truth*," *Mind and Language* 6: 273–83.
——(1996a) *Coming to Our Senses: A Naturalistic Defense of Semantic Localism*, New York: Cambridge University Press.
——(1996b) "The Metaphysics of Nonfactualism," in James E. Tomberlin (ed.), *Philosophical Perspectives, 10, Metaphysics, 1996*, Cambridge MA: Blackwell, 159–76. Reprinted in Devitt 2010.
——(1997a) "Afterword," in a reprint of Devitt 1991b, Princeton: Princeton University Press: 302–45.
——(1997b) "On Determining Reference," in Alex Burri (ed.), *Sprache und Denken/ Language and Thought*, New York: Walter de Gruyter, 112–21.
——(1998) "Naturalism and the A Priori," *Philosophical Studies* 92: 45–65. Reprinted in Devitt 2010.
——. (1999) "A Naturalistic Defense of Realism," in Steven D. Hales (ed.), *Metaphysics: Contemporary Readings*, Belmont, CA: Wadsworth Publishing Company, 90–103.
——(2001a) "Incommensurability and the Priority of Metaphysics," in P. Hoyningen-Huene and H. Sankey (eds.), *Incommensurability and Related Matters*, Dordrecht: Kluwer Academic Publishers: 143–57. Reprinted in Devitt 2010.
——(2001b) "The Metaphysics of Truth," in Michael Lynch (ed.), *The Nature of Truth*, Cambridge, MA: MIT Press, 579–611. Reprinted in Devitt 2010.
——(2002) "Underdetermination and Realism," in Ernest Sosa and Enrique Villanueva (eds.), *Realism and Relativism: Philosophical Issues 12, 2002*, Cambridge, MA: Blackwell, 26–50.
——(2005a) "There is No A Priori," in Sosa and Steup 2005: 105–15.
——(2005b) "Reply to BonJour," in Sosa and Steup 2005: 118–20.
——(2005c) "Scientific Realism," in Frank Jackson and Michael Smith (eds.), *The Oxford Handbook of Contemporary Philosophy*, Oxford: Oxford University Press: 767–91. Reprinted in Devitt 2010.
——(2008) "Resurrecting Biological Essentialism," *Philosophy of Science* 75: 344–82. Reprinted in Devitt 2010.
——(2010) *Putting Metaphysics First: Essays on Metaphysics and Epistemology*, Oxford: Oxford University Press.
——(2011) "No Place for the A Priori," in Michael J. Shaffer and Michael L. Veber (eds.), *What Place for the A Priori?*, Chicago and La Salle: Open Court Publishing Company: 9–32. Reprinted in Devitt 2010.
Dummett, Michael (1978) *Truth and Other Enigmas*, Cambridge, Mass.: Harvard University Press.
——(1993) *The Seas of Language*, Oxford: Clarendon Press.
——(2007) "Reply to Putnam," in Auxier and Hahn 2007: 168–84.
Dupré, John (1981) "Natural Kinds and Biological Taxa," *Philosophical Review* 90: 66–90.
Ellis, Brian (1979) *Rational Belief Systems*, Oxford: Blackwell.
——(1985) "What Science Aims to Do," in Paul M. Churchland and Clifford A. Hooker (eds.), *Images of Science: Essays on Realism and Empiricism, with a Reply from Bas C. van Fraassen*, Chicago: University of Chicago Press: 48–74.
Fales, Evan (1988) "How to be a Metaphysical Realist," in French, Uehling, and Wettstein 1988: 253–74.

Fine, Arthur (1986a) *The Shaky Game: Einstein, Realism, and the Quantum Theory*, Chicago: University of Chicago Press.
——(1986b) "Unnatural Attitudes: Realist and Instrumentalist Attachments to Science," *Mind* 95: 149–77.
French, Peter A., Theodore E. Uehling Jr., and Howard K. Wettstein (eds.) (1980) *Midwest Studies in Philosophy, Volume V: Studies in Epistemology*, Minneapolis: University of Minnesota Press.
——(1988) *Midwest Studies in Philosophy, Volume XII: Realism and Antirealism*, Minneapolis: University of Minnesota Press.
Goodman, Nelson (1978) *Ways of Worldmaking*, Indianapolis: Hackett Publishing Company.
Haack, Susan (1987). "Realism," *Synthese* 73: 275–99.
Heller, Mark (1988) "Putnam, Reference, and Realism," in French, Uehling, and Wettstein 1988: 113–27.
Hesse, Mary (1967) "Laws and Theories," In Paul Edwards (ed.), *The Encyclopedia of Philosophy*, New York: Macmillan, vol. 4, pp. 404–10.
Hooker, Clifford A. (1974) "Systematic Realism," *Synthese* 51: 409–97.
Horwich, Paul (1990) *Truth*, 2nd edn 1998. Oxford: Clarendon Press.
Jennings, Richard (1989) "Scientific Quasi-Realism," *Mind* 98: 223–45.
Kant, Immanuel (1783) *Prolegomena to Any Future Metaphysics*.
Khlentzos, Drew (2004) *Naturalistic Realism and the Anti-Realist Challenge*, Cambridge, MA: MIT Press.
Kim, Jaegwon (1980) "Rorty on the Possibility of Philosophy," *Journal of Philosophy* 77: 588–97.
Kitcher, Philip (1993) *The Advancement of Science: Science without Legend, Objectivity without Illusions*, New York: Oxford University Press.
Kornblith, Hilary (1993) *Inductive Inference and Its Inductive Ground: An Essay in Naturalistic Epistemology*, Cambridge, MA: MIT Press.
Kuhn, Thomas S. (1962) *The Structure of Scientific Revolutions*, Chicago: Chicago University Press. 2nd edn 1970.
Laudan, Larry (1981) "A Confutation of Convergent Realism," *Philosophy of Science* 48: 19–49. Reprinted in Leplin 1984a.
Leeds, Stephen (1978) "Theories of Reference and Truth," *Erkenntnis* 13: 111–29.
Leplin, Jarrett, ed. (1984a) *Scientific Realism*, Berkeley: University of California Press.
——(1984b) "Introduction," in Leplin 1984a: 1–7.
LePore, Ernest, and Barry Loewer (1988) "A Putnam's Progress," in French, Uehling, and Wettstein 1988: 459–73.
Lewis, David (1984) "Putnam's Paradox," *Australasian Journal of Philosophy* 62: 221–36.
Lycan, William G. (1988) *Judgement and Justification*, Cambridge: Cambridge University Press.
McMichael, Alan (1988) "Creative Ontology and Absolute Truth," in French, Uehling, and Wettstein 1988: 51–74.
Matheson, Carl (1989) "Is the Naturalist Really Naturally a Realist?," *Mind* 98: 247–58.
Miller, Alexander (2003) "The Significance of Semantic Realism," *Synthese* 136: 191–217.
Miller, Richard W. (1987) *Fact and Method: Explanation, Confirmation and Reality in the Natural and Social Sciences*, Princeton: Princeton University Press.
Papineau, David (1979) *Theory and Meaning*, Oxford: Clarendon Press.

Putnam, Hilary (1975) *Mind, Language and Reality: Philosophical Papers*, vol. 2. Cambridge: Cambridge University Press.
——(1978) *Meaning and the Moral Sciences*, London: Routledge & Kegan Paul.
——(1981) *Reason, Truth and History*, Cambridge: Cambridge University Press.
——(1983) *Realism and Reason: Philosophical Papers*, vol. 3, Cambridge: Cambridge University Press.
——(1985) "A Comparison of Something with Something Else," *New Literary History* 17: 61–79.
——(1987) *The Many Faces of Realism*, La Salle: Open Court.
——(2007) "Between Scylla and Charybdis: Does Dummett Have a Way Out?," in Auxier and Hahn 2007: 155–67.
Richard, Mark (1997) "Deflating Truth," in Enrique Villanueva (ed.), *Truth: Philosophical Issues 8, 1997*, Atascadero: Ridgeview Publishing Company, 57–78.
Rorty, Richard (1979) *Philosophy and the Mirror of Nature*, Princeton: Princeton University Press.
——(1982) *Consequences of Pragmatism (Essays: 1972-1980)*, Minneapolis: University of Minnesota Press.
Ruse, Michael (1987) "Biological Species: Natural Kinds, Individuals, or What?," *British Journal for the Philosophy of Science* 38: 225–42. Reprinted in *The Units of Evolution: Essays on the Nature of Species*, ed. Marc Ereshefsky, Cambridge, MA: MIT Press (1992: 343–61). [Citation is to Ereshefsky.]
Sosa, E. and M. Steup (eds.) (2005) *Contemporary Debates in Epistemology*, Cambridge, MA: Blackwell.
Stove, D. C. (1991) *The Plato Cult and Other Philosophical Follies*, Oxford: Blackwell.
Tomberlin, James T. (ed.) (1987) *Philosophical Perspectives, 1: Metaphysics, 1987*, Atascadero: Ridgeview Publishing Company.
Wolterstorff, Nicholas (1987) "Are Concept-Users World-Makers?," in Tomberlin 1987: 233–67.
Wright, Crispin (1986) *Realism, Meaning and Truth*, Oxford: Blackwell.

COMMENTS ON MICHAEL DEVITT'S "HILARY AND ME"

Hilary Putnam

Although this is not the paper that Michael Devitt actually delivered at the conference in Dublin,[1] I am very happy to comment on it. After all, much of the pleasure of philosophy lies in debates with one's friends, and Michael Devitt is an old friend. And although the debate between the two of us shows no sign of bringing us closer to agreement, each of us can hope that another round of discussion will help to further clarify the issues and the reasons for our disagreement about them.

Can the Realism issue be stated without reference to semantics?

I am sorry that Devitt is aggrieved at what I wrote about him in "Between Scylla and Charybdis: Does Dummett Have a Way Through?" It will assist my discussion if I quote the passage in full:

> According to Devitt, the realism issue is simply, "Is there a mind-independent reality or not?" (*thump*) and there *that* question has nothing to do with semantics. This short way with the issue reminds one of Lenin's (disastrously incompetent) polemical book against Machian positivism (Lenin 1952). Lenin simply claimed that positivists, since they took human sensations as the class of truth-makers for all propositions (I am using present-day terminology, not Lenin's, of course), could not accept the statement that the solar system existed before there were human beings. This argument simply assumes – what positivists of course deny[2] – that the positivists cannot *interpret* "the solar system existed before there were human beings" in their rationally reconstructed "language of science".
>
> But what of the word "independent" in "the behavior of the stars is independent of human sensations and thoughts and beliefs"? (This is what Devitt portrayed anti-realists as *denying*.)

> Well there are many kinds of independence. Presumably causal independence is what Devitt was talking about, since *logical* independence is a property of *statements* (or, perhaps, of events *under a description*), and whether statements are or are not logically independent is certainly a question about their *semantics*, which Devitt claimed to be irrelevant to the realism issue. But then Devitt's argument once again simply assumes – what anti-realists of course deny – that the anti-realist cannot *interpret* the sentence "the behavior of the stars is independent of human sensations and thoughts and beliefs" in a "justificationist" way, interpret it so that it is 'true' (in the anti-realist sense). Devitt cannot, after all, say "but that's not what the sentence *means*! without engaging in a discussion of – guess what? – semantics."
>
> (Putnam 2007: 159)

As is right, fitting, and proper on the part of a philosopher who has been attacked, Devitt criticizes my description of his position. It remains to see if the criticisms affect my argument in any substantive way at all.

One of his criticisms is that I should have written, "the existence and nature of the stars is independent of our minds" instead of "the behavior of the stars is independent of human sensations and thoughts and beliefs." I do not see the great difference. Moreover, I do not see the great difference between saying that (what Devitt sees as) the realism issue is "Is there a mind-independent reality or not?" and saying that it is about whether the "existence and nature" of things like the stars are "in various ways independent of our minds." But on one thing Devitt agrees that what I wrote was correct, namely that on his view the realism question "has nothing to do with semantics."[3] And it remains to see if what he writes here shows that he can succeed in stating the issue in non-semantic terms.

First: here is Devitt's present formulation of "*Realism*":

> *Realism*: Tokens of most common-sense, and scientific, physical types objectively exist independently of the mental.

Second: Devitt now agrees that the antirealist can interpret "causally independent" (and, obviously, "nature" as well) in such a way that "The existence and nature of the stars is causally independent of our minds" comes out true, according to the antirealist's semantics. (N.B. in the passage Devitt objects to I said that "there are many kinds of independence," and I added that he *presumably* meant causal independence, because I didn't see what *else* he could mean.) I shall now argue that nothing he writes in the present essay responds to this problem.

So *how is the Devittian realist going to explain "objectively exist independently" without reference to semantics?* In the present essay, Devitt twice uses the notion of "constituting":

> (1) In insisting on the objectivity of the world, realists are not saying that it is unknowable. They are saying that it is not *constituted by* our knowledge, by our epistemic values, by our capacity to refer to it, by the synthesizing power of the mind, nor by our imposition of concepts, theories, or languages; it is not limited by what we can believe or discover.

The second occurrence is virtually the same:

> (2) Putnam and Dummett wonder what I mean by 'independent' and see a choice between *logical* and *causal* independence. I am quite explicit about what I mean and it is neither of these. I mean *constitutive* independence: thus, as I say above ... , the known world
>
>> is not *constituted by* our knowledge, by our epistemic values, by our capacity to refer to it, by the synthesizing power of the mind, nor by our imposition of concepts, theories, or languages; it is not limited by what we can believe or discover.

But this is not clear *at all*. If "is not constituted by" does not mean "is not brought into existence by" (which is clearly a causal claim) what *is it* supposed to mean? Is it a rejection of the construction Carnap performed in the *Aufbau*, in which physical objects were identified with logical constructions out of primitive experiences (*Urerlebnisse*)? If so, the "is not constituted by" claim would be acceptable to any antirealist who is *not* a phenomenalist, in particular to Michael Dummett, as Devitt well knows. So *that* can't be what "is not constituted by" means. Can it mean "is not the result of the transcendental ego's imposition of the categories upon the manifold"? Obviously not, because many antirealists reject Kant's metaphysics root and branch, as we all know. I could find only one sentence in Devitt's essay that *might* explain what "is not constituted by" means, and that sentence repeats virtually the mistake I ascribed to Lenin.

Here is the sentence:

> (3) How could dinosaurs and stars be dependent in any way on the activities of our minds? It would be crazy to claim that there were no dinosaurs or stars before there were people to think about them. Constructivists do not seem to claim this. But it is hardly any less crazy to claim that there *would not have been* dinosaurs or stars if there *had not been* people (or similar thinkers). And this

claim seems essential to Constructivism: unless it were so, dinosaurs and stars could not be dependent on us and our minds.

If this sentence is supposed to explain what "is not constituted by" means, then it amounts to the charge that the antirealist (Devitt is here referring to my position in *Reason, Truth and History*) is supposed to accept the counterfactual:

(4) There *would not have been* dinosaurs or stars if there *had not been* people or similar thinkers.

But this is not remotely like anything that I said in *Reason, Truth and History*. What I said there was, "A non-realist or 'internal' realist regards conditional statements as statements which we understand (like all other statements) in large part by grasping their *justification* conditions" (Putnam 1981: 122). And, if asked, I would have said that we determine whether a counterfactual is *justified* by considering the "possible worlds" (i.e. the hypothetical situations) that are relevant to the counterfactual, counting some as more relevantly "similar" to what we take the actual world to be like and others as less similar, and seeing if the consequent of the counterfactual is true in the "most similar" hypothetical situations: in short, the *epistemic* evaluation of counterfactuals is the *same* for the realist and the antirealist.

Devitt will remind me that I said that reality is "mind-dependent" in *Reason, Truth and History* and what could that mean if it didn't mean that reality *would have been different* if our minds had been different? About this I will just make two points:

(1) I called mind-dependence a "metaphor" on the first page of *Reason, Truth and History*, and Devitt's objection shows why I shouldn't have used that metaphor.
(2) Part of its being *merely* a metaphor is that the position I called "internal realism" can be stated without it (at, guess what? the *semantic* level): *Internal realism is the position that truth is idealized warranted assertability.*

Of course, it is no accident that Devitt fastens on the metaphor: it was the one place where I myself seemed (to him) to be stating the realism–antirealism issue in non-semantic terms. The failure of the metaphor illustrates the impossibility of doing that.

To sum up: if "is not constituted by" means simply that the counterfactual (4) is false, then "is not constituted by" can be accepted by an antirealist; it does not succeed in capturing metaphysical realism. (It may be, of course, that Michael does not intend it to do that; perhaps he merely loves to criticize a position that (as he himself mentions) I abandoned in 1990.) If that is not what "is not constituted by" is supposed to mean, then those words have not been given a content. Either way, what I wrote in "Between Scylla and Charybdis: Does Dummett Have a Way Through?" still seems substantially correct to me.

Notes

1 Devitt explains that he substituted this paper for the one he actually gave at the Dublin conference, because that paper "has just been published elsewhere," and he also explains that the paper in question "defended Putnam's position on biological essentialism (1975) from the consensus in the philosophy of biology." However, there are important restatements of and modifications to my 1975 theory in three publications after "The Meaning of 'Meaning'." They are "Meaning Holism" (1986), *Representation and Reality* (1988), and "Aristotle After Wittgenstein" (1994). The latter two defend the thesis that, contrary to what I assumed in "The Meaning of 'Meaning'," the nature (or "essence") of a biological species is *not* given by its molecular constitution. Thus (since 1986) I agree with the critics that Devitt mentions, and *not* with Devitt on this issue.
2 For example, Carnap discusses this sort of statement (his example is "If all minds (or all living beings) should disappear from the universe, the stars would still go on in their courses"), without mentioning Lenin, in "Testability and Meaning," Part II, *Philosophy of Science*, Vol. IV, 1937, pp. 37–38, and concludes that it is both cognitively meaningful and well confirmed.
3 Devitt even expresses agreement with Stephen Leeds' remarkable claim that "to question whether our theories aim at 'picturing' the world' is not to question whether electrons 'really' exist" (Leeds 1978: 119). This reminds me of Rorty's claim "In "Pragmatism, Davidson and truth" (1986) that:

> Using those vocables [the words and sentences of "our language"] is *as direct as contact with reality can get* (as direct as kicking rocks, e.g.). The fallacy comes in thinking that the relationship between vocable and reality has to be piecemeal (like the relation between individual kicks and individual rocks), a matter of discrete component capacities to get in touch with discrete hunks of reality.
>
> (145–46; emphasis added)

The obvious challenge is: "Rorty, how can you use *this* sentence to give an example of a 'piecemeal relation' if there is no determinate relation between the word 'rock' and rocks, and no determinate relation between the word 'kicks' and individual kicks *in this very sentence?*" (Similarly Leeds, in the paper Devitt cites, argues that the use of English does not "single out" any one reference-scheme, while insisting that "electrons really exist.") This "semantics-free" version of realism seems to amount to the claim that to be a realist it suffices to sincerely write or utter the right realist-sounding *sentences*, regardless of the account one gives of *what one is doing* by writing or uttering them.

Bibliography

Leeds, Stephen (1978) "Theories of Reference and Truth," *Erkenntnis* 13: 111–29.
Lenin, V. I. (1952) *Materialism and Empircio-Criticism*, Moscow: Foreign Languages Publishing House.

Putnam, Hilary (1986) "Meaning Holism," in, Lewis E. Hahn and Paul A. Schilpp (eds.), *The Philosophy of W. V. Quine*, La Salle, Ill.: Open Court, 1986, 405–31. Reprinted in *Realism with a Human Face*, Cambridge, MA: Harvard University Press, 1990, 278–302.

——(1988) *Representation and Reality*, Cambridge, MA: MIT Press.

——(1993) "Aristotle after Wittgenstein," in Robert W. Shaples (ed.), *Modern Thinkers and Ancient Thinkers*, Boulder, Col.: Westview; London: UCL Press, 1993, 117–37. Reprinted in my *Words and Life*, Cambridge, MA: Harvard University Press, 1994, 62–81.

——(2007) in Randall E. Auxier and Lewis Edwin Hahn (eds.), *The Philosophy of Michael Dummett*, Chicago: Open Court, 2007.

Rorty, Richard (1986) "Pragmatism, Davidson and truth," in Ernest LePore (ed.), *Truth and Interpretation Perspectives on the Philosophy of Donald Davidson*, vol. 1, New York: Basil Blackwell, 126–50.

3

PUTNAM AND THE PHILOSOPHICAL APPEAL TO COMMON SENSE

David Macarthur

> Then where will be the difference between what the idealist-educated children say and the realist ones? Won't the difference only be one of battle cry?
> (Wittgenstein 1967: #414)

Putnam has described his philosophical life as "a long journey from realism to realism" (Putnam 1999: 49). A parenthetical remark undoes the acute sense of paradoxicality in this formulation: the journey begins with Metaphysical Realism (which he capitalizes for ironic emphasis) and ends with what he variously calls "natural," "pragmatic," or "common sense realism." In this chapter I want to focus on the way the last of these three names for this view gives prominence to common sense; and on Putnam's appeal to "the common man" in his further claim "that progress in philosophy requires a recovery of the natural realism of the common man" (ibid.: 24). One important aim is to try to understand the nature and significance of Putnam's appeal to common sense.

The appeal to common sense occurs as part of a complex diagnosis of the incoherence of traditional formulations of Metaphysical Realism – "the metaphysical fantasy that there is a totality of Forms, or Universals, or 'properties,' fixed once and for all" (ibid.: 6) – one that sees the problem arising from a conception of our cognitive powers as being limited to an inner realm of the mind impinged on at a boundary (or "interface") by causal impacts from the outside world. What Putnam wants to make clear, in particular, is that this picture of cognition does not do justice to our common sense way of thinking about perception. It is in order to suggest what is wrong with Metaphysical Realism – what it excludes from view or overlooks – that Putnam elaborates the view he calls common sense realism, one he takes Wittgenstein, amongst others, to endorse.

Roughly, I claim that we can find three conceptions of common sense in Putnam's *The Threefold Cord* (1999): (1) common sense as a matter of common beliefs (which I call *the positive conception*); (2) common sense as a quietist rejection of representationalist metaphysics and epistemology (which I call *the negative conception*); and (3) common sense as a capacity for good judgment (which I call the Kantian conception). The essay aims to show three things: first, that there is a tension between the appeal to ordinary folk and both of Putnam's positive and negative conceptions of common sense; second, that Putnam's characterization of the positive conception as a version of direct realism in the philosophy of perception should be abandoned, especially given his claim that the interface conception (i.e. indirect realism) is senseless; and, third, that Putnam's general outlook suggests that a better candidate for common sense is the Kantian conception of it. This conception is arguably presupposed by the negative conception and leaves Putnam's criticism of Metaphysical Realism unchanged, except that it would no longer take the form of a positive endorsement of something called "direct realism."

Please note that in the quotations I have taken from Putnam I have, for the sake of emphasis and consistency, used the title "common sense realism" to refer to Putnam's position throughout, even where another title was originally used.

Positive characterization: "common sense" beliefs

In *The Threefold Cord*, Putnam makes an appeal to common sense that he tells us is inspired by, and manifest in the work of, James, Dewey, Husserl, Austin, and Wittgenstein, even in spite of their very different philosophical agendas (Putnam 1999: 5, 10, 24, 41). Wittgenstein, is perhaps the most surprising inclusion on this list since he famously wrote,

> There is no common sense answer to a philosophical problem. One can defend common sense against the attacks of philosophers only by solving their puzzles, i.e., by curing them of the temptation to attack common sense; not by restating the views of common sense.
> (Wittgenstein 1972a: 58–59)

I'd like to begin by considering the apparent tension between Wittgenstein's and Putnam's portrayal of the nature and role of common sense.

When one considers Putnam's philosophical appeal to common sense it is often hard to avoid the impression that, far from endorsing Wittgenstein's attitude to common sense, he is doing precisely that which Wittgenstein rails against: namely, restating "the views of common sense" in order to provide an answer or, answer of sorts, to the philosophical problem of Realism. Consider, for example, the following remarks:

> (I take the label [natural or common sense realism] from William James's expressed desire for a view of perception that does justice

> to the "natural realism of the common man.") A [common sense] realist, in my sense, does hold that the objects of (normal "veridical") perception are "external" things, and, more generally, aspects of "external" reality.
>
> (Putnam 1999: 10)

and

> Common sense realism "involves ... insisting that 'external' things, cabbages and kings, can be *experienced*." (And not just in the Pickwickian sense of causing "experiences," conceived as affectations of our subjectivity).
>
> (ibid.: 20)

In these passages common sense is conceived in positive terms as a more or less fixed set of beliefs attributable to "the common man," which presumably means the vast majority of people. And whilst the role of these common sense beliefs does not constitute an answer to the problem of Realism within the traditional terms of the debate, it *does* provide a direct denial of an unquestioned assumption structuring the debate, namely, that "our cognitive powers cannot reach all the way to the objects themselves" (ibid. 10).

Putnam's appeal to common sense beliefs contests various forms of indirect (or representative) realism in the philosophy of both perception and conception that, on Putnam's account, have dominated philosophy from the scientific revolution of the seventeenth century to the era of materialism and cognitive science in the twentieth century. Being reminded of our common sense commitments outside the study is supposed to help us overcome an interminable oscillation between metaphysical theories that defend or reject Realism inside the study. Whether we think of this as providing an answer or not seems to depend only on our point of view: if we are looking just at the traditional debate between Metaphysical Realism and its deniers then we might say no; but if we widen our view to consider the larger debate between direct or indirect realism in the philosophy of cognition, generally, then we might well say yes.

It is also worth noting that on more than one occasion Putnam states that common sense realism is a version of "direct realism" in the philosophy of perception (Putnam 1999: 10, 24, 151). Again, the contrast with Wittgenstein seems stark. In the *Blue Book*, Wittgenstein distinguishes the common sense philosopher from the common sense man and says that the latter is "as far from realism as from idealism" (Wittgenstein 1972a: 48). I take this to imply that, on Wittgenstein's view, there is no substantial philosophical doctrine that can be attributed to the common man, a reading that seems to confute the idea that common sense is committed to a direct realist or any other philosophical view of perception. The trouble is that in order to see common sense realism as a version of direct realism capable of constituting a move beyond the debate over Metaphysical Realism, Putnam has to employ special *philosophical* language such as the theoretically loaded expressions "'external' things" and "affectation of subjectivity" in characterizing it. Neither expression, we might think, would be clearly understood by the man or woman in the street. Presumably sentences such as "'External' things exist" are not a priori truths; nor are they empirical truths that Putnam has arrived at by gathering empirical evidence such as taking polls or conducting surveys.[1] So with what right can Putnam attribute such beliefs to ordinary folk?[2]

At this point it is worth comparing Putnam's common sense beliefs with those of G. E. Moore. You will recall that Moore begins his famous catalogue of common sense propositions like this:

> There exists at present a living human body, which is my body. This body was born at a certain time in the past, and has existed continuously ever since, though not without undergoing changes ... Ever since it was born, it has been either in contact with or not far from the surface of the earth ... [and, further along] the earth has existed also for many years before my body was born ... [and, further still] I am a human being ...
>
> (Moore 1959: 33)

And so on. In providing evidence for what he calls "the Common Sense View of the World," Moore gives examples of what *he* claims to know with certainty. How, then, does this bear on what others think? In order to effect the shift from "I" to "we," Moore holds that almost every human being knows with certainty propositions *corresponding* to the propositions that he enumerates and knows with certainty. It is important for this purpose that his list contain what he takes to be "obvious truisms" (Moore 1959: 32) that employ nothing but everyday language. In contrast, Putnam's examples are not truistic for the simple reason that, as we have seen, they employ distinctively philosophical language or, as in the case of the term "experienced" (which is italicised in the text), a familiar term that is employed for a distinctively philosophical purpose. This creates a problem for Putnam since in speaking of us as "recovering," "returning to," and on one occasion, "preserving" our common sense realism the implication is that we all, or almost all, share this outlook even if only implicitly.

Of course, I do not mean to suggest that Moore's procedure is without fault. The putatively truistic character of Moore's propositions is undermined by the far-from-everyday manner in which Moore produces them. Moore simply lists his propositions as if that alone is capable of demonstrating a special kind of skeptic-proof knowledge. But one obvious trouble with this is that a simple denial of a not-fully-intelligible conclusion is itself not-fully-intelligible. The philosophical context in which Moore produces his propositions is precisely one in which the meanings of propositions are supposed to be accessible quite independently of any question of use. That particular conception of the relation between meaning and use is one Moore shares with the skeptic. By making a mystery of how his employment of these propositions relates to their ordinary employment Moore robs them of any determinate sense. Like the skeptic, Moore supposes that his words have a clear content when stripped of any natural connection to the history of their significant uses.[3] This forms the basis of one of the overriding themes of Wittgenstein's response to Moore's defense of common sense. For example:

> "I know that that's a tree." Why does it strike me as if I did not understand the sentence? Though it is after all an extremely simple sentence of the most ordinary kind? It is as if I could not focus my mind on any meaning. Simply because I don't look for the focus where the meaning is. As soon as I think of an everyday use of the sentence instead of a philosophical one, its meaning becomes clear and ordinary.
> (Wittgenstein 1972b: #347)[4]

Putnam is at one with Wittgenstein's point here. Much of Putnam's recent work has involved elaborating the radical consequences for much contemporary analytic philosophy – including skepticism about the external world – of a full appreciation of the pragmatic or occasion-sensitive character of semantics.[5]

But while Putnam does not appeal to his examples of common sense beliefs to dogmatically refute the skeptic, it is natural to ask, to whom, or on what occasion, one would say such things as "Successful perception is a *sensing* of aspects of the reality 'out there'" or "The objects of (normal 'veridical') perception are 'external' things" (10). It is hard to imagine *any* context for their use except a *philosophical* context in which these sentences are used in opposition to the indirect or representative realist. But, as Wittgenstein points out, time and again, a philosophical context is typically not a context where a significant use is determined because the philosopher is strongly tempted to consider meanings in abstraction from the specific employment of words for a particular or concrete purpose.

Although Putnam admits to being uncomfortable with the term "direct realism," he seems *forced* to employ philosophical language in his expressions of common sense because, on the one hand, he wants to articulate expressions that his opponent, the indirect or representative realist, cannot say; and, on the other, he is aware that the indirect realist will be perfectly prepared to agree with such familiar claims as "We can sometimes see cabbages and kings." The disagreement is not over *whether* we see cabbages or kings but over what *seeing* is. The problem here seems to be that Putnam does not take seriously enough his own diagnosis of the unintelligibility of indirect realism. If *that* makes no (determinate) sense, then, presumably, neither does its contrary, direct realism – at least when employed to state a philosophical thesis.

The same problem of conceiving common sense in terms of beliefs or knowledge that simply negate a philosophical doctrine also shows up in the skeptical tradition. Skepticism about memory, perception, testimony, or induction is traditionally understood to be directed against the supposedly common sense commitment to the claims that each of these modes of belief-formation is reliable. But it is worth asking whether the unqualified claim that, say, memory is reliable is something that "the common man" is committed to. True, we tend to trust our memories as a matter of course, but that is not the same thing as being committed to the claim that memory is reliable. A young child, for example, can trust her memory without even having a concept of memory. And trusting this faculty in the sense of acting as if one's memories are correct is not the same as claiming that they are. We may well want to make such a distinction with regard to the elderly, the infirm, the mentally retarded, and the forgetful, as well as those who come to realize that their memories are more than a little colored by self-interest or self-image. Similar considerations could be raised with regard to the other faculties. One might reply that second-order beliefs about the reliability of our epistemic faculties are commitments of *normal* people but, then, the suspicion arises that this is circular: that the notion of normal is being spelled out partly in terms of our commitments to the beliefs in question. And what then becomes of the link between normal people, so defined, and "the common man"?

A similar but less apparent problem afflicts external world and other minds skepticism. The skeptic in these cases assumes, and very often manages to get us to assume, that we – that is, ordinary folk – have a *belief* in the existence of the external world or a *belief* in the existence of other minds. It is our apparent inability to justify or defend these supposedly indispensable beliefs that leads to a skeptical crisis. But this assumption, shared by both the skeptic who challenges such "beliefs" and the constructive epistemologist who defends them, can be called into question. Stanley Cavell, for one, has long argued that "our relation to the world's existence is somehow *closer* than the ideas of believing and knowing are made to convey" (Cavell 1981: 145). On his view, the fact that we think, under the pressure of skeptical reasoning, that we have, say, a belief in the external world is itself one of the conjuring tricks that marks our encounter with skepticism. Seeing the world aright is not a matter of finding a justification of this supposedly fundamental "belief" but involves coming to the hard realization that it is neither the case that we believe (or know) that there is an external world, nor the case that we do not believe (or know) this. However commonsensical we might find it in the midst of our philosophical reflections, Cavell's claim is that the concept of belief (or knowledge) just does not do justice to our natural relation to the world.

Negative characterization: quietism

Let us leave aside Putnam's positive conception of common sense in order to consider another. In addition to the conception of common sense as a set of beliefs held by "the common man," Putnam also endorses another quite different *negative* conception. In a number of places in *The Threefold Cord* one can also find remarks such as this:

> "The [common sense] realist account" urged on us by Austin and Wittgenstein, is, in the end, not an "alternative metaphysical account" ... Winning through to [common sense] realism is seeing the needlessness and the unintelligibility of a picture that imposes an interface between ourselves and the world. It is a way of completing the task of philosophy, the task that John Wisdom once called a "journey from the familiar to the familiar."
> (Putnam 1999: 41)

On this characterization, common sense is not conceived as a body of (metaphysical) doctrine so much as a capacity for a certain kind of quietist move that attempts to undermine a false metaphysical picture – which Putnam calls "the interface conception" – without wanting to erect another theory (or "account") in its place. At its heart is an appreciation that the interface conception, which treats the mind as primarily engaged with sense data, impressions, and the like, is explanatorily empty and, when fully thought through, senseless or incoherent. To be a common sense realist, such passages suggest, is a matter of returning to "the familiar" after having felt the temptation to accept, but finally coming to see the emptiness of, a metaphysical account that interposes mental representations between the mind and the world.

This negative conception seems much closer to Wittgenstein's idea that one defends common sense not by restating or justifying common opinions but by solving one's philosophical difficulties. One returns to common sense – or, what Wittgenstein usually calls the "everyday" or "ordinary" (e.g., Wittgenstein 1958: 116, 132) – by overcoming a philosophical attack, although the nature and target of this attack may require reinterpretation. As in the case of modern skepticism, we need not accept the skeptic's own conception of common sense in terms of well-entrenched or widely held beliefs. Common sense or the ordinary, on Wittgenstein's view, is not associated with a statistical likelihood of agreement, confirmable, say, by empirical testing. It concerns the details of our particular uses of words, something that is open to view but strangely hard to see despite or, rather, *because* of that. Wittgenstein writes:

> The aspects of things that are most important for us are hidden because of their simplicity and familiarity. (One is unable to notice something – because it is always before one's eyes.)
> (Wittgenstein 1958: #129)

Apart from more accurately reflecting Wittgenstein's thought, an advantage of this negative conception of common sense is that it is not subject to the threat of emptiness afflicting the positive conception. But a major disadvantage, from Putnam's point of view, is that it involves a highly sophisticated philosophical move – one that requires an appreciation of both the seductive power and eventual senselessness of the metaphysical employment of words – so it, too, is not something that could be attributed to "the common man" if that means something like the normal or average person. And that seems to rob common sense realism of a large part of its original motivation.

Synthesis: second naiveté

These two ways of conceiving common sense are combined under the banner of what Putnam calls a "cultivated" or "second naiveté." For example:

> "second naiveté" [is] a standpoint that fully appreciates the deep difficulties pointed out by seventeenth-century philosophers but overcomes those difficulties rather than succumbing to them – a standpoint that sees that the difficulties do not, in the end, require us to reject the idea that in perception we are in unmediated contact with our environment.
> (Putnam 1999: 44)

The term "second naiveté" perfectly captures the ambivalence of Putnam's treatment of common sense, suggesting both the cultivation of philosophy (especially in its quietist or therapeutic form) and the desire for a return from "metaphysical fantasy" to a "naive" position that characterizes people who have not been corrupted by false philosophizing: a position that is not stupid or ignorant but, rather, *innocent*. Unfortunately, the difficulties that we have so far considered are multiplied: on the one hand, the sophisticated quietist move of appreciating and overcoming the philosophical conundrum over Metaphysical Realism cannot plausibly be ascribed to "the common man"; and, on the other, the talk of an unmediated contact in perception makes no sense unless talk of a mediated contact does, but Putnam himself has persuasively argued that it does not.

Furthermore, although second naiveté involves Wittgensteinian therapy it cannot be equated with Wittgenstein's almost wholly negative characterization of the everyday. When Wittgenstein writes "What we do is bring words back from their metaphysical to their everyday use," it is clear from the context that in this contrast it is the term "metaphysical" that is primary (that wears the trousers, in Austin's phrase). The everyday is not given a positive characterization: it is simply *the non-metaphysical*, where the metaphysical is, paradigmatically, an attempt "to grasp the *essence* of the thing" (Wittgenstein 1958: #116), or a matter of imposing absolute or fixed conditions or demands on explanation or justification.[6]

In Wittgenstein's vision we are repeatedly or incessantly lost in a self-destructive attack on the basis of our mutual intelligibility: on our attunement in criteria for the application of concepts to the world.[7] Whether this is a consequence of skeptical despair or metaphysical ambition, the task is to bring words back to their "everyday use" as a way of overcoming the disorientation of self-imposed exile, of "language ... on holiday" (Wittgenstein 1958: #38). As Stanley Cavell puts it, "the ordinary is precisely what it is that scepticism [or metaphysics] attacks [and] ... is only discovered, in its loss" (Cavell 1996: 89).

Supposing this is on the right path, then, for Wittgenstein, the ordinary depends, constantly, on our shifting sense of what is, and what is not, strange or odd or unfamiliar (Baker 2002). New senses of strangeness discover new senses of the ordinary (Cavell 1998). So the ordinary is not something reified or given (as it is, say, on Moore's picture) but something that only shows up, retrospectively, in its denial.

Although this reading chimes with Putnam's negative conception of common sense it is an open question whether Putnam would endorse this linguistic approach to the ordinary or Wittgenstein's sense of the paradoxicality (or what Cavell calls the uncanniness) of the ordinary; but it is clear that the positive conception of common sense as a version of direct realism held by "the common man" stands in the way of either move.

Another try: a Kantian account

It might seem that I am convicting Putnam of a thoroughly confused position on the nature and philosophical import of common sense, but there is an important aspect to his thinking that has so far escaped attention. I want to argue that Putnam's outlook as a whole suggests an alternative Kantian conception of common sense, one that is presupposed by the negative (quietist) conception, so that Putnam's criticism of Metaphysical Realism can be salvaged, but only at the cost of giving up thinking of common sense realism as a positive philosophical doctrine.

At this stage, let us recall Kant's famous criticism of Thomas Reid and others of the Scottish School of philosophy who appeal to common sense to refute Humean skepticism:

> It is indeed a great gift of God to possess right or (as they now call it) plain common sense. But this common sense must be shown in

action by well-considered and reasonable thoughts and words, not by appealing to it as an oracle when no rational justification for one's position can be advanced. To appeal to common sense when insight and science fail, and no sooner – this is one of the subtle discoveries of modern times, by means of which the most superficial ranter can safely enter the lists with the most thorough thinker and hold his own. But as long as a particle of insight remains, no one would think of having recourse to this subterfuge. Seen clearly, it is but an appeal to the opinion of the multitude, of whose applause the philosopher is ashamed, while the popular charlatan glories and boasts in it.

(Kant 1950: 7)

What I would like to draw attention to in this passage is the contrast between the Reidian notion of common sense as a set of universally held beliefs (which Kant calls "the opinion of the multitude") and the Kantian notion of common sense as a capacity for good judgment (which "must be shown in action by well-considered and reasonable thoughts and words"). A central feature of what Kant means by common sense here is that it cannot be taught by means of rules since, if one insisted upon that, then one would then need further rules to be able to apply these rules and so on ad infinitum. Kant draws the moral:

Judgment is a peculiar talent which can be practised only, and cannot be taught. It is the specific quality of so-called mother-wit.
(Kant 1929: A133/B172)

It seems to me that when we look at Putnam's work as a whole, especially over the past two decades, Putnam's general conception of common sense is most charitably understood in Kantian terms as the capacity for good judgment. Let me explain.

I have so far focused attention exclusively on the term "common sense" as it relates to the position Putnam calls common sense realism, but I'd now like to turn to consider the second half of this title, namely, "realism." Coming to an appreciation of what Putnam means by realism in this context will shed valuable light on what he means, or, rather, what he *ought* to mean, by common sense. If we leave aside the identification of common sense realism with direct realism in the philosophy of perception and concentrate on Putnam's support for small "r" over big "R" realism in his writings then perhaps the best short description of Putnam's realism is to say that it is closer to realism in the novel than to any constructive philosophical thesis. Putnam, as I read him, shares with Wittgenstein what Cora Diamond has called "the realistic spirit" (Diamond 1991: 40): that is, a sense of what normally happens and what does not (e.g. objects do not disappear when unobserved, pigs do not fly, cars do not grow on trees) and of the interconnection between things, the way events normally unfold in time. Realism, we might say, is a grasp of the normal run of things. It is this sense of realism that Putnam means when he refers to, e.g., "our ordinary realism about the past" (Putnam 1999: 54).

Of course, there is an unavoidable vagueness in any positive characterization of this largely implicit understanding or know-how but it is vitally important to all of our inquiries whether they be practical, legal, medical, scientific or philosophical. Indeed it is an important theme of the Deweyan pragmatism that Putnam (1992) endorses that in moral no less than in scientific inquiry we need a sense of what is important and what is not, what to pay attention to and what to pass over, what the relevant grounds for one's judgments are, how much weight they have, and some indication of how they are to be assessed or criticized. In short, we need a sense of realism in *all* of our inquiries, theoretical or practical.

What, then, is the relation between this non-metaphysical conception of realism and common sense? We might put it this way. Kantian common sense is the capacity for realistic judgement in the sense in which both Wittgenstein (on Diamond's reading) and Putnam understand it. Having common sense in the relevant sense is presupposed by more refined abilities such as those involved in, say, being a good judge of people, or having the scientific know-how which gives one a "nose" for when the results are to be trusted, when to check the equipment, when a theory has too many auxiliary hypotheses and so forth.

Kantian common sense is also presupposed in Putnam's larger philosophical ambition to do justice to both "the sense that our practices have for us" (Putnam 1999: 64) and the rich occasion-sensitivity of sense-making (Putnam 1999: 87, 125). And it has an intimate connection with Putnam's conception of the reasonable. Where Kant speaks of "well-considered and reasonable thoughts and words," Putnam writes,

> The meanings of ... words does restrict what can be said using them; but what can be said using them, consistently with the[ir] meaning ... depends upon our ability to figure out how it is *reasonable* to use those words, given those meanings (given a certain history of prior uses), in novel circumstances.
>
> (ibid.)

Indeed, just as Kant draws a distinction between common sense [*Gemeinsinn*] and common human understanding [*gemeinen Menschenverstand*][8] on the ground that the former is ultimately a matter of feeling or sense, rather than rules or concepts, so, too, does connect our powers of judging in accordance with reason with "our full capacity to imagine and feel, in short, [with] our full sensibility" (Putnam 1978: 86). Putnam's Kant-inspired conception of common sense is, ultimately, an appeal to normative but non-rule-governed powers of discrimination and appraisal.

Conclusion

I want to end by suggesting that the tensions in Putnam's philosophical appeal to common sense can only be relieved by giving up the positive conception, essentially the claim that common sense realism is a form of direct realism. Kantian common sense and the negative or Wittgensteinian conception of common sense are mutually supportive since one requires the capacity for good or reasonable judgment in investigating the sense of words on a given occasion of their employment; and having a sense of what makes sense is presupposed by one's capacity to make judgements at all.

Once one has achieved the quietist insight that the indirect realist has hallucinated having a genuine position and having diagnosed the source and power of his confusion, there is no need (and potential harm) in rendering this insight as a positive thesis. It is all very well to say, as Putnam does,

> In my opinion, "direct realism" is best thought of not as a *theory* of perception but as a denial of the necessity for and the explanatory value of positing "internal representations" in thought and perception.
> (Putnam 1999: 101)

But it can only confuse the issue to combine this quietist move with such apparent endorsements of traditional direct realism as that we perceive "external things" or that we sense not a mere affectation of our own subjectivity but aspects of the reality "out there." Having diagnosed the nature, source and power of the metaphysical picture of an interface between the mind and the world, the task, as Putnam himself has brilliantly taught us in other cases, is not to affirm a counter-thesis, nor to try to justify the practice that is under attack.[9] For earning the right not to have to engage in constructive philosophizing involves acknowledging that, as Wittgenstein puts it, "the practice has to speak for itself" (Wittgenstein 1972b: #139).

Notes

1 Some philosophers have attempted this on a small scale. For example, Stephen Stich has conducted tests of his undergraduates' intuitions about knowledge claims.
2 Presumably this is how we are to interpret his reference to "the common man."
3 Moore seems to half-realize this. On the one hand, he supposes that his propositions are not subject to doubt; on the other, he shows signs that he realizes that having said that he *knows* them then the question of *how* he knows is appropriate and requires an answer. For instance, Moore notes that when we reflect on this knowledge we are in the "strange position" (1959: 44) of knowing that we must have evidence for it yet not knowing what that evidence is. This admission destabilizes Moore's "defence." It is as if Moore acknowledges the legitimacy of

the question "How do you know?" whilst at the same time thinking that he has a right to ignore it.
4 Also see Wittgenstein 1972b: #153, #348, #350.
5 Putnam is influenced by the Wittgensteinian idea that sentences admit of an open-ended variety of understandings in their potential employment. Cf. Travis (2000).
6 I take it that the term "metaphysics" is to be understood as a family resemblance concept and that one of the important tasks of philosophy is to discern which utterances are metaphysical and which not. A major problem is that metaphysics typically disguises itself as science (Wittgenstein 1967: #458; 1972a: 18).
7 I am indebted to Cavell's reading of Wittgenstein. See, especially, Cavell (1979).
8 Kant says that this is "the very least that we are entitled to expect from anyone who lays claim to the name of human being" (Kant 1987: 86, §21, §40).
9 "Very often, the problem in philosophy is that a philosopher who knows what he wants to deny feels that he cannot simply do so, but must make a 'positive' statement; and the positive statement is frequently a disaster" (Putnam 1990: 223).

Bibliography

Baker, G. (2002) "Wittgenstein on Metaphysical/Everyday Use," *The Philosophical Quarterly* 52: 289–302.
Diamond, C. (1991) *The Realistic Spirit*, Cambridge, MA: MIT Press.
Cavell, S. (1979) *The Claim of Reason*, Oxford: Oxford University Press.
——(1981) *The Senses of Walden: An Expanded Edition*, San Francisco: North Point Press.
——(1988) *In Quest of the Ordinary*, Chicago: University of Chicago Press.
——(1996) *Contesting Tears*, Chicago: University of Chicago Press.
Kant, I. (1929 [1787]) *Critique of Pure Reason*, trans. N. Kemp Smith. London: Macmillan.
——(1950 [1783]) *Prolegomena to Any Future Metaphysics*, trans. L. White Beck. Indianapolis: Bobbs-Merrill.
——(1987 [1790]) *Critique of Judgment*, trans. W. S. Pluhar. Indianapolis: Hackett.
Moore, G. E. (1959) *Philosophical Papers*, London: George, Allen & Unwin.
Putnam, H. (1978) *Meaning and the Moral Sciences*, Boston: Routledge & Kegan Paul.
——(1990) *Realism with a Human Face*, Cambridge, MA: Harvard University Press.
——(1992) *Renewing Philosophy*, Cambridge, MA: Harvard University Press.
——(1994) *Words and Life*, Cambridge, MA: Harvard University Press.
——(1999) *The Threefold Cord*, New York: Columbia University Press.
Reid, T. (1983) *Inquiry & Essays*, ed. R.E. Beanblossom, and K. Lehrer. Indianapolis: Hackett.
Travis, C. (2000) *Unshadowed Thought*, Cambridge, MA: Harvard University Press.
Wittgenstein, L. (1958 [1953]) *Philosophical Investigations*, Oxford: Blackwell.
——(1967) *Zettel*, Berkeley: University of California Press.
——(1972a [1958]) *The Blue & Brown Books*, Oxford: Blackwell.
——(1972b [1969]) *On Certainty*, Oxford: Blackwell.

COMMENTS ON DAVID MACARTHUR'S "PUTNAM AND THE PHILOSOPHICAL APPEAL TO COMMON SENSE"

Hilary Putnam

David raises an issue that I have wrestled with for many years, namely do I or do I not I agree with what is sometimes described as Wittgenstein's "quietistic" attitude to philosophical problems. Are they "nonsense" to be exposed, as many Wittgensteinians would claim, or do they raise substantive issues? I think I am beginning to find my way out of my perplexity.[1] But it's a way that I think will make David and some other of my former students unhappy. But I'm always doing *that*. And as long as I live I suppose I shall make various former students unhappy.

David finds that when Wittgenstein wrote,

> There is no common sense answer to a philosophical problem. One can defend common sense against the attacks of philosophers only by solving their puzzles, i.e., by curing them of the temptation to attack common sense; not by restating the views of common sense.
> (Wittgenstein 1958: 58–59)

Wittgenstein was anticipating my call for a return to "the natural realism of the common man" in *The Threefold Cord: Mind, Body, and World*, and there are certainly passages in that book that support David's reading. For example, I wrote,

> "The natural realist account" urged on us by Austin and Wittgenstein is, in the end, not an alternative "metaphysical account" ... Winning through to natural realism is seeing the *needlessness* and *unintelligibility* of a picture that imposes an interface between ourselves and the world and this is certainly "Wittgensteinian"!
> (Putnam 1999: 41)

I did not, however, refer to "seeing the *needlessness* and *unintelligibility* of a picture that imposes an interface between ourselves and the world" as *puzzle solving* as Wittgenstein did in *The Blue and Brown Books*; in fact, I find that conception of philosophy, one that I first encountered in the 1950s when I read Gilbert Ryle speaking of other philosophers as committing "howlers" – British schoolboy slang for getting your sums wrong – as extremely likely to backfire. I thought then and still think that if Wittgenstein, or Ryle, or anybody else, manages to convince people that's all there is for philosophy to do – expose howlers – there won't be philosophy departments.

I could end my response here, but that would fail to acknowledge the fact that, as David rightly sees, there has been a change in my position.[2] When I was still in my twenties and early thirties, I was skeptical about the claim of Wittgensteinians that the theses of philosophers are nonsensical. In *The Threefold Cord*, I was less skeptical, but in the end I think that my original skepticism was right.[3]

Notes

1 Now (almost five years later) I would say that while Wittgenstein had many insights, the idea that philosophers habitually talk "nonsense" was a mistake. I explain my reasons for saying this in Putnam (2012a). That's the "way out" I was already contemplating when I responded to David Macarthur's lecture in Dublin.
2 Part of the change is that I no longer find talk of qualia "needless" and "unintelligible." [See my comments on Ned Block's chapter in this volume.] Another part is that I think that finding a picture that satisfactorily shows that conceding the reality of qualia does not require giving up natural realism requires cooperation between philosophy and cognitive science in the widest sense of the term, including brain and behavioural science, and not simply philosophical clarification. See Putnam (2012b).
3 However, at the time of the Conference this book records I was not able to say as clearly as I think I can today why I think it was right. See Putnam (2012a).

Bibliography

Putnam, Hilary (1999) *The Threefold Cord*, New York: Columbia University Press.
——(2012a) "Wittgenstein: A Reappraisal," in Hilary Putnam, *Philosophy in an Age of Science*, ed. Mario De Caro and David Macarthur, Cambridge, MA: Harvard University Press.
——(2012b) "Corresponding with Reality," in Hilary Putnam, *Philosophy in an Age of Science*, ed. Mario De Caro and David Macarthur, Cambridge, MA: Harvard University Press.
Wittgenstein, Ludwig (1958) *The Blue and Brown Books*. Oxford: Blackwell.

Part II

ON WHAT THERE IS

4

PUTNAM VERSUS QUINE ON REVISABILITY AND THE ANALYTIC–SYNTHETIC DISTINCTION[1]

Axel Mueller

I. Introduction

In the following, I want to revisit the criticism of the analytic–synthetic distinction brought forth in Putnam's "The Analytic and the Synthetic" and later writings and compare it with Quine's familiar attack on the same distinction in the last two sections of "Two Dogmas of Empiricism." My purpose in this comparison will be to find the features of Putnam's argument that prepare the ground for his increasingly explicit acknowledgment of the utility of a successor distinction, which sharply separates his pragmatic, induction-based epistemological commitments from Quine's naturalistic rejection of any such project. The following brief review of some doctrinal agreements vis-à-vis logical empiricism will set the stage for specifying the issue between Putnam and Quine regarding the epistemic analytic–synthetic distinction.

Following Quine, Putnam's early writings on the analytic–synthetic distinction criticize the attempt undertaken by logical empiricism (especially Carnap and Ayer) to use a precise and general distinction between analytic and synthetic statements for empirically contentful systems of statements for the purpose of giving a "demystified" account of the special status, interpretation, empirical meaningfulness and justifiability of statements (such as the laws of logic and mathematical truths, statements of semantics, and theoretical statements in scientific theories) that had traditionally resisted – since supposedly independent of experience in content and justification – ready integration into a broadly empiricist methodological outlook. The key to solving all three of the mentioned problems was to first identify apriority, necessity and analyticity, interpret the latter as "truth in virtue of meaning," and then to specify for any empirically contentful language a precise class of analytic statements that gave as much traditional apriorities and necessities (which linguistified the *a priori*) as would be strong enough to explain the interpretability and acceptability-conditions of theoretical statements in terms of observation-statements.[2] Given the underdetermined character of the latter and the multiple options in the choice of linguistic frameworks of empirical justification, conventionalism had the remaining task of explaining the apparent necessity of logic and mathematics (as the choice to retain statements) and the acceptance and meaningfulness of non-observational statements (as the choice of theoretical frameworks for systematizing empirical knowledge). According to conventionalism and linguistified apriority, such choices concern the presuppositions of empirical argument. Since, as presuppositions, they cannot be forced on us by empirical arguments the success of which would have to already presuppose them, their acceptability and actual acceptance have to be due to other sources. Conventionalists overcome the psychologism of their predecessors by attributing these facts of selective, empirically underdetermined acceptance to social agreements on the analyticities to adopt. Likewise, and in parallel fashion, Carnap, Lewis and Ayer believed that the acceptance and empirical meaningfulness of observationally underdetermined theories could be explained as reflecting collective choices as much about connecting principles between observation and theory as about rivals that, given such principles, equally well accommodate the available empirical data. Regarding the explanation of apriority and necessity, it is now our commitment to certain agreed-upon norms of inquiry that explains why the statements expressing these norms are stable under all circumstances as long as the language and framework we use remain the same. This is the thrust of a conventionalist-linguistic explanation of mathematical and logical necessity.[3] Quine and Putnam both reject the idea of taking some statements (many of which are extra-logical) in science as true on merely communal *fiat* instead of empirical argument as incompatible with the empirical nature of the requirements on scientific judgment. Consequently, both oppose the linguistic conception of the substantive *a priori*[4] as much as conventionalism.

As to the first, Putnam is as critical as Quine of the proposal to understand *epistemic* special statuses, insofar as they are present in systems of empirical belief, on the model of *linguistic* stipulations (analyticities), changing or endorsing which is rather a matter of linguistic legislation than of empirical information and argument. On well-known holistic grounds, Quine and Putnam portray this project as an artifact of the requirements imposed by positivistic methodology that has no reasonable basis in the way statements are (epistemically or semantically) assessed in actual scientific practice. The main reasons for this stem from the inseparability of linguistic and empirical information within an empirically contentful system of knowledge. Such inseparability puts into question the idea of there being an identifiable subset of specific statements of the system that merely codifies a special, non-empirical kind of "knowledge of meaning." The particular lines of thought undergirding these critical considerations are three. First, in virtue of the multiple inferential relations of beliefs within these systems, it is futile to non-arbitrarily isolate some of the system's accepted statements as "truths in virtue of language" if they are *logically* candidates for revision in case of conflicts between the system and incoming statements. Second, it is futile to try to trace the empirical significance or testability of statements that employ certain expressions to a given class of statements that allegedly have the sole function of specifying the application conditions of these expressions, since the application of any statement (also the meaning-specifying conditions) requires many stated and tacit auxiliary empirical assumptions which are, since required for application, equally *part of the application* conditions of the expressions. Third, given this inseparability and auxiliary-dependence of empirical applicability, the explanation of conventional-linguistic *constraints* on empirical knowledge would have to portray "knowledge of meaning" as strong enough to constitute *empirically significant* (hence applicable) constraints, and thus would always also articulate ordinary empirical beliefs. But then such knowledge is vulnerable to changes in empirical belief like ordinary empirical knowledge. For these reasons, we fail to obtain the supposed explanans for epistemic priority, necessity and the empirical significance of empirically underdetermined theoretical statements. Consequently, in these writings, Putnam also agrees with Quine that it is an error to regard the ability to draw a fixed dichotomy between analytic and synthetic statements as important for our understanding of the empirical justification of hypotheses. This endorsement of the mentioned doctrines reflects Putnam's commitment to two main methodological tenets that he shares with Quine, holism and the acknowledgement of the indefinite extent to which even deeply entrenched ("a priori") belief is revisable in generalized scientific terms under changes in empirical knowledge, which we could call "fallibilism" or "(indefinitely) general revisability". Both are customarily taken to undermine by themselves the analytic–synthetic distinction.

But, as I mentioned above, these agreements in doctrine do not issue in an agreement of the lessons, and it is in their positions vis-à-vis conventionalism that the differences take shape. While Quine concludes that drawing any kind of analytic–synthetic distinction within the body of our empirical knowledge is "folly,"[5] and that it "has been given *no* tolerably clear meaning *even as a methodological ideal*" (Quine 1956: 132, emphasis added) Putnam claims that drawing a successor distinction "is of logical and methodological significance" (Putnam 1962a: 249) and warns against the "danger of denying its existence altogether" (Putnam 1962: 33). At issue is the methodological significance of an *epistemic* analytic–synthetic distinction, i.e. the significance of an apriori–aposteriori distinction, *given* holism and general revisability.

Succinctly put, Quine's point is that, given confirmation holism, general revisability and a standard empiricist view of the relation between hypothesis and observation, there is and ought to be *no* epistemically significant analytic–synthetic distinction. Now, Quine's wholesale abandonment is often seen (and portrayed by Quine) as a radicalization of empiricism in reaction to the identification of analytic truths with *conventions* by empiricists that I just described. Methodologists as diverse as James, Lewis, Poincare, Carnap and Reichenbach welcomed conventionalism on empiricist grounds as a "demystified" (Friedman 1999: 64) reconstruction of the traditional notion of objective necessity: if statements are held true merely by convention and not held vulnerable to empirical (or other) evidence, then this reflects *our public agreement* to not at the same time hold them as possibly falsified by anything, and access to the set of necessities is just as easy to explain as the consequence of an *actual* and *public* act: we simply *choose* them or commit ourselves to them as fixed guiding principles (cf. Lewis 1923: 15–16). But according to Quine, precisely the empiricist outlook that produced conventionalism ought to prevent the acceptance of *any* empirically immunized assumptions.[6] On his apparently more radical, naturalized empiricism, our decision to *abandon* the search for epistemic analyticity altogether is the final missing move to license the conviction that "all statements are epistemologically on a par." On a par, that is, in being *empirical*.[7]

As I indicated before, Putnam also rejects conventionalism. Furthermore, the motivation for his rejection is the one just mentioned, viz. the view that scientists ought not to be construed as routinely making gratuitous empirically unfounded or immunized assumptions when they are in fact considering the empirical merits of alternative theoretical proposals. But Putnam does *not* claim that all statements are always and under all circumstances on a par. His point is rather that, given holism and general revisibility, confirmation does neither require nor allow, as Carnap suggests, a *general and precise*, but only a *contextual and unpredictable* (i.e. informal) distinction between epistemic priorities. According to Putnam, we ought to *reformulate* epistemic analyticity or apriority as a *contextual and empirically sensitive* notion. This defuses conventionalism in a different way. According to this view, what is an unquestioned guide in inference and epistemic evaluation ("convention") in one context can, without change in meanings or language, appear as a factual assumption in need of empirical support in another. Whether or not it appears as one or the other in a context is likewise a matter of empirically informed argument. Therefore, no acceptance or rejection of scientifically relevant statements or norms can expect to rationally convince without attending to a lot of available empirical information. While the meta-methodological argument just attributed to Quine tends to turn on a philosophical doctrine about how to be a better empiricist, this line of argument emphasizes the *pragmatics* of scientific justification and the normative expectations regarding the sort of reasons in these practices. Thus, Putnam and Quine indeed both reject conventionalism, but on markedly different reasons: Putnam's *pragmatic* rejection requires a flexible distinction of epistemic priorities to make sense, while Quine's *naturalism* claims to do without any. Why would Putnam not have it the simpler, Quinean way? I will suggest that one important reason why a Putnamian, as opposed to a Quinean, would find a successor distinction methodologically *important* (as opposed to merely feasible) is that forcing its abandonment on Quine's reasons requires accepting a thesis that makes a form of confirmation skepticism inescapable and thus results in the collapse of empirical sensitivity for our system of knowledge and belief. However, this would sacrifice precisely the worthiest motive for Quine's suggestion: that changes in empirical information have epistemic effects on the statements we accept, and that we ought not in advance select the points in our system of beliefs where these effects will be noted. Putnam's position can then be seen as an articulation of conditions on empirical belief fixation that avoids this collapse without fear of a successor distinction to the epistemic analytic–synthetic distinction. I will therefore concentrate on the differences between Quine and Putnam in this regard.

For the sake of reconstructing the rift between both philosophers, I will take the constraints of a possible position to be set by the doctrinal agreements reported so far.[8] Thus, avoiding the danger Putnam warns us of has to be

(a) compatible with the insights of a holistic and fallibilistic methodology (i.e. holds even the a priori parts of knowledge sensitive to changes in empirical information)[9] (Quine's lesson) *but* has to
(b) deliver a distinction (the point in dispute) that
(c) forms part of any successful account of the justificatory and epistemic practices of good scientists (Quine's point against imposing a distinction without a difference in practice), such that the result
(d) does not entail a collapse of empirical sensitivity (Quine's problem).

The following discussion will thus move on a mainly *methodological* level.[10] The question is whether the epistemic features of practices of theory-acceptance that endorse holism and general revisability allow or even require a successor distinction to the analytic–synthetic distinction. Framing the issue in this fashion engages the two positions at precisely the level at which Quine, far from simply brushing analyticity aside as old-fashioned positivism, came to see a question of vital importance for his own naturalistic agenda.[11] As he writes: "the philosophically important question about analyticity … is … relevance to epistemology," whereby the restatement of his position runs like this: "a need for analyticity as a key notion of epistemology … lapses when we heed Duhem" (Quine 1986a: 207). The following considerations thus also aim at clarifying some contrasts between naturalist and pragmatic methodologies.

My discussion will follow these steps. I first want to review what I take to be the central move in Quine's recommendation to abandon *any* analytic–synthetic distinction, semantic or epistemic, because of its methodological irrelevance. I will argue that this move rests on a contention that is independent of either holism or fallibilism but symptomatic for Quine's brand of empiricism, and which naturally issues in certain forms of skepticism (II). In the following section (III), I will present those parts of the methodological program that Putnam outlines in "The Analytic and the Synthetic" and subsequent writings that allow bypassing the impasse of Quine's wholesale repudiation of the analytic–synthetic distinction. The crucial idea of this program is to exploit the fact that in actual confirmation practice we evaluate the comparative inductive support for hypotheses on given evidence. Moreover, this inductive approach models what is given as evidence as not hypothetical at the same time as it is used for testing the hypothesis. Such a distinction between hypothetical and non-hypothetical elements in confirmation allows various contextual distinctions between epistemic statuses for parts of our knowledge that satisfy (a)–(d). The result will disallow any principled arguments against minimal degrees of revisability, ensure anti-skepticism, and it will better accommodate evidence that is left out of Quine's picture.

II. Quine's principled argument for rejecting of the distinction

The connection Quine wishes to draw between revisability and the epistemic analytic–synthetic distinction is expressed in the most succinct form in the most famous passage from Quine's "Two Dogmas," where he says:

> Any statement can be held true come what may, if we make drastic enough adjustments elsewhere in the system. ... Conversely, by the same token, no statement is immune to revision. ... A recalcitrant experience can ... be accommodated by any of various alternative reevaluations ... of the total system.
> (Quine 1951: 43–44)

This is surely one of the most puzzling, but also one of the most symptomatic passages in Quine's work. Putnam, for one, has called it at different times a "trenchant paragraph" (Putnam 1983b: 91) and seen it as shot through with "unintelligible" uses of "can" (Putnam 1994a: 256). It has been called the "holism argument" (Berger 2003: 373) and the "revisability passage" (Fodor/LePore 1992). In fact, this suggests two quite distinct roots of the claims, as we will see.

Of course, the passage does occur in the context of Quine's holistic account of the relation between experience and hypothesis that is analogous to points earlier discovered by Duhem. Holism regarding the empirically based acceptance of theories (confirmation holism, for short) arises on acceptance of *Duhem's thesis* that deriving observationally testable predictions from theoretical hypotheses requires taking for granted many additional assumptions from a system of belief, all of which and the hypothesis together imply what either agrees or conflicts with what we actually observe (cf. Duhem 1912: ch. VI, §2, esp. 185ff.). This is often expressed by saying that "no statement is tested in isolation,"[12] a thesis that both Putnam and Quine accept. In "Two Dogmas" Quine even exaggeratedly speaks of the "whole system of science" as the unit of empirical significance, a claim he later retracts. Once this thesis is accepted, one is also committed to the following *logical point*, which Duhem called the *"ambiguity of falsification"*: In the event of an unexpected experience, i.e. one that conflicts with a given prediction, the inference by *modus tollens* is to the falsity of what implied the mistaken prediction. It thus affects not only the hypothesis-statement, but the disjunction of the hypothesis itself along with everything else that contributed to the derivation of the prediction. The upshot of accepting confirmation holism is twofold: (1) the selection of any one involved statement over others for revision is compelled by neither logic nor observational evidence alone but requires an *additional judgment*, and (2) *all* involved statements are *logically* exposed to the threat of being revised on unexpected empirical evidence. That is, holism suggests that confirmation is *not judgment-free* and the *generalization of* empirically (as opposed to, say, skeptically or normatively) induced *revisability*. However, the claims in the quoted passage significantly exceed these generalities in suggesting that the judgments in question are empirically unconstrained or scientifically arbitrary. The quoted passage *does* wear a repudiation of *any* analytic–synthetic distinction on its sleeves. *If* its suggestion is an entailment of holism or the generalization of revisability, then, as so often claimed, the repudiation itself is likewise part of endorsing holism and revisability. But it is doubtful that this is so. For example, the judgments in question could be constrained by further empirical or scientific evidence, as much as many logical *candidates* for revision might be exempt from revision for reasons that are grounded in our overall empirical knowledge. In light of the fact that the thrust of this passage is key for Quine's assessment of the methodological relevance of the analytic–synthetic distinction, we therefore must take a closer look at its connections with holism and revisability. So far, we see that the passage, although sufficient for trivializing the distinction, is not a mere reiteration of trivial consequences of either holism or revisability, and that it is rather unclear what commitment it does in fact express.

Apart from having resisted ready allocation, the overt claims in the passage have immediately provoked obvious criticism. The familiar criticisms of this passage take issue with one of the two categorical claims the passage contains. From early on until late, commentators have found difficulty in making sense of the claim that "all statements are revisable" when it is applied to the logical truths that have to be in place to back up rules of valid deductive inference, because then it seems as if Quine were saying that we have a generally applicable argument of the form *modus tollens* (viz., Duhem's syllogism) that proves the invalidity of *modus tollens*.[13] Likewise from early on, other commentators have found difficulty in making sense of the claim that "all statements are immunizable" when it is applied to appropriately obtained perceptual statements,[14] or taken as a general rule of acceptance for theoretical statements in the empirical sciences.[15] Such critics have taken the passage to face us squarely with the question how some sciences could be so much as *empirical* at all if they were to work as the passage says.

This line is pressed further by another sort of criticism that sees Quine's allegedly empiricist outlook collapse under the pressure of combining both generalizations. Suppose literally everything is revisable, and therefore it is also revisable what follows from what. Then it is unclear how the occurrence of a certain experience can force us to choose either rejection of the experience or changing our web of belief, or at least to epistemically *do something* because we could always revise the rule of inference connecting the inconvenient experience with the hypotheses. By iterating this process on whatever rules we use to defuse the connecting rules, we would embark on an indefinite regress, thus displacing the point of contact between hypothesis and experience equally indefinitely.[16] Once we sever any systematic *mandatory* connections of experiences and the content of our web of belief in this way, we therefore undermine this web's *revisability* on account of experience because we subtract the very *responsivity* to experience required by revisability. This surely shows how everything could be immunizable (in virtue of the free revisability of inferential connections), but at the price of sacrificing experiential constraint on belief.[17] We seem forced to choose between either exempting some statements about connections among statements from revision (i.e. accepting some sort of analytic–synthetic distinction) or embracing skepticism about experiential constraint. The thrust of the passage even seems to have caught Quine himself somewhat off guard. While he initially tried to deflect criticism with the ironically innocent remark that his points were "trivial" and such epistemological quandaries more a defect in the eyes of the beholders,[18] much of his later writings are aimed at showing that the unwelcome consequences pointed at in the criticisms are mostly owed to excessively radical interpretations of his holism.

The latter shows that Quine acknowledges the effects of the passage to be of methodological moment. Accordingly, Quine later moderated his holism ("the whole system of science ... ") in order to shield certain privileged elements in empirical knowledge like observation sentences (Quine 1969: 89; 1981: 71; 1981a: 26; 1992: 7–8)[19] and logical truths (Quine 1991: 268; 1995: 53f) from its effects and to exclude irrelevant statements from its scope (Quine 1986b: 620; 1991: 269). In addition, Quine urges a distinction between a "legalistic" and a "practical" reading for such passages as the above (Quine 1991: 268;

1986b: 620f). Examples of the contrast are that, "legalistically," a scientist could *always* revise geometry and compensate for the reverberations, or "legalistically," scientists always are faced with an indefinitely large array of alternative accommodations even once all the evidence is in, or at least faced with alternatives that are empirically equivalent but incompatible. But "in practice," they respect a "maxim of minimum mutilation," which in fact weeds out a great number of far-out choices, and a number of other rules of thumb. The practical reading would factor this in to explain why not every unpredicted experiential input of some importance produces a dazzling number of equally well-motivated but mutually irreconcilable theories. Quine recommends the practical rather than the legalistic approach and claims that this would defuse most of the mentioned problems.

However, on second thought such maneuvering with holism changes disappointingly little of the methodological substance of this bold passage. Even after all the mentioned moderations, we still get the result that for any hypothesis and relevant set of auxiliaries with a given validly entailed (which relation is now shielded) testable consequence and any given observation (which is now shielded), there are always *legalistically admissible* adjustments of the auxiliaries that save the hypothesis (even though most of them are subsequently overruled as a matter of *practice*). The methodological substance of the passage is apparently located elsewhere than holism. An indication of this is that Quine doesn't declare the legalistic reading false (just "extreme"). This presumably means that it accounts accurately for the actually compelling *logical* and *empirical* constraints on (i.e. all the evidentially relevant parts of) scientific inference.

This impression is furthered when we examine the possible effects of these moderations. Quine argues on account of the ambiguity of falsification that the decision to revise or retain a statement that implies an unsuccessful prediction requires a judgment regarding the systems of belief that would result from various *admissible* ways of "inactivating the false implication" (Quine 1992: 16). Given an array of such possibilities, the "maxim of minimum mutilation" and kindred principles counsel to perform that revision which, all things considered (particularly, all *entailed consequences*), allows the retention of as many past beliefs as possible. But the point is not whether Quine can account for the factors in actual revision behavior, but what Quine has to say about the *prior* question of what makes any such way *eligible* or *admissible* as an "inactivation of a false implication." That alone gives us a clue to what Quine regards as "all the evidence being in" and therefore as evidentially *relevant*. Now, according to Quine's view, the maxim of minimum mutilation (and other principles of judgment) always operates on alternative modifications of the whole web of belief and selects the least disruptive from among them.[20] For this purpose, however, each of the individual modifications has to be an admissible *candidate* for acceptance on the evidence. It is here where the only constraints of generating eligible

153

alternative modifications that Quine accepts are the drawing out of entailed consequences according to the web-internal logical relations to produce predictions (this is the "empirical content" of the web), and to heed the available observational evidence. Therefore, any other candidate of acceptance is *epistemically equivalent* or equally evidentially admissible (no matter how implausible) if and only if it saves the phenomena and is consistent. Whatever else motivates the adoption of one of the candidates as better than others is an epistemically *optional* and *not further evidentially constrained* choice.[21] As to the evidentially relevant stakes of the choice, Quine's position is clear: "Inactivating the false implication is *all* that is at stake" (Quine 1992: 16, emphasis added).

The practical reading is thus *epistemologically inert*. It seems questionable whether Quine's moderation of holism plus pragmatic reading could so much as help defuse the epistemological problems revealed by the quoted passage. It is even less clear how Quine could be *entitled* to advantages of the practical reading such as the elimination of absurd empirically equivalent but incompatible alternative accommodations as – as he put it in the same passage – "intolerable." For, this judgment would require the ability to marshal good reasons ("evidence") against legalistically qualified candidates. But whatever *evidential* status a statement can acquire depends, as the legalistic reading has it, only on the logical and empirical constraints. It follows that whatever *epistemic entitlement* a scientist can claim for her practical decision is fully determined by whatever the legalistic reading gives us. The choices that enable us to disqualify given candidates thus go *beyond* what is evidentially covered. That is, they are, epistemologically speaking, quite arbitrary because (as opposed to the logically worked-out accommodations) they can*not* be motivated by the admissible empirical evidence since the latter is already exhausted by generating the candidates. But this leaves the defense of the claim that a given candidate is "toler*able*" without evidentially relevant resources. And that is exactly the root of the problems the various critics noted. We are thus back to where the critics took off.

Let me take stock: I have argued that the quoted passage is a powerful expression of a basic commitment of Quine's methodology, the logical force of which is not significantly diminished by later modifications of his holism. The point of my argument was that it is not holism, but only holism together with whatever methodological substance is expressed in the passage that produces its claims of revisability and immunizability. I now want to further separate holism from the passage's role in Quine's methodology by spelling out how it functions in the wholesale repudiation of the analytic–synthetic distinction. Insofar as the passage (and the wholesale repudiation) is independent of holism, we then need to clarify what additional substantive commitments enable Quine's repudiation. The rift between a (naturalist) Quinean and a (pragmatic) Putnamian methodology is owed to disagreements in these commitments.

I said before that the thrust of the quoted passage is key for the successful defense of Quine's wholesale rejection of the analytic–synthetic distinction. Let me explain why. This requires shifting attention to the claim that if any statement can be immunized then, *by the same token*, it can be revised. Quine suggests, and has frequently been understood to have successfully argued, that the uselessness and futility of any analytic–synthetic distinction is a consequence of confirmation holism. Representatively, he claims that "methodological monism follows closely on ... holism. Holism blurs the supposed contrast between the synthetic sentence, with its empirical content, and the analytic sentence, with its null content" (Quine 1981: 71). Now, it is indeed obvious how the specific proposal to explicate epistemic priorities in scientific reasoning à la Ayer on the model of analyticity as "null content" or "linguistic convention" crumbles under Duhemian holism. But the further step to "methodological monism" is far less obvious. As illustrated in the case of Carnap, who endorsed Duhemian holism *and* the analytic–synthetic distinction (and, contrary to certain critics (Coffa 1991: 352) was coherent in doing so (cf. Friedman 1999, Isaacson 1992)), or in the case of Putnam, who rejects Carnap's specific proposal but defends a reformed notion of apriority within a holistic methodology, the acceptance of Duhemian holism is not sufficient to force abandoning any methodological a priori–a posteriori distinction as senseless. When Quine speaks of "blurring the distinction" and "methodological monism," however, he has in mind more than the parochial point of having refuted a certain conception of analyticity as inoperative. What Quine is customarily taken to have accomplished with regard to the analytic–synthetic distinction is to have laid one of the foundations for naturalism, namely having shown that "all statements in science are epistemologically on a par," *for all conceptions of epistemic priority worth the name*.[22] It is this more general feat – which is at work in Quine's own view about what can count as established for the purpose of naturalizing epistemology (Quine 1969: 1981: 71–72) – that requires another commitment over and above holism. And the passage quoted from "Two Dogmas" supplies the crucial step for this more general purpose. In my opinion, it is the suggestion that the methodological terms "held true come what may" and "be revised" always apply under the same conditions that forms the backbone of the attempt of what Quine calls "blurring the distinction" (Quine:1981, 71), displaying it as useless in methodology, unintelligible or "folly."[23] To appreciate this, it suffices to distinguish between *criticizing* the analytic–synthetic distinction and certain (or even many) of its theoretical (ab-)uses, on the one hand, and *demonstrating its futility*, on the other. Obviously, the latter project requires a much more stringent argument than the former. My argument is then this: (a) the principled repudiation of the analytic–synthetic distinction is a cornerstone of Quine's "naturalized epistemology," which makes the establishment of the repudiation mandatory for him. (b) Quine does have such a more stringent argument for repudiating the analytic–synthetic distinction, but (c) it seriously undermines empiricism.[24]

The quoted passage culminates in Quine's discussion of the tenability of the distinction between statements that hold "contingent on experience" and the analytic (i.e. a priori) ones that "hold come what may." It says that, whenever it is legitimate to take a statement true come what may on the occasion of an unexpected experience, it is legitimate *without a change in evidence* ("by the same token") to hold that same statement to be revised by that experience, if only one is prepared to pay the price by making consistency-preserving adjustments in the system. This is precisely what I called Quine's *symmetry-thesis* above.

The role of the symmetry-thesis in Quine's rejection of the methodological relevance of an epistemic analytic–synthetic distinction is in fact quite plain. It is clear that it is able to undermine the idea that any such distinction would make methodological sense, because according to the symmetry-thesis, a statement in our knowledge is revisable in a context by a given experience under precisely the same conditions as those under which it is immunizable against that same experience. If this is generally the case, then there is a *guarantee* that, as Richard Creath aptly puts it, "anything can always turn out to be analytic under the criterion" (Creath 2004: 52). Therefore, unfolding a distinction on the basis of these properties on an empirically contentful system of statements *cannot* yield any significant or stable result. The symmetry thesis *excludes* that any proposed epistemic analytic–synthetic distinction could mark out a difference and thus offers a *principled* argument against the analytic–synthetic distinction. No less than this fact – however established – supports the contention that drawing a distinction among statements between those that are more and others that are less vulnerable to revision *cannot* serve any methodological purpose. After all, if there were, in some case, *evidence* to the effect that a certain statement is, given the circumstances, more revisable than any others in a given Duhemian implier, then, in this case, it would be false that this statement under these circumstances could be declared *just as well*, i.e. *without change in evidence*, as immunizable. So: Quine is only entitled to think that the methodological irrelevance of an epistemic analytic–synthetic distinction is established *if* the symmetry-thesis is true. The next question is *whether* the symmetry-thesis is *true*, and what support it has.

To judge whether the symmetry thesis holds, we need to make the conditions more precise under which it would be true. Quine suggests that the quoted passage and the abandonment of a methodologically relevant epistemic analytic–synthetic distinction owe their force to, as he put it, "heeding Duhem." We already saw that the repudiation only follows from holism plus the symmetry-thesis. But perhaps holism suffices as a condition under which the symmetry-thesis is true.

The symmetry of revisability and immunizability for any statement on the occasion of any unexpected experience obtains, in terms of Duhemian holism, if, in a given case, for any revising of a hypothesis in response to a given experience, there is an alternative adjustment of our system of belief that saves the same hypothesis from revision. In particular, this requires that for a set of auxiliaries and hypothesis that accommodates a given unexpected experience, there is a consistent alternative set of auxiliaries such that the denial of the same hypothesis together with them accommodates the same unexpected experience *and* that there is *no further evidence* such that either set is better supported by it than the other. It is only under these conditions that there are no evidentially relevant reasons to decide whether to revise or immunize a given hypothesis on the occasion of a conflict between experience and our system of belief and that there is an equal entitlement to consider the hypothesis as either revisable or immunizable relative to the experience in such a case. This is what the symmetry-thesis requires.

Now, Duhem's logical point shows indeed that it is possible for such circumstances to obtain. Duhemian holism entails that, since no hypothesis entails testable consequences without auxiliaries, there will always be more than one logical possibility of avoiding a mistaken prediction, and that there is always a logically suitable adjustment of auxiliaries that can save a theory from revision and accommodate the same experience. Of course, this by no means shows that all such logically suitable adjustments are in fact *equally scientifically acceptable*. But the mere logical possibility of empirically equivalent adjustments to save a hypothesis is not quite what the symmetry-thesis needs. The symmetry-thesis requires not only that such adjustments be *possible*, so that there might still be an arbitrarily high number of cases where we have only adjustments of the same experience that are evidentially distinguishable from one another. We just saw that such cases need to be excluded if the symmetry-thesis is to be true. The symmetry-thesis requires strictly that it be *inevitably the case* that, whenever there is a set of hypothesis and auxiliaries that entails a mistaken prediction, (1) there is a set of suitable auxiliaries such that the hypothesis can be saved from refutation and accommodate the same experience, and (2) the adjustment of auxiliaries required for saving the hypothesis from refutation and the set of the revised hypothesis and the unadjusted auxiliaries are, when empirically equivalent in the sense of accommodating the same experience, evidentially not further distinguishable. This is a much more stringent qualification of the required evidence than Duhemian holism as such warrants. It implies that all the auxiliaries used in some given case are equally hypothetical and sacrificeable, and requires that whenever two adjustments accommodate the same experience, they are evidentially indistinguishable. If and only if this is the case are all adjustments of our system of beliefs to a given experience equally available and equally scientifically acceptable. Now, we can only take (1) and (2) to hold guaranteed if, holding the experiential statements fixed, and considering only systems of statements that *logically entail them*, we regard all of these systems as (equally) supported by experience.

Let me summarize this by saying that the symmetry-thesis only follows from Duhemian holism if it is *granted* that entailed testable consequences and logical relations among hypotheses, auxiliaries and experiential data exhaust the range of evidentially relevant considerations. For the symmetry-thesis to hold we have to identify empirical equivalence and epistemic indistinguishability. The uncontroversial point Quine seems to appeal to is the *non-uniqueness* of the results of evidential evaluation that follows from Duhemian holism because, given the variety of adjustments allowed by it on unexpected observations, our judgment between adjustments is not determined by logic or the empirical consequences of the statements in the implier (both of which are the same for all candidate revisions) (Fodor/Lepore 1992: 216). But non-uniqueness under empirical equivalence does not imply evidential indistinguishability. What Quine's actual argument *must rely on* is the far more controversial point that *there are no other evidentially serious constraints to be met*. This is the substantive commitment behind the symmetry-thesis, and as such it needs to be supported if the repudiation is to be compelling. I now turn to this question.

In fact, Quine's brand of empiricism never ceased to be, methodologically speaking and with regard to his conception of what it is to be evidentially compelling, thoroughly hypothetico-deductivist. As an empiricist, he says "whatever evidence there *is* for science *is* sensory evidence" (Quine 1969: 75), and regarding how this evidence has to relate to our hypotheses in order to confirm or disconfirm them, he says that the scientific method is the hypothetico-deductive method and little else (Quine 1981: 72; Quine 1981a: 28; see also Quine 1960: §5-6). This issues an *independent* substantive view of what *in principle and in general* is evidentially relevant (and therefore *rationally* responsible for scientific acceptability). It gives us the root commitments from which Quine can actually obtain the symmetry-thesis. Thus, it is here where Quine's repudiation of the methodological relevance of an epistemic analytic–synthetic distinction and his very own substantive commitments (as opposed to Duhem's merely logical point) coalesce and align:[25] to guarantee the methodological inertness of any epistemic analytic–synthetic distinction, the symmetry thesis has to be true, which in turn only is the case if there are no evidentially decidable differences between empirically equivalent accommodations of the same experience, which in turn is only secured by the identification of empirical equivalence and epistemic indistinguishability. The latter, however, is only supported by a commitment to the conception of scientific or epistemic justification that Quine inherits from logical positivism.[26]

The symmetry-thesis thus has deep roots in Quine's methodology. A look at some of the consequences of accepting it illustrates what dangers Putnam warned us of. I just construed the identification of empirical equivalence and epistemic indistinguishability as indispensable support for the symmetry-thesis, but it is also required for Quine's wholesale repudiation of the methodological relevance of an analytic–synthetic distinction. As is well known, when combined with Duhemian holism, this identification simultaneously leads to the underdetermination-thesis (UD). For, any accommodation of an unexpected experience that "saves the phenomena" is, evidentially speaking, as good as any other in virtue of the identification of empirical equivalence and epistemic indistinguishability. In virtue of the ambiguity of falsification resulting from Duhem's thesis, this is so even for cases in which one of the accommodations contains a hypothesis and the other its contrary. Combining both, we get the idea that conflicts with experience open the specter of mutually incompatible, evidentially indistinguishable theories. Because the symmetry-thesis (and its preconditions) occurs in Quine's methodology in a holist setting, it exposes his account to some well-known consequences that any position entailing UD has to face. They form a nested system of increasingly confirmation-skeptical positions.

Excessive epistemic egalitarianism[27]

UD invites us to think that, whenever there is an unexpected experience and a hypothesis we would revise, then there is an evidentially indistinguishable readjustment of our system of beliefs such that we can hold the hypothesis in question true and accommodate the same experience. However, the exclusion of other evidentially relevant considerations for breaking the tie makes it irresistible to continue to the next step by saying that, if any statement may be held true come what may, any statement may also be held true come this or that experience. If, *by the same token*, no statement is immune to revision, then *any* statement held true could be held false, come this or that experience (Laudan 1990: 328). This entails that everything confirms everything *if* "confirmation" is explicated via the hypothetico-deductive method. Quine's view of revisability expressed in the quoted passage thus ultimately seems to collapse into the skeptical "egalitarian thesis" that "every theory is as well supported by the evidence as any of its rivals."[28] Repudiating the methodological relevance of the analytic–synthetic distinction in a principled way thus seems to come at the cost of no longer being able to explain how even deeply entrenched or highly abstract theoretical beliefs can become subject to ordinary empirical (evidence-driven) evaluation and possibly *rationally* revised on the strength of changes in empirical information.

General reversibility of epistemic assessment[29]

The problem pointed at in the egalitarian thesis is that it is unclear how a genuine determinate epistemic warrant for any hypothesis can *exist*. This worry gets exacerbated when we ask how any result in confirmation can actually count as a cognitive entitlement, even supposing some such epistemic relation had been selected somehow. For, suppose we are guaranteed, via the combination of Duhemian holism and the identification of empirical equivalence and evidential indistinguishability for every hypothesis, that there is a consistent accommodation with an adjustment of auxiliaries that entails the contrary of the hypothesis and the same experience. Suppose further that acquiring a rational entitlement for adopting a belief epistemically requires, among other things, exhausting all the available evidence. Then a guarantee of evidentially indistinguishable replacements presumably means that we are equally entitled to each of the two accommodations. Since the argument is perfectly general, the evidence supporting whatever choice we initially make always brings us simultaneously into the possession of an undefeated defeater of the very hypothesis we choose (viz., that same evidence, but used to support the – evidentially indistinguishable – contrary of the hypothesis). The repudiation of the methodological relevance of an epistemic analytic–synthetic distinction thus ultimately disqualifies the acquisition of our empirical entitlements as an essentially self-undermining procedure.

Loss of content[30]

The grounds of Quine's rejection of the distinction ultimately issue in a thesis that is equivalent to the quoted passage, namely that, for all statements we accept on the strength of some experience in some context, we can specify a context in which, given the same experience, this statement is false. But it is by no means clear that we should always have *actual* alternative auxiliaries. It is, for example, much more likely that suspending or denying some auxiliaries like conservation laws regarding energy – which are involved in the planning of many experiments and the derivation of testable predictions from many hypotheses – without supplying adequate replacements disables the derivation of *any* empirical consequences from the hypotheses. However, for all that, nothing in the assumptions undergirding the symmetry thesis prevents setting them as false if only the phenomena are saved. According to the position forced by Quine's symmetry-thesis, we ought to accept the system with the denied conservation principle and the *then* empirically inconsequential hypotheses in question nonetheless as evidentially indistinguishable from those that are actually plausible whenever the conservation principle was part of the Duhemian implier. So, according to Quine, we are generally epistemically entitled to believe that a hypothesis we are testing might at the same time not actually have any specifiable empirical consequences. Of course, lacking empirical consequences because of the defunct indispensable auxiliary, the hypothesis would automatically be immune to revision. We have Quine's desired result, that any hypothesis is revisable iff immunizable. However, when all our hypotheses turn out to only optionally have empirical content and to be immune against any experience in particular, Quine's greatest insight, that revision *on the strength of experience* can strike anywhere and *oblige us* to change our belief somewhere, seems out of reach.

Let me sum up. Quine's principled argument against the methodological relevance of an epistemic analytic–synthetic distinction depends on the symmetry-thesis. Insofar as it does, it does constitute a powerful argument against conventionalism of the Carnapian sort by enabling the overextension-threat. Only given this can Quine suggest that the analytic–synthetic distinction is an independent and spurious addition to Duhemian holism, and that dropping it helps putting conventionalizing pet theories under empirical control, at no extra cost. But the costs of generating the overextension-threat for this argument are in fact quite high, and it also doesn't get at the root of the problem that Quine identifies with conventions (their blocking *empirical* belief-fixation). As Quine leaves intact the combination of the identification of empirical equivalence with evidential indistinguishability with Duhemian holism that characterized much of the logical empiricist conception of evidence and confirmation, his account allows mounting a global underdetermination thesis. This is doubly unfortunate. First, using UD enables privileging some non-revisions over others by *fiat* only, i.e. makes merely positing assertions as true easy. So, Quine's approach cannot undercut conventionalism as radically as talk of naturalism as a "radicalized empiricism" would make us expect. Second, UD inevitably fosters the suspicion that intuitively empirical claims only appear to be sensitive to experience while in fact they cannot be. This is a skeptical result regarding external constraints on rational belief-fixation. I think that both of these reasons play a role in Putnam's resistance to Quinean wholesale repudiations of the distinction.

We saw already that the case is not hopeless. On the one hand, the symmetry-thesis depends not on holism or the acknowledgement of general revisability, but on particular methodological views about what counts as evidence, support and confirmation. They are not without alternatives. On the other hand, we saw that holism does not exclude a contextual analytic–synthetic distinction. So, there is logical space for explicating how holism and a more natural distinction between epistemic priorities conspire to explain epistemic contact between belief and experience. Putnam's view occupies this open methodological space.

III. The methodological significance of a contextual distinction

Putnam's criticism of the attempt to combine empiricism and conventionalism pivots on the following principle of *general revisability*: "any principle in our knowledge can be revised for theoretical reasons" (Putnam 1962: 48). It is hedged by the caveat that "many principles resist refutation by isolated experimentation" (Putnam 1962: 48). How central this caveat is in Putnam's conception becomes patent in the following passage from his "The Analytic and the Synthetic":

> I want to suggest that before the work of nineteenth-century mathematicians, the principles of Euclidean geometry ... had the

following status: no experiment that one could describe could possibly overthrow them, by itself. ... the position was rather different, as physicists soon realized: give us a rival conceptual system, and some reason for accepting it, and we will consider abandoning the laws of Euclidean geometry. ... I mean to group them ... with many other principles: the law "$f = ma$" ... , the principle that the world did not come into existence five minutes ago, the principle that one cannot know certain kinds of facts ... unless one has or has had evidence. These principles play different roles; but in one respect they are alike: They share the characteristic that no isolated experiment ... can overthrow them.

(Putnam 1962: 48)

Putnam adds that the revision of principles with this characteristic is "(a) possible ... but (b) quite a different matter from the revision of an ordinary empirical generalization" (ibid.). To appreciate the full significance of these passages, it is important to attend to three features of Putnam's methodological outlook on the experimental sciences: first, his interactivist view of cognitive contact with the environment, second, his view of theoretical assertions as delivering genuine and irreducible empirical information that can issue fully empirical reasons, and third, his induction-based approach to confirmation, testability and empirical evaluation.

First, in his criticism of the Carnapian analytic–synthetic distinction Putnam importantly speaks always of "experimental results" and similarly large units of empirical significance as the sources of empirical content and evidence, as opposed to Carnap and Quine, who both base empirical appraisal and content on the presence of certain protocol or observation sentences. For Putnam's view it is constitutive that we never deal with single sentences even in the realm of empirical evidence. In consequence, if there is any empirical evidence at all, then certain sets of beliefs that formally are indistinguishable from Duhemian wholes, like reports on experiments, are *correctly* counted as giving *contextually definite results*. While ascertaining empirical results always involves judgments in some sense and is a contrastive affair, such wholes often quite simply reach through to judgments of truth.[31] For Putnam, that is one part of what it means that a body of knowledge is subject to empirical testing: that empirical assertions that are, logically speaking, the conclusions of arguments that conform to Duhemian holism can, ought to, and often do serve as fixed evidence points or *data* for the epistemic assessment of other ("theoretical") statements (Putnam 1965: 88). It is therefore also part of what it means that a body of knowledge is empirically testable that *not all Duhemian wholes are radically underdetermined*. For Putnam, this is a fact about the use of evidence, so that any view that entails a global underdetermination thesis for *all* Duhemian impliers is false of actual empirical science. This rejection of wholesale underdetermination-claims signals, of course, the decidedly anti-instrumentalist conceptions of theoretical statements, as well as of the theory/observation distinction that frames Putnam's own holistic and fallibilistic methodological reflections.[32] But what I am interested in here is the less often observed methodological repercussions of such a rejection of wholesale underdetermination. Putnam regards the relevant difference in epistemic status between data-assertions and others not as the result of the *function* that experimental results are given by competent researchers in *contexts of assessment* (as opposed to a supposed principled difference grounded on, say, epistemic properties, semantic rules, or regularities in acceptance behavior). The key to Putnam's success in *recognizing empirical data as given constraints* while "heeding Duhem" is his repudiation of any a-contextual, general distinctions among empirical statements as to their vulnerability to incoming experience. The same statement can, under relevant changes in context, appear as a testable and tested assumption even though it was correctly used as an evidence-datum before. By itself, Putnam's rejection of wholesale underdetermination thus does not directly commit him to any of the distinctions Quine suggests we should abandon, or beg any of the questions presently at issue.

Second, Putnam is committed (as is Quine) to what Bennett (1971) calls "knowledge empiricism."[33] Knowledge empiricism in the liberal sense here intended demands that whatever status an extra-logical statement may enjoy at a given time, its acceptance or revision cannot be warranted independently of *all* experience, but must involve reference to some experience (Putnam 1962a: 248). So, when Putnam qualifies the revision of the principles in question as being a revision "for theoretical reasons," this is to be regarded as being a revision "for empirical reasons" in spite of not being a refutation by experimental *data*. Settling the truth values of these principles crucially involves reasoning from statements, theories and inferential rules that themselves, as a whole, enjoy empirical support. Putnam's reference to "theoretical reasons" is quite consequential in that it expands the scope of available evidence beyond the observational entailments of a hypothesis on the occasion of a given test, by admitting the independent support that theoretical auxiliary statements involved in such arguments have acquired on other occasions.

Third, the empirical assessment of theoretical principles has, according to this passage, not the form of a hypothetico-deductive argument but that of an inductive, comparative judgment of the relative support enjoyed by one of at least two "rival systems" on the strength of the available evidence. Experimental data are one important factor in determining which of the two theories is better supported by the evidence, but not necessarily the only one. Such judgments are *essentially* non-monotonic and context-dependent, i.e., not determined by deductive relations among the statements related as evidence and hypothesis alone, and sensitive to changes in the alternatives as much as in the sort of empirical data. Although these two features cast a shadow on the identification of empirical equivalence and evidential indistinguishability and thus are indirectly relevant for evaluating the reasons for the rejection of the distinction, the fact that the judgments are contrastive is methodologically directly relevant. It means that, when two theories are compared as to the empirical support lent to each by *the same or shared* empirical evidence, not all involved statements can be equally revisable in this context. In order for there to *be a comparison*, at least the shared evidence has to remain invariant when other statements are up for grabs. As invariant for the purpose, these statements are thus less revisable in this context than those of the theory.

Putnam's conception of the peculiarities of the epistemic status for the framework statements is roughly this. In light of the general outlook along these three commitments, the confirmation and revision of the principles is not experimentally determined (because they are not capable of direct experimental test), but it is not therefore empirically unconstrained. But it is important to note what special roles the principles play for inquiry. For example, Putnam explains, they are "employed as auxiliaries to make predictions in an overwhelming number of experiments, without themselves being jeopardized by any possible experimental results" (Putnam 1962: 48). That is, they are *recurrent* parts of many Duhemian impliers, in all of which they do not count as good candidates for revision but are rather taken for granted or *counted among what is given* in a confirmation argument: "one is not expected to give much of a reason for" them (Putnam 1962a: 240). As a first approximation, we can say that we are, at a given stage of inquiry, not *normally* required to give any further support for assuming and not revising the statement. Instead, Putnam says, "holding them immune from revision [is] good methodology" (Putnam 1965: 92) so that their special status is that of not being seen *de facto* as rationally revisable at a certain stage of inquiry. Clearly, this status is a feature not of the statement, nor of its empirical consequences, but of the context and the way in which it is used that can, under the changed conditions of a later stage of investigation, become capable of being revised (and known to be false) on the strength of empirical evidence available then.

With regard to justification, the "special status" thus cannot be that of classical apriority. For, if it is a traditional sense of a priori justification that it is justification by reasoning from principles the acceptance of which does not require any empirical information, then the framework principles Putnam talks about cannot be traditionally a priori. Their revision is supposed to be neither experimental nor non-empirical,[34] that is: not purely a priori, but also not analytic, if the latter is understood as "factually vacuous."

In my view, the most fruitful way of explicating Putnam's remarks about statements with this status is to embed them in a pragmatic or "default" conception of epistemic entitlement combined with a "defence commitment" (Williams 2001: 25) on the part of their users in this way: (a) as long as someone who *requires* a justification fails to produce credible circumstances that offer a counterexample to the statement, we are *normally* entitled to take it for granted without *further* empirical justification (Harman 2003: 23–34). (b) Putnam's claim that "holding [the principles] immune from revision [is] good methodology" (Putnam 1965: 92) means that as long as we are entitled to take something for granted without further empirical justification, the presumption is that *there are no good reasons against it*. Statements satisfying (a) and (b) are *not hypothetical in a context*.

Putnam's conception of evidence and confirmation combined with this view of epistemic entitlement has the consequence that there are statements that we are normally entitled to hold true without previous experimental test or further experimental reasons and which it is, under the given circumstances, *irrational to give up* without adequate replacement. Combined with the contextual nature of the status, the special status of the principles is then that we are entitled and required to use them in the relevant contexts of confirmation without further empirical reasons unless *special conditions* obtain where this ceases to be the case. A somewhat surprising but welcome effect of the position developed so far is that the possibility for such statements is a consequence of the principle of general revisability when the latter is embedded in the same conception of epistemic entitlement. For, if a statement in our knowledge can be revised for at least theoretical reasons and if we are entitled to hold true principles in our knowledge unless there are available theoretical principles against it, then there can be principles in our knowledge that we are entitled to hold because we do *not* have *any* theoretical reasons against them. That is the case when certain principles are needed as auxiliaries in a wide array of Duhemian impliers and we do not possess adequate replacements for them. Let me refer to statements for which we possess (or could adduce) support by past evidence and for which we do not need to give further evidence to be justified in employing them as auxiliaries in Duhemian impliers as *non-hypothetical*.

We now face two questions. On the one hand, why are such statements not just another version of the conventionalist's arbitrary stipulative exemptions from empirical revision? On the other hand, precisely insofar as they are not, why are they not just *plain revisable statements* like all others? Why regard "non-hypothetical" as epistemologically exciting if they remain revisable in some context? The induction-based outlook described above gets explanatory bite right here, because the answer requires attention to the *relative* support enjoyed by certain contrasting statements in *given* situations.

That certain statements in Duhemian impliers are less hypothetical than others is actually not uncommon, and in relatively few cases does this have anything to do with conventions. It is, for example, a feature of statements that we take for granted as auxiliaries in a particular context of confirmation, but which are independently testable (say, assumptions about the reliability of a thermometer under certain conditions). Intuitively, when such statements are challenged and independently tested, the resulting support in case of a positive result of the test makes them less revisable than the other auxiliaries in the same context that are similar in initial credibility but merely taken for granted without additional test. So, independently testable auxiliaries can indeed be non-arbitrarily epistemically privileged members of Duhemian impliers. However, since they acquire this status in virtue of *being tested* and therefore not "without further empirical investigation," they can only be contextually *non-hypothetical* but not even contextually *a priori*. But it is important to recognize that testables independently have this status. For this *already* shows that Duhemian impliers do not simply comprise equally contextually hypothetical statements, and also that the empirical import of a Duhemian implier does not simply consist in the observational entailments in a particular situation. Independent tests offer an *unimplied source of support and evidence*. We have driven the first wedge between empirical equivalence and evidential indistinguishability by specifying parts of the evidence that are available in a given context but not encoded in the particular Duhemian implier as such.

Now consider the case of recurrent statements – like fundamental statements of physical geometry or conservation laws, or similar high-level theoretical principles. Suppose we took such a statement – say, a conservation law – for granted as an auxiliary in an experiment that tests some theory by displaying scatters of particles on a screen, and that the experiment showed an unexpected result. Then the special status of a statement like the conservation principle can be illuminated in terms of Duhemian holism in three directions: (a) vis-à-vis the theoretical statements under scrutiny (our hypothesis), (b), vis-à-vis independently testable auxiliaries, and (c) vis-à-vis the testability-conditions for hypotheses.

(a) Duhemian holism exposes the auxiliary statement, our law of conservation, to possible revision. This might seem to suggest that, in spite of its apparent epistemic priority, there could be experimental reasons for doubting this statement just if there are such for doubting the hypothesis and all the other statements involved in deriving the prediction. However, this does not work. Suppose, for example, that we deny the conservation law and in this way no longer derive the prediction about our particle scatter that conflicted with the observation. But the reason for this is that we can no longer predict *any* reaction of the screen *rather than another* on the basis of our hypothesis and the remainder of auxiliaries. Moreover, the same crumbling of determinate empirical consequences happens in most *other* cases where the conservation law plays a role in prediction. In this sense, we actually would not have specified any *empirical* context of which the conservation law is clearly false. Moreover, once suspended, the absence of the conservation principle will likewise block the derivations of many other empirical consequences in past cases that were not actually at issue. Therefore, we can take our lack of relevant empirical evidence for each of the simultaneous failures of prediction that we would produce by suspending the conservation principle as empirical information capable of preventing its revision. Of course, there is an appearance of circularity here, since the empirical information on which we rest our retention of the conservation principle is partly dependent on that same principle's application. But the considerations at issue are in an important sense *contrastive* and therefore not exhausted by a simple reinstatement of the conservation principle. The retention of the principle does not merely "rest on" its successful applications, but also on the fact that the alternative is an empirically entirely unmotivated and inexplicable wholesale loss of large stretches of empirical information and support in unrelated cases, which is equivalent to assuming a miracle (viz., that a failed experiment can remove conservation). If the alternative were more empirically palatable, so many successful applications of the principle might not be able to save it *even if its success in predicting the cases remains constant*. Its privilege is thus *not merely conventional* and not simply by "default."[35] Rather, the unproblematic status it has as a default can – in case anyone were to propose sacrificing the principle – be itself defended as a result of assessing empirical information we possess, even though not of any particular experimental result.[36]

(b) But – in contrast to the independently testable hypotheses considered before – it also does not seem quite right to take the auxiliary as more *supported* than before by such considerations. It is correct, of course, that we did not turn up any experimental evidence against holding the conservation law. But the alternatives in which the conservation law was considered as false (and presumably "found true" via *reductio*-arguments) were not seriously considered by us as other *empirically specified* contexts. We just found that they were not such in the first place. Therefore, they are also not contexts in which *any* empirical support could accrue, positive or negative. So it is not the case that the fact of lacking evidence against the conservation law *independently* contributes to the *support* of the statement. Conversely, in virtue of the absence of an adequate set of empirically specifiable contexts for its empirical re-evaluation, it is also not properly regarded as just one more *plain revisable statement* because we *can* have no theoretical or experimental reasons against it. We can thus explain how some statements that are members of Duhemian impliers in the context of confirming particular hypotheses at a given stage of inquiry can be relatively non-hypothetical while their acceptance is not contingent on further empirical evidence, or a priori. The contextual status they have is due to a significant, albeit quite un-empiricist and non-physicalist (i.e. neither logical nor observational), collection of facts, viz. the historical and social facts that make up a situation of which it is true that there actually are no adequate alternatives to a given statement in the field, and no empirical counter-examples available.[37] I think this fairly captures an intuitive, generic notion of contextual apriority.

(c) The impression that such a methodologically motivated notion of contextual apriority is even *positively suggested* by Duhem's thesis acquires more force when we add another consideration about confirmation practice, the fact that in most cases, theoretical hypotheses are not tested by exposing them to refutation, but by weighing the support they gather by given observations *relative to salient competitors*. Thus, what a given observation actually tests is an *array* of related theoretical hypotheses, and what we want to find out is which of these is *most supported* by the evidence. The most obvious case for this are estimated quantitative predictions like "given experiment E and the mutually exclusive theoretical hypotheses T1 and T2, the quantity Q will either (case 1) be between n and m, or (case 2) between k and l, or (case 3) between j and i; case 1 will support T1, case 2 be neutral, and case 3 support T2." According to Duhem's thesis, each of the theories, T1 and T2, require auxiliaries to predict any values of Q, given E. Now, given the problem, E is a means of determining the value of Q. Therefore, no matter which of our hypotheses we take E to test, we will have to use that *common* set A which (together with, respectively, T1 and T2) allows predicting values of Q given E. In our example, the value of Q confirms T1& a iff it conflicts with the prediction from T2& a and vice versa, such that there would always *seem* to be a possibility to revise A, *if it weren't that the evidence for doing so entails* A. No matter whether T1 or T2 turn out true or false, A is needed for supplying the evidence in *any* of the possible outcomes. A is thus *invariant* under the outcomes of the test; therefore, it is *not* tested when any of the alternative theoretical hypotheses are. Wherever we regard testing in this way as an essentially *contrastive* affair, then there are, *precisely for Duhemian reasons*, always some shared background auxiliaries that enable the shared evidence for any of the considered outcomes.[38]

The methodological cash value of these reflections is that principles that we don't have theoretical reasons to regard as actually revisable in this way become *part of the evidence* brought to bear on the assessment of hypotheses, even though they are, by nature, theoretical principles and as such in a formal sense "revisable" because they appear, as auxiliaries, in a Duhemian implier. But, for all that, they are *neither hypothetical* in the relevant contexts *nor* justified in the context of their use on the strength of independent confirmation. This is what justifies calling them "a priori." Since they can become part of the *undisputed* evidence only in this status, their possessing this status is evidentially relevant. Drawing an a priori–a posteriori distinction in a context in this sense and finding statements with this status thus *affects the available evidence* and failing to draw it *changes the available evidence* by misrepresenting non-hypothetical elements from the auxiliaries as hypothetical and thus not part of the evidence.

The lesson from this is that the *evidence* for or against a statement is constrained but not determined by the formal relations between the hypothesis and its entailed empirical consequences. An actual determination of what the relevant evidence in a case is can only come from factoring in and prudently judging doxastic and non-doxastic contextual information. Clearly, such differences in revisability-conditions within Duhemian impliers crucially depend on non-arbitrary doxastic and non-doxastic features of our epistemic situation[39] and the contexts in which statements are used, both of which are not in our hands and open-ended. In light of this, adjustments of our system of belief that accommodate a given unexpected experience and retain a given hypothetical statement at the cost of violating either independently testable or contextually a priori parts of the relevant Duhemian implier are *evidentially distinguishable* in the relevant contexts from adjustments that accommodate the same experience but consider the hypothetical statements as revised. The fact that two adjustments are empirically equivalent is thus not generally sufficient for their evidential indistinguishability because in actual fact, auxiliaries as such most of the time carry information about their previous confirmation and contexts of their further employment with them into Duhemian impliers.[40] Thus, when unexpected results occur, revision does not strike indiscriminately. As this undercuts the symmetry-thesis, no general UD-threat follows.

Recall that Quine's principled argument against the methodological relevance of any epistemic analytic–synthetic distinction ultimately rested on the identification of empirical equivalence and evidential indistinguishability. Giving it up has the cost of sacrificing the symmetry-thesis and Quine's principled argument. But the methodologically relevant a priori–a posteriori distinction in terms of degrees of hypotheticity in Duhemian impliers does not oblige us to accept any non-empirical sort of justification, and the context-sensitive strategy it is part of captures much more of the actually available evidence. Quine's principled argument is thus uncompelling in the light of alternatives like the Putnamian line here presented. Breaking the Quinean grip leaves it open whether more "traditional" approaches to epistemic privilege for areas of inquiry like the understanding of logical necessity are needed, and how adequate notions of epistemic priority can be developed for such purposes on the model of the pragmatic, contextual notion laid out here. The need is illustrated when even Quine in his late work resurrects the very account of logical necessity (Ayer's) that he combated in "Two Dogmas." Putnam's current work[41] as well as that of many others (Floyd, Casullo, Field, etc.) explores the latter question. Contrary to Quine, finding ways of drawing the epistemic analytic–synthetic distinction is still of central methodological importance.

Notes

1 This chapter is the result of a long process during which many people helped it grow. Throughout, discussions of the various stages with Cristina Lafont were a continuous source of improvement. When I read sections at the Central Division meeting of the APA in April 2003, Jay G. Campbell and Louise Antony made

me see important points. The adjusted chapter profited from comments of Carlos Pereda, Maite Ezcurdia at the UNAM in Mexico, and at the Alice Berlin Kaplan Center for the humanities from comments by Tom McCarthy, Bob Gooding-Williams and Tom Ricketts. I am especially grateful for encouraging feedback I received from Arthur Fine, and for Thomas Ricketts' continuous incisive, patient and collegially cordial criticism. Colloquia at Grinnell College and the University of Illinois Urbana-Champaign brought additional valuable comments from the audiences. The final and most enormous debt I owe, of course, to Maria Baghramian and Hilary Putnam for giving me the opportunity to present the final version at the conference in honor of Putnam's 80th birthday at University College in Dublin. There, Alan Berger's and Hilary Putnam's extensive direct comments on the chapter, but also many other papers and conversations, enriched me more than I can have been able to express. My deepest thanks go to all of them.
2 For a succinct representative account that explicitly makes the claim that logical and mathematical necessity as well as epistemic necessity (irrevisability) is to be reduced to analyticity (understood as empirical vacuity or "being a tautology"), cf. Ayer (1936: 39). For more technical presentations of the identification of necessity, analyticity and apriority, cf. the joint product of Carnap (1934: §§ 52, 67–69 and 79), as well as, in semantic terms, Carnap (1956: §§ 2) (translates 'analytic' as "L-true") and 39 (identifies "necessary" and "L-true"), for the identification of analyticity and apriority, Carnap (1974: ch. 18, esp. 181–82).
3 The claim that conventionalism accounts for the necessity of mathematical and logical truth should not be confused with the claim that there is a conventionalist account of the *grounding* or *generation* of logical truth. The latter was trenchantly rebutted in Quine (1934) and Quine (1956). The difference between both projects is illuminatingly pointed out in Hellman (1986), as well as in Putnam (1994a, esp. 248).
4 Cf. Putnam (1962): "analytic statements ... are true because they are accepted as true, and because this acceptance ... has no systematic consequences beyond ... allowing us to use pairs of expressions interchangeably" (68–69), and Quine (1986): "I see little use for [the psychogenetic notion of analyticity] in the epistemology or methodology of science" (95). For an excellent recent exposition and discussion of the thesis that analyticities are one and all epistemologically harmless, cf. Nimtz (2003).
5 Quine (1951): "it becomes folly to seek a boundary between ... statements, which hold contingently on experience, and ... statements, which hold come what may" (43).
6 Quine (1970) deems the linguistic conception as "too generous" because it "views these domains [logic and mathematics] as immune likewise to empirical refutation" (99).
7 The fundamental significance of Quine's attack on Carnap's way of drawing the distinction for the development of the program of philosophical naturalism has been stressed by Quine throughout his work. That this rejection *has to* take the form of a *principled* rejection of *any* successor distinction and the counter-thesis that all statements are empirical has been forcefully argued by Friedman (1997 and 2000). That this form of rejecting the distinction in principle has the same foundational and, as it were, transcendental role for the defense of naturalism as the defense of the analytic–synthetic distinction had for Carnap's program of the logic of science has been recognized and argued by Lepore (1995), and is supported by reflecting on the role of logic as a fundament, which Quine's philosophy transforms relative to Carnap but never abandons, as Ricketts (2004) argues. A particularly uncompromising representative of a naturalist

program in regard to the methodological non-role of the a priori is Devitt (forthc.).
8 This distinguishes the argument here proposed from criticisms of skeptical consequences of Quine's methodology that are intended as proofs of traditional a priori claims, like BonJour (1998: 62–97).
9 Putnam and Quine are here in the same camp in comparison with neo-rationalists like BonJour or Katz, who defend certain forms of a priori justification. While Katz's account is heavily bent on maintaining the connection between apriority and linguistic meaning, BonJour (1998) takes on the question of the distinction in the explicitly epistemological/methodological way here pursued. Cf. ibid., 76.
10 I am thus sidelining more general discussions of a priori knowledge as such, but also much of the literature on holism and analyticity, which mostly concentrates on issues in the theory of meaning. In doing so, I simply take for granted with both authors that the linguistic conception of apriority is not an option for the reasons sketched above.
11 Which, as is well known, has as one of its foundational axioms the futility of *any* such distinction. Cf. Quine (1969: 82ff.), Friedman (1997).
12 An additional complication arises, of course, from the fact that theoretical hypotheses in technical languages are typically formulated with the help of "cluster terms" (Putnam 1962). I will neglect this meaning-holistic aspect in what follows and concentrate on the confirmation relations between *understood* theoretical hypotheses and the evidence. My working hypothesis is that what I will say will apply, mutatis mutandis, to Duhemian impliers that are expanded so that they capture the relevant parts of the theory needed to specify the use and application of the hypothesis.
13 Bennett (1958–59) was the first to note this problem; more recently, Berger (2003) gives an illuminating account.
14 Numerous epistemologists have taken Quine to task on this point. A thorough and elucidating example is Travis (2004).
15 Popper (1963/2002), Grünbaum (1960), (1962), and Wedeking (1963) critically scrutinize Quine's argument in this direction early. More recently, the most compelling and sustained criticism has been formulated by Laudan (1990) and Laudan/Leplin (1991).
16 This line of criticism originates in Bennett (1958–59) and Frankfurt (1960). Dummett (1973: 596–608) constitutes another milestone, clarified by Williams (1998: 239). More recent kindred arguments to the conclusion that Quine's methodology is incoherent on account of the general revisability thesis can be found in Wright (1986: 196ff.), and in BonJour (1998: 90–97).
17 This is one of the issues raised by McDowell (1994), who comments on Quine's deflation of apriority in terms of centrality, i.e. "the relative likelihood, in practice, of our choosing one statement rather than another for revision in the event of recalcitrant experience," that this means that for Quine, "it is not that it is right to revise one's belief system thus and so in the light of such-and-such experience, but just that that revision is what would probably happen" (133). McDowell observes that this converts Quine's talk of beliefs "facing the tribunal of experience" into empty rhetoric, leaving us with "the awkward position of experience in Quine's thinking" (135).
18 Quine (1963: 133). Ricketts (1982) takes this reaction as a clue to explaining Quine's strategy in "Two Dogmas." He argues that Quine's "Duhemian argument" is overrated because it is mistaken to make an epistemologically interesting point where it is best understood as a trivializing argument against yet another

candidate for an analyticity-criterion. It goes without saying that he does not think that this deflation of the argument would be damaging to Quine's overall philosophy, or particularly, to non-trivial readings of his revisability-theses (e.g. as basically negative contributions to research into confirmation theory). In what follows, I agree with Ricketts that the "Duhemian argument" might be *intended* as a trivializing argument, but I disagree with the suggestion that it is itself inconsequential ("trivial") or that Quine's methodology could live without the non-trivial, epistemological readings of what's behind the passage. Instead, the trivialization comes at a *high price*.

19 Quine (1975: 314–16) speaks of the "strong presumption in favor of the observation statements ... that makes science empirical"; Quine (1991a: 109): "piecemeal is how the sentence relates to theory."

20 M. Williams notes that Quine's view of the application of the maxim is predicated on the assumption that holism means that "local justification presupposes global" (Williams 1991: 292).

21 That this is Quine's view of the matter becomes particularly evident in his expanded explanation of how "centrality" can account for the apparent necessity of mathematical truth. He writes:

> why is mathematical truth necessary rather than contingent? ... Holism's answer is that when a critical mass of sentences jointly implies a false prediction, *we are free to choose* what component sentence to revoke so as to defuse the implication. In so choosing we choose to safeguard any purely mathematical truths among those sentences.
> (Quine 1999: 22 (emphasis added))

See also Quine (1992: 15–16). Clearly, the work in this explanation is not done by Duhemian holism, but by Quine's insistence on the freedom to choose.

22 Isaacson (2004) speaks fittingly of the "impossibility argument in 'Two Dogmas'" (242).

23 When Quine, pressed by Hookway's criticisms, claims at a later point that he "never found these [passages, AM] useful or illuminating" (Quine 1994: 503), this confirms my suspicion that the *principled* argument against the analytic–synthetic distinction (as opposed to other, more local ones) is not even by his own lights Quine's best. But that does not mean there'd be a better one. The wholesale repudiation (needed for grounding Quinean naturalism) could be *ill-motivated*.

24 Lepore (1995: n. 6) makes a similar point in the context of determining the scope of Quine's semantic holism when he adverts that even though there is an interpretation of Quine's criticism (one of Putnam's) that comes to saying that "Quine rejects the a/s distinction because it has no role to play in accounting for knowledge. Since there are no a priori truths, we don't need an a/s distinction to account for them," this interpretation "can't be the entire story" because it "is consistent with the a/s distinction being perfectly intelligible; it is merely superfluous." The latter, however, is incompatible with Quine's claim that the distinction "has not been given any methodological sense."

25 Quine affirms his commitment to hypothetico-deductivism until his last and definitive work on scientific method:

> On the heels of observation sentences we saw science emerging with the inception of observation categoricals. ... The categorical was a miniature scientific theory. Its antecedent clause was the experimental condition, and

> its consequent clause the prediction. ... observation categoricals ... are the lifeline of science; for I see them not just as miniature scientific theories individually, but as the ultimate checkpoints of science generally. A theory is tested by *deducing an observation categorical from it and testing the categorical*.
> (Quine 1995: 43–44, emphasis added)

Since the observation categorical's relation to its compound observation sentences is likewise deductive in virtue of its being an implication (cf. *Pursuit of Truth*, p. 12), we arrive at full-fledged hypothetico-deductivism. Thus, whereas in the practical decisions of scientists

> much ... is accepted without thought of its joining forces with other plausible hypotheses to form a testable set[,] ... having reasonable grounds is one thing, and implying an observation categorical is another. / ... implication ... is the lifeblood of theories, or perhaps better the finger of their fate. *It is what relates a theory to its checkpoints* in observation categoricals.
> (ibid. 48–49/51)

26 It is very important not to confuse the point I just made with the very different claim, which I do not endorse, that Quine's *explanation of acceptance-behavior* regarding scientific theories or scientific/epistemic *reasoning* did not advance over his logical positivist predecessors. Quite the contrary. But while Quine pushes for the recognition of the *inevitable encroachment of pragmatic arguments* in scientific *reasoning*, he does *not* adopt a non-traditional, pragmatic conception of *evidence* (according to which such things as historically salient alternatives, known limitations on instrumentation to test predictions, available and plausible idealizations and background theories, appreciation of the support of theories on account of other parts of the empirical knowledge with which they make epistemic contact, etc., get to be part of calculating the *evidence* or the *support* of theories, and thus of the justification of selecting some but not others on account of the available perceptual, hypothetico-deductive *and other* evidence). To be sure, Quine's holism was one of the most important turning points in making such conceptions available, but *Quine himself* did not significantly stray from the reductive picture of evidence that he inherits from traditional logical empiricist methodology.
27 The line of criticism rehearsed in this paragraph has been most convincingly developed in Laudan (1990) and Laudan/Leplin (1991).
28 I take the formulation and name of the thesis from Laudan (1990: 324).
29 For this line of objection, see Bergström (1993), Bergström (2004).
30 The expansion from confirmation skepticism to loss of content is famously developed in McDowell (1994: 130–35).
31 I borrow this expression from Fine (1996: 153).
32 These commitments, unequivocal anti-instrumentalism about scientific theories and a total rejection of the theory-observation distinction, are two further salient methodological incompatibilities between Putnam and Quine. Quine's wavering between what he calls "robust realism" and instrumentalist passages is notorious, and his pursuit of a modified theory–observation distinction is clearly present in his persistent preoccupation with an adequate definition of observation sentences, the parts of the web of belief that are (a) exempt from Duhemian considerations, (b) universally accepted on the same causal prompts, (c) basic justifiers, and (d) the *only* source of empirical content. Given some adequate and complete conception of observation sentences, and given the semantic and

epistemic roles Quine attaches to observation sentences, a resurrection of the theory–observation distinction as that between observation sentences (and simple compounds thereof, as observation categoricals) and the rest of the web is inevitable. Quine is *de facto* elaborating a variant of precisely the theory–observation distinction that Putnam completely abandons without remnant in favor of a contextual distinction between justifying and to-be-justified beliefs as early as "What theories are not" (1960). For an illuminating discussion of the role of this point in Quine's naturalized epistemology, cf. Williams (1991: 261–65).

33 Cf. Bennett (1971). The reference to knowledge empiricism is often used in similar ways as I do here by Boyd (cf. Boyd 2002: sec. 2).

34 In Putnam's words, they are "empirical in the sense of being about the world" (Putnam 1967: 109).

35 I use this expression in the sense of Field (2000), who calls a statement "default reasonable" when "it is reasonable to believe or employ it without first adducing evidence or arguments in its favour" (124).

36 John Earman argues a similar point with the example of determinism. In an epistemic situation where we don't yet know exactly in many important contexts how to transform the existing deterministic laws in not-yet-existing indeterministic laws, for example, that fact would engender "a scientific claim to be argued over the way one argues over other deep scientific claims, *none of which* ever gets *definitely* settled by the dictates of experimental evidence" (Earman 1993: 14).

37 In the case of what is nowadays referred to as "folk psychology," he says: "The acceptance of [a] conceptual system, or explanatory scheme, is justified, as is the acceptance of many an empirical hypothesis, by the joint facts of explanatory power and no real alternative" (Putnam 1969: 447). Recently, Philip Kitcher defends the contextuality of the a priori on precisely this reason, which he terms the denial of identifying the apriority of a part of knowledge with its "tradition-independence" (Kitcher 2000: 90). Historical experience (or experience of working with a theory) is here on the same epistemological footing with sensory experience when it comes to explaining the (un-)revisability of parts of scientific knowledge (like mathematics) that serve as a priori in the weak sense.

38 This defense of methodological apriority has been argued in great detail in Sober (1999) and Sober (2000), esp. § 12 ("Duhem's Thesis").

39 Allison (1983: ch.1) uses the term "epistemic condition" in a similar sense. The term also occurs in a similar context in Putnam (1994a: 258).

40 This point has been convincingly argued in Laudan/Leplin (1991). My argument can be seen as parallel to that of Stathis Psillos, who uses Leplin/Laudan's insights to construct an argument in favor of realism by exploiting its power to disarm underdetermination-based anti-realist ploys (cf. Psillos 1999: 168–71). Relatedly, Okasha (2002), argues on account of Duhem's thesis, i.e. the need for determinate auxiliaries in order to derive *any* empirical consequences, that holism is incompatible with global underdetermination (307ff.). In a similar way, I am using both points to disarm Quine's principled argument against the methodological relevance of the a priori–a posteriori distinction insofar as it must be based on the global (proto-underdeterministic) symmetry-thesis.

41 The *generic* notion of apriority developed in the text is not, like traditional apriority concepts, modeled on the paradigm of logical truth but developed from within the practice of empirical justification. The relevant distinction there is between hypothetical and non-hypothetical elements in justification, which itself presupposes standards of valid deductive inference. Thus, as such, it is of only limited immediate explanatory use for the status of logical truth. On its own, moreover, this concept of apriority does not suggest the idea of statements that

are impossibly false but rather that of fixed points of a particular inquiry. Putnam noted this in Putnam (1983a) and Putnam (1994), where he says that reflecting on logical truth shows that their status and unrevisability is not merely owed to contextual apriority of the kind involved in the role of, e.g., conservation principles in physics. But then again, it surely is no mistake to represent logical truths as non-hypothetical and contextually a priori. The notion turns out norms of deductive inference expressed in logical truths as in most (in the core of first order logic: *all*) cases non-hypothetical. The real complaint might be that this is *too little* to get right the *specific way* in which logical truths are non-hypothetical, and too little to make us see why *all* logical truths are equally non-hypothetical if any are, and how they can *acquire* this status when the rules of inference they articulate are everywhere presupposed. This is right, but perfectly consistent with saying that we have no theoretical reasons to revise any of them, as trifling and quaint as that may be. The most basic laws of logic might, for all we know, turn out to be non-hypothetical and contextually a priori *for all debatable cases* (i.e. "in all possible worlds") and thus preclude evaluable talk of their "revisability." It would be the task of philosophers of logic to spell out what specific kind of privilege these laws have, and what its basis is. That a notion of epistemological privilege that grows out of methodological concerns that have their paradigms in principles of the *empirical sciences* would not automatically come equipped with an account of logical truth but rather require us to work one out as a *special and peculiar case* should come as no surprise.

Bibliography

Where possible, I have preserved the original date of publication as the citation of the articles used to preserve a sense of chronology, although the actual quotes mostly are from the reprints in the collections given in the bibliography.

Allison, H. (1983) *Kant's Transcendental Idealism. An Interpretation and Defense*, New Haven and London: Yale University Press.
Ayer, J.A. (1936) "The Apriori," in P. K. Moser (ed.), *A Priori Knowledge*, Oxford: Oxford University Press, 1987, 26–41.
Ben-Menahim, Y. (2006) *Conventionalism*, Cambridge: Cambridge University Press.
Bennett, J. (1958–59) "Analytic and Synthetic," *Proceedings of the Aristotelian Society*: 163–88.
——(1971) *Locke, Berkeley, Hume*, Oxford: Oxford: University Press.
Berger, A. (2003) "The Quinean Quandary and The Indispensability of Nonnaturalized Epistemology," *The Philosophical Forum* 34(3–4): 367–82.
Bergström, L. (1993) "Quine, Underdetermination, and Skepticism," *Journal of Philosophy* 90: 331–58.
——(2004) "Underdetermination of physical theory," in R. Gibson (ed.), *The Cambridge Companion to Quine*, Cambridge: Cambridge University Press, 91–114.
BonJour, L. (1998) *In Defense of Pure Reason*, Cambridge: Cambridge University Press.
Boyd, R. (2002) "Scientific Realism," *The Stanford Encyclopedia of Philosophy (Summer 2002 Edition)*, Edward N. Zalta (ed.), URL = <http://plato.stanford.edu/archives/sum/entries/scientific-realism/>.
Carnap, R. (1934) *Logische Syntax der Sprache*, Vienna: Julius Springer.
——(1956) *Meaning and Necessity*, 2nd edn, Chicago: University of Chicago Press.

——(1974) *Philosophical Foundations of Physics*, ed. M. Gardner, New York: Basic Books.
Coffa, J. A. (1991) *The Semantic Tradition from Kant to Carnap*, Cambridge, MA: Cambridge University Press.
Creath, R. (2004) "Quine on the Intelligibility and Relevance of Analyticity," in R. Gibson (ed.), *The Cambridge Companion to Quine*, Cambridge MA: Cambridge University Press, 47–64.
Devitt, M. (forthc.) "No Place for the A Priori," in M. J. Shaffer and M. Weber (eds.), *New Views of the A Priori in Physical Theory*, Vienna: Rodopi Press.
Duhem, P. (1912) *The Aim and Structure of Physical Theory*, New York: Atheneum, 1962.
Dummett, M. (1973) *Frege. Philosophy of Language*, Cambridge, MA: Harvard University Press.
Earman, J. (1993) "Carnap, Kuhn, and the Philosophy of Scientific Methodology," in P. Horwich (ed.), *World Changes. Thomas Kuhn and the Nature of Science*, Cambridge, MA: MIT Press, 9–36.
Field, H. (2000) "Apriority as an Evaluative Notion," in P. Boghossian and C. Peacocke (eds.), *New Essays on the Apriori*, Oxford: Oxford University Press, 117–49.
Fine, A. (1996) *The Shaky Game. Einstein, Realism, and the Quantum Theory*, 2nd edn, Chicago: University of Chicago Press.
Fodor, J. and LePore, E. (1992) *Holism. A Shopper's Guide*, Oxford: Blackwell.
Frankfurt, H. (1960) "Meaning, Truth, and Pragmatism," *Philosophical Quarterly* 10: 171–76.
Friedman, M. (1997) "Philosophical Naturalism," *Proceedings and Addresses of the American Philosophical Association* 72(1): 7–21.
——(1999) "Geometry, Convention, and the Relativized A Priori," in F. Friedman, *Reconsidering Logical Positivism*, Cambridge, MA: Cambridge University Press, 59–70.
——(2000) "Transcendental Philosophy and A Priori Knowledge: A Neo-Kantian perspective," in P. Boghossian and C. Peacocke (eds.), *New Essays on the Apriori*, Oxford: Oxford University Press, 367–84.
Gregory, Paul (2003) "'Two Dogmas' – All Bark and No Bite? Carnap and Quine on Analyticity," *Philosophy and Phenomenological Research* 67/3: 633–48.
Grünbaum, A. (1960) "The Duhemian Argument," *Philosophy of Science* 27: 75–87.
——(1962) " The falsifiability of theories: Total or partial? A contemporary evaluation of the Duhem-Quine thesis," *Synthese* 14: 17–34.
Harman, G. (2003) "The Future of the Apriori," in *Philosophy in America at the Turn of the Century*, Bowling Green: Philosophy Documentation Center, 23–34.
Hellman, G. (1986) "Logical Truth by Linguistic Convention," in P. A. Schilpp and L. E. Hahn, (eds.), *The Philosophy of W.V.O. Quine*, La Salle: Open Court, 189–205.
Hylton, P. (1982) "Analyticity and the Indeterminacy of Translation," *Synthese* 52: 167–84.
Isaacson, D. (1992) "Carnap, Quine and Logical Truth," in D. Bell and W. Vossenkuhl, (eds.), *Science and Subjectivity. The Vienna Circle and Twentieth-Century Philosophy*, Berlin: Akademie Verlag, 100–30.
——(2004) "Quine and Logical Positivism," in R. Gibson (ed.), *The Cambridge Companion to Quine*, Cambridge, MA: Cambridge University Press, 214–69.
Kitcher, Ph. (2000) "A Priori Knowledge Revisited," in P. Boghossian and C. Peacocke (eds.), *New Essays on the Apriori*, Oxford: Oxford University Press, 65–91.

Laudan, L. (1990) " Demystifying Underdetermination," reprinted in M. Curd, and J. A. Cover (eds.), *Philosophy of Science. The Central Issues*, New York and London: Norton & Co., 1998, 320–53.

Laudan, L. and Leplin, J. (1991) "Empirical Equivalence and Underdetermination," *Journal of Philosophy* 88: 449–72.

LePore, E. (1995) "Two Dogmas of Empiricism and the Generality Requirement," Nous 24: 468–80.

Lewis, C. I. (1923) "A Pragmatic Conception of the A Priori," repr. in P. K. Moser (ed.), *A Priori Knowledge*, Oxford: Oxford University Press, 1987, 15–25.

McDowell, J. (1994). *Mind and World*, Cambridge, MA: Harvard University Press.

Nimtz, C. (2003) "Analytic Truths – Still Harmless After All These Years?," in H. J. Glock, K. Gluer,and G. Keil (eds.), *Fifty Years of Quine's 'Two Dogmas'*, Amsterdam and New York: Rodopi, 91–118.

Okasha, S. (2002) "Underdetermination, Holism and the Theory/Data Distinction," *The Philosophical Quarterly* 52: 303–19.

——(2002a) "How To Be a Selective Quinean," *Dialectica* 56: 37–47.

Popper, K. (1963/2002) "Truth, Rationality, and the Growth of Scientific Knowledge," in K. Popper, *Conjectures and Refutations*, London: Routledge, 2002, 291–340.

Psillos, S. (1999) *Scientific Realism: How Science Tracks Truth*, London: Routledge.

Putnam, H. (1960) "What theories are not," in Putnam 1975: 215–27.

——(1962) "The Analytic and the Synthetic," in Putnam 1975a: 33–69.

——(1962a) "It Ain't Necessarily So," in Putnam 1975: 237–49.

——(1965) "Philosophy of Physics," in Putnam 1975: 79–93.

——(1967) "An Examination of Grünbaum's Philosophy of Geometry," in Putnam 1975: 93–129.

——(1969) "Logical Positivism and the Philosophy of Mind," in Putnam 1975a: 441–51.

——(1975) *Philosophical Papers I. Mathematics, Matter And Method*, Cambridge: Cambridge University Press.

——(1975a) *Philosophical Papers II. Mind, Language, and Reality*, Cambridge: Cambridge University Press.

——(1983a) "There is at least one Apriori Truth," in H. Putnam, *Philosophical Papers III. Realism and Reason*, Cambridge: Cambridge University Press, 98–114.

——(1983b) "'Two Dogmas' Revisited," in H. Putnam, *Philosophical Papers III. Realism and Reason*, Cambridge: Cambridge University Press, 87–97.

——(1994) *Words and Life*, Cambridge, MA: Harvard University Press.

——(1994a) "Rethinking Mathematical Necessity," in Putnam 1994, 245–63.

——(1999) *The Threefold Chord. Mind, Body, and World*, New York: Columbia University Press.

Quine, W. V. (1934). "Truth by Convention," in W. V. Quine, *The Ways of Paradox and Other Essays*, Cambridge, MA: Harvard University Press, 1976, 77–106.

——(1951) "Two Dogmas of Empiricism," in W. V. Quine, *From a Logical Point of View*, Cambridge, MA: Harvard University Press, 1980, 20–46.

——(1956) "Carnap on Logical Truth," in W. V. Quine, *The Ways of Paradox and Other Essays*, Cambridge, MA: Harvard University Press, 1976, 107–32.

——(1960) *Word and Object*, Cambridge, MA: MIT Press

——(1963) "A Comment on Grünbaum's Claim," in S. Harding (ed.) *Can Theories be Refuted? Essays on the Duhem–Quine Thesis*, Kluwer: Amsterdam, 1976, 133.

——(1969) "Epistemology Naturalized," in W. V. Quine, *Ontological Relativity and Other Essays*, New York: Columbia University Press, 69–90.
——(1970) *Philosophy of Logic*, Englewood Cliffs: Prentice-Hall.
——(1975) "Empirically Equivalent Systems of the World," *Erkenntnis* 9, 313–28.
——(1981) "Five Milestones of Empiricism," in W. V. Quine, *Theories and Things*, Cambridge, MA: Harvard University Press, 67–72.
——(1981a) "Empirical Content," in W. V. Quine, *Theories and Things*, Cambridge, MA: Harvard University Press, 24–30.
——(1986) "Reply to Bohnert," in P. A. Schilpp and L. E. Hahn (eds.), *The Philosophy of W.V.O. Quine*, La Salle: Open Court, 93–96.
——(1986a) "Reply to Geoffrey Hellman," in P. A. Schilpp and L. E. Hahn (eds.), *The Philosophy of W.V.O. Quine*, La Salle: Open Court, 206–8.
——(1986b) "Reply to Jacques Vuillemin," in P. A. Schilpp and L. E. Hahn (eds.), *The Philosophy of W.V.O. Quine*, La Salle: Open Court, 619–22.
——(1991) "Two Dogmas in Retrospect," *Canadian Journal of Philosophy* 21: 265–74.
——(1991a) "In Praise of observation sentences," *Journal of Philosophy* 90: 107–16.
——(1992) *Pursuit of Truth*, Cambridge, MA: Harvard University Press.
——(1994) "Responses," *Inquiry* 37: 495–506.
——(1995) *From Stimulus to Science*, Cambridge, MA: Harvard University Press.
——(1999) "Quine speaks his mind," interview in A. Pyle (ed.), *Key Philosophers in Conversation. The Cogito-Interviews*, London: Routledge, 17–25.
Reichenbach, H. (1920) *Relativitätstheorie und Erkentnnis A priori*, Berlin: Springer.
——(1924) *Axiomatik der relativistischen Raum-Zeit-Lehre*, Braunschweig: Vieweg.
Ricketts, T. (1982) "Rationality, Translation, and Epistemology Naturalized," *Journal of Philosophy* 79: 117–37.
——(2004) "Frege, Carnap, and Quine: Continuities and Discontinuities," in S. Awodey and C. Klein (eds.), *Carnap Brought Home*, La Salle: Open Court.
Ryckman, T. (2005) *The Reign of Relativity. Philosophy in Physics 1915–1925*, Oxford: Oxford University Press.
Sober, E. (1999) "Testability," *Proceedings and Addresses of the American Philosophical Association* 73: 47–76.
——(2000) "Quine's Two Dogmas," *Proceedings of the Aristotelian Society*, Supplementary Volume 74: 237–80.
Travis, C. (2004) "The Twilight of Empiricism," *Proceedings of the Aristotelian Society* 104 (1): 247–72.
Wedeking, G. (1963) "Duhem, Quine and Grünbaum on Falsification," reprinted in S. Harding, *Can Theories be Refuted? Essays on the Duhem-Quine Thesis*, Dordrecht: Kluwer, 1976.
Williams, Me. (1998) "The Etiology of the Obvious," in Me. Williams, *Wittgenstein on Mind and Meaning*, London: Routledge, 216–39.
Williams, M. (1991) *Unnatural Doubts*, Oxford: Blackwell.
——(2001) *Problems of Knowledge*, Oxford: Oxford University Press.
Wright, C. (1986) "Inventing Logical Necessity," in J. Butterfield (ed.), *Language, Mind and Logic*, Cambridge: Cambridge University Press, 187–209.

COMMENTS ON AXEL MUELLER'S "PUTNAM VS. QUINE ON REVISABILITY AND THE ANALYTIC–SYNTHETIC DISTINCTION"

Hilary Putnam

Axel Mueller's essay is a deep study of the similarities and differences between Quine's "Two Dogmas" and my "The Analytic and the Synthetic." For the most part, I have only admiration for what he writes, and I recommend his analysis to all students of these issues.

However, while I agree that there are serious differences between my analysis of the issues and Quine's various analyses, I also think that Mueller is unnecessarily uncharitable to Quine. Without disagreeing with Mueller's criticisms of some of Quine's views, I do want to say that there is an analytic–synthetic dichotomy that Quine demolished. As Mueller explains, I have long defended the view that there are statements in science at any given period – I have sometimes called them "a priori relative to a body of (putative) knowledge" (and more recently simply "framework principles" (Putnam 2012)) – which play a special epistemological role, and which are such that, at least in that scientific period, we cannot make sense of the idea that they might be false, or, more precisely, we are totally unable to say *how* they could be false (and hence the question of "justifying" them does not arise). This is what Mueller sees as my "epistemological" successor to the analytic–synthetic dichotomy. If Quine wrote things that were supposed to rule out such a successor, then Quine erred. But, I repeat, there *was* an analytic–synthetic distinction that Quine demolished, and what I wrote in "The Analytic and the Synthetic" certainly built on Quine's achievement.

Quine's target was Carnap's claim that the epistemology of mathematics and logic is no longer a problem once we see that mathematics is just logic (and, of course, that logic and mathematics are both "analytic"). As Carnap himself put it "On the basis of the new logic, the essential character of logical sentences can be clearly recognized. This is of the greatest importance for the theory of mathematical knowledge ... ." Nor were the positivists the only philosophers who thought that important philosophical problems could be solved by declaring various propositions "analytic."[1] I do not agree that Quine's arguments all depended on what Mueller calls his "symmetry thesis." Quine also – too briefly, but very definitely – appealed to the history of science to show that propositions that were not unreasonably regarded as analytic at one time *have* often later turned out to be false, and this is something that my "The Analytic and the Synthetic" went into at length. And I like very much Quine's statement in "Carnap and Logical Truth" that the question "which statement in physics are definitions?" is a bad question in the same way that the question, "which places in Ohio are starting points?" is a bad question. (It all depends on what journey you want to take.)

I would now like to make some remarks about a different issue, which receives brief mention in Mueller's chapter. As Mueller reminds us, Quine said in a famous passage that any statement "can be held true come what may," and Mueller rightly said early on I found the passage "trenchant," but I later saw it as it "as shot through with 'unintelligible' uses of 'can'." It may help our discussion if I explain what I meant by speaking of the "cans" in Quine's "revisability passage" as "unintelligible."

The claim that a particular proposition (say, the principle of mathematical induction) is one that underlies virtually all of our mathematical practice, and that we cannot, given our body of (putative) knowledge, and our whole body of what we take to be coherent alternatives to that "knowledge," see any way in which it could be false, is one that I find undeniably true. The further claim that it is beyond the power of human minds (but perhaps not the minds of extraterrestrials much smarter than we?) to describe something which could be rationally described as a way in which the principle of mathematical induction could be false is, however, obviously very vague. And the still further claim that it is *metaphysically impossible* for there to be any such description, which is what the claim that the principle is "apriori" in the traditional sense comes to, is a claim which employs a modal operator, "metaphysically possible" (or more precisely its negative, "metaphysically impossible") that, I have argued,[2] has not been given any clear sense.

Thus, I would not say that any statement can be revised, because this "can" is just the modal "metaphysically possible." But neither would I say "Some statements are unrevisable." I would not say "Every statement can be revised," nor would I say "Some statements can't be revised." But we can certainly say that some statements are contextually necessary truths, or even conceptual truths, in the epistemological and "pragmatic" sense that Mueller very well describes.

A corollary of my view is that fallibilism is really hard to state. If what I have just said is right, then one cannot state fallibilism by simply saying "any statement can be revised." So what does "fallibilism" mean?

I think fallibilism is best construed as a recommendation, an attitude. Namely, if someone is intellectually respectable – of course you can make a big mistake about that – but if someone intellectually respectable defends a view that you are inclined to say "couldn't be true," a view whose negation you find contextually unintelligible, and that person says, "No, you're wrong," *you should listen to her arguments.* You shouldn't say "I don't have to listen to the arguments, I have this conviction or intuition that the conclusion can't be right!" If a logician that I respect claimed even to have found a contradiction in first-order arithmetic, I would look at her proof!

Notes

1 An important essay that documents this claim that I recommend reading alongside Mueller's essay is Pidgen (1987).
2 See Putnam (1990).

Bibliography

Pigden Charles (1987) "Two Dogmatists," *Inquiry*, 173–93.
Putnam, Hilary (1990) "Is Water Necessarily H₂O," in Putnam, *Realism With a Human Face*, ed. James Conant, Cambridge: MA: Harvard University Press, 1990, 54–79.
——(2012) "Reply to Gary Ebbs," in Randall Auxier (ed.),*The Philosophy of Hilary Putnam*, Chicago and La Salle, IL: Open Court.

5

PUTNAM ON EXISTENCE AND ONTOLOGY*

Charles Parsons

The origin of this chapter lies in a puzzlement I have felt about how Putnam understands Quine's views on existence and ontology. I have found it difficult to put my finger on what his quarrel with Quine about this has been. But one could also see it as a fragment of a commentary on the following recent remark of Putnam. Speaking of the lectures "Ethics Without Ontology" published in the book of that name, Putnam writes that they

> ... provided me with an opportunity to formulate and present in public something that I realized I had long wanted to say, namely that the renewed (and continuing) respectability of Ontology (the capital letter here is intentional!) following the publication of W. V. Quine's "On what there is" at the midpoint of the last century had disastrous consequences for just about every part of analytic philosophy.
>
> (Putnam 2004: 2)

It will be pretty clear from what follows in the lectures themselves that Putnam is largely concerned with a rather broad philosophical tendency that followed Quine's essay (Quine 1948) and not directly with Quine's views themselves. He is not very explicit about the extent to which he holds Quine responsible for what he deplores. In various writings Putnam has written quite a lot about Quine. He has not, however, written a lot on Quine on ontology. What I discuss will be based on a relatively small number of texts. I hope they represent his thought well enough for this exercise to be worthwhile. Although Quine's views and Putnam's view of them will be prominent in what follows, I hope to offer more than just a commentary on the Putnam–Quine relation.

I might frame an issue rather crudely by distinguishing between what could be called a modest and extravagant sense of, and concern with, ontology. Quine's discussion of ontological commitment belongs in the first instance to the modest side. Ontological commitment as Quine understands it is a property of theories. The question of the ontological commitment of a theory can be discussed in abstraction not only from the question whether the theory is true or to be accepted, but also from the question how much it takes in, how comprehensive it is. Extravagant views in ontology are in all the examples I can think of views about what there is. Quine does not commit himself to such views in "On what there is," and to the extent that he gives indications of his views there, they tend to be either deflationary, on the matter of universals and possibilia, or tentative, as on the matter of physicalism versus phenomenalism.[1]

Putnam's concern with ontology in his later writings seems to be with views that can be rather tendentiously classified as extravagant. To the extent that he is quarreling with the Quine of 1948, it is with the idea that one can have an ontology at all, not a view of ontological commitment but a view of what there really is. Does such an aspiration commit one to an extravagant ontology or at least the program of seeking one? I think this raises questions of ontological and other forms of relativity, about which both Quine and Putnam have had things to say.

I

In the case of Quine, "On what there is" seems to license a concern with ontology, although apparently not with extravagant ontology. Sometimes Quine does flirt with ontological extravagance, although usually in a negative rather than a positive sense, as when he suggests much later that physical objects might be eliminated from our theory in favor of sets (thus producing economy, since on his view we need sets anyway) (Quine 1981: 17–18 and 1976). The views about reference that he advances in "Ontological relativity" and later do imply that even given a manual of translation that determines the truth-values of the sentences of a theory, it is not settled what objects are referred to. But both his views on assessing ontological commitment and his own firm theoretical preferences mean that the options will be different domains of objects for a first-order theory.

Putnam's early writings indicate an inclination to downplay the significance of ontology. He mentions equivalent descriptions in physics, and it is likely that that phenomenon made an impression on him at the very beginning of his career. About mathematics, he has always tended to treat ontology as secondary. Thus in his important early paper "Mathematics without foundations" (henceforth MWF) he writes, "In my view the chief characteristic of mathematical propositions is the wide variety of equivalent formulations that they possess" (Putnam 1967: 45). Then he singles out two ways of formulating mathematical statements that he regards as equivalent in roughly the same sense, Mathematics as Modal Logic and Mathematics as Set Theory. The second is just the familiar framing of classical mathematics in axiomatic set theory, ZF or some extension by additional axioms. The first is illustrated by translating a number-theoretic statement as a modal statement asserting that, necessarily, if the axioms of arithmetic hold, then the statement holds.[2] In MWF he proposes a more complicated method of translating statements of set theory into a modal language.[3] In both cases Putnam avoids explicit statements of the existence of the relevant mathematical objects, but the method does presuppose the *possible* existence of objects that stand in relations corresponding to the structure of the mathematical domain in question. Unlike the ontological relativity discussed by Quine just a little later, this way of formulating mathematical theories changes the logical form in such a way that however one describes the change, it's not just a change in what objects are referred to.

Putnam also differs from most writers influenced by his construction, who took it as a way of eliminating or at least greatly limiting reference to mathematical objects. Taken in that way it is subject to some criticisms.[4] Putnam, however, viewed the more conventional set-theoretic formulation of mathematics and the modal-logical formulation as equivalent descriptions, each corresponding to different pictures in something like Wittgenstein's sense. Each would shed light in its own way on the concepts involved. For example, the set-theoretic formulation serves to make clear at least the logic of the modalities, while the modal formulation brings out what is limited in the sense in which mathematics postulates objects (MWF, p. 49). Putnam does not say in so many words that the two formulations differ in their ontology, but this is clearly implied by some of his statements (e.g. ibid. 48). I think he wants to conclude that its ontological commitment, whether in the precise sense derived from Quine or some other, is not an essential or intrinsic feature of a mathematical theory. Rather than accepting or rejecting the "mathematical-objects picture" outright, his aim is to relativize it.

One of the features of the "metaphysical realism" that Putnam began to attack in the late 1970s is that according to it what objects there are and their individuation is fixed by "reality" independently of our theories and their formulation (Putnam 1978). As regards mathematical objects, Putnam did not hold this view even in his early essays. To that extent, he was never a metaphysical realist about mathematics. However, he seems to have thought that some degree of "ontological relativity" was compatible with metaphysical realism (Putnam 1978: 132). In MWF, however, he advances equivalent descriptions in which the objects of one do not arise in the other even as constructions. That appears to be a more radical departure from metaphysical realism as he formulated it later. So far as I know, however, he does not address the question of the compatibility of the view of MWF with metaphysical realism. It may be that the ontological side of the rejection of metaphysical realism in the late 1970s represents an extension to reference in general of a view that he already held about mathematical reference.

II

I now turn to an early text where Putnam does engage to some extent with views of Quine on ontology, the little book *Philosophy of Logic* (1971). But I confess I also have the aim of reminding us of something about Quine, which is easily forgotten especially if one concentrates on the metaphysical flights of some philosophers influenced by him. I hesitate a little in using this work for the purpose, for two reasons. First, it was evidently intended as an introductory book and so might simplify issues more than he would in another context. Second, in much of it he adopts nominalism as his target. In fact the book is probably now best known for its presentation of an "indispensability argument" for admitting mathematical objects. And in that place he makes clear his *agreement* with Quine. If by nominalism one means the rejection of abstract objects, the refusal to quantify over them, then of course Quine was no nominalist. Even his experimental interest in seeing how far one could go on a nominalist basis, reflected in the well-known paper Goodman and Quine 1947, was quite temporary.

Nonetheless I think there is a nominalist tendency in Quine, not about mathematical objects but about meaning. It is certainly connected with his skepticism about the notion of meaning but appears to have been formed earlier. I would also argue that it has merits independent of that skepticism.

What I have in mind is Quine's view of predication and the notions of proposition, property, and attribute. His reserve toward these notions is one of his earliest philosophical stances. As regards propositions, it is expressed in "Ontological Remarks on the Propositional Calculus," his first philosophical publication (Quine 1934). It is worth noting that Quine was willing to use the adjective "ontological" in the title of this paper and again in a lecture of 1939 that I will mention. He may already have had the attitude toward the word "ontology" that he expresses in a later discussion of Carnap:

> I might say in passing, though it is no substantial point of disagreement, that Carnap does not much like my terminology here. Now if he had a better use for this fine old word 'ontology', I should be inclined to cast about for another word for my own meaning. But the fact is, I believe, that he disapproves of my giving meaning to a word which belongs to traditional metaphysics and should therefore be meaningless. ... Meaningless words, however, are precisely the words which I feel freest to specify meanings for.
> (Quine 1951: 203)

In the paper of 1934 Quine argues that understanding propositional logic (or the "theory of deduction," as he also calls it) as a theory about propositions, so that the letters $p, q, \ldots$ range over propositions, amounts to treating sentences as names of propositions. He makes it clear that in his view this is a quite optional way of viewing the theory:

> Without altering the theory of deduction internally, we can so reconstrue it as to sweep away such fictive considerations; we have merely to interpret the theory as a formal grammar for the manipulation of sentences, and to abandon the view that sentences are names. Words occurring in a sentence may be regarded severally as denoting things, but the sentence as a whole is to be taken as a verbal combination which, though presumably conveying some manner of intelligence (I write with deliberate vagueness at this point), yet does not have that particular kind of meaning which consists in denoting or being a name of something.
> (Quine 1934: 267)

Although it is not as explicit as in later writings such as *Methods of Logic*, Quine's reading of the letters of propositional logic as schematic letters for sentences is essentially there in 1934.[5] At the end of the paper, Quine does suggest another reading in which the letters are true variables ranging over sentences.[6] But that reading also doesn't imply that sentences designate anything or commit him to propositions.

Another central element of Quine's nominalistic side emerges in a paper written and presented in 1939, "A Logistical Approach to the Ontological Problem" (Quine 1966a).[7] A large part of Quine's view of ontological commitment is already there, including the slogan "To be is to be the value of a variable." The main idea is simply that whether an expression names something or is "syncategorematic" turns on whether the place where it occurs is subject to existential generalization. In his original example, "Pebbles have roundness," "roundness" names something just in case the sentence implies "$(\exists x)$(pebbles have x)." The mark of a name is this connection with quantification. He considers the possibility that the "entities" involved might be fictions and admits this if the quantifiers can be eliminated by suitable definitions, as could be done in one case he cites: the addition of "propositional" quantifiers to truth-functional logic, as was done in the interwar Polish school.

One could certainly infer from this paper that already in 1939 Quine held that predicates as such do not designate anything. It *would* be an inference: he does not discuss that case explicitly, even to discuss the relation between "Pebbles are round" and "Pebbles have roundness." But the inference is buttressed by his closing claim that we can obtain a language adequate for science by adding to the first-order language of set theory a number of empirical predicates.

> For this entire language the only ontology required – the only range of values for the variables of quantification – consists of

concrete individuals of some sort or other, plus all classes of such entities, plus all classes formed from the thus supplemented totality of entities, and so on.[8]

(Quine 1966a: 201)

Quine's view that the use of predicates does not unavoidably involve us in commitment to properties or attributes emerges in "On what there is." He argues against his fictitious McX, who maintains that red houses, red roses, and red sunsets must have something in common, which is what he calls redness. McX is willing to accept the denial that "red" in such uses *names* redness, and he retreats to the position that it at least has a meaning and that this meaning is a universal. Quine replies:

For McX, this is an unusually penetrating speech; and the only way I know to counter it is by refusing to admit meanings. However, I feel no reluctance toward refusing to admit meanings, for I do not thereby deny that words and statements are meaningful

(Quine 1948: 11)

Synonymy, which he does not question in this context, would allow meanings in by the back door, as equivalence classes of synonymous expressions. But then they would not be "special and irreducible intermediary entities" that are supposed to have "explanatory value" (ibid. 12).

The point of view where general terms and predicates are explained as true or false of certain objects (so that "elephant" or "x is an elephant" is true of each elephant) underlies the treatment of quantificational logic in *Methods of Logic* (Quine 1950: especially §12 and §17). Properties and attributes that might be meant in some sense by such expressions are hardly mentioned, although he does make the following remark in explaining why he uses "is true of" rather than "denotes":

'Denotes' is so current in the sense of 'designates' or 'names', that its use in connection with the word 'wicked' would cause readers to look beyond the wicked people to some unique entity, a quality of wickedness or a class of the wicked, as named object. The phrase 'is true of' is less open to misunderstanding; clearly 'wicked' is true not of the quality of wickedness, nor of the class of wicked persons, but of each wicked person individually

(Quine: 1950: 65)

I shall call the collection of views mentioned here Quinean nominalism.[9]

Let us now turn to Putnam's *Philosophy of Logic* (1971). Early in the book Putnam focuses on a simple syllogism:

All S are M. All M are P. Therefore all S are P.

He considers the contemporary textbook view to be that this syllogism is valid if it is so "no matter what *classes* may be assigned to S, M, and P" (Putnam 1971: 324, emphasis in the text). He probably has in mind standard model-theoretic definitions of validity and consequence, although he doesn't put it that way. In fact he focuses on an "object language" formulation:

(A) For all classes S, M, P: if all S are M and all M are P, then all S are P.

Shortly after, at the beginning of the next chapter, Putnam introduces nominalism. As I have said, his target is full-blooded nominalism rather than Quinean nominalism. However, about the above syllogism, what he offers as the nominalist's substitute for the formulation in terms of classes is a formulation close to one that Quine would also use:

> The following turns into a true *sentence* no matter what *words* or *phrases* of the appropriate kind one may substitute for the letters S, M, P: 'if all S are M and all M are P, then all S are P'.
> (ibid. 325, emphasis in the text)

However, it doesn't seem to be Quine's use of it that Putnam has in mind. He worries about what is meant by the appropriate kind of word, and writes that "what is meant is all *possible* words or phrases of some kind or other, and that *possible words and phrases* are no more 'concrete' than classes are" (ibid. 326, emphasis in the text).

This example shows that it is not so easy to tell where and to what extent Putnam dissents from Quinean nominalism. Quine's point of view, as we noted, depends on treating sentences as truth bearers, and at one point Putnam seems to deny this (ibid. 327), but a little later he considers arguments on the issue and ends with an inconclusive result.

A more definite disagreement arises when the immediate issue is the scope of logical truth. He mentions that according to Quine quantification theory does not really assert (A) but rather something without the class quantifiers, in which S, M, and P are schematic letters for predicates. Since by "quantification theory" Quine surely means first-order logic, Putnam could hardly quarrel with the first part of Quine's claim: (A) is no theorem of first-order logic, and after all first-order logic is complete. But he rejects the view that such instances of the schema as

> (9) If all crows are black and all black things absorb light, then all crows absorb light.

are truths of logic, while evidently they are paradigm truths of logic according to Quine. Putnam writes:

> In my view, logic, as such, does *not* tell us that (9) is true; to know that (9) is true I have to use my knowledge of the logical principle

> (A), *plus* my knowledge of the fact that the predicates 'x is a crow', 'x is black' and 'x absorbs light' are each true of just the things in a certain class, namely the class of crows, (respectively) the class of black things, (respectively) the class of things which absorb light.
>
> (ibid. 335)

This argument clashes pretty directly with Quinean nominalism, but I find it pretty dubious. Putnam seems to be saying that to know (9) we have to infer it with the help of (A) and comprehension principles such as

$(\forall y)(y \in \{x: x \text{ is a crow}\} \longleftrightarrow y \text{ is a crow})$.

That would be a more complicated quantificational argument than the syllogism (and perhaps conditionalization) involved in arriving at (9) without any appeal to classes. There is a kind of circularity: in order to arrive at a certain first-order logical conclusion I have to appeal to a more complex, second-order piece of reasoning. I doubt that this argument really expresses Putnam's considered view.

I suspect that the more important point from Putnam's point of view is the observation that he goes on to make, first, that there is an idealization involved in treating the predicates contained in (9) as well-defined, and second, that "knowing a good bit about both language and the world" is involved.

> That 'x is a crow' is a pretty well-defined predicate, 'x is beautiful' is pretty ill-defined, and 'x is a snark' is meaningless, is not logical knowledge, whatever kind of knowledge it may be.
>
> (ibid.)

However, I don't think this point locates the disagreement with Quine. It would lead to the conclusion that there is not an autonomous body of logical knowledge, knowledge that one can arrive at without at any point making commitments that are not logical. But I doubt that Quine thinks otherwise; his holism would suggest a similar conclusion.

Putnam also remarks that insofar as the logician working with first-order logic makes assertions, they are assertions of such properties as validity:

> ... when a logician builds a system which contains such theorems as (5'), *what does he mean to be asserting?* ... The simple fact is that the great majority of logicians would understand the intention to be this: the theorems of the system are intended to be valid formulas. Implicitly, if not explicitly, the logician is concerned to make assertions of the form 'such-and-such is valid', that is, assertions of the kind (A). Thus even first-order logic would normally be understood as a "metatheory".
>
> (ibid.: 336)

Now notions of validity and consequence that involve quantification over classes or sets are entirely standard in logic.[10] One would have to be a nominalist in the general sense, not just the Quinean sense, to refuse to appeal to them. Still, this remark enables us to identify the disagreement between Putnam and Quine. It is in part about the demarcation of logic (e.g. whether it is reasonable to regard second-order logic as logic), but I think it is really about the status or interest of different kinds of statement a logician (or even someone reasoning logically) might make.

Let us consider three cases, (9), by Quine's lights a logical truth, and two formulations of the general principle that it instantiates:

(A′) For any classes α, β, γ, assigned to the letters S, M, P as their extensions, the conditional 'If all S are M and all M are P, then all S are P' is true.

(B) No matter what *terms* or *predicates* are instantiated for S, M, and P, 'If all S are M and all M are P, then all S are P' is true.

Here terms and predicates are to be understood as linguistic items. Quine, of course, has no quarrel with either of these formulations. I think Putnam's reservations about (B) would disappear if one thinks of it as presupposing a definite language, definite enough so that anything that counts as a term will be true or false of any element of the domain.

Putnam seems to be arguing in *Philosophy of Logic* that (A′) is the proper formulation of the general logical principle and that (B) is in some way derivative. Quine does not directly engage this issue, but the procedure of his own *Philosophy of Logic* (written about the same time as Putnam's) suggests a certain primacy to (B), since it is what is arrived at after his discussions of truth-bearers, grammar, and truth (Quine 1970). (B) has a well-known problem, in that it only accords with intuitions concerning logical truth if the language is sufficiently rich. And (A′) has the advantage that it need not refer to a particular language, particularly if it is emended in the natural way so as also to generalize over the domain of quantification. In the end Quine seems to give some fundamental role to both, as well as to the syntactic characterization by a proof procedure.

We are left with less clarity concerning Putnam's attitude toward Quinean nominalism than we would wish for.

III

Putnam does discuss logical relations with an eye to ontological issues in *Ethics without Ontology*. He seems to admit that it is natural to use the language of objects in discussing cases of logical validity. However,

> few philosophers today think it right to take talk of "describing relations between statements" with inflationary metaphysical earnestness,

> that is, to think we are literally *describing* a certain sort of *relation* between certain *intangible objects* when we point out the validity of a simple logical inference in this way.
>
> (Putnam 2004: 56)

He then points out that in mathematical logic the terms of logical relations are typically sentences or formulae. However, he seems to regard the notions used in mathematical logic as ersatz:

> The standard way of treating "validity" in mathematical logic is a way of *doing without* the notion, not a way of analyzing it.
>
> (Putnam 2004: 57)

His meaning might be better expressed by saying that it is a way of giving and operating with a mathematical model of these notions.

Putnam goes on to take up, with a reference to *Methods of Logic*, the question of definitions of validity like (B) above. He is critical of such a definition, partly on grounds familiar from *Philosophy of Logic*. But unlike there, however, he does not seem to be breaking a lance for an alternative like (A′), although one of his objections, that the definition of "tautology" in *Methods* (Quine 1950) "fails to capture what may be called the *universality* of logical truth" (Putnam 2004: 57), may point in that direction, since he interprets Quine as intending to apply his definition to a particular formalized language. As an interpretation of *Methods* this does not strike me as obvious, since so much of the book is devoted to analyzing inferences in natural language.

It's not so clear what the specific criticisms of Quine have to do with the main theme Putnam is pursuing in the lecture. That one shouldn't "take talk of 'describing relations between statements' with inflationary metaphysical earnestness" is a recommendation that Quine and many other logicians agree with. The relative roles of statements of principles of logic involving linguistic items, classes, and propositions or attributes still give rise to delicate questions. Are they in the end not ontological?

I'm a little troubled by the position Putnam takes here because he seems to want to give up what I myself see as one of the insights achieved by more formal analytic philosophy, in particular Quine's writing on quantification and ontology. One might put it by saying that Quine offered a way of making reasonably definite and tractable questions about when we are making reference to objects and committing ourselves to their existence. The effect of this in his own work (already anticipated in many respects by Frege and Carnap) was to forestall the kind of metaphysical inflation that Putnam is most concerned to combat.

IV

Putnam suggests that the passages we have just discussed are a non-technical restatement of parts of his extended paper "Was Wittgenstein *really* an anti-realist about mathematics?" (Putnam 2001). There we do find a more direct criticism of Quine's views on existence and ontology, with the focus more on mathematics. Early in this discussion he makes a very strong assertion:

> Wittgenstein believes – and I think he is right – that it does not make the slightest sense to think that in pure mathematics we are talking about objects.
>
> (Putnam 2001:150)

I don't want to enter into Wittgenstein's views. My own interpretation of Quine has something in common with what Putnam proposes on the next page, that he "has interpreted the statement that in mathematics we are talking about objects in a way that totally robs it of its supposed metaphysical significance" (ibid. 151). I'm not sure what "metaphysical significance" is, but I do think that in talking about ontological questions about mathematics Quine is in the sphere of modest rather than extravagant ontology and that that is true of most of his writing about ontology generally. That is not always the case, and this bothers Putnam. To state in simple terms what bothers him, it is that Quine holds that what there really is is determined in the end by science, but science rather narrowly conceived. Scientific truth does not uniquely determine ontology (as we have noted), but it does greatly constrain it. And in later writings Quine is not sure to what extent scientific truth is itself uniquely determined.

But I want to return to modest ontology. Putnam refers in a footnote to remarks of his own on continually extending the sense of the word "object," but he seems curiously to resist the very well-entrenched extension involved in understanding first-order logic and its application to mathematical theories. His Wittgenstein sees the difference between the use of quantifiers in talking of ordinary objects and talking of objects in pure mathematics as "just too great" (Putnam 2001: 150). Putnam writes that Paul Benacerraf's "Mathematical truth" (Benacerraf 1973)

> clearly assumes that if we take the quantifiers in classical mathematics to be "objectual" quantifications in Quine's sense, then we are committed to regarding them as ranging over objects in a sense perfectly analogous to the sense in which quantifiers over the books in my office range over objects.
>
> (Putnam 2001: 151)

Whether or not Benacerraf regards the two senses as "perfectly analogous," he makes himself vulnerable by arguing that to understand knowledge of objects, the best available theory (as of 1973) is a causal theory. That is obviously a specific epistemological assumption, in no way part of Quine's view of what ontological commitment involves, and even for the Benacerraf of 1973 a separate thesis. Many later writers who have argued that Benacerraf has raised a serious problem for mathematical knowledge have not adopted this epistemological thesis but have sought an alternative that would do the same critical work (see Field 1989, in particular the introduction and the title essay).

The analogy that exists between the use of quantifiers over numbers (natural, real, and complex) and over the books in Hilary Putnam's office is first of all formal: reasoning about both can be modeled by first-order logic. I would guess that children begin to use the determiners of natural language that are modeled as quantifiers with respect to numbers fairly early. I have argued elsewhere that it is logic that tells us what an object is, or better, perhaps, what the concept of object is (Parsons 2008: ch. 1). That makes the concept of object a formal concept. It certainly doesn't give encouragement to the idea that Putnam has so often objected to since the late 1970s, that Reality (presumably including "mathematical reality") consists of a fixed totality of objects with determinate properties.

It is also true that the articulation of such a concept of object is a modern development. It is at most hinted at by Kant, even though the notion of object is a central part of his conceptual apparatus. But Kant's developed conception is that of an object of experience, which will precisely not be an abstract object according to a common way of demarcating abstract objects, which I myself favor, since a Kantian object of experience is located in space and time and enters into causal relations. Probably the first articulation of something close to the formal conception of object was by Frege, although there are probably other nineteenth-century sources.

This, I think, offers the way to look at Putnam's suggestion in a footnote that "of course if one wants to simply extend the notion of object by speaking of 'mathematical objects' in connection with mathematical propositions, that is something different" (Putnam 2004: 151 n. 18).[11] This extension was not just a late invention of philosophers, but a gradual development whose important background was the nineteenth-century transformation of mathematics.

Putnam raises a substantial issue in noting that the language of mathematical logic might be viewed as "the skeleton of an *ideal* language," a view that he says drives Quine's philosophy, or one can regard it as "simply a useful canon of rules of inference, and of formalization as simply a technique of idealization that facilitates the statement of these rules, their representation as (recursive) calculating procedures, and so on" (ibid. 152).

If we mean by the former outlook that the language is supposed to be language as it ought to be, that represents the world as it is while the language we ordinarily use (even in mathematics) is only a rough-and-ready approximation, then it is hard not to discern metaphysical excess. It's a delicate question of Quine-interpretation to what extent Quine's view of the language of science leads him into such excess. Although Putnam is suggesting that it does, I don't think that he means to retract here his earlier statement that Quine is not a metaphysical realist (Putnam 1983: 232, 1987: 31, 1994: 362). In view of his thesis of the inscrutability of reference, Quine could hardly be a metaphysical realist in Putnam's sense, even though Putnam is critical of that thesis.

But seeing mathematical logic as working with a "language" that is an idealized model of actual language does not mean that it is not as workable a model for many purposes as models in science generally are. The application of logic that Putnam might be inclined to question is in developing theories of meaning and reference in natural languages. But in practice he does not question it in application to mathematics, for example that Gödel's incompleteness theorem tells us something about what certain means of proof cannot achieve. Another example would be independence proofs in set theory. Consider the statement "All Σ_2^1 sets of real numbers are Lebesgue measurable." This is one of a number of statements that the classical descriptive set theorists of the early twentieth century tried to prove. They failed. Gödel already showed that this particular statement is refutable if one assumes $V = L$, so that it could not be proved in ZFC. A forcing model showed in the 1960s that it could not be refuted in ZFC. It follows that the methods the classical theorists used could not have decided this question. But that follows only if the representation of their methods of proof in the formal theory ZFC did not lose anything essential about what could be proved and what not.

I doubt that Putnam means to dispute any of this. But he does seem to resist applying the same point of view to ontology.

V

My own puzzlement about Putnam's view of Quine on ontology began with hearing him say in seminars that according to Quine, "exists" is *univocal*.[12] This was something he wished to deny. My first reaction was that this could not be a fundamental question for Quine, because it would make it a substantial issue whether the difference in the use of "exist" in "Tables and chairs exist" and "Complex numbers exist" is a difference of meaning. I don't think he would have been much moved by the comment that these statements represent a different *use* of "exist"; too many possible distinctions could be intended in talking of different uses. He would, however, observe that the difference between the basis on which we judge that tables and chairs exist and the basis on which we judge that complex numbers exist is better described as resting on a difference between tables and chairs and complex numbers, rather than on a difference in what we mean by "exist." Could we use "exist" in the tables-and-chairs sense and consider "Complex numbers exist" so understood? Maybe; it seems that the answer would be that they don't, so that that might capture the nominalist's intention. But then it seems there would be no argument about nominalism; it would just turn on an ambiguity. Leaving Quine aside, that is not what Putnam thinks.

In the paper discussed in the last section, Putnam discusses two more substantially different uses of the existential quantifier, as substitutional and as meaning $\neg\forall\neg$ in the fragment of intuitionistic logic that obeys the classical laws. I wouldn't myself object to saying that these represent a different meaning of the quantifier. Quine considers the substitutional quantifier as offering only an ersatz concept of object and existence. I proposed otherwise some years ago. I don't think the issue is of great moment.[13] If one enters into the intuitionistic way of thinking, which of course Quine does not, one may be tempted to say that it is also not important whether one says that the intuitionistic $\neg\forall\neg$ expresses a different meaning of the existential quantifier from the classical logician's. For lower levels of mathematics it is probably not. For higher set theory, matters are more complicated than I can go into here.

The remark about Benacerraf that we quoted above suggests that it is the objectual interpretation, as opposed to the substitutional, that incorporates allegedly unique meanings of "object" and "exist." Quine says that in the case of a language like that of arithmetic, where for each element of the domain there is a term designating it, there is no difference between the two interpretations. That suggests that he doesn't assign any special metaphysical force to the objectual reading. The substitutional reading is unavailable in cases where the language's provision of names is inadequate, most prominently with the variety of very local objects that we encounter in perception and, at the other end as it were, where uncountable totalities are involved.

VI

Here again, I don't think I have succeeded in putting my finger on what troubles Putnam. Although I am not sure I can attribute this view to Quine, I would suggest that what the univocality claim amounts to is that there is a common formal structure, first-order logic, and that in fact theories can be formulated, admittedly in the idealized way that the application of symbolic logic implies, so as to maintain this structure and still be quite comprehensive, though not perfectly so. However, at least one type of gap in comprehensiveness is corrected by talking of an expanded domain of objects, still within this framework.

This is in keeping with the view of the concept of object as a formal concept, briefly set forth in section IV and developed in more detail in my own writings. Invoking it brings us to one of the deeper disagreements between Putnam and Quine, about the inscrutability or indeterminacy of reference. In a late essay Putnam writes:

> And I still see ontological relativity as a refutation of any philosophical position that leads to it. For what sense can we make of the idea

that the world consists of objects any one of which is a quark in one admissible model, the Eiffel tower in a second admissible model, but is no more intrinsically one of these than any other? Surely the very notion of "object" crumbles if we accept this. The reason that Quine does not see that it does is, I think, his belief that the laws of quantification theory by themselves give enough content to the notion of an object to render notions like "object" and "ontology" usable in metaphysics.

(Putnam 1993: 280–81)

In a footnote Putnam says that he argues against "this view" in the first lecture of *The Many Faces of Realism* (Putnam 1987). By "this view" he seems to refer to the belief he attributes to Quine. I am not sure what argument from that lecture he has in mind. It may be the introduction in the last part the lecture of the idea of conceptual relativity, which is deployed again in the second lecture (see also Putnam 1987a).

The main theme of these lectures is criticism of the view that we can make at a global level a distinction between discourse and theory that represents the world "as it is in itself" and other discourse that is in one way or another second class. The example with which he begins is Wilfrid Sellars's contrast between the manifest image of the world and the scientific image. Much of Putnam's argument in this lecture does not engage the issue of a general concept of object at all, although he might very well say that a metaphysical realist view implies that there is a single "objective" conception of object.[14] Since he doesn't regard Quine as a metaphysical realist, that would not help with my present puzzlement.

Where he does touch on these issues is in introducing the idea of conceptual relativity, which he illustrates by an example of a simple world with three atomic individuals and the contrast between two ways of conceiving it, a "Carnapian" way in which the three individuals are all there is in that world, and a "Polish logician's" way in which there are also mereological sums of these objects (Putnam 1987a).

Evidently this example is meant to offer a very simple model of more serious cases where different conceptual schemes talk of objects in very different ways, with far-reaching consequences as to what, according to the scheme, there is. Putnam writes:

> And so it is no accident that metaphysical realism cannot really recognize the phenomenon of conceptual relativity – for that phenomenon turns on the fact that *the logical primitives themselves, and in particular the notions of object and existence, have a multitude of different uses rather than one absolute 'meaning'*.
>
> (Putnam 1987: 19)

> What is right about the second of the ways we considered of reconciling the two versions or 'worlds' – reinterpreting the existential quantifier – is that the notions of 'object' and 'existence' are not treated as sacrosanct, as having just one possible use. It is very important to recognize that the existential quantifier itself can be used in different ways – ways consonant with the rules of formal logic. What would be wrong ... would be to accept this idea, and then go on to single out *one* use as the only metaphysically serious one.
>
> (ibid. 35)

It is not clear to me whether Putnam means in these passages (or in the larger text of which it is a part) to offer an argument against the understanding of the concept of object as a formal concept. In the situation of the simple model, singling out one of the uses as "the only metaphysically serious one" would necessarily involve putting more into that use than the basic formal concept, which would only decide between the two ways of describing the toy world if we beg the question by assuming that the formal logic underlying the object concept includes mereology. That would not fit Quine's understanding, in view of his privileging of first-order logic. As for my own view, I don't privilege any particular logic, but I also haven't taken a position on whether changing the logic (e.g. adding modality, or going intuitionistic) changes the concepts of object. I do think that certain steps, in particular using modal logic or the most plausible version of the Meinongian idea of nonexistent objects, does introduce ambiguities about *existence* that are glossed over by Quine's view.[15]

Examples of this kind make plausible the view that a formal concept of object is a sort of skeleton, which is amplified in actual applications, possibly by a more determinate choice of logic, but more fundamentally by the flesh that is put on such a skeleton by various instances of objective reference, particularly the most basic, such as that to bodies and other objects of our immediate environment.

Some of Putnam's more everyday examples are probably meant to suggest that even a more liberal version of the skeleton, such as I have sketched here, will not be adequate to the data. I will defer this question for the moment. Already relevant to the univocality issue is that this more liberal attitude toward logic than Quine's introduces what I have described as ambiguities.

The remark at the end of the above quotation from "Realism without Absolutes" suggests a different objection to Quine: that a concept of object along roughly these lines suffices for *metaphysics*. The reply that the formal concept gives only the most general concept of object and that in particular cases (e.g. common sense or fundamental physics) something more needs to be added would, if I am reading Putnam right, be seen as conceding the criticism rather than answering it. Although the reply is one that I might make, I don't think that Quine would make it, given his thesis of the inscrutability of reference. Roughly, the possibilities of reinterpretation that imply that there is no fact of the matter about which objects individual predicates of a theory are true of also affect the predicates that would lay out the "something more" that would distinguish other fundamental kinds of objects.[16]

Already in *The Many Faces of Realism* (1987), and even more in later writings, Putnam engages in a defense of common sense. Of course that separates him from Quine in many ways. I am in general sympathetic to this project and to the complaint that *perception* does not get its due in Quine's account of reference, probably not even in his genetic accounts. But my main concern is with the question whether Putnam has grounds for objecting to the formal concept of object, or at least objecting to reading discourse in which objective reference occurs in such a way as would fit it.

I don't know of a place where he focuses on the issue in this way. However, he appears to raise doubts about it in the first Dewey Lecture. He gives a variety of examples: the sky, mirror images, intentional objects that don't exist, a lamp in his house whose shade falls off whenever it is moved (so that its parts do not in general move together), and particles in quantum mechanics (Putnam 1999: 7–8). The context is the question whether the questionable objects should be recognized as objects by a realistic *theory*. That makes it unclear whether the examples are meant to show a fundamental inadequacy in the formal concept of object.

However, we can consider the examples without answering this question about Putnam's intentions. The most challenging may be that of quantum particles, and here I don't have the knowledge to give an answer.[17] Intentional objects, in my view, are just objects in some other sense talked of in intentional contexts, so that the problems they present are those of intentional contexts. Mirror images seem to me to be objects in a perfectly straightforward sense: they are phenomena as objective as is required by reference in everyday contexts, and spoken of with the same general devices of reference as other everyday "objects," even though they are not bodies. One can say much the same about the sky and about Putnam's lamp; the latter, in fact, is much closer to being a body.

Leaving aside the case of quantum particles, then, I don't see these examples as counterexamples to the formal concept of object.[18]

In this chapter I have surveyed some things Putnam has said about ontology, especially as Quine conceives it. I have not always been successful in making the issues clear. I hope my attempt will stimulate the author and others to help me out. In some cases, where there is disagreement, I have tried to make out that a view either Quine's or close to it can be defended.

Notes

* Sections I–V of this chapter are a revision of my lecture at the Dublin conference, March 11, 2007. Section VI has been added.
1 However, in later writings of Quine, phenomenalism drops out as an option.

2 For first-order arithmetic, the antecedent would have to be the conjunction of some finite subset of the axioms, since first-order arithmetic is not finitely axiomatizable.
3 Putnam never published the technical details of this translation, and his readers have had some difficulty working out his sketch. However, constructions serving the same end have been worked out by others, most extensively by Geoffrey Hellman; see Hellman 1989.
4 Putnam himself deflates the claim made by some writers that such a modal translation avoids the epistemological problem widely thought to exist for reference to mathematical objects. Whether in the case of higher set theory the possibility statements referred to above can be cashed in by objects that are in any plausible sense concrete or nominalistically admissible is questioned in §6 of Parsons 1990. That point affects remarks Putnam makes but, it seems to me, not the issues discussed in the text.
5 As he wrote later in Quine 1986: 14.
6 I conjecture that this paper represents a rather rapid response to his encounter with Tarski in 1933, when he must have learned something of Tarski's work on truth, although it was only in 1935 that the *Wahrheitsbegriff* was published in a language Quine could read. Central to both the non-propositional readings that Quine proposes is the idea that sentences can be treated as truth vehicles. However, Quine mentions Wittgenstein's *Tractatus* and reads it as identifying propositions with sentences, so that one can't be certain about Tarski's decisive influence.
7 Actually, Quine 1966a is an abstract of the lecture. On the complicated publication history of the lecture, see Parsons 2011: 214–15.
8 Curiously, the formulation suggests the "iterative conception of set," which is hardly mentioned in Quine's writing about set theory. I now (December 2011) think it more likely that Quine had in mind the simple theory of types.
9 Further to this theme see Parsons 2011.
10 I don't know whether Putnam speaks of classes rather than sets to accommodate the case where predicates involved might not have sets as their extensions.
11 Putnam goes on to say that "then the application of 'intangible' makes no sense, since the tangible/intangible distinction goes with the ordinary, unextended use." I am not persuaded. Why should that not have been extended as well? What is Putnam to make of "intangible drilling costs" in the Federal income tax code? There is even a Wittgensteinian reply suggested by statements in writings of William Tait: to say that numbers are "intangible" is a grammatical remark, roughly that it does not make sense to say that we touch them.
12 Putnam does say this in print in a note to his first Dewey Lecture (Putnam 1999: 179 n. 12). (I had not noticed this before the Dublin conference.) Putnam seems to recognize there that the question of the univocality of "exist" should not be a fundamental one for Quine, but he says that Quine's practice with regard to issues of ontology is inconsistent with this. The explanation I would offer is that according to Quine, questions of ontological commitment properly arise only for statements and theories regimented in first-order logic. I think he takes that to imply not that the words "object" and "exist" as we inherit them are univocal in a way in which other philosophically significant words are not, but rather that the schematic and formal concepts of object and existence embodied in first-order logic suffice for his philosophical purposes, and possibly for any serious discussion of ontology. Like Putnam, I have argued that Quine's framework is too narrow, but Putnam's objection is much more far-reaching.
13 However, the substitutional interpretation is a sort of first approximation to the understanding of quantifiers in constructive type theories such as Per Martin-Löf's; see Parsons 1986.

14 There is a connection between metaphysical realism and the recently much discussed question about quantification over absolutely everything, whether it makes sense, or at least makes sense in the way that quantification ordinarily does. I have argued (Parsons 2006) that the affirmative view implies a form of metaphysical realism. That the converse does not hold, that someone holding the negative view need not deny metaphysical realism, is argued in Glanzberg 2004.

My claim would not have been news to Putnam, who, in the context of explaining his rejection of metaphysical realism, writes of the notion of object as "inherently extendable" and glosses conceptual relativity as "the idea that there are many usable extensions of the notion of object, and many alternative ways of describing objects" (Putnam 1994: 305).

15 On modality and its relation to mathematical existence, see Parsons 1983, Essays 1, 7, and 10; on non-existent objects see Parsons 2008, §6.

16 An instructive treatment of the issues is Hylton 2004. Putnam is not mentioned in Hylton's essay, but it makes clear how deep the differences are that underlie Putnam's rejection of Quine's indeterminacy thesis.

17 It appears that the issue might be put as one about their individuation. They may challenge any account of the notion of object. Interestingly, Quine mentions puzzles about quantum particles as a reason for adopting an ontology that dispenses with matter in favor of space-time regions and ultimately sets (Quine 1976: 498–500).

18 It must be admitted, however, that as usually described (in particular by me) this conception does involve some idealization. For example, the application of logic usually does not take account of vagueness, which can affect even identity statements. In the above I have taken this as going without saying.

Bibliography

Note that papers by Putnam and Quine reprinted in their collections are cited according to the reprints, in the latest edition where applicable.

Benacerraf, Paul (1973) "Mathematical Truth," *The Journal of Philosophy* 70: 661–79.
Field, Hartry (1989) *Realism, Mathematics, and Modality*, Oxford: Blackwell.
Glanzberg, Michael (2004) "Quantification and realism," *Philosophy and Phenomenological Research* 69: 541–72.
Goodman, Nelson and W. V. Quine (1947) "Steps toward a constructive nominalism," *The Journal of Symbolic Logic* 12: 105–22, reprinted in Goodman, *Problems and Projects*, Indianapolis: Bobbs-Merrill, 1972, 173–98.
Hellman, Geoffrey (1989) *Mathematics without Numbers: Toward a Modal-Structural Interpretation*, Oxford: Clarendon Press.
Hylton, Peter (2004) "Quine on Reference and Ontology," in Roger F. Gibson, Jr. (ed.), *The Cambridge Companion to Quine*, Cambridge: Cambridge University Press, 115–50.
Parsons, Charles (1983) *Mathematics in Philosophy: Selected Essays*, Ithaca, NY: Cornell University Press.
——(1986) "Intuition in Constructive Mathematics," in Jeremy Butterfield (ed.), *Language, Mind, and Logic*, Cambridge: Cambridge University Press, 211–29.
——(1990) "The Structuralist View of Mathematical Objects," *Synthese* 84: 303–46.
——(2006) "The problem of absolute universality," in Agustín Rayo and Gabriel Uzquiano (eds.), *Absolute Generality*, Oxford: Clarendon Press, 203–19.

——(2008) *Mathematical Thought and its Objects*, Cambridge: Cambridge University Press.
——2011 "Quine's nominalism," *American Philosophical Quarterly* 48: 213–28.
Putnam, Hilary (1967) "Mathematics without foundations," *The Journal of Philosophy* 64: 5–22, reprinted in Putnam 1975: 43–59.
——(1971) *Philosophy of Logic*, New York: Harper and Row, reprinted in Putnam 1975 (2nd edn only): 323–57.
——, 1975. *Mathematics, Matter, and Method. Philosophical Papers*, vol. 1, Cambridge: Cambridge University Press. 2nd edn 1979.
——(1978) "Realism and Reason," in *Meaning and the Moral Sciences*, London: Routledge and Kegan Paul.
——(1983) "Realism and Reason," in *Philosophical Papers*, vol. 3, Cambridge: Cambridge University Press.
——(1987) *The Many Faces of Realism*, La Salle, Ill.: Open Court.
——(1987a) Truth and convention," *Dialectica* 41, 69–77, reprinted in Putnam, *Realism with a Human Face*, ed. James Conant, Cambridge, MA: Harvard University Press, 1990, 96–104.
——(1993) "Realism without Absolutes," *International Journal of Philosophical Studies* 1: 179–92. Reprinted in Putnam 1994.
——(1994) *Words and Life*, ed. James Conant, Cambridge, MA: Harvard University Press.
——(1999) *The Threefold Cord*: Mind, Body and World, New York: Columbia University Press.
——(2001) "Was Wittgenstein *really* an anti-realist about mathematics?," in Timothy McCarthy and Sean C. Stidd (eds.), *Wittgenstein in America*, Oxford: Clarendon Press, 140–94.
——(2004) *Ethics without Ontology*, Cambridge, MA: Harvard University Press.
Quine, W. V. (1934) "Ontological Remarks on the Propositional Calculus," *Mind* 43, 472–76. Reprinted in Quine 1966.
——(1948) "On What There Is," *The Review of Metaphysics* 2: 21–38. Reprinted with additions in *From a Logical Point of View*, Cambridge, MA: Harvard University Press, 1953, 1–19.
——(1950) *Methods of Logic*, New York: Holt. Citations will fit the second edition (1959) but not necessarily later editions.
——(1951) "On Carnap's Views on Ontology," *Philosophical Studies* 2: 65–72. Reprinted in Quine 1966.
——(1966) *The Ways of Paradox*. New York: Random House, 2nd edn, expanded, Cambridge, MA: Harvard University Press, 1976. All essays in the first edition of this work are also included in the second.
——(1966a) "A Logistical Approach to the Ontological Problem," in Quine 1966: 64–69.
——(1970) *Philosophy of Logic*, Englewood Cliffs, NJ: Prentice-Hall, 2nd edn, Cambridge, MA: Harvard University Press, 1986.
——(1976) "Whither Physical Objects?," in Robert S. Cohen, Paul K. Feyerabend, and Marx W. Wartofsky (eds.), *Essays in Memory of Imre Lakatos*, Boston Studies in the Philosophy of Science, vol. 39, Dordrecht: Reidel, 497–504.
——(1981) *Theories and Things*, Cambridge, MA: Harvard University Press.
——(1986) "Autobiography of W. V. Quine," in Lewis Edwin Hahn and Paul Arthur Schilpp (eds.), *The Philosophy of W. V. Quine*, La Salle, Ill.: Open Court, 3–46.

COMMENTS ON CHARLES PARSONS' "PUTNAM ON EXISTENCE AND ONTOLOGY"

Hilary Putnam

I am not surprised that Charles Parsons thinks I have misinterpreted or misrepresented some of Quine's views. That is simply what happens when one criticizes great philosophers. If you criticize any of them, someone will always say that you have misunderstood. I also know that one can play the game of always seeking an interpretation that makes one's favorite philosopher come out *completely right*. That was my own attitude towards Quine's philosophy when I came to UCLA as a graduate student in 1949; at the very first meeting of Reichenbach's seminar, he asked me to talk about Quine's views on ontology. And Reichenbach was impatient with my endorsement of those views, and he said to me "So, you are saying that the existence of sets, is just like the existence of electrons." Over the years (and it took me decades) I have come to the conclusion that, "Yes, that *was* Quine's view, and it's wrong." I no longer interpret Quine so that he always comes out right. For example, Quine says in *Theories and Things* (1981) that the numbers five and twelve are "intangible objects"; that might be a good description of *photons* but it makes five and twelve *much too much* like photons. I now believe that Quine did fall into the error that Reichenbach rightly foresaw, the error of *assimilating the epistemology of mathematics to the epistemology of theoretical physics*.

Beyond these words, I'll only offer two clarifications of my past criticisms of Quine. One of my criticisms was in a sense terminological. I criticized his claim that the term "logic" should not apply to any part of set theory in my *Philosophy of Logic* (1972). There I pointed out that the statement "The syllogism All S are M, all M are P, therefore all S are P is valid" seems, on Quine's view, to be a statement of *set theory*, not a statement of logic (because the definition of "valid" involves a quantifier over set-theoretic entities, viz. interpretations). And that seems to me a very unnatural way to restrict the term "logic."

The second clarification, or piece of background information, is that I have claimed in print that Quine's way of treating validity, which is the standard way in mathematical logic, is a way of *doing without the notion* and not a way of analyzing it. Moreover, I have a similar claim to make concerning Tarski's so-called "semantical conception of truth" (Tarski 1944). First, I've argued in a number of papers starting with "A Comparison of Something with Something Else" that Tarski's definition of truth is only correct *provided the mathematical axioms of the metalanguage are true* – and that proviso uses the very notion of truth that some people claim Tarski completely explained for us! Why do I say this? Well, remember that Tarski's criterion of adequacy is that *all the T-sentences must be theorems of the metalanguage*. If the metalanguage is *incorrect* and it can be *incorrect without being inconsistent*, a truth predicate can be *adequate in Tarski's sense and extensionally incorrect!* And that is very often forgotten. In any case, I regard a Tarskian truth definition as certainly not *intensionally* correct (that is, it does not provide any predicate which is conceptually equivalent to "true") for reasons I gave in "A Comparison of Something with Something Else." Quite simply, if the sentence "Snow is white" is TR, where TR is the predicate Tarski shows us how to define, then it would have *that* property TR *no matter what the words "snow" and "white" meant*, as long as snow was still that color. "Snow is white" is TR even in worlds in which the words "snow" and "white" have different meanings.

There is a little elementary school joke that I like to use to illustrate this point, namely "What colour would snow be (or would coal be) if the word 'white' meant *black* and the word 'black' meant *white*?" The correct answer is, "It would still be white" (and coal would still be black). Similarly, the *words* in which the Tarskian definition of truth are stated would obviously change their meaning in a world, call it W, in which "snow" changed its meaning. So in English$_W$ the sentence "Snow is white" would be true only if snow is black, but the famous T-sentence ["'Snow is white' is TR if and only if snow is white"] would still be true (however it would *mean* "Snow is white" is TR if and only if snow is black – "TR" would denote a different property, because its definition would have a different meaning). But the property TR that *Tarski* defines in the actual world when *he* gives the same truth definition is a property that the sentence "snow is white" would *not* have in W, even though "Snow is white" would be *true as understood in* W. Again I think it's a slightly hard point and it illustrates just how deep that joke we heard in elementary school about coal and snow is and what would happen if white and black shifted. However, I would of course grant that Tarski did show us a way to give an *extensionally correct* definition of true in L – language by language. But the notion of *truth in L where L is a variable over languages* – which I think is an indispensable one even if, in terms Parsons has used in his papers on the Liar paradox, it can only be explained "schematically," is not analyzed at all. And we do have to speak of "all languages" and of truth in an arbitrary language.

Bibliography

Putnam, Hilary (1972) *Philosophy of Logic*, London: Allen and Unwin.
——(1985) "A Comparison of Something with Something Else," *New Literary History* 17(1): 61–79. Reprinted in *Words and Life*, Cambridge, MA: Harvard University Press, 1994, 330–50.
Quine, W. V. (1981) *Theories and Things*, Cambridge, MA: Harvard University Press.
Tarski, Alfred (1944) "The Semantic Conception of Truth," *Philosophy and Phenomenological Research* 4(1): 341–75.

6

SOME SOURCES OF PUTNAM'S PLURALISM

Russell B. Goodman

> Reason has so many forms that we do not know which to resort to: experience has no fewer.
>
> (Montaigne 1991: 1207)

I am interested in the lives of certain ideas, in their adventures as Whitehead put it (Whitehead 1933). One of these ideas is pragmatism, which lives in a tradition of largely but not entirely American thought, in which Hilary Putnam has a stellar place. Another is pluralism, an allied tradition of thought, or what can be seen as an alternative version of the same tradition. My thesis here is that Putnam has a place in this tradition as well. Philosophical pluralism was first canonized in a book published in 1920 by a young Frenchman, Jean Wahl, who went on to become a professor at the Sorbonne, the teacher of Jean-Paul Sartre, and the author in the 1930s of influential books on Hegel and Kierkegaard. Wahl's book on pluralism, entitled *Les philosophies pluralistes d'Angleterre et d'Amérique*, was published in an English version by Routledge in 1925 as *Pluralist Philosophies of England and America*.

In Wahl's lineup of pluralist thinkers, William James occupies the central place, not least for his book *A Pluralistic Universe* (1909). Wahl discusses James's philosophy as a whole from a pluralist perspective, focusing on his "cult of the particular," "polytheism," "temporalism," and "criticism of the idea of totality." He also includes many other writers in his pluralist panorama: Gustav Fechner, Hermann Lötze, Wilhelm Wundt, Charles Renouvier, John Stuart Mill (to whom James dedicated *Pragmatism*), John Dewey, Horace Kallen, George Santayana, Ferdinand Canning Scott Schiller – even George Holmes Howison of Berkeley, said to be a "pluralist idealist" of the "Californian School," and Bertrand Russell and G. E. Moore, said to be aligned with pluralism because of their views about temporality.

What then does Wahl mean by pluralism? He offers no one definition but rather a plurality of them, a plurality of pluralisms, and he acknowledges that Arthur Lovejoy might easily follow up his already classic paper

"The Thirteen Pragmatisms" with a similar paper on the many pluralisms. Wahl beats him to it, however, by distinguishing among noetic or epistemological, metaphysical, aesthetic, moral, religious, and logical pluralisms. Following James, for example, he states that noetic pluralism is the view that "the facts and worths of life need many cognizers to take them in. There is no point of view absolutely public and universal" (Wahl 1925: 155). Speaking more generally, he writes that "pluralism is a philosophy which insists by preference on diversity of principles ... it asserts both the diverse character and the temporal character of things" (Wahl 1925: 275). A few pages later Wahl writes that "pluralism is the affirmation of the irreducibility of certain ideas and certain things," and also that it is a form of realism: "pluralism is ... a profound realism that asserts the irreducibility of phenomena. ... the irreducibility of one domain of the world to another" (Wahl 1925: 279). Wahl notices the confluence between pragmatism and pluralism, but he denies their identity: "Speaking generally, pluralism is a metaphysic of pragmatism; though pragmatists cannot hold the monopoly of this metaphysic. It is usually associated with a realistic tendency which is particularly strong in the United States" (Wahl 1925: 273).

The convergence of pragmatism, pluralism, and a strong "realistic tendency" is again to be found in the United States, in the work of our contemporary Hilary Putnam. Let me briefly consider some ways in which Wahl's words are true of Putnam. Regarding irreducibility, and leaving aside his work in the philosophy of mind, consider Putnam's conclusion from a section entitled "Conceptual Pluralism" in *Ethics Without Ontology*. Putnam is considering the long-standing problem of how what he calls the "fields and particles scheme" of physics and the everyday scheme of "tables and chairs" relate to one another. He writes: "That we can use both of these schemes without being required to reduce one or both of them to some single fundamental and universal ontology is the doctrine of pluralism" (Putnam 2004: 48–49).

Elsewhere, Putnam does not speak of the everyday as a "scheme," and instead follows Husserl and Wittgenstein in defending the authority and legitimacy of what he calls "the lebenswelt." Complaining that philosophy makes us "unfit to dwell in the common" (Putnam 1990: 118), Putnam urges us to "accept" "the *Lebenswelt*, the world as we actually experience it" (Putnam 1990: 116).[1] The verb "accept" is crucial here, because Putnam does not think that the existence of the world can be proven, and he does not think that the everyday world is the subject of a theory that is in competition with science. It is at this point that his thought converges with that of his Harvard colleague Stanley Cavell, who wrote in "The Avoidance of Love" (1969) that "what skepticism suggests is that since we cannot know the world exists, its presentness to us cannot be a function of knowing. The world is to be accepted; as the presentness of other minds is not to be known, but acknowledged" (Cavell 1969: 324). This is not meant to be a refutation of or even an avoidance of skepticism, but rather the recognition of a difference. It is a difference that is obscured, Putnam holds, in the search for "the One Method by which all our beliefs can be appraised" (Putnam 1987: 118).

Pluralism shows up in Putnam's work not only in the contrast between science and the everyday – a species of what several recent writers have called "vertical pluralism," the pluralism of different domains or discourses – but in his discussions of truth, even truth within science. This latter is "horizontal pluralism," the claim, as Maria Baghramian puts it, "that there can be more than one correct account of how things are in any given domain" (Baghramian 2004: 304). In his pragmatist period Putnam defends a conception of truth that owes something to Charles Sanders Peirce, who wrote that the "opinion which is fated to be ultimately agreed to by all who investigate, is what we mean by the truth" (Peirce 1992: 139). Putnam states that "a true statement is one that could be justified were epistemic conditions ideal" (Putnam 1987: vii). Unlike Peirce, however, Putnam asserts that there need not be only one such scheme. Why, he asks, "should there not sometimes be equally coherent but incompatible conceptual schemes which fit our experiential beliefs equally well? If truth is not (unique) correspondence then the possibility of a certain pluralism is opened up" (Putnam 1987: 73).

These incompatible schemes fit the experiential beliefs of a community of inquirers, as wave and particle schemes appeal to the community of physicists. Putnam goes further, however, in asserting what amounts to another form of pluralism in *Realism with a Human Face* when he denies that truth can conceivably be attained by a single community. It is not that the community will in the long run find several schemes that fit their experiential beliefs, but that no single community can know all the truth.

> People have attributed to me the idea that we can sensibly imagine conditions which are *simultaneously ideal* for the ascertainment of any truth whatsoever, or simultaneously ideal for answering any question whatsoever. I have never thought such a thing. ... There are some statements which we can only verify by failing to verify other statements.
>
> (Putnam 1990: viii)

This statement chimes with James's claim, quoted by Wahl, that there is "no absolutely public and universal point of view."

There is yet another site in Putnam's writing where a kind of pluralism emerges. This is in "James's Theory of Perception," in *Realism with a Human Face*, one of the most sympathetic and imaginative discussions of James's so-called "radical empiricism" to be found in the literature. For a Darwinian like James, Putnam argues, no two individuals are identical, so that although "there is a 'central tendency,' this tendency is simply an average; Darwin would say that it is a mere abstraction." For Darwin, Putnam concludes, "the reality is the variation," not the type (Putnam 1987: 235). James's criticism of the power of concepts to capture reality is a reminder, Putnam argues, "that even though the rationalistic type of thinking has its place – it is sometimes pragmatically effective – once it becomes one's only way of thinking, one is bound to lose the world for a beautiful model" (Putnam 1987: 236). The world one loses is the world of concrete particulars, of "variations." This is a pluralism not of schemes or truths, but of particulars, and it is aptly rendered by James's explicitly pluralistic slogan quoted above, namely: "Something always escapes."

I have now touched on Putnam's defense of common sense against scientific reductionism, and of the possibility of incompatible schemes at the limit of inquiry, and his idea that no community could be in the position to justify every true statement. I want now to consider even more briefly three other characteristics of pluralism mentioned by Wahl: their focus on temporality, their realism, and their pragmatism.

Temporality appears not in Putnam's metaphysics but in his epistemology. The term "history" in Putnam's title, *Reason, Truth, and History*, for example, refers to the view of knowledge that he learns not only from James and John Dewey, but also from Thomas Kuhn, Michel Foucault, and even Ludwig Wittgenstein. Putnam reads Foucault's historical studies, for example, not as those of a relativist who is concerned to argue that "past practices were more rational than they look to be," but as those of a fallibilist, for whom all practices, including our own, are less rational than they appear to be. Putnam concedes that rationality cannot be "defined by a 'canon' or set of principles," and that our conceptions of the cognitive virtues evolve, but he at the same time asserts the authority of regulative ideas, such as that of "of a just, attentive, balanced intellect" (Putnam 1987: 163). In *Ethics Without Ontology* Putnam finds a continuing basis for agreement with Foucault's idea that our concepts have histories:

> Although "analytic" philosophers still often write as if concepts were a-historic entities (which is exactly how they were conceived by the fathers of analytic philosophy, Moore and Russell), there is no reason for their latter-day successors to deny that concepts have a history, and that conceptual analysis and historical analysis can fruitfully enrich each other ...
> (Putnam 2004: 113)

I shall be even briefer with regard to Putnam's realism and pragmatism. Putnam is of course a major contributor to the revival of pragmatism in the last decades of the twentieth century, and his pragmatist period is marked by a vigorous attempt to defend a form of realism. Following Kant and James, he attempts both to credit the human contribution to the world we know – enunciated in the slogan he draws from James, that "the trail of the human serpent is over everything" – and at the same time to assert the reality and objectivity of that world. Putnam called one such attempt "internal realism," and later chose "pragmatic realism" when the "internal" in "internal realism" seemed to suggest a lack of contact with the world or an excessive subjectivity. In any case, it is only "metaphysical realism" – the fantasy of a "God's eye view of the world" – that Putnam rejects, not the realism of common sense or of science. In his book *The Many Faces of Realism*, as in its title, Putnam asserts both plurality and realism.

Finally, Wahl states that pragmatists tend to be pluralists, and so it is in the case of Putnam, who accounts for the connection in the statement cited above. If "the world" is the world as we conceptualize and encounter it, a world bearing the marks of the human serpent, then, as Putnam says, a certain possibility of plural schemes is opened up.

In the rest of this essay I want to consider three figures in the background of Putnam's pluralism. Two of them, like Putnam himself, are self-identified pragmatists who taught at Harvard: William James[2] and Nelson Goodman. The third is Ludwig Wittgenstein, neither a pragmatist nor a Harvard professor, whose importance for Putnam and in general for what we know as "neo-pragmatism" is immense, and whose relation both to pragmatism and to pluralism is interestingly complicated.

The term *pluralism*, the *Oxford English Dictionary* tells us, originally had an ecclesiastical use, indicating the practice of holding more than one office at a time. It first makes its way into philosophy only in the late nineteenth century. James employs the term in *The Varieties of Religious Experience* (1902), and in *A Pluralistic Universe*, where he defines pluralism as "the doctrine that [the universe] is many." He goes on to state:

> Everything you can think of, however vast or inclusive, has on the pluralist view a genuinely 'external' environment of some sort or amount. Things are 'with' one another in many ways, but nothing includes everything, or dominates over everything. The word 'and' trails along after every sentence. Something always escapes. 'Ever not quite' has to be said of the best attempts made anywhere in the universe at attaining all-inclusiveness. The pluralistic world is thus more like a federal republic than like an empire or a kingdom.
> (James 1902–1910: 776)

The dominating unity of James's day was the Hegelian and Neo-Hegelian Absolute Spirit propounded by his contemporaries Thomas Hill Green and F. H. Bradley, but James also wished to counter an emerging scientific reductionism. His position is both metaphysical and epistemological: there is no one overarching entity, and no all-inclusive explanation of the world. James develops the idea of multiple systems of truth, multiple useful ways of making our way through the world. In *Pragmatism's* (1907), chapter on "Pragmatism and Common Sense," James writes that our common "ways of thinking," "concepts" or "categories" have a history, and that our notions of "One Time," "One Space," "Bodies," "Minds," "Thing," "Kinds," "causal influences" and "Subjects and attributes" are useful tools "by which we handle facts by thinking them" (James 1902–1910: 561). These ways of thinking, he suggests, are discoveries of "prehistoric geniuses whose names the night of antiquity has covered up" and which then "*spread*" over long periods of time "until all language rested on them and we are now incapable of thinking naturally in any other terms" (James 1902–1910: 566). "There are many conceptual systems," James holds, including the categories of common sense, the theories of science, the criticism of philosophy – all of them means of "rationalizing" the "everlasting weather of our perceptions" (James 1902–1910: 562). James presses the question, so important for Putnam, of which of these schemes is the true one, and he answers that although each is useful for one sphere of life or another, there

> is no *ringing* conclusion possible when we compare these types of thinking, with a view to telling which is the more absolutely true. ... Common sense is better for one sphere of life, science for another, philosophic criticism for a third; but whether either be *truer* absolutely, Heaven only knows.
>
> (James 1902–1910: 569)

If Putnam wants to admit into his republic the language and practices of ordinary life, including those of morality, James wants to admit not only science and common sense, but religion in at least some of its aspects. James was a scientist: he attended the Lawrence Scientific School at Harvard, not Harvard College, and spent his junior year abroad floating down the Amazon with Louis Agassiz. His graduate degree was in medicine and his first appointments were teaching anatomy and physiology at Harvard, though he soon moved to psychology and then philosophy. He begins *The Varieties of Religious Experience* with a chapter on religion and neurology, but it is in the conclusion to that work that he makes some of his most provocative statements about the sciences. "The scientist" he states "is, during his scientific hours at least, so materialistic that one may well say that on the whole the influence of science goes against the notion that religion should be recognized at all" (James 1994: 533). James nevertheless speaks up for religion not as a set of doctrines or practices, but as an example of certain modes of experiencing and conceptualizing the world.

> It is the terror and beauty of phenomena, the "promise" of the dawn and of the rainbow, the "voice" of the thunder, the "gentleness" of the summer rain, the "sublimity" of the stars, and not the physical

laws which these things follow, by which the religious mind still continues to be most impressed ...

(James 1994: 541)

James is impressed too, and he sees the source of religion's authority in the personal point of view. "Science" (with a capital "S") is "impersonal" (James 1994: 543) by its very nature, and therefore, James argues, it is not equipped to register the world in these ways. The sciences offer us ways of knowing the world, but there are other ways which science cannot duplicate or reduce to its terms. The universe is:

a more many-sided affair than any sect, even the scientific sect, allows for. ... the world can be handled according to many systems of ideas, and is so handled by different men, and will each time give some characteristic kind of profit, for which he cares, to the handler, while at the same time some other kind of profit has to be omitted or postponed.

(James 1994: 137–38)

James defends these personal and humanized ways of thinking against the charge that they are just survivals that must be eliminated in the course of a general "deanthropomorphization of the imagination." James's call not only to retain and develop but to recognize the authority of an anthropomorphized imagination is echoed ninety years later in Putnam's assertions of the objective validity of the human point of view. "There *are*," Putnam tells us in *The Many Faces of Realism*, "tables and chairs and ice cubes. There are also electrons and space-time regions and prime numbers and people who are a menace to world peace and moments of beauty and transcendence and many other things" (Putnam 1987: 16). These tables and chairs are James's subject in "Pragmatism and Common Sense," and these moments of beauty and transcendence are his subjects in *The Varieties of Religious Experience*.

Putnam acknowledges the importance of Nelson Goodman for his own pragmatism in many places in his writing. In "After Empiricism," for example, he links him with Husserl, Merleau-Ponty, Austin, and Wittgenstein in countering Hume's project of dividing reality into "the Furniture of the Universe" on the one hand and "our projections" on the other (Putnam 1987: 52). In his earlier review of *Ways of Worldmaking* (1978), Putnam states that "the heart of Goodman's book ... is its defense of pluralism." For example, he takes Goodman as saying that while both physicalism and phenomenalism are good "research programs," if they become "dogmatic monisms ... there is everything wrong with both of them" (Putnam 1983: 155).

Putnam entitles a section of his review "one world or many?" and this is the question I now want to consider, with the help of an earlier paper by

Goodman that Putnam does not mention, entitled "The Way the World Is" (1960). In this paper, published, appropriately enough, in *The Review of Metaphysics*, Goodman takes up the question of the way the world is by first considering how it is given to us, a question to which he argues there is no clear answer. He next turns to the question of how the world is best seen, and he argues that the answers are many:

> For the ways of seeing and picturing are many and various; some are strong, effective, useful, intriguing, or sensitive; others are weak, foolish, dull, banal, or blurred. But even if all the latter are excluded, still none of the rest can lay any good claim to be the way of seeing or picturing the world the way it is.
> (N. Goodman 1972: 29)

Goodman's central claim, embedded in the following passage, is that there is no *one* way the world is, but that the world is *many* ways:

> If I were asked what is *the* food for men, I should have to answer 'none'. For there are many foods. And if I am asked what is the way the world is, I must likewise answer, 'none'. For the world is many ways. ... For me, there is no way that is the way the world is; and so of course no description can capture it. But there are many ways the world is, and every true description captures one of them.
> (N. Goodman 1972: 31)

Whereas in *Ways of Worldmaking*, Goodman speaks of "multiple actual worlds" (N. Goodman 1978: 6), here he speaks of the many ways the world is. Putnam calls the multiple actual worlds position "naughty" (Putnam 1987: 42), presumably because it clashes with our commonsense view that there is just the world. That is why I like the language of "The Way the World Is." However, Goodman argues that it makes little difference how we speak about the matter, that whether there are many worlds or one world with many versions depends on how we take things:

> As intimated by William James's equivocal title *A Pluralistic Universe*, the issue between monism and pluralism tends to evaporate under analysis. If there is but one world, it embraces a multiplicity of contrasting aspects; if there are many worlds, the collection of them all is one. The one world may be taken as many, or the many worlds taken as one; whether one or many depends on the way of taking.
> (N. Goodman 1972: 2)

I would want to say, then, that I find it most profitable and least confusing to take the one world as many rather than to speak of many worlds. I think also that the idea of contrasting aspects is worth considering, for its implication that multiplicity is a feature not just of our schemes, theories, or versions, but of the world itself. How much distance, I wonder, is there between Putnam's "many faces of realism" and Goodman's "multiplicity of contrasting aspects"?

Before leaving "The Way the World Is," I want to consider Goodman's statement that: "If I were asked what is *the* food for men, I should have to answer 'none'. For there are many foods." Goodman is a pluralist about foods. He gives no examples, but it is easy to think not just of different bowls of cornflakes and multiple hamburgers, but of different systems, cultures of foods: Sichuan, Tunisian, Italian, Mexican, paella, fejoado, poi, bagels, collard greens, nettle stew, and Cashel blue. It is so hard *not* to agree with Goodman that there is no one food for human beings that I am reminded of Wittgenstein's statement in the *Investigations* that if one were to try to advance theses in philosophy it would be impossible, because a philosophical thesis is one to which everyone would agree (Wittgenstein 1953: 128). The pluralist seems sometimes not so much to be advancing a thesis as attempting to remind us of something – "for a certain purpose," as Wittgenstein says (Wittgenstein 1953: 127). What are Goodman's purposes in reminding us about the plurality of foods and asserting the plurality of worlds?

Goodman raises just this question in *Ways of Worldmaking* when he writes:

> in what non-trivial sense are there ... many worlds? Just this, I think: that many different world-versions are of independent interest and importance, without any requirement or presumption of reducibility to a single base. The pluralist, far from being anti-scientific, accepts the sciences at full value. His typical adversary is the monopolistic materialist or physicalist who maintains that one system, physics, is preeminent and all-inclusive, such that every other version must eventually be reduced to it or rejected as false or meaningless. ... But the evidence for such reducibility is negligible. ... (How do you go about reducing Constable's or James Joyce's world-view to physics?) ... A reduction from one system to another can make a genuine contribution to understanding the interrelationships among world-versions; but reduction in any reasonably strict sense is rare, almost always partial, and seldom if ever unique. ... .The pluralists' acceptance of versions other than physics implies no relaxation of rigor but a recognition that standards different from yet no less exacting than those applied in science are appropriate for appraising what is conveyed in perceptual or pictorial or literary versions ...
> (N. Goodman 1978: 4–5)

As it is for Putnam, reductive physicalism is Goodman's main enemy, but in contrast to both Putnam and James, Goodman makes art a central concern. It is Constable's or Joyce's "world-view" from which we are said to learn, just as we learn from those of Aristotle or Einstein. Constable, Picasso, Fra Angelico, and the unnamed wall painters of ancient Egypt all show us aspects of the world, according to Goodman. In *Languages of Art* Goodman argues that both art and language can refer to or depict the world, and he draws attention to art's capacities for exemplification and expression. In *Ways of Worldmaking* he argues that expression and exemplification add to the ways in which we understand the world – add to the worlds we make, as he prefers to put it: "Worlds are made not only by what is said literally but also by what is said metaphorically, and not only by what is said either literally or metaphorically but also by what is exemplified and expressed – by what is shown as well as by what is said" (N. Goodman 1978: 15). In his review of *Ways of Worldmaking*, Putnam pushes Goodman toward an even wider pluralism that would acknowledge the moral underpinnings of his project: "Goodman recognizes that we wish to build worlds because doing so enriches us in many ways. And this, it seems to me, requires him to recognize that the notions of truth and rightness subserve a vision of the good" (Putnam 1987: 168–69). Putnam's critique not only looks forward to his concern with what he calls "the collapse of the fact/value dichotomy," but, as he is well aware, back to William James's view in *Pragmatism* that truth is "one species of good" (James 1902–1910: 520).

Wittgenstein is an important influence on Putnam, but he is neither a pragmatist nor a self-identified pluralist. Nevertheless, his later philosophy is deeply concerned with plurality, multiplicity, and variety, and this is one reason, I have argued, for the deep affinity he felt for William James, despite his hostility to pragmatism (R. Goodman 2002). Wittgenstein does not, however, assert a multiplicity of world versions or worlds, but rather a "multiplicity" of language-games and concepts. He states that there are "*countless*" different kinds of use of words and sentences, and that

> It is interesting to compare the multiplicity of the tools in language and of the ways they are used, the multiplicity of kinds of word and sentence, with what logicians have said about the structure of language. (Including the author of the *Tractatus Logico-Philosophicus*.)

This multiplicity, he also states, has a temporal structure: it "is not something fixed, given once for all; but new types of language, new language-games, as we may say, come into existence, and others become obsolete and get forgotten" (Wittgenstein 1953: 23). Wittgenstein considered as an epigraph for the *Investigations* a quotation from *King Lear* – "I'll teach you differences." His book teaches the differences among such concepts as intending, deciding, hoping, thinking, conversing, reading, and confessing, and among the language-games we play in describing things, giving orders or measurements, making up a story, telling jokes, playing chess, and translating from one language into another.

Wittgenstein also teaches the difference between the methods of science and the methods of philosophy. As Jim Conant points out in "Putnam's Wittgensteinianism," a section of his introduction to *Realism with a Human Face*, Wittgenstein warns in *The Blue Book* against our "craving for generality" and its source in

> our preoccupation with the method of science ... , the method of reducing the explanation of natural phenomena to the smallest number of primitive natural laws. ... Philosophers constantly see the method of science before their eyes, and are irresistibly tempted to ask and answer questions in the way science does. This tendency is the real source of metaphysics, and leads the philosopher into complete darkness.
>
> (Putnam 1987: xlix)

This is a Wittgensteinian source for Putnam's "vertical pluralism."

Although Wittgenstein emphasizes the multiplicity of language-games, he does not assert the multiplicity of human forms of life. He tests the limits of our human form of life – for example, in his discussions of hypothetical tribes who measure the quantity of a stack of wood by how much ground it covers, and he observes that "one human being can be a complete enigma to another" (Wittgenstein 1953: 223). Yet his emphasis is on what is common, on the human form of life that we share, not on ways in which we are different. He contrasts the human form of life not with other actual or possible human forms, but with those of dogs – who are said not to be capable of believing that their masters will be at the door tomorrow – and lions – whom we could not understand, even if they could speak.

There is this difference also. The pragmatist pluralists James, Goodman, and Putnam are all epistemologists, whereas Wittgenstein is centrally concerned not with knowledge or metaphysics, but with language and philosophical psychology. In *On Certainty*, the one work of Wittgenstein's where knowledge comes to center stage, he does not assert a plurality of schemes, theories, or ways of worldmaking, but writes of a "world-picture [that is] the substratum of all my enquiring and asserting" (Wittgenstein 1969: 161). This world-picture, which includes "the existence of the earth" for many years in the past (Wittgenstein 1969: 209), is not only my picture, but "our" picture: "it gives our way of looking at things, and our researches, their form. Perhaps it was once disputed. But perhaps, for unthinkable ages, it has belonged to the *scaffolding* of our thoughts" (Wittgenstein 1969: 211).

The world-picture evolves, perhaps at a rate as slow as that of common sense as James understands it in *Pragmatism*, but Wittgenstein does not conceive of the world-picture as "knowledge." That is part of his quarrel with Moore and implicitly with James. "Why," Wittgenstein asks,

> should the language-game rest on some kind of knowledge? Does a child believe that milk exists? Or does it know that milk exists? Does a cat know that a mouse exists? Are we to say that the knowledge that there are physical objects comes very early or very late?
> (Wittgenstein 1969: 477–79)

The answer to all these questions is presumably "no," and Wittgenstein's point is that knowledge is not the foundation for our language-game. For James – at least in his pragmatist guise – and I think for Goodman, our relation to the world is fundamentally one of knowing it. With his Wittgensteinian focus on the *lebenswelt*, and his exploration of what he calls our "moral images," Putnam has a wider view of that relation.

To conclude: I have been considering some sites of pluralism that resonate with Putnam's work in the writings of William James, Nelson Goodman, and Ludwig Wittgenstein. If Jean Wahl were updating *Pluralist Philosophies of England and America* today he would clearly have to add some more chapters. "Pluralism," like "pragmatism," "romanticism," and "religion," is a family resemblance term (cf. James 1994: 31), but running through many of its uses is the idea that there are multiple ways of understanding a given subject, range of phenomena, or just the world, with no one way adequate for a full account of it all.[3]

It seems to me that philosophers are in a particularly good position to appreciate pluralism so construed, for two reasons. First, because we are the custodians and producers of ethical theories, and although most of us have our favorites, we also know that each of the standard models – deontology, utilitarianism, and virtue ethics – has both strong and weak points, and that none is completely adequate to our moral intuitions and experience. So it is with philosophy itself, and this is my second reason for thinking that philosophers already have an intimate pluralistic understanding. If someone asked me what is *the* philosophy to study I would say along with my namesake Nelson Goodman: "none"; for to study philosophy is to study not just one person or theory, but a range of them. Whitehead said that all philosophy is a footnote to Plato, and Aquinas thought of Aristotle as "the philosopher," but we do not teach our students that there is just one philosopher or philosophy. James gives us a reason for our approach and a reason for believing that it will never be otherwise in his emphasis on the *humanity* and *personality* of philosophical writing. He states in *Pragmatism* that the history of philosophy is a study in individual points of view and individual temperaments, and that "the finest fruit of our ... philosophic education" is our understanding of the "essential personal flavor" of these strange and profound views of the world (James 1902–1910: 502). In *A Pluralistic Universe* he writes that a philosophy is "the expression of a man's intimate character," and that a philosopher's "vision is the great fact about him" (James 1902–1910: 639).

As I think about Putnam, I keep coming back to a sort of energetic happiness expressed in all his writing, from early papers like "It Ain't Necessarily So" through *Reason, Truth, and History* and beyond. It is a joy in his own powers and insights, melded with a penetrating intellectual and moral seriousness. Putnam reminds us not only of the many faces of realism but of the many human faces of philosophy – among which his is one of our time's most probing, imaginative, and sane.

Notes

1 See also MFR, 4-5 and James Conant's introduction to RHF, xliv ff.
2 For a comprehensive discussion of James and pluralism, see O'Shea (2000).
3 Compare Baghramian and Ingram (2000: 1–2).

Bibliography

Baghramian, Maria (2004) *Relativism*, London: Routledge.
——, and Attracta Ingram, eds. (2000) *Pluralism: the philosophy and politics of diversity*, London: Routledge.
Cavell, Stanley (1976) *Must We Mean What We Say?* Cambridge: Cambridge University Press.
Goodman Nelson (1972) "The Way the World Is," in *Problems and Projects*, New York: Bobbs-Merrill.
——(1978) *Ways of Worldmaking*, Indianapolis and Cambridge: Hackett.
Goodman, Russell B. (1995) *Pragmatism: A Contemporary Reader*, London: Routledge.
——(2002) *Wittgenstein and William James*, Cambridge: Cambridge University Press.
James, William (1902–1910) *Writings*, New York: Library of America.
——(1994) *The Varieties of Religious Experience*, New York: Random House.
Montaigne, Michel de (1991) *The Complete Essays*, trans. M. A. Screech, London: Penguin.
O'Shea, James (2000) "Sources of Pluralism in William James," in Baghramian and Ingram 2000: 17–43.
Peirce, Charles Sanders (1992) *The Essential Peirce*, vol. 1, ed. Nathan Houser and Christian Kloesel, Bloomington and Indianapolis: Indiana University Press.
Putnam, Hilary (1981) *Reason, Truth, and History*, Cambridge: Cambridge University Press.
——(1983) *Realism and Reason* (*Philosophical Papers*, vol. 3), Cambridge, MA: Cambridge University Press.
——(1987) *The Many Faces of Realism*, La Salle, IL: Open Court.
——(1990) *Realism with a Human Face*, Cambridge, MA: Harvard University Press.
——(2004) *Ethics Without Ontology*, Cambridge, MA: Harvard University Press.

Wahl, Jean (1925) *Pluralist Philosophies of England and America*, trans. Fred Rothwell, London, Routledge (translation of *Les philosophies pluralistes d'Angleterre et d'Amérique*, Paris: F. Alcan, 1920).
Whitehead, Alfred North (1933) *Adventures of Ideas*, New York: Macmillan.
Wittgenstein, Ludwig (1953) *Philosophical Investigations*, trans. G. E. M. Anscombe, New York: Macmillan.
——, 1969, *On Certainty*, trans. G. E. M. Anscombe and G. H. von Wright, Oxford: Blackwell.

COMMENTS ON RUSSELL GOODMAN'S "SOME SOURCES OF PUTNAM'S PLURALISM"

Hilary Putnam

Russell Goodman's elegant and erudite chapter locates me in the "pluralist" tradition, and I am happy with that placement. I greatly appreciate his compliments (especially the one about my "energetic happiness"), and I have learned from his account of the history of pluralism. What I want to do in this comment is (1) make two important corrections to his account of my views; (2) distinguish my pluralism from Nelson Goodman's; and then (3) comment on a few of Goodman's remarks, in the order in which they appear in his lecture.

First correction: "Putnam is of course a pragmatist"

I just wrote, "corrections to [Goodman's] account of my views," but in fact Goodman refers to views I have held at different times, and the reader should keep that in mind in reading these comments. For example, Goodman writes, "Putnam is of course a pragmatist." The reader may thus be surprised to find that in my comment on Richard Boyd's essay I wrote, "I've written a lot about Pragmatism, and in every single paper I say that I don't think that the Pragmatist theories of truth – *any* of the Pragmatist theories of truth – Peirce's, James' or Dewey's – were right." Since the classical Pragmatists all thought that one had to accept some such theory (in spite of their disagreements among themselves!) to count as a "Pragmatist" (or, in Peirce's case, as a "Pragmaticist"), that means I have never been what the fathers of the movement would have counted as a Pragmatist. How can one reconcile what Goodman writes with what I wrote in my response to Boyd?

Part of the answer is that, in the comment on Boyd's essay, I immediately followed those words by writing,

> Fortunately, Dewey never really *depended* on the Pragmatist theory of truth. He has one footnote in the *Logic*, saying that Peirce's

theory is right, but what Dewey is concerned with is *warranted assertibility*, and that means that, fortunately, his belief that Peirce got the definition of truth right actually plays no real role in anything Dewey does. But in any case, one can learn from a philosopher without believing everything he says, or even believing everything he regards as tremendously important.

(from Putnam's response to Boyd in this volume, p. 96)

This is still what I think. I regard the classical Pragmatists as pioneers in a number of areas – for example, in beginning the important work of showing the incoherence of the still-popular fact/value dichotomy – and I do share their antireductionism (I am a "pluralist" in *that* sense), but I would not today call myself a "Pragmatist" (although I have applied the term to my views in the past on one or two occasions).

However, my reasons for not accepting any of the Pragmatist theories of truth today are not the reasons I had in my "internal realist" period (approximately 1976–90). Then, I myself identified being true with being warrantedly assertible under epistemically ideal conditions,[1] and I was concerned to distinguish my account from the classical Pragmatist identification of truth with being the consensus that would be reached from a certain point on if inquiry were continued forever. Consensus theories of truth make the truth of statements about the past dependent on what happens in the future, or would happen in the future if inquiry were infinitely prolonged in Peirce's case, and I believe that this simply cannot be right (Putnam 1997). But later I attacked the classical Pragmatist theories of truth on a *different* ground, a ground which also rules out "internal realism": namely – I argued – truth does not imply verifiability – not verifiability in the long run, a là Pragmatism, and not verifiability under good enough conditions, a là "internal realism."[2] (I explained this in "Pragmatism," a paper I published in 1995.)

Second correction: re "equally coherent but incompatible conceptual schemes"

Goodman writes,

> Putnam states that "a true statement is one that could be justified were epistemic conditions ideal" (Putnam 1987: vii). Unlike Peirce, however, Putnam asserts that there need not be only one such scheme. Why, he asks, "should there not sometimes be equally coherent but incompatible conceptual schemes which fit our experiential beliefs equally well? If truth is not (unique) correspondence then the possibility of a certain pluralism is opened up" [(Putnam 1987: 73)].

(Goodman, this volume, p. 207)

Goodman's quotation is accurate, but it is important to remember that it comes from my "internal realist" book, *Reason, Truth and History* (1983). I have not believed anything *like* this at least since I realized that the verificationist semantics which was the heart of "internal realism" was a mistake in 1990.[3] As Goodman (correctly) explains the passage in *Reason, Truth and History*, the thought was that it is at least logically possible that two "ideal theories," total alternative systems of scientific knowledge, should fit our "experiential beliefs" equally well, and meet such constraints as "simplicity" equally well, although they disagree on the nature and behavior of unobservables, *and in that case both would be true, even though incompatible.* This argument for the possibility of "incompatible true theories" depends essentially on the premise that all that is required for truth is correct prediction (fit with our "experiential beliefs") plus "simplicity," and similar "theoretical virtues." Today I would say that if we ever face such a situation, then what we should say is that *we can't tell* which theory is true (if either), but *not* that both are true.

Some additional comments

(1) "In any case, it is only 'metaphysical realism' – the fantasy of a 'God's eye view of the world' – that Putnam rejects, not the realism of common sense or of science." There are two separate issues here, what "metaphysical realism" means, and what "God's eye view of the world" means. With respect to the former, Goodman delivered his talk before my concluding lecture (see the Prologue) of course, so he could not know that I would explain in it that there is an important sense in which I *am* a metaphysical realist, even if I am not a "Metaphysical Realist" (Putnam 1990: 30–42) in the very special sense I gave those words in *Reason, Truth and History*. What I say in "From Quantum Mechanics to Ethics and Back Again" is:

> As I explained "metaphysical realism" ... what it came to was precisely the denial of conceptual relativity. My "metaphysical realist" believed that a given thing or system of things can be described in exactly one way, if the description is complete and correct, and that way is supposed to fix exactly one "ontology" and one "ideology" in Quine's sense of those words, that is, exactly one domain of individuals and one domain of predicates of those individuals ... it cannot be a matter of convention, as I have argued that it is, whether spacetime points are individuals or mere limits ... To be sure, this is *one form* that metaphysical realism can take. But if we understand "metaphysical realist" more broadly, as applying to all philosophers who reject all forms of verificationism and all talk of our "making" the world, then I believe it is perfectly possible to be a metaphysical realist in *that* sense and to accept the phenomenon I am calling "conceptual relativity."
> (this volume, p. 27)

And with respect to "God's eye view of the world," Goodman is right that I reject that idea. Our concepts are anthropocentric because *homo sapiens* is the species to which we belong; but a concept can be anthropocentric and guided by objective features of the world, even if those features are ones that it takes our sort of brain and nervous system (and the possession of our particular interests) to detect. For example, the physical properties that lead us to call certain objects "red," certain other objects "green," and so on, are highly disjunctive, and of no interest whatsoever to elementary particle physics; but they are genuine properties of objects for all that, and they enable us to do certain things, for example to recognize the same object again in certain cases. The fact that we do not have a "God's eye view of the world" doesn't mean that we have a *false* image of the work. Contrary to philosophers like Wilfrid Sellars, the "manifest image" is not false. Here Goodman gets me right, and he is also right that rejecting a "God's eye view of the world" does not entail any sort of antirealism on my part, either with respect to the common-sense image of the world or the scientific image.

(2) I like the following passage very much:

> James ... speaks up for religion not as a set of doctrines or practices, but as an example of certain modes of experiencing and conceptualizing the world.
>
> It is the terror and beauty of phenomena, the "promise" of the dawn and of the rainbow, the "voice" of the thunder, the "gentleness" of the summer rain, the "sublimity" of the stars, and not the physical laws which these things follow, by which the religious mind still continues to be most impressed ...
> (James 1994: 541)

> James is impressed too, and he sees the source of religion's authority in the personal point of view. "Science" (with a capital "S") is "impersonal" (James 1994: 543) by its very nature, and therefore, James argues, it is not equipped to register the world in these ways. The sciences offer us ways of knowing the world, but there are other ways which science cannot duplicate or reduce to its terms.
> (from Goodman in this volume, p. 211)

(3) "Putnam acknowledges the importance of Nelson Goodman for his own pragmatism [*sic!*] in many places in his writing." In "After Empiricism," for example, he links him with Husserl, Merleau-Ponty, Austin, and Wittgenstein in countering Hume's project of dividing reality into "the Furniture of the

Universe" on the one hand and "our projections" on the other (1987: 52). In his earlier review of *Ways of Worldmaking* (1978), Putnam states that "the heart of Goodman's book ... is its defense of pluralism."

While I agree with Goodman that we need many different (but not genuinely incompatible!)[4] "versions," I do not agree with Goodman's self-styled "irrealism" at all. In fact, there is a book titled *Starmaking: Realism, Anti-Realism, and Irrealism* in whose pages Israel Scheffler and I, on the one side, and Goodman, on the other, debate the question whether there is any sense in which Goodman's claim that "we make the stars" is true, and Scheffler and I argue that there isn't. Different versions, yes; different worlds, no.

(4) I like very much what Goodman writes about Wittgenstein. I am glad that Goodman does not discuss the passages in which Wittgenstein suggests that philosophers are talking "nonsense" and that we need a "therapy" to "cure" them, because that is the aspect of Wittgenstein's thought that I *don't* agree with, as I explain in my response to David Macarthur's talk. But I do agree with the aspects of the thought of the later Wittgenstein that Goodman beautifully discusses here. And I greatly appreciate his concluding remarks.

Notes

1 I once wrote,

> By an ideal epistemic situation I mean something like this: If I say 'There is a chair in my study', an ideal epistemic situation would be to be in my study, with the lights on or with daylight streaming through the window, with nothing wrong with my eyesight, with an unconfused mind, without having taken drugs or having been subjected to hypnosis, and so forth, and to look and see if there is a chair there. Or to drop the notion of 'ideal' altogether, since that is only a metaphor, I think there are *better* and *worse* epistemic *situation with respect to particular statements.*
>
> (Putnam 1990a: viii)

In the same place I distinguish this from the Peircean conception. Being what the community of scientists would "converge" to if inquiry went on forever is neither necessary or sufficient for being what would be warrantedly assertible if conditions were, actually, "good enough" in the sense I described. Of course, I now reject both these theories of truth for reasons given in the text.

2 For example, I believe that most statements about what there is outside the light-cone of the human species are unverifiable for physical reasons, but conjectures about that are true or false. Every cosmologist would say that certain such conjectures are probably true and others are probably false, and I believe they are not talking nonsense.

3 I renounced "verificationist semantics" in my reply to Simon Blackburn at the Gifford Conference in my honor at St. Andrews in November 1990, published in Clark and Hale 1994.

4 For an explanation of the distinction between versions that are incompatible if taken at face value and genuinely incompatible versions see "From Quantum Mechanics to Ethics and Back Again" in this volume.

Bibliography

Clark, P. and Hale, B. (eds.) (1994) *Reading Putnam*, Cambridge, MA and Oxford: Blackwell.
Dewey, John (1938) *Logic: the Theory of Inquiry*, New York: Henry Holt.
James, William (1994) *The Varieties of Religious Experience*, New York: Random House.
Putnam, Hilary (1990) "A Defense of Internal Realism," in Putnam 1990a, 30–42.
——(1990a) *Realism With a Human Face*, Cambridge, MA: Harvard University Press.
——(1994) "Comments and Replies," in Clark and Hale 1994: 242–95.
——(1995) "Pragmatism," *Proceedings of the Aristotelian Society* 95(3): 291–306.
——(1997) "James's Theory of Truth," in Ruth Anna Putnam (ed.), *The Cambridge Companion to William James*, Cambridge: Cambridge University Press, 166–85.

7

PHYSICS AND NARRATIVE

David Z. Albert

I'm not going to attempt anything along the lines of a summing up of what Hilary has meant, and what he continues to mean, to my own particular corner of philosophy here. But it needs at least to be mentioned – on an occasion like this – that Hilary has thought about the foundations of physics harder, and longer, and more deeply, and with more openness, and with more wonder, and with more determination, and with more courage, than anyone now living. Sidney Morgenbesser used to say that Hilary was the most quantum-mechanical philosopher in the world, because he and his philosophical position could not simultaneously be identified. And that (as with all of Sidney's jokes) is exactly right. Nobody, to this day, is as young, and as curious, and as willing to be surprised, and as ready to turn his back on everything he has ever believed, and as full of the exuberant expectation of the impossible, as Hilary. And this is how to learn about the world.

And I want to do something in that spirit here. There is a topic that Hilary and I have been talking and talking and talking to one another about for decades, and about which we have both lately been surprised, about which we have both lately come to understand that we never really knew anything at all. And that's what I want to talk about today.

I'm going to start off with some mildly technical remarks about the behaviors of quantum-mechanical wave-functions under Lorentz-transformations. But bear with me just a bit – I think something of what's at stake in these considerations, something of what's philosophically interesting, will come through well enough later on, whether you're able to follow the quantum mechanics or not.

Consider a system of four distinguishable quantum-mechanical spin-1/2 particles. Call it S. And suppose that the complete history of the motions of those particles in position-space – as viewed from the perspective of some particular Lorentz-frame K – is as follows: Particle 1 is permanently located in the vicinity of some particular spatial point, and particle 2 is permanently located in the vicinity of some *other* spatial point, and particles 3 and 4 both move with uniform velocity along parallel trajectories in space-time.[1] The trajectory of particle 3 intersects the trajectory of particle 1 at space-time

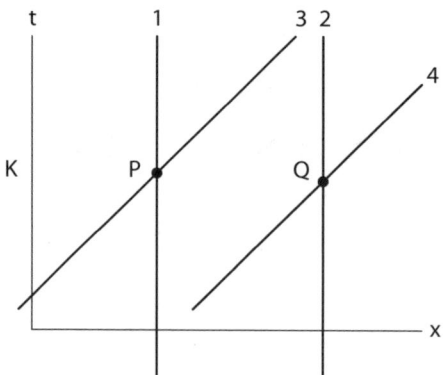

Figure 7.1

point P – as in Figure 7.1 – and the trajectory of particle 4 intersects the trajectory of particle 2 at space-time point Q. And P and Q are simultaneous, from the perspective of K.

And suppose that the state of the *spin* degrees of freedom of S, at $t = -\infty$, is $[\varphi>_{12} [\varphi>_{34}$, where

$$[\varphi>_{AB} = 1/\sqrt{2}[\uparrow>_A[\downarrow>_B - 1/\sqrt{2}[\downarrow>_A[\uparrow>_B. \qquad (1)$$

I want to compare the effects of two different possible *Hamiltonians* on this system. In one, S evolves freely throughout the interval from $t = -\infty$ to $t = +\infty$. The other includes an impulsive contact interaction term that *exchanges spins* – a term (that is) which is zero except when two of the particles occupy the same point, and which (when it *isn't* zero) generates precisely the following unitary evolution:

$$\begin{aligned}
&[\uparrow>_A[\downarrow>_B \to [\downarrow>_A[\uparrow>_B \\
&[\downarrow>_A[\uparrow>_B \to [\uparrow>_A[\downarrow>_B \\
&[\uparrow>_A[\uparrow>_B \to [\uparrow>_A[\uparrow>_B \\
&[\downarrow>_A[\downarrow>_B \to [\downarrow>_A[\downarrow>_B
\end{aligned} \qquad (2)$$

A minute's reflection will show that the entire history of the quantum state of this system, from the perspective of K – the complete temporal sequence (that is) of the instantaneous quantum-mechanical *wave-functions* of this system, even down to the overall phase, from the perspective of K – will be *identical* on these two scenarios. On both scenarios (that is) the state of S, from the perspective of K, throughout the interval from $t = -\infty$ to $t = +\infty$, will be precisely $[\varphi>_{12} [\varphi>_{34}$.

And what's interesting is that the situation is altogether *different* from the perspective of every *other* frame. On the first scenario – the scenario in which S evolves freely – the state of S is going to be precisely $[\varphi>_{12}[\varphi>_{34}$, in *every* frame, at every time, throughout the interval from $t = -\infty$ to $t = +\infty$.[2] But on the *second* scenario, when viewed from the perspective of frames other than K, the interactions at P and Q occur at *different times*. In those other frames, then, at all times throughout the interval between P and Q, the state of S is going to be $[\varphi >_{14}[\varphi >_{23}$.

And it follows immediately that the complete temporal sequence of the quantum states of S in frames *other* than K cannot be deduced, either by means of the application of a geometrical space-time point-transformation or *in any other way*, from the complete temporal sequence of the quantum states of S in K – because the transformation in question would need (*per impossibile!*) to map *precisely the same* history in K into one of two *entirely distinct* histories in K', depending on which one of the above two *Hamiltonians* obtains.

* * *

All of this is as easy as can be. And all of it has been taken note of, on a number of different occasions, in the literature of the foundations of quantum mechanics. It was pointed to in a 1984 paper by Yakir Aharonov and myself – for example – and in a paper by Wayne Myrvold from 2002, and it must at least have occurred in passing to a great many people.[3] But nobody seems to have been able to look it *straight in the face*, nobody seems to have entirely *taken it in*.[4]

Let's back up (then) and slow down, and see if we can figure out what it means.

Call a world *narratable* if the entirety of what there is to say about it can be presented as a single *story*, if the entirety of what there is to say about it can be presented as a *single temporal sequence* of *instantaneous global physical situations*.

The possible worlds of Newtonian Mechanics can each be presented, in its entirety, by means of a specification of the local physical conditions at every point in a four-dimensional manifold. And there is a way of *slicing that manifold up* into a one-parameter collection of infinite three-dimensional hyperplanes such that the dynamical *significance* of the parameter in question – the dynamical *role* of the parameter in question – is precisely that of a *time*.[5] A Newtonian-Mechanical *instantaneous global physical situation*, then, is a specification of the local physical conditions at each one of the points on any particular one of those infinite three-dimensional hyperplanes. And since all of those instantaneous global Newtonian-Mechanical physical situations taken together amount – by construction – to a specification of the local physical conditions at every point in the manifold, the possible worlds of Newtonian Mechanics are invariably *narratable*. Moreover, they are *uniquely* narratable, in the sense that the number of different ways of slicing the manifold up in such a way as to *satisfy* the conditions described above – in a Newtonian-Mechanical world – is invariably, precisely, *one*.

The possible worlds of *Non-Relativistic Quantum Mechanics* can each be presented, in its entirety, by means of a specification of the values of a real two-component field – a specification, that is, of the quantum-mechanical *wave-function* – at every point in a 3N+1 dimensional manifold (where N is the number of particles in the world in question). And there is a way of *slicing that manifold up* into a one-parameter collection of infinite 3N-dimensional hyperplanes such that the dynamical role of the parameter in question is precisely that of a time. A *Non-Relativistic Quantum-Mechanical* instantaneous global physical situation, then, is a specification of the local physical conditions at each one of the points on any particular one of those infinite 3N-dimensional hyperplanes. And since all of those instantaneous global Non-Relativistic Quantum-Mechanical physical situations taken together amount to a specification of the local physical conditions at every point in the manifold, the possible worlds of Non-Relativistic Quantum-Mechanics are invariably narratable. And the narratability here is again *unique*, in the sense that the number of different ways of slicing the manifold up in such a way as to *satisfy* the conditions described above is invariably, precisely, *one*.

The possible worlds of *Classical Relativistic Maxwellian Electrodynamics* – just like those of Newtonian Mechanics – can each be presented, in its entirety, by means of a specification of the local physical conditions at every point in a four-dimensional manifold. And there is, again, a way of *slicing that manifold up* into a one-parameter collection of infinite three-dimensional hyperplanes such that the dynamical significance of the parameter in question is precisely that of a *time*. And so a Classical Relativistic Maxwellian instantaneous global physical situation is a specification of the local physical conditions at each one of the points on any particular one of those infinite three-dimensional hyperplanes. And since all of those instantaneous global Classical Maxwellian physical situations taken together amount to a specification of the local physical conditions at every point in the manifold, the possible worlds of Classical Relativistic Maxwellian Electrodynamics are narratable. But in *this* case the narratability is manifestly *not* unique – Classical Relativistic Maxwellian Electrodynamics is (rather) *multiply* narratable. In the case of Classical Relativistic Maxwellian Electrodynamics, each different *Lorentz-frame* is plainly going to correspond to a different way of slicing the manifold up so as to satisfy the conditions described above.

But Relativistic *Quantum* Theories are an altogether different matter. In both the non-relativistic and the relativistic cases, an instantaneous Quantum-Mechanical *state of the world* – an instantaneous Quantum-Mechanical *global physical situation* – is a specification of the expectation-values of all of the local and non-local quantum-mechanical observables that refer exclusively to the time in question. And the lesson of the example we went through above is that the entirety of what there is to say about a Relativistic Quantum-Mechanical world cannot be presented as a one-parameter family of situations like that. The lesson of the example we went through above (more particularly) is that any one-parameter family of situations like that is necessarily going to leave the expectation-values of non-local Quantum-Mechanical observables that refer to several *different* times – the expectation-values of non-local Quantum-Mechanical observables (that is) which are instantaneous from the perspective of *other* Lorentz-frames – unspecified. In order to present the entirety of what there is to say about a Relativistic Quantum-Mechanical world, we need to specify, *separately*, the Quantum-Mechanical state of the world associated with *every separate space-like hypersurface*. If the theory is to be relativistic in the sense of Einstein, in the sense of Minkowski, nothing less is going to do.

* * *

The relationship between the quantum-mechanical states of the world associated with any set of space-like hypersurfaces and the quantum-mechanical states of the world associated with any *other* set of space-like hypersurfaces is therefore, invariably, a matter of *dynamical evolution* – even (for example) if one of those sets happens to be the complete family of equal-time hyperplanes for K and the other one of those sets happens to be the complete family of equal-time hyperplanes for K'.[6]

Moreover, the elementary *unit* of dynamical evolution here is plainly not an infinitesimal *translation in time* (which is generated by the global Hamiltonian of the world H, as in Figure 7.2a) but an arbitrary infinitesimal *deformation*, an arbitrary infinitesimal *undulation*, of the *space-like hypersurface* (which is generated by the *local Hamiltonian density* of the world dH, as in Figure 7.2B).

The dynamical laws of the evolutions of relativistic quantum-mechanical systems therefore have a much richer mathematical structure than the laws of the evolutions of *non*-relativistic quantum-mechanical systems do. Suppose (for example) that we should like to calculate the wave-function of some particular isolated quantum-mechanical system on hypersurface b, given the wave-function of that system on some *other* hypersurface a – where a may be either in the past of b or in its future. In the *non*-relativistic case, which is depicted in Figure 7.3A, there is always exactly *one* continuous one-parameter family of hypersurfaces – the continuous one-parameter family of *absolute simultaneities* between a and b – along which a calculation like that is going to have to *proceed*, along which the system in question can be pictured as *evolving*. In the relativistic case, on the other hand, there is invariably an *infinity* of continuous one-parameter families of space-like hypersurfaces along which such a calculation can proceed, and along which the system in

Figure 7.2

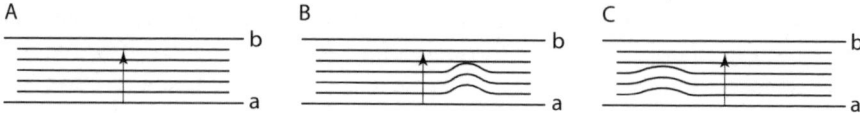

Figure 7.3

question can be pictured as evolving. Two such families are displayed in Figures 7.3B and 7.3C. And one of the necessary conditions of the *existence of a solution* to the dynamical equations of motion of a theory like this, one of the necessary conditions of the *internal consistency* of the dynamical equations of motion of a theory like this, is that the calculation that proceeds along the route pictured in Figure 7.3B and the calculation that proceeds along the route pictured in Figure 7.3C, so long as they both *start out* with precisely the same wave-function at *a*, will both necessarily *produce* precisely the same wave-function at *b*.

And while there can be no such thing as a Lorentz-transformation of the complete temporal sequence of the quantum states of any isolated system S in frame K into the complete temporal sequence of quantum states of that system in frame K′, there is nonetheless a perfectly clear and perfectly explicit idea of the Lorentz-transformation of any *comprehensive summary of the world*; there is a perfectly clear and perfectly explicit idea (that is) of the Lorentz-transformation of any assignment of states to every space-like hypersurface. Given any such assignment, the way to Lorentz-transform it is just to assign the same set of states to a *Lorentz-transformed* set of *hypersurfaces*, and we speak of a set of dynamical laws of the evolutions of wave-functions as *Lorentz-Invariant* just in case any Lorentz-transformation of any comprehensive summary of the world which is in accord with those laws yields another comprehensive summary of the world which is in accord with those laws.

* * *

Here are two stories – which pull in very different directions – about where all this might leave us:

STORY 1

This story is about the *collapse* of the wave-function. And it will work best – for the moment – to tell it in the language of the old-fashioned and idealized and unscientific and altogether outmoded postulate of collapse on which collapses are brought about by means of the intervention of localized, external, un-quantum-mechanical *measuring-devices*. On this picture, collapses involve a discontinuous and probabilistic projection of the wave-function of the *measured* system, the *quantum-mechanical* system, onto an eigenfunction of some particular one of its *local observables* (the observable, that is, which the external device in question is designed to measure) at some particular *space-time point* (the so-called "measurement-event" – the point at which the measured system *interacts* with the measuring-device). The probability of a projection onto this or that particular eigenfunction of the measured observable is determined, in the familiar way, by the Born rule.

On the *non-relativistic* version of the collapse postulate (which is depicted in Figure 7.4A) the collapse occurs as the "now" sweeps forwards across the measurement-event – the collapse (that is) affects the wave-function of the system in question in the *future* of that event, but not in its *past*. And twenty or so years ago, I wrote a paper with Yakir Aharonov which proposed a manifestly Lorentz-invariant *relativistic* version of that postulate (which is depicted in Figure 7.4B) on which the collapse occurs as an *undulating space-like hypersurface, any* undulating space-like hypersurface, *deforms* forwards across the measurement-event – on which (that is) the collapse affects the wave-function of the system in question on those space-like hypersurfaces that intersect the *future light-cone* of measurement-event, but not on those space-like hypersurfaces that intersect its *past light-cone*.

Suppose (then) that we are given the wave-function of some isolated relativistic quantum-mechanical system S along some space-like hypersurface a, and suppose that we are given the addresses of all of the space-time points in the future of a at which measurements of local observables of S are to be carried out, and suppose that we are told what particular local observable of S each particular one of those measurements is to be a measurement *of*. The relativistic postulate of collapse just described – together with the deterministic laws of the ordinary dynamical evolutions of the wave-functions of *isolated* relativistic quantum-mechanical systems under infinitesimal deformations of the space-like hypersurface – will assign a definite probability to any particular assignment of *outcomes* to those measurements, and it will assign a definite probability to any particular assignment of a quantum-mechanical *wave-function* to any particular space-like hypersurface b which is entirely in the *future* of a, and (moreover) it will do both of those things *uniquely* – completely independent (that is) of which one of the above-mentioned *routes* the calculation of those probabilities takes.

The *trouble* here – or so I imagined until now – is that the possible worlds of this sort of a theory aren't going to be *narratable*. Suppose (for example)

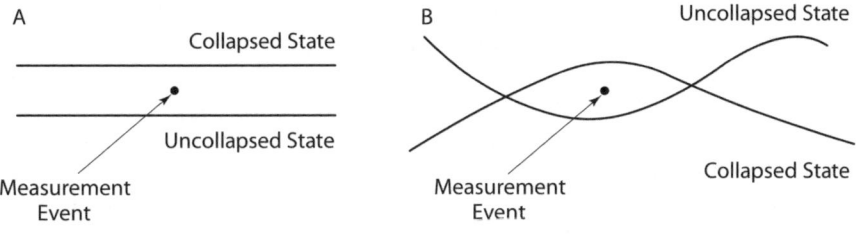

Figure 7.4

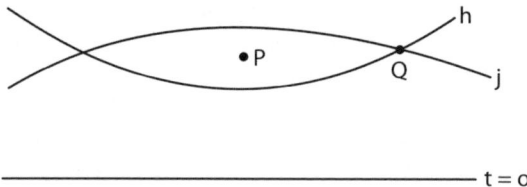

Figure 7.5

that the momentum of a free particle is measured along the hypersurface marked t = 0 in Figure 7.5, and that later on a collapse leaves the particle localized at P. Then the projection-postulate that Aharonov and I proposed is going to stipulate (among other things) that the wave-function of the particle along hypersurface h is an eigenstate of momentum, and that the wave-function of the particle along hypersurface j is (very nearly) an eigenstate of *position*. And so the quantum-mechanical wave-functions associated with hypersurfaces h and j, in this example, are going to disagree with one another even about the expectation-values of *local* quantum-mechanical observables at points like Q, where they intersect.[7] And that (of course) puts narratability quite decisively out of the question.

But a case might be made that the example we went through at the outset of this essay sheds a very different light on all this. We can now see – it might be argued – that the narratability of Relativistic Quantum Theories is dead before the measurement problem ever even *comes up*, before the non-locality that Bell discovered ever even *enters the picture*. Adding a postulate of the collapse of the wave-function to a Relativistic Quantum Theory, on this view, solves the measurement problem, and costs *nothing*. The Lorentz-invariance of the theory is preserved perfectly intact, and as for the failure of *narratability, that* price turns out to have been *paid*, unbeknownst to us, long before the question of measurement ever arose.

If all this is right, then many-worlds and many-minds and many-histories theories have no advantage whatever – in so far as questions of Lorentz-invariance are concerned – over collapse theories. The Lorentz-invariance of many-worlds and many-minds and many-histories theories comes, after all, at the price of a failure of narratability – just as that of collapse theories does.

Moreover, there is now reason to hope that these considerations may turn out *not* to depend all that sensitively on the unrealistic idealizations of the measurement-process I described a few paragraphs back. A talented young German physicist named Roderich Tamulka has recently published a fully relativistic version of the GRW collapse-theory for non-interacting particles – a theory (as it turns out) that fits around the schematic general principles that Yakir and I laid out twenty years ago like skin. It still remains – and it may turn out to be a highly non-trivial business – to generalize Tamulka's theory to the case of interacting particles and to fields. We shall have to wait and see. But what Tamulka has already accomplished represents an immense and encouraging step in the right direction.

STORY 2

This is a story about the linear, unitary, deterministic evolution of the wave-functions of quantum-mechanical systems, altogether unadorned by any mechanism of collapse. Consider a Relativistic Quantum-Mechanical world W in which the free Hamiltonian of a certain pair of electrons is identically zero, and in which the *wave-function* of that pair, along every space-like hypersurface whatever, is precisely the wave-function [φ > $_{12}$ of equation (1). And let t' = a be a flat space-like hypersurface all of whose points are simultaneous with respect to some particular Lorentzian frame of reference K'. And imagine an experiment designed to measure and record the total spin of that pair of electrons along t' = a. The experiment involves two localized pieces of apparatus, which have previously been brought together, and prepared in a state in which certain of their internal variables are quantum-mechanically entangled with one another, and then separated in space. One of those pieces of apparatus then interacts with particle 1 at point L (in Figure 7.6) and the other interacts with particle 2 at point Q. And the positions of the relevant *pointers* on those two pieces of apparatus, at the *conclusions* of those interactions, are measured, and the values of those positions are transmitted to F, and those values are mathematically combined with one another in such a way as to determine the outcome of the measurement of the total spin of the pair of electrons along t' = a, and (finally) that outcome is *recorded*, in ink (say), in English, on a piece of paper, at G.[8] No such experiment is actually *carried out* in W – mind you – but it is a fact about W that *if* such an experiment *were* to have been carried out, it would with certainty have been recorded at G that the total spin of that pair along t' = a was zero.

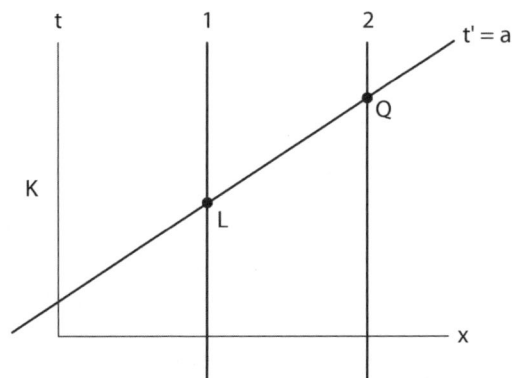

Figure 7.6

Now, the most obvious and most straightforward way of *accounting* for that fact, the most obvious and most straightforward way of *explaining* that fact, is to point out (1) that the state of the electron-pair, along the hypersurface t' = a, is [φ > $_{12}$, and (2) that [φ > $_{12}$ is an eigenstate of the total spin of that pair, with eigenvalue zero, and (3) that a *measurement* of the total spin of that pair along t' = a – if it had been carried out – would therefore, with certainty, have found that the total spin of that pair *is* zero. Note that this explanation depends only on the *state* of the pair of electrons at t' = a, and not *at all* on the *dynamical laws* by which that state *evolves*.[9]

But another explanation has – or rather a *continuous infinity* of other explanations has – plainly got to be available as well. If (for example) we trace out the development of the world exclusively along the continuous one-parameter family of hypersurfaces of simultaneity in K, the experiment in question is going to look not so much like an *instantaneous measurement* as an extended sequence of *dynamical interactions*. At t = 0, the state of the electron-pair is [φ >$_{12}$, and the pair of *apparatuses* are in the specially prepared quantum-mechanically entangled state – call it [1 > – alluded to above. Then – at L – electron 1 interacts with one of the localized pieces of apparatus, and this interaction leaves the *electron-pair* quantum-mechanically *entangled* with the pair of *apparatuses*. Then – at Q – electron 2 interacts with the *other* localized piece of apparatus in precisely such a way as to *undo* that latter entanglement – leaving the electron-pair once again in the state [φ >$_{12}$ and the pair of apparatuses once again in the state [1 >. Thereafter, the various transmitters and receivers and compilers and recorders go to work, and the end-product of all this activity – the end-product (that is) which is *entailed* with *certainty* by the state of the world along t = 0 and the deterministic quantum-mechanical equations of motion, no matter *which* continuous one-parameter family of space-like hypersurfaces the intervening calculation traces through – is a sheet of paper at G, bearing the inscription "total spin equals Zero."

This particular experiment's having this particular outcome, then, can be given a *complete* and *satisfactory* and *deterministic* explanation which traces out the development of the world *exclusively* along the continuous one-parameter family of hypersurfaces of simultaneity in K, and which makes *no mention whatsoever* of the state of the pair of electrons – or of anything else – at t' = a.

And we are plainly going to be able to produce very much the same sort of an explanation – very much the same *continuous infinity* of explanations – of the outcome in any hypothetical experiment whatsoever.

And this suggests a way of picturing relativistic quantum-mechanical worlds – for a price – as *narratable*. All that needs to be given up is the Einsteinian insistence that the unfolding of the world in every separate Lorentz-frame and along every continuous one-parameter family of space-like hypersurfaces all be put on an *equal metaphysical footing*. Suppose – on the contrary – that it is stipulated that an assignment of a quantum state of the world to every one of the hypersurfaces of simultaneity of (say) K – and to no *other* space-like hypersurfces – amounts in and of itself to a complete and exhaustive and unaugmentable account of the world's history. Then there would be no facts at all about the "state of the world" along, say, t' = a. And all *talk* of such "facts" in the physical literature would need to be reinterpreted as shorthand for *counterfactual* talk about how this or that hypothetical *experiment* – if it were to be performed – would come out. The world would be narratable – and (moreover) *uniquely* so.

On this way of thinking, the impulse away from an *Einsteinian* understanding of special relativity – the impulse (that is) towards a *Lorentzian* understanding of special relativity – would arise not (in the first instance) from the *non-locality* of the *collapse*, but *earlier* and *farther down*, from *the geometry of the Hilbert space* and the demand for *narratability*. And the way would seem to be open to trying out new fundamental theories of the world which violate Lorentz-invariance – a little bit – even in their empirical predictions.[10]

Notes

1 This sort of permanent localization can be accomplished, say, by placing the particles in boxes, or by making their masses large.
2 I am going to be supposing, throughout, that the velocities of these other frames with respect to K are small compared to the speed of light, so that the effects of Lorentz-transformations on the spins can be neglected. The effects of transforming to other frames that are going to interest us here can all be made as large as one likes, even at small relative velocities, by separating the two particles from one another by a great spatial distance.
3 The example presented here, however, is a good deal cleaner and more perspicuous than either the one discussed by Aharonov and Albert 1984 or the one discussed by Myrvold 2002. The example cited in the paper by Aharonov and myself involves *measurement*-type interactions, and the one Myrvold presents involves an external field that violates Poincare-invariance. Neither of those sorts of distractions come up, however, in the example presented here.
4 What Aharanov and I had to say about it (Aharanov and Albert 1984) was that in so far as frame K is concerned, the interaction "disrupts (as it were) the *transformation* properties of the state and disrupts its *covariance*, without in any way disrupting the history of the state itself." But precisely how it is that the *transformation* properties of something can be disrupted without *in any way* disrupting *the history of the thing itself* I confess I can no longer imagine. It seems panicked – looking back on it now – and incoherent, and mad.

Professor Myrvold (on the other hand) thinks it shows that the Lorentz-transformation of quantum-mechanical wave-functions is not so much a *geometrical* or even a *kinematical* matter as it is a matter of *dynamics*, a matter of the *Hamiltonian* of the system whose wave-function is being transformed. According to Professor Myrvold, the business of performing a Lorentz-transformation on the complete temporal history of the wave-function of an isolated system is in general going to require that we know, and are able to solve, the system's *dynamical equations of motion*. But if we go *that* route, nothing whatever is going to remain of the intuition that carrying out such a transformation is merely a matter of looking at *precisely the same set of physical events* from two different *perspectives*, from two different *points of view*. Dynamics – after all – is not the business of changing one's perspective on already *existing* events, but of generating entirely *new* ones!

5 It means a host of things, by the way, to speak of the parameter in question here as "playing the dynamical role of a time." It means (for example) that the trajectory of every particle in the world intersects every one of the three-dimensional hyperplanes in question here exactly once, and it means that the total energy on any one of these hypersurfaces is the same as the total energy on any *other* one of them, and it means (principally and fundamentally and in sum) that the equation $F = m(\partial^2 x/\partial \rho^2)$, where ρ is the parameter in question, is true.

6 In this respect, then, Professor Myrvold (see note 4) is perfectly right. Where Myrvold goes wrong is in imagining that a relationship like that is consistent with the claim that an assignment of a quantum state of the system in question to every one of the equal-time hyperplanes of K can amount to a complete *history* of that system – where he goes wrong (that is) is in imagining that a relationship like that can leave the world *narratable*.

7 Note, however, that the expectation-values of all local observables at Q *given the state along* $t = 0$ will still be completely independent of the *route* by which one chooses to *calculate* from $t = 0$ to Q. On *certain* routes (for example) Q is going to come up as an element of h, and on certain *others* it will come up as an element of j. If Q comes up as an element of h, then the expectation-values of all local observables at Q, given the state along $t = 0$, will be determined – in the familiar way – by the state at h. But if Q comes up as an element of j, then the expectation-values of all local observables at Q, given the state along $t = 0$, will be determined by a *probability-distribution* over various different *possible* states at j – corresponding to the different possible outcomes of the measurement at P. The Lorentz-invariance of the dynamical equations of motion and the collapse-postulate, however, will guarantee that those two sets of expectation-values will invariably be identical.

8 Detailed instructions for the construction and preparation of measuring apparatuses like these – using only local interactions – can be found in an old paper of Yakir Aharonov's and mine ...

9 The account *does* depend on the dynamics of the two pieces of *measuring apparatus* – of course – and on the dynamics of the mechanism whereby the positions of the relevant pointers on those two pieces of apparatus are *transmitted to* F, and on the dynamics of the mechanism whereby those position-values are mathematically combined with one another in such a way as to determine the *outcome* of the total-spin measurement, and (finally) on the dynamics of the mechanism whereby that outcome is *recorded* at G – but it doesn't depend *at all* on the dynamics of the pair of electrons *themselves*.

10 Acknowledgement: I am grateful to my son, Ben Albert, for doing such a wonderful job with the diagrams.

Bibliography

Aharonov, Y., and Albert, D. (1984) "Is the usual notion of time evolution adequate for quantum-mechanical systems? II. Relativistic considerations," *Physical Review D*, 29: 228–34.

Albert, David Z. and Putnam, Hilary (1995) "Further Adventures of Wigner's Friend," *Topoi* 14(1): 17–22.

Myrvold, W. C. (2002) "On Peaceful Coexistence: Is the Collapse Postulate Incompatible With Relativity?," *Studies in History and Philosophy of Modern Physics* 33: 435–66.

COMMENTS ON DAVID ALBERT'S "PHYSICS AND NARRATIVE"

Hilary Putnam

David Albert has proved an important theorem, a surprising one, which certainly has relevance to the way we will understand quantum mechanics in the future. Whether its moral is really the "non-narratibility" of the history of the quantum world is, however, dependent on interpretative questions about which philosophers and physicists – even philosophers and physicists who, like David Albert and myself, are looking for what the late, great, J. S. Bell called an "unromantic" interpretation of quantum mechanics – are sure to disagree. In this brief comment I want to say what Albert has certainly *shown*, and what depends on those interpretative questions (and, of course, what those questions are). By an "unromantic" interpretation, what Bell meant is an intelligible and mathematically precise interpretation in which there is no talk about "consciousness" reducing the wave packet, "measurements" are simply described as a subclass of physical interactions, and, of course, there is no loose talk about the world consisting of "information."

What Albert has shown is that there is no transformation which will always give you the complete history of the evolution of the wave-function of "the world" (of an arbitrary quantum mechanical system) in one frame, or family of spacelike hypersurfaces (henceforth "one foliation") given the history in an arbitrary different foliation. A *fortiori*, there is no Lorentz-transformation that will do this: Lorentz-transformations do not act on the wave-function. (One philosophically significant consequence is that the Many Worlds interpretation of quantum mechanics – an interpretation in which there is "only the wave-function" – does *not* give us one single Lorentz-invariant "narrative" of the history of the world.)

The interpretative issues

Albert's interpretation of the, so to speak, metaphysical significance of his theorem is that the physical world has a family of *foliation-dependent histories*, not one unique history. The history of the evolution of the world is not completely capturable by a single "narrative." But there are other possible interpretations. That is what I want to explain.

To do this, it will be useful to explain a term introduced into the discussion by John Stewart Bell, the term "beable." A "beable" is an entity that a theory postulates as being physically real. In "The Theory of Local Beables," Bell wrote,

> The word "beable" will ... be used here to carry [the distinction] familiar already in classical theory between 'physical' and 'non-physical' quantities. In Maxwell's electromagnetic theory, for example, the fields E and H are 'physical' (beables, we will say) but the potentials A and φ are 'non-physical.' Because of gauge invariance the same physical situation can be described by very different potentials. It does not matter that in Coulomb gauge the scalar potential propagates with infinite velocity. It is not really supposed to be there. It is just a mathematical convenience.
>
> (Bell 1993: 53)

And further:

> We will be particularly concerned with the *local* beables, those which (unlike, for example, the total energy) can be assigned to some bounded spacetime region. For example, in Maxwell's theory, the beables local to a given region are just the fields E and H and all the functionals thereof. It is in terms of local beables that we can hope to formulate some notion of local causality.
>
> (ibid.)

All realistic interpretations of quantum mechanics postulate the existence of some beables or other (that is what makes them *realistic* interpretations), but they do not all postulate the existence of *local* beables. In the Many Worlds interpretation, for example, the wave-function itself is a "beable," one might call it a "global beable," but there are no local beables. In Roderich Tumulka's (Tumulka 2006),[1] version of the GRW (Ghirardi–Rimini–Weber) interpretation however, the wave-function is not regarded as a beable, but simply as a mathematical object that represents the probability distributions over the beables, and the only beables – and they *are* local ones – are the "flashes," that is the point-like events that occur when a particle (which prior to such an event has only a potential existence) momentarily "flashes" into existence (Bell 1987). In the Bohm interpretation, the wave-function seems once again to be a global beable (at least this is how Bohm seems to have thought of it), but there is a full complement of local beables: the particles. But the Bohm interpretation does not pretend to be Lorentz-invariant, so the history of the world in the preferred frame is *the* history.

Equipped with these concepts, we can now return to Albert's example of a system with the remarkable property that, if we follow the time evolution of its wave-function in one foliation, call it "Alice," then there the spin of a certain particle a is *always* perfectly correlated with the spin of its distant "twin" a', while if we follow the time evolution of its wave-function in anther foliation, call it "Bob," then there is a period of time during which the spin of a is correlated with the spin of a different particle b', and not correlated with the spin of a'. Alice and Bob "tell" entirely different stories about the correlations between the spins of four particles, a, a', b, b' (I have left out the part of the story that concerns b and a').

But are spins (or correlations between spins of separated particles) *beables*? According to Tumulka's version of GRW (with the "flash" ontology) they are not. In the "world" Albert describes there are no collapses, and hence no "flashes." It is a world where a number of things *could have happened* (there was a positive probability of a "flash"), but, as luck would have it, nothing did happen. And that's an easy history to narrate: *nothing happened*. Is this the right interpretation of quantum mechanics? Time will tell.

Moral: the ultimate evaluation of the significance of Albert's result will have to wait, as so much else about quantum mechanics will, until we arrive – if we ever do – at an interpretation of quantum mechanics that satisfies us (and that, we hope, does so because it is the right one).

Note

1 An account of Tumulka's model that presupposes only elementary mathematics is chapter 10 of Maudlin (2011).

Bibliography

Bell, John Stewart (1993) *Speakable and Unspeakable in Quantum Mechanics*, Cambridge: Cambridge University Press.
——(1987) "Are There Quantum Jumps?," in *Speakable and Unspeakable in Quantum Mechanics*, Cambridge: Cambridge University Press, revised edition 2004, 201–12.
Maudlin, Tim (2011) *Quantum Non-locality and Relativity: Metaphysical Intimations of Modern Physics*, 3rd edn, Oxford: Wiley-Blackwell.
Tumulka, Roderich (2006) "A Relativistic Version of the Ghirardi–Rimini–Weber Model," *Journal of Statistical Physics* 125(4): 821–40.

8

HILARY PUTNAM'S MORAL PHILOSOPHY

Ruth Anna Putnam

For more than a quarter of a century Hilary Putnam has been concerned to undermine the fact–value dichotomy. Indeed, his *The Collapse of the Fact–Value Dichotomy and Other Essays* (Putnam 2002) is entirely devoted to that effort. Two years later, in *Ethics without Ontology* (Putnam 2004a), he returned to the question of the objectivity of ethics. During the same period he has become more and more interested in the writings of the classical Pragmatists, in particular, those of William James and John Dewey. The aim – to defend the objectivity of ethics – and the interest – in Pragmatism – are, of course, connected. The Pragmatists, Dewey explicitly and James implicitly, rejected the fact–value dichotomy; both defended, as does Hilary Putnam, the objectivity of moral judgments. Indeed, one might say that one attacks the fact–value dichotomy in order to establish the objectivity of ethics, for what masquerades as the fact–value dichotomy is actually the thesis that ethical judgments are not factual.

However, subjecting the fact–value dichotomy to critical examination reveals more than that ethical judgments can be objective. It reveals, for example, the crucial role epistemic values play in science. This was, in my opinion, Hilary Putnam's most important early contribution to the philosophical debate concerning the status of values. Critical examination also reveals that our moral lives – our moral lives as we actually live them – involves the use of "thick" concepts, concepts that have both evaluative and descriptive content. Both points demonstrate what Putnam calls "the entanglement of facts and values."[1]

1. Epistemic values

Defenders of the fact–value dichotomy, at any rate in the early phases of the debate, dealt only with so-called "thin" ethical concepts – good, right, ought – making it appear plausible that all sentences could be easily classified as either factual or ethical. Of course, there are difficulties even if one eschews all thick concepts. How would one classify mathematical truths? As Hilary Putnam has pointed out, they are classified as analytic, i.e. non-factual when the dichotomy in view is that of the analytic versus the synthetic (factual), but these "non-factual" sentences are clearly not ethical. Moreover, as the emotivists knew well, not all uses of the basic value words "good," "right" and "ought" are ethical. But once one admits non-ethical uses of these words, the task of classifying judgments into ethical or non-ethical is no longer simple; it requires attention to context and content.

Reflecting on Quine's critique of the analytic–synthetic distinction and on his own critique of the fact–value dichotomy leads Putnam to make several points that I want to mention in passing. First, the fact that a concept C is not sharply defined need not mean that there are no cases that fall clearly under C and others that equally clearly do not fall under C. Thus Putnam denies neither that there are paradigmatic moral judgments nor that there are paradigmatic judgments that are not moral judgments. Second, a concept C may isolate a fairly well-circumscribed class of things (actions, judgments) that fall under it, while the complement class (the class of things not falling under it) is a motley collection of things that have nothing interesting in common. Thus non-ethical judgments include non-ethical value judgments (aesthetic, economic, epistemic, etc.), descriptive judgments, scientific theories, mathematical statements, etc., etc. Thus, while there are contexts in which it is useful to distinguish between ethical judgments and other judgments, nothing metaphysical or epistemological follows from this; just as no such consequences follow from the fact that it is useful in some contexts to distinguish between chemical judgments and those that do not belong to chemistry.

Suppose a defender of the fact–value dichotomy were to suggest now that the difficulties just raised hinge on the notion of the *ethical*, while what is at stake is a dichotomy of facts on the one hand and *all kinds of values* on the other. Putnam's first move in his attack on the fact–value dichotomy can be seen as a reply to this suggestion since he drew attention to non-ethical, namely, epistemic, values. How could non-cognitivist philosophers like Carnap and Reichenbach, philosophers who contributed so significantly to philosophy of science, fail to notice that such notions as coherence, relevance, simplicity, warrant, etc., are evaluative? I suggest that they failed to notice this because they thought of value judgments as judgments containing the words "good," "right" or "ought" and their opposites. To be sure, they sometimes mentioned aesthetic judgments in passing, and they put aside as "factual" and thus unproblematic judgments of instrumental value. In contrast, Putnam took the term "value" seriously, and so uncovered the indispensable role of epistemic value judgments in the practice of science. Descriptions of observations, theoretical statements, and judgments of epistemic value are inextricably intertwined in the development and selection of scientific hypotheses and theories. Consequently, if value judgments are not objective, neither are scientific theories. But scientific theories are supposed to be paradigms of objectivity! I shall return to this matter, but it is time to say something about the relevance of "thick" concepts to our topic.

2. Thick concepts

Such terms as "cruel" or "generous" do not merely describe an action or character trait, they also evaluate it. An action is not generous if it does not confer a benefit of some sort or other; it also fails to be generous if it is not at least somewhat supererogatory; a generous action confers a benefit in excess of what is strictly speaking required. Of course, Hilary Putnam was not the first to notice the crucial role played by these concepts. Socrates, it will be recalled, did not ask, "What is Good?" he asked, "What is Piety?," "What is Justice?," etc. The important role played in our moral lives by thick ethical concepts is cited by opponents of the fact–value dichotomy as evidence that there is no such dichotomy, for judgments using these concepts are at once descriptive and prescriptive. Defenders of the dichotomy respond either (a) by trying (unsuccessfully) to factor the thick concepts into mutually independent descriptive and evaluative components, or (b) by retreating into one sort of relativism or another. I call the latter move a retreat, because it retreats from plain non-cognitivism into a limited or relative cognitivism. However, that cognitivism is embedded in a fundamental non-cognitivism, for it is accompanied by the claim that cross-cultural value judgments are nonsense, at least in some cases.[2] Hilary Putnam has argued repeatedly that neither move succeeds in rescuing the fact–value dichotomy. Thick concepts cannot be factored into a descriptive and an evaluative component. For example, a generous action is not simply an action that confers a benefit (pretending that "benefit" is not already evaluative!); a generous action confers a greater benefit than justice requires. Putnam finds relativism indefensible, even when it avoids being self-refuting, because it presupposes a notion of culture that cannot survive Michele Moody-Adams' devastating critique (Moody-Adams 1997).

3. Facts

In an important new critique of the fact–value dichotomy, Putnam points out, "In the writings of the positivists, in the case of both the dualism of analytic and factual statements and the dualism of ethical and factual statements, it is the conception of the 'factual' that does all the philosophical work" (Putnam 2002: 21). And he suggests, helpfully, that what masquerades as a dichotomy is actually a thesis, namely, "that 'ethics' is not about 'matters of fact'" (Putnam 2002: 19).

This insight prompts then a careful examination of the development of the philosophical, specifically the empiricist, notion of fact, beginning with David Hume and ending with Carnap's position late in his career. At that point Carnap held that scientific theories have factual content (are cognitively meaningful, confront experience) only as wholes, but that the language of science could be neatly divided into a theoretical and an observation vocabulary. As Putnam summarizes, the theoretical terms "were regarded as mere devices for deriving the sentences which *really* state the empirical facts, namely the observation sentences" (Putnam 2002: 119). According to Carnap, there is room for ethical terms in neither the observation nor the theoretical vocabulary. They are nonsense.

Here I would like to note that Carnap's examples of observation terms often refer to so-called secondary qualities, for example, "hot" or "blue" – terms which, like "large," are clearly relative or subjective. Carnap's notion of fact – what is stated in observation statements – thus differs radically from Bernard Williams' notion; for Williams the facts are what will be stated in the best future physics, and that physics will refer only to primary qualities. I conclude that Putnam's examination of the *fact* side of the supposed fact–value dichotomy serves to undermine it, as did his earlier examination of the *value* side. Of course, what undermines the fact–value dichotomy is not the mere disagreement on what is to count as "factual." Rather the disagreement seems to force us to be aware of a third class of judgments, judgments that are neither value judgments nor factual in whatever sense of "factual" is chosen. In the case of Carnap, these are the theoretical scientific statements; in the case of Williams, they are the statements that are NOT part of the best physical theories. It seems that precisely what Carnap accepts as factual is characterized by Williams as insufficiently objective. In view of Putnam's concerns in *Ethics without Ontology* (Putnam 2004a), I note that neither Carnap's distinction between theoretical and observation terms nor Williams' distinction between, in effect, terms referring to primary and those referring to secondary qualities leaves room for terms of mathematics. Yet no modern theory in the physical sciences can do without these. In any case, a re-examination of the tacit identification of factual and objective that underlies the debate may be in order. Putnam indeed continues his examination of the factual by drawing attention, once again, to the "thick" concepts.

As is well known, Bernard Williams admits that judgments containing thick ethical concepts have truth values within a culture that has the corresponding concepts, while Carnap would presumably reject them as nonsense. As Putnam put it, "Non-cognitivism has been rebaptized as relativism" precisely because philosophers have become aware of the importance of thick ethical concepts and come to agree that they cannot be analyzed as conjunctions of a descriptive and an evaluative component (Putnam 1990b: 165). Williams, according to Putnam, replaced the fact–value dichotomy by a distinction between truth and absoluteness, or between what is true only from within a local perspective and what is true independent of us. Putnam finds the latter dichotomy as indefensible as the former.

Williams' notion of an absolute conception of the world, a conception that will correspond to how the world is independent of any human perspective, what I called above "the best future physics," is rejected by Putnam as resting on an indefensible, indeed an incoherent, metaphysics. Williams assumes that science will converge to a single theoretical account, an account that will be forced upon scientists because it "corresponds" to the way things are. But that assumption presupposes the existence of a unique relation of correspondence "independent of us" between words in our language and things "in the world." It would lead me too far afield to rehearse here Putnam's multiple arguments against this assumption.[3] He summarizes his critique as follows.

> Williams tacitly assumes a correspondence theory of truth when he *defines* the absolute conception, and then forgets that he did this when he suggests that we do not need to assume that such semantic notions as the 'content' of a sentence will turn out to figure in the absolute conception itself.
> (Putnam 1990a: 174)

In other words, Williams' absolute conception of the world is too impoverished to account for itself. This is, of course, not a critique of physics; it merely points out that even the best future physics will not be a theory of everything, if "everything" includes everything human beings need to talk about, for example, the content of sentences or the grandeur of Mt. Fuji. However, the target of Putnam's critique is not merely Bernard Williams' notion of the absolute conception of the world but contemporary naturalism in general.

Recently Putnam has contrasted naturalism with his own conceptual pluralism, i.e. with the claim that statements in ethics, statements about meaning and reference, statements in history, etc., are as subject to standards of truth and rationality as are statements of physics (Putnam 2004b). Although it would lead us too far outside the confines of the present essay to consider Putnam's detailed critique of naturalistic reductionism and naturalistic eliminationism, I would like to quote what he regards as the starting point of an alternative picture.

> [I]t is only in the context of such a practice as *talking about cats* that such a sentence as 'Tabitha won't drink milk' constitutes a *statement*. And ... there is not even a way to begin to talk about that practice without talking about the various things we do with cats ... starting with *perceiving* them – that is, *talking about things* is a vast and ever-expanding motley of *world-involving practices*.
> (Putnam 2004b: 65)

I want to draw attention here to the emphasis on world-involving practices. Just as an adequate account of intentionality requires us to consider language in the context of a world-involving practice, so we will not give an adequate account of ethics unless we see ethical judgments in the context of a world-involving practice. Ethics is *world-involving*, i.e., not *a priori*, and it is a *practice*, i.e., it concerns conduct. Putnam concludes his discussion of naturalism – I shall return to this below – by suggesting that naturalists are motivated by a fear of the normative. That fear is due to the mistaken idea that bona fide indicative statements must *describe* reality; hence, if value judgments are bona fide indicative statements, then there must be values in the sense of entities. A similar mistake leads to postulating mathematical entities. Putnam argues against identifying objectivity with description of objects.

4. Entanglement again

As mentioned above, Putnam has cited both the indispensability of epistemic values in the practice of science and the indispensability of thick concepts in our moral lives as objections to the fact–value dichotomy; both entanglements also play key roles in the argument of The Collapse of the Fact/Value Dichotomy. Here I want to interject that, of course, coherence, relevance, warrant, etc., are themselves thick concepts. One should also note that not only epistemic but also moral values are "entangled" in the practice of science, and indeed in belief formation in everyday life. This last point calls for some elaboration.

Putnam writes, "The concern that is – obviously – connected with the values that guide us in choosing between hypotheses (coherence, simplicity, preservation of past doctrine, and the like) is the concern with 'right description of the world'" (Putnam 2002: 31–32). But in doing science we (a) do not merely choose between hypotheses on the basis of characteristics of the hypotheses themselves, we choose also on the basis of relations between hypotheses and experimental results. Therefore, (b) we do not merely select theories, we design and run experiments and note the results. Science is, in other words, a world-involving *practice* that calls for certain character virtues in scientists: honesty, diligence, carefulness, etc. How "right" a description of the world scientists produce depends in part on their possession of these virtues.

The moral virtues are relevant in yet another way. Although philosophers and scientists may dream of a complete description of the world, or, somewhat more realistically, of a collection of complete descriptions from various perspectives (a complete physical description, a complete description of the bio-sphere, a complete account of the human mind/psyche, a total history of humanity, etc.), in practice, we must be satisfied with very much less. Financial and human resources are limited; choosing where to employ these limited resources calls upon further moral as well as intellectual virtues.

I am not suggesting that all research should be "applied." Not only is it well known that applied research will soon dry up without a foundation of pure research, but the human interest in knowledge for its own sake is itself to be cherished and fostered. But there is no algorithm determining the proper balance between pure and applied research or between different investigations on either side. In this connection one should also mention ethical considerations in relation to research on human or animal subjects. Sometimes one may have to forego a certain kind of knowledge because acquiring it (or acquiring it by the only method now known to us) would cost too much in human or animal suffering. The moral judgments made in the course of choosing research projects thus have a bearing on the subject matter though not upon the specific content of our scientific hypotheses.

Putnam has pointed out yet another way in which morality enters into the conduct of science. He writes,

> Moreover, it is not just that, on Dewey's conception, good science requires respect for autonomy, symmetric reciprocity, and discourse ethics ... but that, as already observed, the very *interpretation* of the *non*-algorithmic standards by which scientific hypotheses are judged depends on cooperation and discussion structured by the same norms. Both for its full development and for its full application to human problems, science requires the *democratization of inquiry*.
> (Putnam 1994b: 173)

Putnam summarizes these reflections by saying that *science* is a normative notion.

5. Pragmatism

Recently Putnam has formulated the view just discussed in a form that makes its descent from Pragmatism apparent and has indeed set it in a wider Pragmatist context (Putnam 2002: ch. 8). Here are the formulations in question.

(1) Knowledge of (particular) facts presupposes knowledge of theories (where that includes all generalizations).
(2) Knowledge of theories (in the wide sense of 1) presupposes knowledge of (particular) facts.
(3) Knowledge of facts presupposes knowledge of values.
(4) Knowledge of values presupposes knowledge of facts.

While Putnam accepts all four claims, he emphasized in the final chapter of *The Collapse of the Fact/Value Dichotomy* that he was concerned to defend (3), and that it could be understood as making two separate claims: (i) that the activity of justifying factual claims presupposes value judgments; and (ii) that we must regard these value judgments as capable of being *right* or objective if we want to avoid subjectivism with respect to factual claims.

To the best of my knowledge, Putnam has never claimed that justifying factual statements in the narrow sense of (1) and (2), for example a Carnapian observation sentence ("the cat has a white spot on its nose"), presupposes value judgments. His arguments have always concerned what are here called "theories." In (3) but perhaps not in (4) – which is directed against a priori ethics – "factual" is understood broadly to include empirically grounded theories. I believe that the arguments already rehearsed make clear that such theories cannot be justified without an appeal to value judgments. However, to speak of justifying a Carnapian observation report appears to be problematic. Carnapian observation statements are supposed to be capable of being established by a few simple observations. If the demand for justification is not to be an invitation to skepticism, it must, as John Austin (1970b) pointed out long ago, rest on a specific doubt ("maybe it is milk; I just saw her drinking"). Such doubt may concern the epistemic conditions ("it is too dark to see clearly") and thus call for a judgment of epistemic value, but it may, as in the case I envisaged, call merely for further observation. Does the spot disappear as the cat licks its nose? I am not suggesting that observation reports are incorrigible – they are not; I am suggesting that for the most part observation reports do not call for justification.

In any case, I believe that Putnam would subscribe to (3) even if "facts" is taken to refer to observation reports as well as to scientific theories. For, contrary to Carnap and some, but not all, other non-cognitivists, we may *observe* that a so-called thick concept is instantiated. Coming upon some boys about to set fire to a gasoline-drenched live cat (the gruesome example is due to Harman 1977: 4) we see that what they are about to do is cruel. We could not see that if we were not conscious of the wrongness of what the boys are about to do. Neither could we see it if we knew nothing about the nature of gasoline (if we did not believe a "theory" in the sense used in (1) or a "fact" in the sense used in (4)). In other words, knowing that what the boys are about to do is cruel presupposes knowing both facts and values; it is itself an entanglement of facts and values.

But are there no facts untainted by values? How about the fact mentioned above that the cat has a white spot on its nose? Of course, in any easily thought-of context my saying that the cat has a white spot on its nose is all the reason you need to believe that the cat has a white spot on its nose. It would be pathological if you were to ask yourself whether I can be trusted or whether the very idea of a cat with a white spot on its nose is coherent. Of course, there are, and Putnam cheerfully admits that there are, purely factual statements. He also grants that there are purely ethical judgments.[4] So what? If these statements and these judgments are of any interest at all, they will be linked to that great web of beliefs that is, to use an image of Quine's improved by Vivian Walsh, black with fact, white with convention, and red with value, in other words, a pinkish grey (Putnam 2002: 30 quotes Walsh 1987). The objectivity of facts and theories is inextricably linked to that of values.

6. Moral skepticism

But it would be rash for defenders of the objectivity of moral judgments to declare victory. There are those who will conclude from the above that so-called factual judgments are indeed not objective, at least not as objective as Hilary Putnam would claim them to be. Putnam has defended his qualified realism in his long-lasting debate with the late Richard Rorty. Those arguments lie outside the confines of this essay. Here I am concerned with moral skepticism, J. L. Mackie's label for his version of the view that value judgments, and in particular moral judgments, have no truth values, or are not objective (Mackie 1977). Since the history of philosophy shows that skepticisms cannot be defeated on their own grounds, Mackie's label serves as a useful warning. To defeat skepticism, one must refuse to play the skeptic's game.

Mackie denies that values exist on the grounds that, if they existed, they would be "queer." Putnam's refutation of Mackie's argument does not consist in showing that *values* are not "queer," nor in showing that values exist; it consists in showing that value *judgments* do not work the way Mackie thinks they work. For what makes values queer, according Mackie, is that, according to him, value judgments are motivational in a very strong sense. And this – not that values are queer, but that value judgments are motivational in a very strong sense – is a view that was, and perhaps still is, widely shared by non-cognitivists. Putnam summarizes the view as follows: "An adjective whose semantic content is that something possesses intrinsic value (or disvalue) is such that anyone who uses such an adjective without hypocrisy or insincerity must be *motivated* to approve or disapprove of it" (Putnam 2002: 36).[5] He then quotes with approval Elizabeth Anderson's objection that for various psychological reasons (boredom, despair, etc.) one may fail to desire what one judges to be good (Anderson 1993). Moreover, Putnam points out, a value may be overridden by a competing value. Thus, one may acknowledge that one is rude, but consider rudeness an appropriate response to a racist joke.

Of course, value judgments are among the reasons we have for acting in whatever way we act, but any value judgment may be overridden by another or ignored for various other reasons. Moreover, some value judgments neither are nor are meant to be action guiding, e.g. judgments concerning persons in the distant past. I cannot go into these issues here. The important point here is, rather, that rejecting the claim that values, if they existed, would be queer does *not* commit one to the *existence* of values, whatever that might mean. It commits one only to the view that there are valuable things and valuable states of affairs, not merely things and states of affairs that are valued by someone or other, but things or states of affairs that are found *valuable upon reflection*. The new idea here introduced is the idea of reflection. We cannot refute the moral skeptic, I believe, but we can evade moral skepticism by finding the grounds of objectivity not in the existence of "non-natural" objects but in the practice of reflection.

7. Objectivity without objects

I belabor this point because when Hilary Putnam asserts that value judgments have truth values or are objective, he is *not* saying that there are "objects" that these judgments are about. Although he has sometimes called himself a moral realist, he is, in fact, not a moral realist in the sense in which, for example, Plato and G. E. Moore were moral realists. In "Objectivity without Objects" (Putnam 2004a: ch. 3) Putnam recalls two persistent philosophical errors: (1) that if a judgment is objective there must be some objects to which it corresponds, and (2) that if there are no "natural" objects to play this role, then it must be played by "non-natural" objects. Plato's theory of ideas and Moore's claim that good is an unanalyzable non-natural property are examples of this tendency. To speak of "facts" as entities to which all true statements are said to correspond is another manifestation of the same error. There are no "facts" over and above the things (including human beings and their thoughts and feelings) that our true statements describe in so far as they are descriptive.

Very briefly, Putnam defends "objectivity without objects" case by case. Concerning logic, Putnam points out that one comes to know what a logical truth is not by becoming acquainted with a set of Platonic objects but by learning how to construct proofs, i.e., by learning something about the *practice* of logic. Again, he points out that positing objects – numbers, sets, functions, etc. – that are said to be described by (true) mathematical statements adds nothing to mathematical *practice*. Suppose there were such objects and one day they were all to be wiped out, mathematicians would go on doing mathematics just as successfully as before, and grocers, engineers, bankers, etc., would continue to go about their business, and perform their calculations just as successfully as before. The *practice* of mathematics would not be affected because the posited entities were said NOT to interact with anything in the world. (See Putnam 2001.)

Finally, concerning judgments of epistemic value, Putnam maintains,

> ... just as the ethically important adjectives 'cruel' and 'compassionate' describe properties that human beings may have or lack, not supernatural properties, but also not properties that one can simply perceive (or 'measure') without having understood or learned to imaginatively identify with a particular evaluative outlook, so 'simple' and 'coherent'

(in their scientific applications) describe properties that certain human products, namely, scientific theories may have or lack, and that one cannot perceive without having understood and learned to imaginatively identify with a particular evaluative outlook.

(Putnam 2004a: 69)

Generally the point of such judgments is not to describe; it is certainly not to describe some non-natural entities. It is to evaluate. The capacity to make such judgments is learned in the course of one's scientific training and practice.

The point of this brief review of statements other than ethical that tempt some philosophers to become Platonists and others to become nominalists or skeptics is twofold. First, to recall that moral concepts, whether "thick" or "thin" are not unique in presenting this temptation, and second, to note that *Putnam avoids the temptation by changing the ground on which he takes his stand.* The Platonizing temptation arises from the mistaken view that the point of every genuine statement (declarative sentence in the indicative mood used seriously and sincerely) is to describe "reality"; so that where there is no reality apparent, one must be posited. Speakers (and also hearers) are assumed to be mere spectators. They do not interact with the world they attempt to describe, and so it is hardly an objection to point out that the abstract or otherwise non-natural entities they posit also do not interact with the world. In contrast, Putnam takes on the *agent* point of view. This is how he refuses to play the skeptic's game.

8. Practice

Although the expression "agent's point of view" does not occur in Putnam's most recent writings, I interpret them as elaborations of and additions to things written earlier in which he referred explicitly to the agent's point of view. I do this because I see defending the objectivity of ethics not as an end in itself but as a means to a better ethics; I believe that this is also the basis of Hilary Putnam's interest in this subject. Here it is interesting to note the following contrast. Emotivists, and more generally non-cognitivists, have argued that their meta-ethical position leaves the moral life untouched, although some non-cognitivists have in fact defended or criticized certain types of moral reasoning.[6] Still, the official non-cognitivist position is, must be, that, *as a matter of logic*, no moral judgment (no judgment of intrinsic value of any kind) *can* follow from any meta-ethical statement. On the other hand, if one rejects the fact–value dichotomy, if one insists on the objectivity of at least some moral judgments, then the meta-ethics/ethics dichotomy is also deflated. It too is a mere distinction useful sometimes, but without any particular epistemological or ontological implications.

If moral judgments *can* be objective, and now I stress "can," then we are obligated to try to get them right. Note that this is itself a moral judgment.

But what is involved in that effort? There is no simple answer to this question, because there are many different kinds of ethical judgments. But in various writings, Hilary Putnam has mentioned features that are, or should be, present in what we may loosely call moral reflection. I choose this broad term deliberately. Moral reflection calls for reasoning, perception, imagination, and a certain perspective in various combinations at various times. In the next few paragraphs I want to mention briefly Putnam's widely scattered contributions to what John Dewey called "reflective morality."

Hilary Putnam pointed out quite some time ago that "What we require in moral philosophy is, first and foremost, a moral image of the world" (Putnam 1987: 52). Kant, with his notion of a kingdom of ends, of a community of beings who think for themselves, has provided a moral image of the world, a moral image which inspires and makes sense of the Categorical Imperative in both its formal and its material version. But Putnam also thought that this moral image needed supplementation, for example, by the idea that we are all members of one human family. "A moral image," he explained,

> in the sense in which I am using the term is not a declaration that this or that is a virtue, or that this or that is what one ought to do; it is rather a picture of how our virtues and ideals hang together with one another and what they have to do with the position we are in.
> (Putnam 1987: 51)

A moral image of the world is not a morality, but every genuine morality is said to reflect a moral image. A moral image is how we see ourselves and each other. Putnam returned to this notion, which I regard as his most fruitful contribution to moral reasoning, in his Oxford Amnesty Lecture "Cloning People" (Putnam 1999). He developed there a moral image of the family that included valuing diversity. For, he argued, one's moral image of the family influences one's moral image of society, but a moral image of society that scorns diversity has led to untold human suffering. One need think only of the Thirty Years War, of the Eugenics movement in America, and of the destruction of European Jewry.

I wish to appeal to Putnam's notion of a moral image to improve on his claim that

> if one did not at any point share the relevant ethical point of view one would never be able to acquire a thick ethical concept, and that sophisticated use of such a concept requires a continuing ability to identify (at least in imagination) with that point of view.
> (Putnam 2002: 37–38)

The phrase "relevant ethical point of view" requires interpretation. Relativists will happily agree that each "culture" has a particular ethical point of view and that, of course, one cannot master a culture's thick concepts without, at least imaginatively, sharing that point of view. But Putnam is not a relativist. Needless to say, merely substituting "moral image" for "relevant ethical point of view" is not enough. I wonder whether Putnam would not, in fact, agree with the following account. One cannot acquire any ethical concept, thick or thin, without participating in the ethical life of some group of people. In infancy and early childhood one's group is very small; it expands as one grows older. Adults may participate in the life of more than one group, though these will overlap; that is one way in which, as already mentioned, the borders of these groups become blurred and porous. One will acquire, at least if all goes well, not merely a set of ethical concepts, nor that plus some principles or rules and some ability to apply them thoughtfully, nor all that plus some ideals and some virtues, one will also acquire a moral image of the world, a way of seeing oneself and others. I am not suggesting that one shares a moral image with all the members of the overlapping groups to which one belongs: citizens of one's country, co-religionists, fellow professionals, etc. Nor am I suggesting that all members of any one of these groups share a moral image. But neither am I suggesting that one's moral image is idiosyncratic; rather one finds like-minded people in any of the groups to which one belongs. They are the people whose moral judgments one trusts, whose judgments one expects to agree with one's own, who will frequently see without need for argument what one sees oneself. If, then, to one's astonishment and, perhaps, grief, one finds oneself disagreeing with some person like that, one will take the opposing view very seriously; one will respect it even if one does not share it. I do not believe that learning a moral concept presupposes having a moral image; I rather think that moral maturation proceeds, so to speak, on all fronts simultaneously. But this is not an essay in moral psychology.

One acquires, I said, in the course of one's moral maturation, concepts, rules, and principles, that is, one acquires the intellectual wherewithal to reason about moral issues, and one learns to recognize when such reasoning is called for, or when such concepts apply, that is, one's moral perception develops. Certain philosophers whom Hilary Putnam admires, in particular Martha Nussbaum and Iris Murdoch, emphasize the crucial role played by perception. Nussbaum quotes with approval Aristotle's dictum, "the discernment rests with perception" (Aristotle, *Nicomachean Ethics* 1109b in Nussbaum 1990: 69). In "Taking Rules Seriously" (in Putnam 1990a), Putnam worries that a morality based entirely on perception, or a morality that emphasizes too much that rules have exceptions or fails to hedge any exceptions carefully, is in danger of collapsing into an empty situation ethics. On the other hand, he also quoted with approval, as he continues to do to this day, George Eliot's remark, "There is no general doctrine which is not capable of eating out our morality if unchecked by the deep-seated habit of direct fellow-feeling with individual fellow-men" (*Middlemarch*, ch. 61). To balance this, one needs to mention, however, that Putnam also likes to quote Dewey's remark concerning the scope and limits of sympathy. "Sympathy ... is a precious instrumentality for the development of social insight and socialized affection; *but in and of itself it is on the same plane as any natural endowment*" (Putnam 2004a: 102 quoting Dewey and Tufts 1932: 347). Dewey explains that sympathy may cause one to shrink from misery, or even if it moves one to helpfulness, ignorance or lack of thoughtfulness may cause one to do harm rather than good. He points out also that sympathy may cause one to be so partial to one's small circle that one will actually commit injustice to those outside it. Putnam emphasizes that sympathy needs to be transformed, that one needs to be "*educated* into the ethical life" (Putnam 2004a: 102).

None of this adds up to a moral methodology; nor should it. I began by noting that Putnam's increasing preoccupation with "collapsing" the fact–value dichotomy has gone hand in hand with an increasing interest in the philosophy of John Dewey. Dewey, as is well known, replaces traditional epistemology, with its search for foundations of knowledge, with what he calls a "theory of inquiry." Inquiry begins whenever one finds oneself in a problematic situation, and one brings to that situation both "facts" and "values". In other words, we do not begin with, nor do we seek, a foundation; we begin where we are. We *can* only begin where we are; any other story is a philosophical fairy tale. But in the course of further investigation, some, though never all, of our present beliefs and/or valuations will be called into question, may be warranted or modified or even completely rejected. All our experiences are shot through with valuations (with attractions and repulsions, with seeking and fleeing, with longing and dread), but only valuations that survive criticism turn into objective value judgments (evaluations, in Dewey's language).

Space constraints prevent discussion of Dewey's theory of inquiry. In any case, while the sort of value inquiry that is *like any other kind of inquiry* is an enormously important part of our moral lives, it is not all there is to the moral life. It is indeed important to point out to Kantians of various stripes, as Putnam does in his ongoing debates with, for example, Habermas and Korsgaard, that while we need norms, norms are not enough. We also need values; and it is values that become warranted in a process of inquiry that is like any other process of inquiry. But even norms and values are not enough. Both Dewey and William James point out that in the most difficult moral situations one confronts not the question "What will I do?" but "What kind of person will I become?" Finally, Putnam points out – this he has learned from Levinas – "what could be *more* irreducible than my knowledge, face to face with a needy human being, that I am *obliged* to help that human being" (Putnam 2002: 132).

9. Ethics

What then are the practical consequences of this Aristotelian–Kantian–Deweyan–Levinasian normative outlook? In recent years Putnam has advocated the democratization of inquiry, and that involves the democratization of public life. He has defended what he calls the "third enlightenment," the pragmatist enlightenment, and by implication the two preceding enlightenments, that begun by Socrates and the seventeenth–eighteenth-century Enlightenment (see Putnam 2004a: part II). In the third of the Rosenthal lectures (which make up the first three chapters of *The Collapse of the Fact/Value Dichotomy*) Putnam illustrates the effects of meta-ethical commitments on economic theory and through that on political decisions affecting large numbers of people. He ends his brief survey of a hundred years of economics with a discussion of Amartya Sen's "capabilities" approach to problems of poverty and deprivation. A capability is a *valuable* functioning; thus value judgments are unavoidable. Therefore, the need for inquiry as a democratically structured social enterprise is built deeply into this approach to, for example, development economics. Putnam concludes, agreeing with Sen, that economists must learn from ethicists and vice versa.

Putnam's early attempts to collapse the fact–value dichotomy have seemed to me to be located too exclusively in philosophy of language and philosophy of science. As I suggested above, one needs to step outside those confines, away from the spectator's point of view, to escape the unending discussion between "skeptics" and "anti-skeptics." I believe and have tried to show in this essay that in his recent work Putnam has taken that step. It will be interesting to see where he will go from here.

Notes

1 Hilary Putnam's earlier work in ethics and meta-ethics is discussed in R. A. Putnam 2002. While some repetition is inevitable, this essay deals primarily with his most recent writings in these areas.
2 Bernard Williams suggests that cross-cultural judgments make sense only when the choice between the cultures in question is for us a live one. For Williams' views discussed in Putnam 2002 and alluded to in this essay, see Williams 1985 and Williams 1978.
3 Putnam has raised objections against metaphysical realism for many years; his recent critique of Bernard Williams' position uses these earlier arguments. I hope that other contributors to this volume will address these issues.
4 I am not convinced of this last. He has suggested "murder is wrong" as an example, but *murder* seems to me to be a thick concept not analyzable into separate descriptive and evaluative components. To be sure, we don't call a killing murder if we think it was justified or accidental. So, we call an action murder if and only if we think that it was a *wrongful* killing. But if that is all that is meant by "murder is wrong," then it seems to me trivially true, not an ethical statement in any interesting sense.
5 Putnam refers here not to Mackie but to Hare 1981. Hare considered "rude" to be not evaluative because one might not care that one is rude.
6 For example, J. L. Mackie defended a kind of utilitarianism in Mackie 1977 while Bernard Williams raised trenchant objections against (act) utilitarianism in Smart and Williams 1973.

Bibliography

Anderson, Elizabeth (1993) *Value in Ethics and Economics*, Cambridge, MA: Harvard University Press.
Austin, J. L (1970a) *Philosophical Papers*, 2nd edn, ed. J. O. Urmson and G. J. Warnock, Oxford: Oxford University Press.
——(1970b) "Other Minds," in Austin *Philosophical Papers*, 2nd edn, ed. J. O. Urmson and G. J. Warnock, Oxford: Oxford University Press.
Burley, Justin (ed.) (1999) *The Genetic Revolution and Human Rights: The Oxford Amnesty Lectures 1998*, Oxford: Oxford University Press.
De Caro, Mario and David Macarthur (2004) *Naturalism in Question*, Cambridge, MA: Harvard University Press.
Dewey, John and James Tufts (1932) *Ethics*, in *The Later Works of John Dewey*, ed. Jo Ann Boydston, Vol. 7, Carbondale: University of Southern Illinois, 1981–90.
Harman, Gilbert 1977. *The Nature of Morality: An Introduction to Ethics*, Oxford: Oxford University Press.
Hare, R. M. (1981) *Moral Thinking*, Oxford: Oxford University Press.
James, William (1975-) *The Works of William James*, 17 vols, Cambridge, MA: Harvard University Press.
Mackie, J. L. (1977) *Ethics: Inventing Right and Wrong*, Harmondsworth: Penguin.
McCarthy, Timothy and Sean C. Stidd (eds.) 2001 *Wittgenstein in America*, Oxford: Oxford University Press.
Moody-Adams, Michele (1997) *Fieldwork in Familiar Places: Morality, Culture and Philosophy*, Cambridge, MA: Harvard University Press.
Murdoch, Iris (1971) *The Sovereignty of Good*, New York: Schocken Books.
Nussbaum, Martha (1990) *Love's Knowledge: Essays on Philosophy and Literature*, Oxford: Oxford University Press.
Putnam, Hilary (1987) *The Many Faces of Realism*, Peru, IL: Open Court Publishing Company.
——(1990a) *Realism with a Human Face*, ed. James Conant, Cambridge, MA: Harvard University Press.
——(1990b) "Objectivity and the Science/Ethics Distinction," in Putnam 1990a: 163–78.
——(1994a) *Words and Life*, ed. James Conant, Cambridge, MA: Harvard University Press.
——(1994b) "Pragmatism and Moral Objectivity," in Putnam 1994a: 151–81.
——(1999) "Cloning People," in Burley 1999: 1–13.
——(2001) "Was Wittgenstein Really an Antirealist about Mathematics?," in McCarthy and Stidd 2001: 140–94.
——(2002) *The Collapse of the Fact–Value Dichotomy and Other Essays*, Cambridge, MA: Harvard University Press.
——(2004a) *Ethics without Ontology*, Cambridge, MA: Harvard University Press.
——(2004b) "The Content and Appeal of Naturalism," in de Caro and Macarthur 2004: 59–70.
Putnam, Ruth Anna (2002) "Moralische Objectivität und Putnam's Philosophie," in Raters and Willaschek 2002: 225–44.
Raters, M.-L. and M. Willaschek (eds.) (2002) *Hilary Putnam und die Tradition des Pragmatismus*, Frankfurt: Suhrkamp.

Smart, J. J. C. and Bernard Williams (1973) *Utilitarianism: For and Against*, Cambridge: Cambridge University Press.
Walsh, Vivian (1987) "Philosophy and Economics," in *The New Palgrave: A Dictionary of Economics*, vol. 3, ed. J. Eatwell, M. Milgate, and P. Newman, London: Macmillan, 861–69.
Williams, Bernard (1978) *Descartes: The Project of Pure Inquiry*, Harmondsworth: Penguin.
——(1985) *Ethics and the Limits of Philosophy*, Cambridge, MA: Harvard University Press.

COMMENTS ON RUTH ANNA PUTNAM'S "HILARY PUTNAM'S MORAL PHILOSOPHY"

Hilary Putnam

Ruth Anna Putnam's profound essay does not simply get my principal views about values and facts *right*; it "pulls them together" in a way I have not done myself up to now. In particular, her rational reconstruction (for that is what it is) of what I have written about the importance of moral images of the world in ethics and in life is not just a restatement of what I have written, but a statement of what I *should* have written on this topic, and I am profoundly grateful for it, as for so much that she has given me in the course of the more than a half century since we met at a luncheon in honor of Rudolf Carnap in August of 1960.

Only on one significant point do we perhaps differ. With regard to skepticism she writes, "Since the history of philosophy shows that skepticisms cannot be defeated on their own grounds, Mackie's label serves as a useful warning. To defeat skepticism, one must refuse to play the skeptic's game." This suggests that simply viewing things as we actually do when we are actually engaged in ethical judgment, in science, in arguing about whether the bird we saw in the bush was a bittern, or whatever, and refusing to discuss the epistemologist's "how do you know" question, is the right, and indeed the only, way to deal with the skeptic. To put it more crudely than Ruth Anna does, "Just tell the skeptic to get lost." Although my own position on what to do about skepticism has vacillated, this is not a view that I have ever held.

Re skepticism

In several essays (Putnam 1998 and 2012: chs 29–32) I defended the view that the classical skeptical arguments depend on treating "know" as if it were a completely bivalent and context-insensitive verb. For the skeptic, *of course* it is true or false that at this moment I *know* that I am not dreaming, and similarly it is true or false that I *know* I am typing these words on my computer. And I believe that, at least on the use of "to know" that is relevant to skepticism, both of these assumptions are incorrect; I think that the question as to whether I know either of those things simply does not arise in the present context. Of course, I am not the first to argue that ignoring context-sensitivity is the flaw in the traditional skeptical arguments (Malcolm 1949),[1] and the view has itself been sharply challenged by Barry Stroud, whose arguments I in turn criticized in detail in an essay I published in 2001 (Putnam 2001).

In an essay I published in the closing years of the twentieth century I wrote:

> The reason skepticism is of genuine intellectual interest – interest to the *nonskeptic* – is not unlike the reason that the logical paradoxes are of genuine intellectual interest: paradoxes force us to rethink and reformulate our commitments. But if the reason I undertake to show that the skeptical arguments need not be accepted is, at least in part, like the reason I undertake to avoid logical contradictions in pure mathematics (e.g., the Russell Paradox), or to find a way to talk about truth without such logical contradictions as the Liar Paradox; if my purpose is to put my own intellectual house in order, then what I need is a perspicuous representation of our talk of "knowing" that shows how it avoids the skeptical conclusion [the reference is to context-sensitive semantics, as applied to the verb "to know"], and that my *nonskeptical* self can find satisfactory and convincing. (Just as a solution to the logical paradoxes does not have to convince the skeptic, or even convince all philosophers – there can be alternative ways to avoid the paradoxes – so a solution to what we may call "the skeptical paradoxes" does not have to convince the skeptic, or even convince all philosophers – perhaps here too there may be alternative solutions.) It is not a good objection to a resolution to an antinomy that the argument to the antinomy seems "perfectly intelligible," and, indeed, proceeds from what seem to be "intuitively correct" premises, while the resolution draws on ideas (the Theory of Types, in the case of the Russell Paradox; the theory of Levels of Language in the case of the Liar Paradox – and on much more complicated ideas than these as well, in the case of the follow-up discussions since Russell's and Tarski's) that are abstruse and to some extent controversial. That is the very nature of the resolution of antinomies. What I have tried to provide [by rebutting the skeptic's arguments with the help of context-sensitive semantics] is an argument *that convinces me* that *the skeptic cannot provide a valid argument from premises I must accept to the conclusion that knowledge is impossible*. In the same way, Russell showed that (after we have carefully reconstructed our way of talking about sets)

> a skeptic – or whoever – cannot provide a valid argument from premises we must accept to the conclusion that mathematics is contradictory, and Tarski showed that (after we have carefully reconstructed our talk about truth) a skeptic – or whoever – cannot provide a valid argument from premises we must accept to the conclusion that talk about truth is contradictory.
>
> (Putnam 1998: 256)

I said above that my view on skepticism has "vacillated." In fact, in an essay I published in 2006, I described the above words as "not exactly wrong, but superficial" (ibid.: 120). But in the revised version of that paper (Putnam 2012: ch. 32), I replaced this with "I now think that although what I wrote was correct, it is insufficient" (not, NB, "superficial"). What I thought needed to be added was an examination, along lines pioneered by Stanley Cavell, of the reasons that drive us to skepticism, including forms of skepticism that we do not realize are skepticism. And this is still my position; skeptical arguments do need to be reflected on and addressed *as arguments*, although that is not all that there is to say about skepticism. That is different from simply telling the skeptic to get lost. It isn't, however, simply "playing the skeptic's game," which is why I said that Ruth Anna and I *perhaps* differ here; I hope she will not, in fact, disagree with my present position.

Three further points

(1) Ruth Anna is absolutely right that I criticize reductionist and eliminationist versions of naturalism. But I now regret having at times *given* the good Deweyan word "naturalism" to reductionists and eliminationists. In my Prometheus Prize Lecture titled "Corresponding with Reality" (Putnam 2012a) and subsequently I describe myself as a "liberal naturalist."[2]

(2) I agree with Ruth Anna that *for the most part* observation reports do not call for justification. But there is a host of occasions on which they do, as a day spent in a law court listening to a series of cases will convince anyone. When the question is not one of what one oneself is observing right now, but of whether to trust reports of past observations, and especially which ones to trust, when there is disagreement, the values of coherence, plausibility, and the like enter into the decision much as they do in science. And in experimental science, *past observations*, no matter how carefully made, are constantly re-examined.

(3) As Ruth Anna says, I did point out that one comes to know what a logical truth is not by becoming acquainted with a set of Platonic objects but by learning how to construct proofs, i.e., by learning something about the *practice* of logic. But I have found that others (though not Ruth Anna) have misunderstood this as implying that what one *means* by a logically valid statement is one that can be proved. If that were right, then

Gödel's Completeness Theorem for First Order Logic would have been otiose! Although one first acquires the notion of validity by learning to construct proofs, one learns to understand the notion also in cases in which one cannot, in actual fact, verify that it applies. The argument for verificationism, in logic or in empirical science, from "how we learn to use the words" is one I have never accepted (Putnam 1995).

Notes

1 A similar view was defended by Norman Malcolm, for example, although in company with claims that I think are incorrect.
2 For an articulation of *liberal naturalism* and a defense of its advantages over contemporary forms of reductive or scientific naturalism see De Caro and Macarthur (2004 and 2010).

Bibliography

de Caro, Mario and David Macarthur (eds.) (2004) *Naturalism in Question*, Cambridge, MA: Harvard University Press.

——(2010) *Naturalism and Normativity*, New York: Columbia University Press.

Malcolm, Norman (1949) "Defending Common Sense," *Philosophical Review* 58(3): 201–20.

Putnam, H. (1995) "Pragmatism," *Proceedings of the Aristotelian Society* 95(3): 291–306.

——(1998) "Skepticism," in Marcelo Stamm (ed.), *Philosophie in synthetischer Absicht*, Stuttgart: Klett-Cotta, 239–68.

——(2001) "Skepticism, Stroud and the Contextuality of Knowledge," *Philosophical Explorations* 4(1): 2–16, reprinted in Putnam 2012.

——(2006) "Philosophy as the Education of Grownups: Stanley Cavell and Skepticism," in Alice Crary and Sanford Shieh (eds.), *Reading Cavell*, London and New York: Routledge, 117–28.

——(2012) *Philosophy in an Age of Science*, Cambridge, MA: Harvard University Press.

——(2012a) "Corresponding with Reality," *Philosophy in an Age of Science*.

Part III

PERCEPTION

9

SOME REMARKS ON "EXTERNALISMS"

Tyler Burge

As far as I know, the term "externalism" is not used *prominently* by any of the philosophers on this panel to describe his own views.[1] The popularity of the term has been, I think, inversely proportional to its clarity. Like the term "naturalism," "externalism" warmly welcomes a running together of different doctrines, perhaps in the interests of a felt solidarity among those in need of asserting allegiance to a cause. Much of the problem lies in unclarity about what is external to what. Some answers to such a question use terms like "meaning," "proposition," and "content" whose uses vary widely among philosophers. I want to make a few remarks about important differences among views that have been labeled "externalist." I will lay aside epistemic externalisms and focus entirely on externalisms relevant to language and mind.

One family of views often termed "externalist" concerns language. It is trivial that many entities that are in fact objects of linguistic reference are external to – independent for their nature and existence of – language. It is *not* trivial that some factors *constitutively determining* which objects linguistic terms refer to are irreducibly external to – independent of – idiolects, dialects, and communal languages. Such factors include causal chains, contextual parameters, and molecular structures, none of which individuals need not be able to specify. This point was established, I think, by Strawson for demonstrative reference (Strawson 1959), by Saul and Keith Donnellan for proper names (Donnellan 1970; Kripke 1972), and by Saul and Hilary for natural kind terms (Kripke 1972; Putnam 1975b, 1975c). I certainly endorse the point. It marks one sort of view often termed "externalism."

There are many importantly different and incompatible views about *meaning*, as distinguished from reference, that are called "externalist views." A hyper-Millian view holds that the meaning, or the specifically semantical contribution, of names and perhaps other terms is *exhausted* by its referent. No one on this panel is committed to this position. There is the less committal but still Millian view that elements of linguistic meaning, or linguistic propositional content – particularly, elements of the meaning of proper

263

names and natural kind terms – *include* objects of reference in the physical environment. Hilary accepted such a view in the 1970s and Saul has shown some sympathy for it. I am non-committal, shading toward the doubtful.

I think that the notion of meaning has a root conceptual connection to the notion of potential understanding. I think that a direct connection between understanding and physical objects has never been made clear or plausible. Understanding is certainly always perspectival. The idea of understanding, or indeed perceiving, a physical object (even as a *component* of meaning) *neat* is, I think, incoherent. So if physical objects in the environment are to be considered components of meaning, some account of meaning that loosens its relation to understanding must be developed. Clearly, *some* sort of understanding, some sort of psychological competence, is associated with proper names and natural kind terms. A serious development of the fundamental notions of meaning and understanding that underlie even this moderate Millian view has never, to my knowledge, been undertaken. I believe that if semantical discussion is to get beyond the impasses that have faced it in the last couple of decades, more attention needs to be devoted to the conceptions and motivations that underlie various notions of meaning and understanding. So I believe that the moderate Millian view is at best unclear.

It does not help to add the negative point, originally made by Hilary, that for "externalists" meaning is not in the head. Insofar as meaning is shareable, even those who are labeled "internalists" can and should say that meaning is not in the head. I believe that meaning is an abstraction, hence not located anywhere. So I am doubtful that there is an acceptable notion of externality according to which it is true, interesting, and distinctive, to claim that *components* of meaning are external to language, the individual, or what not. But such a claim is commonly associated with the term "semantic externalism." I think that the term is so associated with unclarity and dispute on these issues that it is better to drop it. "Semantic," "meaning," and "understanding" are sufficiently in need of explication that adding another term "externalism" to the mix just piles up intellectual debts.

In any case, I think that the power and interest of the arguments regarding linguistic reference that were given by Donnellan, Saul, and Hilary transcend technical issues about exactly how to regard meaning or linguistically expressed propositions. To return to something I said earlier, the constitutive *determiners* of reference are partly independent of individuals' idiolects and of communal languages. Perhaps here we have a position that the three of us share that is very close to what is popularly understood as "externalism" about language.

Let us turn from language to mind. In my view, the positive results on linguistic reference are ultimately founded on a broader set of phenomena regarding mind. And the fact that the determiners of reference are external to idiolects, dialects, and communal languages is ultimately to be understood in terms of the independence of such determiners from individuals' psychologies.

The term "externalism" is if anything less well anchored with respect to mind than it is with respect to language. Many associate the term with the view that representational mental contents or, even worse, mental states and events, are somehow in the wider environment beyond the individual. Although such fringe views haunt the landscape, no major figure I know of holds any such view. Some of Saul's followers, though not Saul himself, maintain that whereas linguistic meaning includes or is exhausted by objects in the environment, representational mental content is purely descriptive. Thus referents of representational mental content are determined by description. Proponents of this two-dimensional view are sometimes counted "externalists," although their position is "internalist" on the most elementary aspect, viz. reference, of the most fundamental matter, viz. thought. I leave perception aside here. The original arguments by Saul and Hilary (and by Donnellan) regarding linguistic reference can be trivially adapted to show that reference in thought cannot be fixed by descriptive capacities of individuals, or even whole communities. Since much reference in thought is not indexical, where reference is not fixed by descriptive capacities, representational thought content cannot be either. I am simply not generous enough to share an unqualified label "externalist" with such philosophers.

The view about mind that I provided a series of arguments for, beginning in the late 1970s, which I call "anti-individualism," is that the constitutive determiners of the natures of many mental states include relations between the individual in those mental states and elements of the wider physical and social environments (Burge 2007). This is emphatically not primarily a view about representational mental content, but about mental states and events. It is about what representational mental content mental states or events constitutively have and can have.

The view is also not that the representational mental content is external to the individual. Again, I think of the content as abstract, and not anywhere. Moreover, *thinkings* of the content are always in the individual's mind or head, if they are anywhere. (I think that claiming that there is an *exact* spatial location for higher-level mental events like thoughts may be pointless.) Thus externality to the individual concerns the *constitutive determiners* of the mental states' representational content – and ultimately of the nature and identity of the mental state or event – *not* the content itself or the mental states or events themselves. The key point is that some constitutive determiners need not be part of or immediately accessible to the individual's psychology. In this sense, elements beyond the individual – entities in the physical environment, and non-psychological, causal relations to them, for example – are among the constitutive determiners of the individual's psychology. This view is not a trivial corollary of the work on linguistic reference.

Putnam's work in "The Meaning of 'Meaning'" (1975d) was at best ambivalent with respect to anti-individualism. But he came to endorse it fully. I think that it is the doctrine that underlies and helps explain the views about linguistic reference that I characterized some paragraphs back. That is, I think anti-individualism is more fundamental than the views about linguistic reference that are often called "semantical externalism." Language is an expression of mind.

"Externalism" about language should be firmly distinguished from "externalism" about mind. "Externalism" about constitutive determiners of the natures and identities of psychological (or mental) states or events should be sharply distinguished from "externalism" about the nature of meaning, representational content, and referents.

Even once such parameters are set, what externality precisely consists in is in many instances in need of clarification. I think that this label has encouraged sloppy thinking. Although proposals for linguistic reform are rarely heeded – and I do not expect this one to be – I believe that it would serve philosophy either to drop the term "externalism" altogether, or always to qualify it, so that the relata that are external to one another are clearly specified, and the particular relation of externality is clarified. Such usage would be less snappy. But short-hand has rarely served philosophical reflection.

Let me turn to a more broad-based observation about the currents in philosophy that I have been discussing. In retrospect, I am struck by the relatively compartmentalized focus on language that marked their beginnings. In the first half of the twentieth century, mainstream philosophy, especially in Britain and the United States, had focused on perception almost as much as on language. With the demise of sense-data views at mid-century, interest in perception abruptly faded. So the initial work on linguistic reference at mid-century was almost completely divorced from any discussion of perception.

Strawson is a partial exception to this remark. His work on demonstrative reference in the 1950s was linked to powerful points about the perception of duplicate scenes (Strawson 1959). He noted that a perception of a scene that is indiscernible from a perception that would be obtained from a similar scene that occurs elsewhere in the universe would nevertheless be a perception of, and only of, the scene by which it is causally occasioned. Here perceptual reference depends on causal relations to a scene and cannot be determined fully by discriminations available to the individual. In my view, Strawson failed to exploit this insight because of his descriptivist leanings with respect to names and his insistence on criteria for the application of general terms. In the early phases of the work on linguistic reference, no one besides Strawson thought hard about perception. Such was the tendency to reflect on language as an autonomous phenomenon.

Although this narrow focus on language reaped obvious rewards, I think that it also carried serious disadvantages. Sometimes perception was, and still is, regarded as dependent on language for making singular reference to entities in the physical environment, or as dependent on language for categorizing entities under general types. Both ideas are completely out of step with what is known from science. More broadly, if a reasonable conception of perception had been central to these early discussions, the discoveries regarding linguistic reference and mental states would have come more easily. The discoveries about language would have been made in a broader and more natural setting. And deeper understanding of the origins of reference would have been attained.

For example, the Kripke–Donnellan points about reference of names have obvious analogs for perception. An object can be seen even though the perceiver could not perceptually distinguish the object – given the perceiver's looking angle and background knowledge – from a look-alike that might have been substituted for the object. This point is analogous to the point that a language speaker can refer to an object with a name or to a kind by a natural kind term, even though the perceiver cannot distinguish the name's or term's bearer from other entities, except by use of the name or term. Perceptual reference is not carried out purely by perceptual attributives or perceptual categories in the perceiver's (or perceptual system's) repertoire, just as reference in language is not carried out purely by descriptive resources in the speaker's repertoire. Perceptual reference, like reference with many names and kind terms, is partly and irreducibly determined by causal relations to the referent.

Similarly, perceptual reference is compatible with being perceptually wrong about most of the salient properties of the perceived object. The color, shape, sortal type, and position of an object can be misperceived, all at once, even as the object is perceived. Here we have a clear analog of a standard and deep point made about the use of names, natural kind terms, and so on. An individual can succeed in referring to the bearer of a name or to the referent of a natural kind term, even though most of the individual's associated descriptions are false of the referent.

What was unfortunate about the narrow focus on language is not just a failure to exploit analogies between perceptual reference and linguistic reference. There was a failure to follow reference back to its roots. (I believe that this point bears on disquotationalist views of reference.) In many paradigmatic cases, the association of a name with its bearer, or of a natural kind term with the relevant kind, depends ultimately on perception. Elementary linguistic reference is, I think, to a large extent grounded in perception. There are forms of reference that are not obviously empirical – reference with numerals, for example. And there are empirical mechanisms beyond perception: chains of communication, introduction of kind terms through hypothesis or theory, and so on. But, obviously, the roots of reference for these more complex mechanisms, at least in empirical cases, lie in perception.

Even in my own work on mind, I did not center on perception until the early and mid-1980s, after I had studied David Marr's psychology of vision in classes at MIT while I was a visiting professor there. Hilary does give serious attention to perception in 1994 in his Dewey Lectures (Putnam 1994). In my view, however, these lectures do not make any serious use of the *science* of visual psychology – an area of psychology, almost the only area, that had matured well before then into a mathematically rigorous science. There is not a single serious reference to any of the methods or theories in empirical perceptual psychology in those lectures. In fact, much that Hilary says in those lectures seems to me to be incompatible with what had been known in the science for some decades.

A full conception of objective representation must develop accounts of mechanisms for linguistic reference in the light of a scientifically informed account of perception. I found it striking that in the roundtable on perception given at the Dublin conference – at least in the oral form that it took during the conference – there was not a single serious mention, much less extended discussion, of the considerable body of knowledge in the science of perception, particularly visual perception.[2]

Anti-individualism applies to perceptual states. Most of the anti-individualistic elements in thought and in language must be understood as grounded in antecedent perceptual representation. (I say more about these matters in Burge 2005, 2007, 2010.)

I turn now to a brief appreciation of Hilary's contributions, and some questions about them. I think of Hilary's work on reference, which really goes back to "It Ain't Necessarily So" (1975a), as brilliantly imaginative. The work is carried out with a nuance, depth, and freedom that make it entirely admirable. I think that it will prove to be one of his lasting contributions to philosophy. I would like to ask two questions about middle-level components of this work.

One is about stereotypes. Stereotypes were introduced, I think, in "Is Semantics Possible?" (1975b), as short dictionary-type explications of a term, anchored by a further component – the referent itself. I am primarily interested in the explication component of the stereotype. Such explications were accorded the function of conveying, in short-order, an understanding of the term that might get a novice started at applying it to its referents. Hilary rightly found remarkable the power of a short description to teach a language learner a new term, even though the description normally does not determine a unique referent, and normally is not even close to being synonymous with the term. He emphasized that the descriptive elements in the stereotype need not be *true* of all (or in the limit, perhaps any) of the entities to which the term applies, as long as those elements enable users to agree on a use with respect to standard or paradigmatic examples.

I regard this notion as an imaginative contribution to our thinking about meaning and reference. It is intriguing in that it does not fit into any of the standard slots in semantical thinking. I seriously doubt that the descriptive elements in stereotypes are, except perhaps in the loosest sense, any part of the literal meaning of the terms to which they are attached. They can change with circumstance, context, and time in ways that terms' meanings do not seem to. The explicative, descriptive elements seem arguably a part of linguistic theory. They seem to be an important element in linguistic practice. But as I said, they do not seem to fit into any of the standard slots – literal meaning, implicature, or what not.

My question is how Hilary now regards this contribution – in particular, the explicative descriptive component of the stereotype – and whether he foresees ways of developing the notion further.

The other question is about twin-earth methodology. I owe much to Hilary's introduction of this methodology. I believe that it is an exceptionally imaginative and effective way of discussing examples. My attitude is not shared even by all who accept the conclusion of arguments that make use of the methodology. There are those who think that such dramatic fiction should play no role in philosophy, that the thought experiments are too strange to carry conviction, and so forth. I will not engage with wholesale doubts about the methodology, except to say that thought experiments using the methodology *did* carry conviction. I do believe that all the points made with the methodology can in principle be made without it. But discovery and imagination are often aided by just such thought experiments. They seem to be at least an epistemically valuable prompt for reflection.

What I want to focus on is a particular aspect of the thought experiments. In the literature subsequent to Hilary's publication of the initial twin-earth thought experiment, it was often noted that the thought experiment that centered on water describes a situation that is strictly impossible (Putnam 1975d). It seemed important to the thought experiment that it concern actual human usage. And it seemed important to the thought experiment that it concern a simple everyday kind like *water*. But one simply cannot have a duplicate twin of a human being or human body in a world in which there is no water.

From the moment the point was articulated, I believe that all philosophers with judgment, including Hilary of course, recognized that in some sense the impossibility did not matter to the point and force of the thought experiment. Even though the thought experiment rested on an impossible state of affairs, it made its point. How did it do so?

A possible view is that there are other thought experiments not involving water that postulate such duplications that are possible. But it seems that no thought experiment that takes a human being as one of the protagonists and that concerns the stuff *water* could possibly do the job. Deprive twin-earth of water and one cannot have a physical duplicate of a human being on twin-earth. Then why is it that the thought experiment is persuasive specifically regarding the referential relation between the term "water" and *water*?

It seems to me that the answer has to do with the point of the thought experiment. The main point is not what it first appears to be. The main point is not to show that it is metaphysically possible that physical duplicates can have terms with different referents. The main point is not about the failure of local supervenience of linguistic reference on the physiology of the individual language user. This point can be made using other thought experiments. Hilary's water thought experiment does suggest how to construct such thought experiments.

But I think that the value of the twin-earth thought experiment that centers on *water* is not adequately accounted for by calling it a near miss. Its value is not best accounted for by saying that it fails on its own terms, but helps us think up better thought experiments that succeed. I believe that these reflections indicate that the point about the failure of local supervenience of linguistic reference on the physiology of individual language users is not properly thought of as the basic philosophical point (or objective) of Hilary's original thought experiment. The basic point is rather to bring to consciousness an awareness of what factors constitutively bear on reference, and on aspects of meaning that determine reference.[3] The impossible fiction contains pointers to what factors are and what factors are not decisive in determining the nature of the referential relation, at least in the cases of a large class of kind terms. Even though strict duplicates are impossible, the postulation of the duplicates reminds us that what sorts of fluid are contained in an individual's body are not any more determinative of the referents of the individual's terms than are what sorts of connections obtain between the individual's synapses or what sorts of bodily movements the individual engages in, considered in themselves.

The science fiction makes a point that does not lie in a strict modal counter-example to the view that sameness of bodily constitution and behavior is compatible with difference in reference. The science fiction helps one reason more clearly about what factors are relevant and what factors are irrelevant to reference. I would like to understand better the relation between the fiction in the thought experiment – a fiction that makes its point even though it is quite literally an impossible fiction – and thought experiments that *depend* on citing a genuine possibility.

I am interested in what Hilary thinks about these matters. His use of science fiction in making philosophical points is unsurpassed. Perhaps there are epistemic insights embedded in his methodology that might help us better understand not only modal epistemology, but the epistemology of reflection on constitutive matters.

Notes

1 This piece is a lightly edited and lightly supplemented version of a talk given at a panel discussion whose designated title was "Externalism." The discussion occurred at the conference in honor of Hilary Putnam in Dublin, Ireland, March 2007. The other panelists were Saul Kripke and Hilary Putnam. I have retained first names for these colleagues in order to emphasize the informality of both my contribution and the occasion.

2 The chapters by Travis and McDowell in this volume.
3 The essay is advertised as being about meaning, but I believe that Hilary's discussion of meaning in the essay is confused. I think that the main insights are into reference and derivatively into aspects of meaning that are different if reference is different. For some discussion, see my "Other Bodies" and Introduction in Burge 2007.

Bibliography

Burge, Tyler (2005) "Disjunctivism and Perceptual Psychology," *Philosophical Topics* 33: 1–78.
——(2007) *Foundations of Mind: Essays by Tyler Burge*, vol. 2, Oxford: Oxford University Press.
——(2007a) "Other Bodies," in *Foundations of Mind: Essays by Tyler Burge*, vol. 2, Oxford: Oxford University Press, 82–99.
——(2009) "Perceptual Objectivity," *Philosophical Review* 118(3): 285–324.
——(2010) *Origins of Objectivity*, Oxford: Oxford University Press.
Donnellan, Keith (1970) "Proper Names and Identifying Descriptions," *Synthese* 21: 335–358.
Kripke, Saul (1972) *Naming and Necessity*, Cambridge, Mass., Harvard University Press.
Putnam, Hilary (1975a) "It Ain't Necessarily So," in *Philosophical Papers*, vol. 1, Cambridge: Cambridge University Press, 237–49.
——(1975b) "Is Semantics Possible?," in *Philosophical Papers*, vol. 2, Cambridge: Cambridge University Press, 139–52.
——(1975c) "Explanation and Reference," in *Philosophical Papers*, vol. 2, Cambridge, Cambridge University Press, 196–214.
——(1975d) "The Meaning of 'Meaning'," in *Philosophical Papers*, vol. 2, Cambridge: Cambridge University Press, 215–71.
——(1994) "Sense, Nonsense, and the Senses: An Inquiry into the Powers of the Human Mind," *The Journal of Philosophy* 91: 445–517.
Strawson, P.F. (1959) *Individuals*, New York: Doubleday and Company, 1963, ch. 1, sections 1–2.

COMMENTS ON TYLER BURGE'S "SOME REMARKS ON 'EXTERNALISMS'"

Hilary Putnam

Tyler Burge and I have long been allies in the struggle against individualistic accounts of meaning and of mental contents generally. We have influenced each other through the years. And we certainly agree that the "determiners" of mental states do not lie inside our heads. But Burge has qualms about my counting the things in the extension of a natural kind term as components of the meaning of the term. (He describes himself as "non-committal, shading toward the doubtful.") The clearest statement of these qualms occurs early in his talk, when he writes:

> I think that the notion of meaning has a root conceptual connection to the notion of potential understanding. I think that a direct connection between understanding and physical objects has never been made clear or plausible. Understanding is certainly always perspectival. The idea of understanding, or indeed perceiving, a physical object (even as a *component* of meaning) *neat* is, I think, incoherent. So if physical objects in the environment are to be considered components of meaning, some account of meaning that loosens its relation to understanding must be developed.
> (Burge in this volume, p. 264)

I want to respond to his qualms. The project of trying to describe what an ideal dictionary entry for a word might look like, and what evidence would be relevant, was central to my "The Meaning of 'Meaning'" (written in 1972) and its predecessor "Is Semantics Possible?" (written in 1968). As I explain in "The Meaning of 'Meaning'," counting the extension of a natural kind term as part of what I called its "meaning vector" does *not* mean that the linguist is visualized as attributing to the native speaker the ability to *describe* that extension non-tautologically. (Of course, the native speaker can describe it tautologically by saying that, e.g., "gold" refers to gold.) So the link between meaning and understanding *is* loosened in my account. (But the other components of my meaning vector – the syntactic and semantic markers, and the stereotype – do describe the speaker's understanding of the term in question.)

Why did I loosen the link between meaning and understanding in this way? Because I wanted to represent the fact that when the reference of a term is different in two communities, we *count* that as a difference in meaning. The overwhelming majority of philosophers of language and cognitive scientists apparently share my intuition here, I am happy to report.

Stereotypes

I am happy to find Burge writing,

> I regard this notion [the stereotype] as an imaginative contribution to our thinking about meaning and reference. It is intriguing in that it does not fit into any of the standard slots in semantical thinking. I seriously doubt that the descriptive elements in stereotypes are, except perhaps in the loosest sense, any part of the literal meaning of the terms to which they are attached. They can change with circumstance, context, and time in ways that terms' meanings do not seem to. The explicative, descriptive elements seem arguably a part of linguistic theory. They seem to be an important element in linguistic practice. But as I said, they do not seem to fit into any of the standard slots – literal meaning, implicature, or what not.
>
> (Burge in this volume, p. 268–69)

I understand very well why Burge hesitates at saying, as I do, that if we change or abandon the stereotype associated with a natural kind term, that should count as a change in the meaning of the term. Let me mention that in 1968 (when I first taught my view of the meaning and reference of natural kind terms to a class in the Philosophy of Language), I told the class that what I was constructing was what I called "a mild rational reconstruction" of just the customary sense of the notion of meaning among people interested in language from a linguistic point of view (*not* the various notions of meaning put forward by philosophers). I called it a "rational reconstruction" because I was aware that my proposal would have some counterintuitive consequences, but I think any reconstruction will have some. Sometimes change in a stereotype might not be considered a change in meaning; yet it does seem to me that if we no longer associate tigers with *stripes* at all, that should count as a change in the "meaning" of the term. But, as is always the case in rational reconstruction, there is room for alternatives here. And I called it "mild" because I hope that the more precise concept of meaning I propose is still close to customary usage.

Twin Earth

Lastly, I want to respond to Burge's request that I say more about my Twin Earth thought experiment. Here are some sentences that I wrote in *Reason, Truth and History* that describe how to modify it so as to avoid the objection "but it's physically impossible." I repeat them, because few philosophers seem to be aware of them:

> [T]he liquid on Twin Earth need not be *that* similar to water. Suppose it is actually a mixture of 20% grain alcohol and 80% water, but the body chemistry of Twin Earth people is such that they do not get intoxicated or even taste the difference between such a mixture and H_2O. Such a liquid would be different from water in many ways; yet a *typical* speaker might be unacquainted with these differences, and thus be in exactly the same mental state[1] as a *typical* speaker in 1750[2] on earth. Of course, Twin Earth water tastes different from Earth water to *us*; but it does not taste different to *them*. And it behaves differently when you boil it, but must an English speaker have noticed exactly when water boils and exactly what takes place in order to associate a fairly standard conceptual content with the word "water"?
>
> (Putnam 1981: 22)

Notes

1 I should have written "brain state" and not "mental state" of course. This mistake is part of what led me to the misguided "internal realist" position that I defended in that book. And it is not essential to the modified Twin Earth thought experiment that Oscar and Twin Earth Oscar be microphysical duplicates, or that their brains be microphysical *duplicates*: it is enough if their brains are in sufficiently similar states with respect to those systems that enable the appropriate use of words.
2 I set the scene at a time when the chemical composition of substances was supposed to be unknown both on Earth and on Twin Earth. I argue both in this passage and in "The Meaning of 'Meaning'" that changes in scientific knowledge about water should not count as changes in the linguistic meaning of the word "water."

Bibliography

Putnam, Hilary (1970) "Is semantics possible?," *Metaphilosophy* 1(3): 187–201.
——(1975) "The Meaning of 'Meaning'," *Minnesota Studies in the Philosophy of Science* 7: 131–93.
——(1981) *Reason, Truth and History*, Cambridge: Cambridge University Press.

10
WITTGENSTEIN AND QUALIA[1]

Ned Block

Introduction

The representational content of an experiential state can often be described in public language partly in terms of qualities of objects that bear some salient relation to the state, for example, "looks red" or "feels like sandpaper" or "smells rotten," but it is the contention of this chapter that public language terms including terms for such properties of objects do not fully capture the contents. Qualia in my terminology are ways things look red or feel like sandpaper or smell rotten. If things can look red in more than one way – as I will be arguing – "looks red" does not fully capture the content of the state. Qualia can be referred to in public language, for example as the quale I get when I see green things. But that reference to the quale does not fully capture its content – it does not capture the individuating particularity about the way that I see green that is different from the way others may see green. Similarly, I can refer to the content of a thought as "the content of the thought I had at 11:33 AM" without fully capturing its content.[2]

We have a notion of the content of an utterance or thought which can be fully captured without specifying anything about modes of presentation. If I say "Napoleon is buried in Paris," we can fully capture an important content of that utterance by saying it is the content that Napoleon is buried in Paris, even though that way of putting it does not attempt to specify my eccentric ways of thinking of Napoleon and Paris. But the experiential aspect of the content of an experience just is a kind of mode of presentation, so a notion of the content of an experience that left out the mode of presentation would be defective.

Note that I am assuming color realism, i.e. that there are facts about the colors of things and those facts involve things actually having colors, for example that fire hydrants are often red and grass is often green. This position contrasts with error theories that say that nothing really is colored but rather color involves an erroneous projection of mental properties onto the world (Boghossian and Velleman 1989, 1991).

In other work, I have defined qualia as qualities of experience that cannot be defined in terms of their representational,[3] functional[4] or cognitive properties. And I have used the inverted spectrum hypothesis (1990, 1994, 1999; Block and Fodor 1972) in those arguments. The word "qualia" is often used to indicate a putative feature of our experience whose existence is disputed. Here the focus is on the ineffability of experience, and so it is convenient to use the term "qualia" to denote features of experience that have the kind of ineffability just mentioned.[5]

Two inverted spectrum hypotheses

Wittgenstein's "Notes for Lectures on 'Private Experience' and 'Sense Data'" (Wittgenstein 1968) were written in English, apparently between 1934 and 1936 (Rhees 1968). Wittgenstein is notoriously difficult to interpret, even to the extent that scholars cannot agree whether claims that are clearly formulated in his writings are being asserted or denied or something else. I will put forward an interpretation of Wittgenstein's view of the inverted spectrum hypothesis and of the nature of sensory experience, not as a proposal that meets the standards of Wittgenstein scholarship, but rather as a suggestion in a recognizably Wittgensteinian framework that is worthy of discussion (and refutation) on its own merits. When I attribute a view to Wittgenstein, you may wish to understand that as "Wittgenstein-according-to-one-non-expert." The seeming endorsement of the possibility or at least coherence of one kind of spectrum inversion (the kind I am calling "innocuous") begins in this passage:[6]

> The normal use of the expression "he sees [red] where ... " is this: we take it as the criterion for meaning the same by 'red' as we do, that as a rule he agrees with us in giving the same names to the colours of objects as we do. If then in a particular instance he says something is red where we should say that it's green, we say he sees it different from us.
>
> Notice how in such a case we would behave. We should look for a cause of his different judgment, and if we had found one we should certainly be inclined to say he saw red where we saw green. It is further clear that even before ever finding such a [[284]] cause we might under circumstances be inclined to say this. But also that we can't give a strict rule for ...
>
> Consider this case: someone says "it's queer/I can't understand it/, I see everything red blue today and vice versa." We answer "it must look queer!"' He says it does and, e.g., goes on to say how cold the glowing coal looks and how warm the clear (blue) sky. I think we should under these or similar circumst[ances] be incl[ined] to say that he saw red what we saw [blue].[7] And again we should say that

we know that he means by the words 'blue' and 'red' what we do as he has always used them as we do.

(Wittgenstein 1993: 231)

I will be arguing that the kind of inverted spectrum hypothesis that Wittgenstein endorses (as possible or at least coherent) in this passage commits him to something he would not agree with, so a defender of Wittgenstein might respond that after proper consideration, Wittgenstein would not have endorsed it.[8] However, I think what Wittgenstein describes here is obviously coherent. Further, subsequent technological developments have shown that something near enough is possible, even technically feasible now. Colors are easily reversed in digital television. I myself have appeared, inverted in color, in an interview on a German television station. And it is feasible right now for virtual reality goggles to make use of such technology in producing that inversion experience in a subject. With a relatively small investment, such virtual reality goggles could be produced now. I think most vision scientists would agree that the same transformations could in principle be accomplished by circuits embedded between the eye and the brain, although no one knows how to do this now. (I will describe this science fiction scenario as having "wires crossed" in the visual system: a terminology that I think was first used by Putnam (1981: 80).)

Later in these notes (Rhees 1968: 316, Stern: 285), Wittgenstein confirms the endorsement and introduces the version of the inverted spectrum hypothesis that he rejects – what I will call the "dangerous" type. (This is my terminology, not Wittgenstein's – I mean dangerous for a Wittgensteinian point of view.)

... We said that there were cases in which we should say that the person sees green what I see red. Now the question suggests itself: if this can be so at all, why should it [not] be always the case? It seems, if once we have admitted that it can happen under peculiar circumstances, that it may always happen. But then it is clear that the very idea of seeing red loses its use if we can never know if the other does not see something utterly different. So what are we to do: Are we to say that this can only happen in a limited number of cases? This is a very serious situation. – We introduced the expression that A sees something else than B and we mustn't forget that this had use only under the circumstances under which we introduced it.[9] Consider the prop[osition]: "Of course we never know whether new circ[umstance]s wouldn't show that after all he saw what we see." Remember that this whole notion need not have been introduced. "But can't I imagine all blind men to see as well as I do and only behaving differently; and on the other hand imagine them really blind? For if I can imagine these possibilities, then the question, even if never answerable makes sense." Imagine a man, say W., now blind, now seeing, and observe what you do? How do these images give sense to the question? They don't, and you see that the expression stands and falls with its usefulness.

The idea that the other person sees something else than I, [[317]] is only introduced to account for certain expressions: whereas it seems that this idea can exist without any reference to expressions. "Surely what I have he too can have".

(Wittgenstein 1993: 285)

Note the words "We said that there were cases ... " suggesting that those cases are coherently describable and perhaps possible. (Some may say that those words are not meant to be understood as Wittgenstein's own view, but it is hard to read this material without seeing that Wittgenstein supports the idea that, in certain circumstances, there would be a use to the idea that the other person sees things as green what we see as red.) What is the difference between the innocuous and dangerous cases? In the innocuous case, colors are inverted but certain properties of them – warm and cool – are not, and this happens suddenly to someone whose color experience has been normal before. So it is detectable because of two significant changes: (1) Things the subject knows to be red such as hot coals and blood look green and things the subject knows to be green such as grass look red and (2) Blood suddenly seems cool colored and grass seems warm colored. The dangerous scenario is widespread and is not behaviorally detectable.

There is an immediate problem in figuring out what is supposed to be happening in the dangerous scenario. The most straightforward way for the innocuous case to become widespread would be if the odd thing that happened to the subject of the innocuous inverted spectrum scenario simply happened repeatedly, the result being many inverted people who saw blood as green and cool colored and grass as red and warm colored and were aware of this fact about their vision. But that is not what Wittgenstein intends in the dangerous scenario, since he takes the dangerous scenario to be one that is behaviorally indetectable. He says about the dangerous scenario that "we can never know if the other does not see something utterly different."

A proponent of qualia could suppose that the odd thing that happened to the subject in the innocuous scenario happens in the dangerous scenario at or before birth, making the inversion widespread but not detectable. For the inverted people have not experienced a change and they have learned to use color words and the word "cool" in conjunction with the color experiences they get on seeing, for example, grass. So the proponent of qualia could take the dangerous scenario to be one in which warm and cool are inverted along with the colors themselves (Block 1990: footnote 16; Levine 1991), and in which the subject has no memories of things having looked differently in the past. What Wittgenstein seems to be saying is that the legitimate use of the locution "The person sees green what I see red" would not apply to such a scenario.

The inner arena model

This paper started life as a comment on a chapter of Paul Horwich's book in progress on Wittgenstein (Horwich, forthcoming). Horwich – like Wittgenstein – contrasts a form of inverted spectrum involving experiential contents that can be captured in ordinary language with another form of inverted spectrum which cannot, and so, in my terms involves qualia. I am grateful to Horwich and his chapter for inspiring me to try to elaborate the case for qualia from considerations of inverted and shifted spectra – the subject of this chapter.

Horwich, interpreting and elaborating Wittgenstein's ideas, argues that (what I would call) the dangerous inverted spectrum hypothesis presupposes a private arena model according to which experiences are observed directly by the person whose arena it is, but only indirectly by others. And observation of experience is not just a matter of having the experience. On Horwich's account, the private arena model motivates a conception of experience as essentially subjective and ethereal and not constituted by anything objective and concrete. He contrasts these ideas unfavorably with the claim that the meaning-constituting use of "I am in pain" should be taken instead to be an expressive use in which those words are substituted for a natural expression of pain. On this account, the reference of "pain" is not involved in fixing the meaning of the term. He also links the private arena model to the idea that there must be determinate answers to questions about the sensations of others, e.g. whether computers can have pains. A related view of the "Cartesian Theater" has been advocated by Dennett (1991).

I will argue that an inner arena model has little to do with the argument for inverted or shifted spectra.

It is not easy to find contemporary philosophers who have argued for the possibility of an inverted spectrum and who can also reasonably be said to accept a private arena model. D. M. Armstrong (1968; Bacon, Campbell, and Reinhardt, 1993, reply to Martin) accepts an observational model of introspection and something that might be called an inverted spectrum, but the issue is complicated by his eliminativism about experiential qualities. Sydney Shoemaker (1982) has argued strongly for the possibility of an inverted spectrum but equally strongly against an observational model of introspection (1994b; 1996b, including footnotes not in the journal version). As Shoemaker notes, it is not clear that even Locke accepted an observational model of perception, given that his theory of perception involves causal signals from external objects affecting sense organs so as to produce ideas in our minds that represent those external objects. This is a reliable but fallible process as contrasted with introspection, in which for Locke there is no gap between appearance and reality.

Shoemaker gives a detailed analysis of what is wrong with various observational models of introspection. For example, perception involves an organ of perception but there is no organ of introspection; perception involves experiences of what is perceived but there are no experiences of experiences in introspection; there are no different introspective perspectives on the same experiences in the way that there are different perceptual perspectives on the same perceived object; the relation between the pain and the introspective belief about it is more intimate than an observational relation: the pain is more like a part of the introspective belief than a reliable cause of it; the objects of perception often exist completely independently of the perception of them and the perceivers who perceive them, but what is introspected cannot be independent of the introspection and introspector in this way. Shoemaker emphasizes a version of the self-intimating nature of experience in relation to introspection which has no analog in observation. His overall viewpoint provides a serious challenge to the idea that a dangerous inverted spectrum necessarily involves an observational model of introspection.

I am another example of someone who argues for an inverted spectrum but does not accept the observational model of introspection. I agree with the points just mentioned about what is wrong with the observational model of introspection, but unlike Shoemaker, I think that one can attend to one's own experiences. (And in that respect, my view is more like an observational model than Shoemaker's.) Shoemaker's view is shared by Fred Dretske (1995), Gilbert Harman (1990), Michael Tye (1995, 2000) and many others who advocate what G. E. Moore termed the diaphanousness (or sometimes the transparency) of experience. Harman (1990) puts the point by saying that the more one tries to attend to one's experience of the tree, the more one attends to the real tree instead. Although Moore is sometimes cited as the originator of this point, he did not actually accept it. I have heard him quoted saying " ... the moment we try to fix our attention upon consciousness and to see what, distinctly, it is, it seems to vanish: it seems as if we had before us a mere emptiness. When we try to introspect the sensation of blue, all we can see is the blue; the other element is as if it were diaphanous." (Moore 1903) But these words are followed by what I regard as a more significant truth: "Yet it can be distinguished if we look attentively enough, and know that there is something to look for." (See Amy Kind's treatment in her 2003.)

If we want to appreciate the case for the claim that we can attend to our own experiences, we would do well to avoid examples like Harman's in which one is looking at a tree, trying to attend to one's experience instead of the tree. An example I have used (Block 1995): you are engaged in an intense conversation, realizing suddenly that for some time, you have been hearing street-drilling outside and have even raised your voice to compensate for it. At the moment of the sudden realization, you switch at least some of your attention to the experience of the sound, and not just to the sound itself. For another type of example, consider the difference between blurry vision as of something, say a movie, whose lines may be clear and crisp, as contrasted with clear and crisp vision of a blurry movie (Block 1996, 2003). There is an introspectible difference that cannot be appreciated without attending to the experience as well as to what the experience is of. What we experience is closely tied to what concepts we bring to bear in experience and introspective experience is no exception. Of course these examples are the beginning of an argument, not the end.[10]

Another way in which I differ from the private arena model as sketched by Horwich is that I do not take experience to resist objective concrete constitution. The view of qualia advocated here is, at least according to me, fully compatible with physicalism. I also doubt that the private arena model motivates the claim that experience resists objective concrete constitution. I take what Dennett (1991) calls the Cartesian materialist picture to be one that combines a private arena view with materialism.

Still another way in which I differ from the private arena model at least in Horwich's version is that I do not think that questions about other minds need have determinate answers. An example that I have given elsewhere (Block 2002) is that belief in qualia does not require a determinate fact of the matter as to whether fish have qualia.

Horwich takes the difference between the innocuous and dangerous inversion hypotheses to be the difference between a case that can be described in public language with expressions like "smelling a rose," "painful" and the like, and a case that requires a private way of describing experience not expressible in public language. In my terms, the difference is qualia. He takes the rules of use for mentalistic expressions to dictate that your experience when you look at red things in normal circumstances is just like mine. There can be no further question of what it is like for you to see red as compared with me. To ask what looking red is like is like asking how long five feet is. Here, I disagree, as will become clear in the sections below on shifted spectra and inverted spectra. Horwich argues that the dangerous form of the inverted spectrum hypothesis derives from the internal arena model, especially the conflation of first-person sensation reports – which he construes as expressions of sensation (on the model of natural expressions of pain) – with observations. As I have mentioned, many contemporary advocates of inverted spectra do not accept key tenets of the internal arena model and the observational view of introspection. Of course, what one explicitly advocates and what one presupposes are two different things. In introducing a materialistic version of the "Cartesian Theater," Dennett allows that "Perhaps no one today explicitly endorses" such an idea. Indeed, "Many theorists would insist that they have explicitly rejected such an obviously bad idea" (Dennett 1991: 107). But, he insists, the picture he has sketched nonetheless plays a behind-the-scenes role. And perhaps Horwich would suppose something of this sort too. But Horwich and Dennett give no reasons for thinking that actual contemporary arguments for the possibility of dangerous inverted spectra really do presuppose the mistaken models.

In my view, Wittgensteinians who emphasize the observational model of qualia are barking up the wrong tree. The view of qualia that leads to the epistemic problems that exercise Wittgensteinians is that that there are determinate facts of qualia independently of our cognitive access to those facts. A Wittgensteinian might call it the "inner light" model.[11]

Intrasubjective vs. intersubjective

Let us now return to the issue of what the difference is between the innocuous and dangerous inverted spectrum scenarios. Philosophers have made much of the difference between an intrasubjective spectrum inversion – in which a person at one time is said to be inverted with respect to the same person at another time – and an intersubjective spectrum inversion in which one person is said to be inverted with respect to another (Putnam 1981; Shoemaker 1982, 1996a). The key dialectical difference can be explained as follows. Suppose we have a pair of identical twins at birth, one of whom has had the wires crossed in his visual system. The twins are raised normally and acquire color terminology in the normal way. On the point of view that I favor, it is possible (as far as we know) that the way red things (which they agree are red) look to one twin is the same as the way green things (which they agree are green) look to the other. Now a vulnerability in this line of thought stems from the following objection (Block 1990, 1994; Harman, 1990).

Notice that it is not possible that the brain state that one twin has when he sees things that both twins call "red" is exactly the same as the brain state that the other twin has when he sees things that they both call "green." At least, the total brain states can't be exactly the same, since the first causes the subject to say "It's red," and to classify what he is seeing as the same color as blood and fire hydrants, whereas the second causes the other twin to say "It's green," and to classify what he is seeing with grass and Granny Smith apples. Here is an example. Suppose that the color-relevant brain state that the normal twin (the one who has had no operation) has when he sees red things and that the abnormal twin has when he sees green things is R-oscillations in area V4, whereas the color-relevant brain reaction in the normal twin to green and to the abnormal twin to red is G-oscillations in area V4. If the proponent of the possibility of an inverted spectrum says this is evidence for inversion, the objector can say that phenomenal properties should not be thought to be based in brain states that are quite so "localized" as R-oscillations in V4 or G-oscillations in V4, given that R-oscillations lead to different reports in the different twins. Rather color experience should be seen as based in more holistic brain states that include the brain bases of reporting and classification behavior. (I am assuming agreement on an extremely weak form of physicalism.)[12] Thus the objector whom I am thinking of will want to say that one twin's holistic brain state that includes R-oscillations and the other twin's holistic brain state that includes G-oscillations are just alternative realizations of the same experiential state: that experiential state has a disjunctive realization. So the fact that red things cause R-oscillations in one twin but G-oscillations in the other doesn't show that their experiences are inverted.

Of course the G to R transition within a single person is a transition in the way things look. However, that experiential difference has only been demonstrated intrasubjectively, keeping constant the larger brain state that specifies the roles of R- and G-oscillations in classifying things. The R/G difference in each subject grounds a color experience difference, but this gives us no knowledge of cross-person comparisons. The objector can insist on typing brain states for interpersonal comparisons holistically. And most friends of the inverted spectrum are in a poor position to insist on typing experiential states locally rather than holistically, given that they normally emphasize the "explanatory gap," the fact that there is nothing known about the brain that can adequately explain the facts of experience. So the friend of the inverted spectrum is in no position to insist on local physiological individuation of qualia. At this stage, the debate seems a standoff, and that is where the intrasubjective inverted spectrum comes into the picture.[13]

The intrasubjective inverted spectrum scenario can be seen as a way for the defender of the inverted spectrum to evade this objection, for if the change happens in the life of an individual person, we have introspective and behavioral evidence of an inversion and so can avoid the issue of whether brain states should be thought of in a localistic or holistic manner (Block 1990, 1994; Shoemaker, 1982).

I agree with this superiority of the intrasubjective inverted spectrum scenario, and will be pursing it in detail later. But for now, my point is that the intra vs. inter difference is not directly involved in the difference between the innocuous and the dangerous inverted spectrum. What is involved, as I will be arguing, is whether the inverted pair are both normal, since that is what is relevant to the expressibility of phenomenal character in ordinary language.[14]

Normality

So what is the difference between the "innocuous" inverted spectrum case, the one Wittgenstein regards as at least coherent, and the "dangerous" case, the one that he rejects? One difference is that the innocuous case occurs suddenly and "under peculiar circumstances": the subject agrees that fire and the sky now "look queer"; whereas in the dangerous case "it may always happen," even not under peculiar circumstances. Another difference is that the innocuous case is behaviorally detectable because the subject says, e.g., coal looks coal colored, whereas what Wittgenstein is suggesting in the dangerous case is an inverted person who is not behaviorally detectable. I would guess that the behavioral indetectability of the dangerous inversion was extremely important to Wittgenstein's rejection of it. (This comes out in the second quote from Wittgenstein together with the passages in the text surrounding it.)

However, there is another difference that does not depend on behavioral indetectability, and this difference is the one I am going to focus on here. I will argue that the dangerous scenario can be used to argue for qualia even if it is behaviorally detectable. Qualia, you will recall, are features of experience that are not expressible in ordinary language, including terms for properties of objects. One cannot express what red things look like colorwise in normal circumstances using color terms as in "looks red," since things that look the way red things look to me (in normal circumstances) may look to you the way green things look to me. So among qualia are ways things can look red. Something might look red to two people in different ways. And I think a crucial difference between the innocuous and dangerous cases relevant to qualia is whether normal people (or one normal person at different times) in normal circumstances can be said to be color inverted or shifted with respect to another normal person in normal circumstances. In the innocuous case, the color inverted person is abnormal. But if "one section of mankind has one sensation of red and another section another" (Wittgenstein 1958, section 272, p. 95) then it would seem that normal people can have inverted color experience with respect to one another, and that is enough to produce a "very serious situation."[15] Here is why.

It is incoherent to suppose that there are normal people in normal viewing circumstances for whom red things look green. To see this, suppose you are one of those putatively normal people for whom red things always look green. Suppose that you and I agree that there is a difference between us in ways that things look color-wise, and that the difference can be described by the locution: "Things we agree are red look to you the way things we agree are green look to me." I say to you that whereas red things look red to me, red things look green to you. You can object to the idea that red things look green to you. You can reply: "Who says that red things look green to me? Why are you the one for whom red things look red? I can with equal justification say that red things look red to me and green to you!"

If we are both normal, you have as good a case as I do. Since we are both normal, the right response is that neither you nor I have a superior claim to be the one for whom red things look red and green things look green. The situation is relevantly symmetrical. What we should say instead is that the way red things look to me is the same as the way green things look to you, and in allowing that there are ways things look that cannot be expressed in terms of "looking red" or "looking green" or any phrase of the form "looking F" where F is a color name, we step into the realm of qualia. (Given what I mean by "qualia,", this is definitional.)

Using the familiar "what is like" terminology (Farrell 1950; Nagel 1974), the point is that if we acknowledge the existence of an innocuous inverted spectrum scenario, we can say that green is what it is like for the abnormal person to see red, whereas for the normal person, red is what it is like to see red. So the innocuous scenario does not require us to suppose that there are color experiences that cannot be expressed in terms of properties of things. However, if we allow the existence of a dangerous scenario, in which normal perceivers are inverted with respect to one another, we cannot say of either of them that green is what it is like to see red. If we acknowledge the existence of an inverted spectrum in this sense, we have to agree that no color name expresses what it is like for either one of the inverted people to see red. There are ways things look red, and those ways are qualia. (Whether the actuality of a dangerous scenario is required for qualia or whether its possibility will do will be taken up later.)

Note that I am not denying that what it is like for them to see red can be referred to in English. For example, we can refer to it by saying "What it is like for that person to see red." What we cannot find is a color name "F" such that what it is like for one of these people to see red can be expressed in the form "looking F," and in that sense we can say that the experiential property is an ineffable quale.

To repeat: I am not denying that Wittgenstein was concerned with the behavioral indistinguishability of the persons in the dangerous inverted spectrum case. If there could be an inverted but behaviorally indistinguishable pair of people, then it is hard to see how the difference between them could be relevant to any everyday use of terms. My point is rather that an inverted pair both members of which are normal, is problematic for Wittgenstein even if they are not behaviorally indistinguishable.

Sydney Shoemaker (Shoemaker 1982) distinguishes between intentional and qualitative similarity. If something looks red to you and me, then our experiences are thereby intentionally similar, but if your spectrum is inverted relative to mine, our experiences are thereby qualitatively dissimilar. (Although I have not yet argued for the possibility of the dangerous kind of inversion, I will assume it here to get the conceptual groundwork in place.) If something looks red both to you and to me, our experiences thereby have a shared intentional content, but if our spectra are inverted with respect to one another, and if you are looking at a red thing and I am looking at a green thing, our experiences have a shared qualitative content. Looking red is an intentional content of color experience, not a qualitative content. For both members of the inverted pair, red things look red and green things look green. Color language in application both to the outer and the inner is keyed to intentional contents of experience (Block 1990). States that have qualitative contents are just qualia, and it is the existence of qualitative contents that poses the challenge to expressibility of qualia in language.

It may seem from what I have said so far that the issue of qualia is the issue of whether the phenomenal character of experience goes beyond its representational content, that is, the issue of representationalism, or representationism as I call it (Block 1990, 2003). But that is not the case, as can be seen by a brief consideration of a view held by Shoemaker (1994a, 1994b) and Michael Thau (2002). In Shoemaker's version, the view is that when one looks at a ripe tomato, one's experience represents the tomato as having two distinct kinds of color-relevant properties, as being red and as having a certain "phenomenal property." If your spectrum is inverted with respect to mine, and we are looking at different items with complementary colors (e.g. you a red thing, me a green thing), our experiences represent those items as having the same phenomenal property and as having different colors. These phenomenal properties are definable in terms of qualia. As far as what I have said so far is concerned, one might think of them as qualia projected onto objects – but Shoemaker does not think of them that way, since he holds they are causally efficacious, indeed defined in terms of their production of qualia. So Shoemaker is a kind of representationist, and that allows one to see that one can be both a representationist and a believer in qualia. On Shoemaker's view, color experience has two kinds of representational contents. One of them is what I have been and will be calling intentional contents, namely color-representing representational contents, contents that represent something as, e.g., red. But the other kind of representational content (the kind that represents phenomenal properties) is not expressible in public language. The issue of qualia is not the issue of whether the mental properties of experience can be fully captured in terms of what is represented by experience, since it may be that what is represented by experience cannot always be fully captured in public language.

I endorse the principle that normal perceivers in normal circumstances see red things as red, and thus that public language attributions of color experience express intentional contents of experience rather than qualitative contents. We could call this principle the Principle of Normality.[16]

Gottlob Frege held a somewhat similar view:

> The word 'white' ordinarily makes us think of a certain sensation, which is, of course, entirely subjective; but even in ordinary everyday speech, it often bears, I think, an objective sense. When we call snow white, we mean to refer to an objective quality which we recognize, in ordinary daylight, by a certain sensation. If the snow is being seen in a coloured light, we take that into account in our judgement and say, for instance, 'It appears red at present, but it is white.' Even a colour-blind man can speak of red and green, in spite of the fact that he does not distinguish between these colors in his sensations; he recognizes the distinction by the fact that others make it, or perhaps by making a physical experiment.

> Often, therefore, a colour word does not signify our subjective sensation, which we cannot know to agree with anyone else's (for obviously calling things by the same name does not guarantee as much), but rather an objective quality.
>
> (Frege 1884/1953: §26, quoted in Byrne 2006)

And, although my interpretation is not standard, one can see Wittgenstein's beetle in the box passage as compatible with a similar view.[17] The idea would be that the thing in the box – a quale – is irrelevant to the language game, which involves only what I am calling intentional contents (that is, color-representing contents). But qualia can exist and be important for some purposes even if the language game that Wittgenstein has in mind has no need of them.

In a comment on a version of this chapter at Hilary Putnam's 80th birthday conference, Pierre Jacob noted, correctly I think, that belief contents do not mirror intentional contents of perception in the sense in which I am using the term. If our putative inverted twins both see a ripe tomato and have intentional color contents representing it as red (and the same shade of red) but have different qualitative contents, we would be reluctant to say that they have exactly the same color-relevant beliefs about the tomato. For the twins have different qualitative beliefs about the color of the tomato, where a qualitative belief is a belief that includes a color quale (or, alternatively, a belief that represents the tomato as having a certain phenomenal property in Shoemaker's sense of the term). Another way of seeing Jacob's point would be to think of the intentional contents of perception as individuated both in terms of reference and mode of presentation, where qualia are taken as modes of presentation of those referential contents as suggested by Tyler Burge (2003). Nothing hangs on how we use the term "intentional content" (and I will continue to use the term to mean color-representing purely referential content). The important point is that if normal people can be inverted with respect to one another, there is an aspect of color experience that cannot be captured in ordinary language in terms of properties of objects.

The Normality Principle links public language color terminology to intentional rather than qualitative contents of experience. I now turn to the argument for that link, and then to arguments for shifted and inverted spectra.

Color terms express intentional not qualitative contents

Assuming without argument at this point that the dangerous scenario is possible, what exactly is the argument that color terminology ("red,", "green," etc.) is keyed to color-representing intentional contents rather than qualitative contents?

In daily life, we do not distinguish between intentional and qualitative content, just as we do not normally distinguish between weight and mass or between rest mass and relativistic mass. Shouldn't we suppose that there is some sort of indeterminacy, as with "mass," where ordinary uses of the term "mass" partially denote both, as argued plausibly by Hartry Field (1973)? In Block (1990), I argued that if spectrum inversion is known to be rife, we should think of our tacit semantic policy as one of using color terms as applied to experience to denote intentional contents of experience, since when we say of someone that the fire hydrant looks red to him, we often know what the intentional content is, but not what the qualitative content is. So how can we be understood as attributing a qualitative content? However, we do not know whether spectrum inversion is actually rife (cf. Byrne 2006: §3.8). Is there an argument from our lack of knowledge whether or not inversion is rife to the same conclusion?

Yes, a similar argument applies. If phrases like "looking red" were intended to apply to qualitative contents, we would have a vulnerability to widespread error that we tacitly assume that we do not have. Of course if everyone has the same spectrum except for a few defectives who see red things as green, we do think that stoplights do not look red to the defectives. But if spectra vary from normal person to normal person, we would not take that to impugn our judgment that stoplights look red. For what would the alternative be? The Principle of Normality reminds us that we can't suppose that stoplights look green to some normal people or yellow to other normal people. So even if spectra vary from one person to another, we must suppose that stoplights look red to all normals, and that shows that "looking red" is keyed to intentional content and not qualitative content.

I have some agreement with Frege when he says "Often, therefore, a colour word does not signify our subjective sensation, which we cannot know to agree with anyone else's." I would take the "cannot know" to mean in practice rather than in principle, since I think perceptual neuroscience is making great strides in the direction of such knowledge. The Fregean point is very easily available to language users. I became aware of it as a child. And my daughter at age seven commented on first hearing the inverted spectrum hypothesis that it explained why some people didn't have purple as their favorite color.[18]

Shifted spectra

The chapter now shifts gears to two arguments for the possibility of spectra that are inverted or shifted. I have not said what sense of "possible" is at issue. The relevant notion, I think, is metaphysical possibility, but there is no need to go into the matter because I will be arguing for a stronger thesis. In the case of shifted spectra, my conclusion will be that there is reason to think they are actual and in the case of inverted spectra I will be arguing for nomological possibility with an eye to actuality.

Thus far, I have argued that we do not take our attributions of looking red to be shown false or otherwise problematic by the discovery of qualia, thus indicating that our tacit semantic policy is to key "looking red" to intentional contents rather than qualitative contents. But I have not yet argued that there really are states with qualitative contents, that is, I have not argued for qualia. In this section I argue that individual variation in the phenomenology of color vision at least sometimes goes beyond variation in the use of public color terminology. I argue that this fact can be used to argue for the existence of qualia and moreover that its appreciation by us provides further support for the claim of the last section that attribution of looking red is keyed to intentional contents rather than qualia. (See Block 1990, 1999 and Putnam's example of the Ixxzians (Putnam 1999: 162–66).)

The first premise in the argument is the fact that there is enormous variation in the physiology of color vision in the normal population, which leads to enormous variation in color phenomenology. For example, there are large differences among normal perceivers in peak sensitivity of cones in the retina. There is a 51.5%/48.5% split in the population of two types of long-wave cones that differ by 5–7 nm, roughly 24% of the difference between the peak sensitivities of long and middle wave cones (Neitz and Neitz 1998). This characteristic is sex-linked. The distribution just mentioned is for men. Women have smaller numbers in the two extreme categories and a much larger number in between. As a result, the match on a common test "most frequently made by female subjects occurs where no male matches" (Neitz and Jacobs 1986: 625). (See Block 1999 for further explanation.)

Further, variation in peak sensitivities of cones is just one kind of color vision variation. In addition, the shape of the sensitivity curves vary. These differences are due to differences in macular pigmentation, which vary with "both age and degree of skin pigmentation" (Neitz and Jacobs 1986: 624). Hence races that differ in skin pigmentation will differ in macular pigmentation. There is also considerable variation in amount of light absorption by pre-retinal structures. And this factor also varies with age.

I emphasize gender, race and age to stifle the reaction that one group should be regarded as normal and the others as defective.

Premise 1 said that that there is enormous variation in the physiology of color vision in the normal population which leads to enormous variation in color phenomenology. Premise 2 says that the variation in the phenomenology of color vision must obtain even among those whose use of color terms is the same because the borders for our application of color terminology to objects must to some extent be constrained by needs of communicating and cooperating with other people.

Imagine, contrary to fact, that we were all given rigorous training in the application of accepted color terminology to the point where variation in application of color terms among us was minor. Things we almost all categorize as "borderline between red and purple" will still look quite different to us, just as, in the inverted spectrum scenario, a fire hydrant that the members of the inverted pair both categorize as "red" looks different to them. My premise

2 is that to some extent that is the way things are. That is, color terminology is to some extent subject to social and linguistic constraint.

How do we know that? Normal people see colors as having the same similarity relations. In the Farnsworth–Munsell 100 hue test, subjects are asked to arrange 100 chips in a circle with one chip fixed as the starting chip. Normal subjects make nearly the same arrangement (Hilbert and Kalderon 2000). One of the things social and linguistic influence does is to impose a set of categories on that similarity space. Before the introduction of oranges into England, the color we call "orange" was considered a shade of "red." (The OED's first listed use of "orange" as the name of a color is from 1512.) Cultural and linguistic influences no doubt affect the borders of our color categorizations. And of course culture also affects our shade categories. I am sure that those who were of school age in the USA after 1949 will agree pretty much on the forty shades of Crayolas introduced then and in use (with more added and a few subtracted in 1958, 1972, 1990, 1993 and 1998) since then, such as turquoise blue – despite variation in the way those colors look to us.

The upshot is that there are likely to be many normal cases of same use of public color terminology, different phenomenology – and that is what I am calling shifted spectra. If red things look slightly different to you than to me, there is no saying that either of us perceives more veridically than the other, since we are both normal perceivers, and so there is no way of capturing the difference in external terms. (A number of replies are canvassed in my 2003.) So there are qualia.

An objection to this line of reasoning: red things may look slightly different to you than to me, but that difference may be describable in ordinary language. For example, a red thing may look yellower to you than to me. Here is an argument to support the objector. Many people report slightly different color vision in their two eyes, e.g. things look yellower through one eye than through the other. (Hilary Putnam mentioned that he sees colors differently in different eyes at the Putnam at 80 conference mentioned in note 1.) Suppose Putnam's left eye could be copied twice and inserted in both eyes of one member of a set of identical twins at birth, Lefty, and copies of his right eye inserted into Righty. If Putnam sees yellower through the left eye, we have reason to think that Lefty sees yellower than Righty. So here is a difference that is effable.

Suppose Lefty and Righty are looking at a wall painted an orange that is perfectly balanced between yellow and red. One possibility is that Righty says it is pure orange but Lefty says the wall is slightly on the yellowish side of orange. However, another possibility – and one that my argument of this section militates towards as a reality and not just a possibility – is that both Lefty and Righty say and think that the wall is pure orange. One would expect that if both were trained on Crayolas! And there is no reason to suppose that the way it looks to them deviates systematically from their thought and talk. The situation is then that they both see it as pure orange but one sees it as yellower than the other. How can that be? The best way to understand how that could be is to acknowledge that there are ways of seeing orange, that those ways can differ from person to person. The objection that we are considering notes that we can compare these ways in ordinary language. And here is the reply: yes we can compare them in ordinary language, but that does not show that we can fully capture these contents in ordinary language. Lefty and Righty differ in their color vision, but they may have equal claim to see orange as orange. This very simple argument shows that in a reasonable sense of the term "qualia," there are qualia.

Points similar to the ones mentioned here were made in Block (2003) where I was arguing (as against representationism) that the phenomenal character of experience outruns its representational content. I claimed that two phenomenally slightly different experiences could nonetheless represent the same color (in different phenomenal ways), even the same minimal shade. Much of that paper was concerned with the issue of whether the phenomenally different experiences that represented the same color could nonetheless be said to have different representational contents. However, the point argued for in this paper is much weaker than the earlier argument, as can be seen by noting that even if the slightly phenomenally different experiences are also different in representational content, they are still qualia if those representational contents cannot be expressed in public language. That is, even if my argument against representationism fails, the argument for qualia in the present sense can succeed.

The picture that emerges is that there is a structured space of color qualia that determines the structure of real world colors themselves. Normal people have pretty much the same similarity relations in their structured spaces (as shown by the experiment with the 100 hue test mentioned earlier) but differ in correspondences between that space and colors in the world, probably because of variation in the retina and in pre-retinal structures. Relations among color qualia are determined by the shared structured qualia space, and so those relations can be expressed in terms of the colors themselves (e.g. "yellower"), but there is no objective "location" of color qualia in real world color space because of the differences among people in correspondence between the space and actual colors.[19]

The point about qualia being comparable but not expressible in ordinary language applies also to inverted spectra. In the Lefty/Righty shifted spectrum case, Lefty and Righty differ by a rotation of the color circle – slightly towards yellow in Lefty. In the usual ROYGBIV depiction of the color circle, that corresponds to a clockwise rotation. In the inverted spectrum cases to be discussed below, one twin differs from the other by a 180° rotation, which is the same in both directions.

These points will be the basis of my discussion below of the "Frege–Schlick" view.

To summarize: the Putnam two-eye example suggests that qualia can at least sometimes be compared across people. One person's color experience is yellower than another's or one person's color experience is "complementary" to another's. Does this show that the contents are expressible in public language after all and so are not qualia? No: qualia can be compared in public language without being fully capturable in public language. Even if your experience is yellower than mine, it can nonetheless be the case that there is no color term F such that your experience of red things is describable as "looks F."

Behavioral indistinguishability

My arguments for qualia on the basis of the shifted and inverted spectrum do not presuppose that the shifted or inverted perceivers are behaviorally indistinguishable from one another. For example, the 51.5%/48.5% split in the population that I mentioned could, for all I know, determine the extent to which warm colors advance (i.e. project forward) or are exciting compared to cool colors. If half of mankind is inverted with respect to the other half, the inversion shows the existence of qualia even if the inverted spectrum is behaviorally detectable – unless one half is thereby seen to be abnormal or unless the behavioral difference undermines the claim of inversion. To see this, note that the little dialectic I rehearsed earlier about who has authority over the word "red" would apply to the two normal groups as well as to two normal individuals. Neither group could pretend to be "the" group for which red things look red. If it is alleged that for members of one group, red things look green, the other group can complain that the situation is relevantly symmetrical, whether or not there are differences in which colors advance and which recede.

Virtually all arguments that inverted spectra are impossible that I have read or heard appeal to one or another sort of asymmetry in color space.[20] (I am talking about arguments that spectrum inversion is impossible, not that it makes no sense or is otherwise problematic, as alleged in the arguments by Robert Stalnaker that will be considered later.) For example, Bernard Harrison (1973) argues that there are more colors between red and green going one way around the color circle (via blue) than going the other way (via yellow). A far more significant asymmetry is that the most saturated colors differ in their lightness levels from color to color. If you decrease the lightness of a sample of yellow you get a different color (brown), but the same is not true for green or blue. The most saturated reds are darker than for other primary colors. Further, desaturated red is pink but desaturated green is green, so hue is not symmetrical with regard to saturation.[21] These are not just differences in categorization, but also differences in similarity. A light and dark blue look much more similar to one another than do light yellow and dark yellow, i. e. brown (Hilbert and Kalderon 2000). Just how significant such asymmetries are is hotly debated. Stephen Palmer (1999) discusses a far larger number of ways in which the color space can be mapped onto itself than had appeared in the prior literature, some of which may avoid such problems although Justin Broackes (2007) argues otherwise. In addition, as Shoemaker notes, it is not clear why minor asymmetries ought to be significant given that we could imagine a slight variant of human color vision in which those asymmetries are absent but color experience is much the same as ours. But this argument is unsound according to Daniel Dennett (1991). Dennett notes that red is advancing, warm and exciting, whereas green is receding, cool and calming, claiming that such asymmetries in function are what make the colors look different from one another. So, according to Dennett, Shoemaker's imagined race for whom these "minor" asymmetries are ironed out, could not have color experience much like ours. Others (Block 1994) argue that these differences in reaction may not be intrinsic to color experience, their widespread presence in different cultures being explained by environmental regularities that are not necessary at least to the basics of color experience.[22]

But this whole set of controversies can be sidestepped – at least if the existence of qualia is the issue. For as I have noted, the argument for qualia that I am talking about depends not whether the inversion or shift is behaviorally undetectable but whether the groups that are inverted or shifted with respect to others are normal. If it turns out – and as I argued, the evidence points in that direction – that a person's spectrum is very often shifted with respect to his neighbor, I don't think anyone should conclude that this shows that defective color vision is widespread.

In the rest of this chapter, I will discuss an argument that an inverted spectrum is possible. I will focus on an intrasubjective inverted spectrum because of the advantage I mentioned earlier. I will be considering an inversion in which the inverted pair are roughly functionally equivalent but not necessarily exactly functionally equivalent. For example, perhaps one member of the pair experiences red things as exciting and advancing whereas the other experiences them as calming and receding. (Earlier versions are in Block 1990, 1994.)

I say that an argument that an inverted spectrum is possible is an argument for qualia. "But doesn't a possible inverted spectrum show at most that qualia are possible rather than actual?" The argument from the possibility of inverted spectra to qualia is this. Suppose an inverted spectrum is possible but non-actual. If we manage to create an inverted spectrum (a procedure that may work is described below), it would be wrong to suppose that we have created qualia where they did not already exist. The fundamental nature of experience does not change because we create a situation that exhibits a fundamental feature of it! So the possibility of an inverted spectrum is sufficient for the existence of qualia.

Inverted spectra

I have made the case for actual shifted spectra. Now I will argue that inverted spectra are possible and perhaps actual. Let us start with a

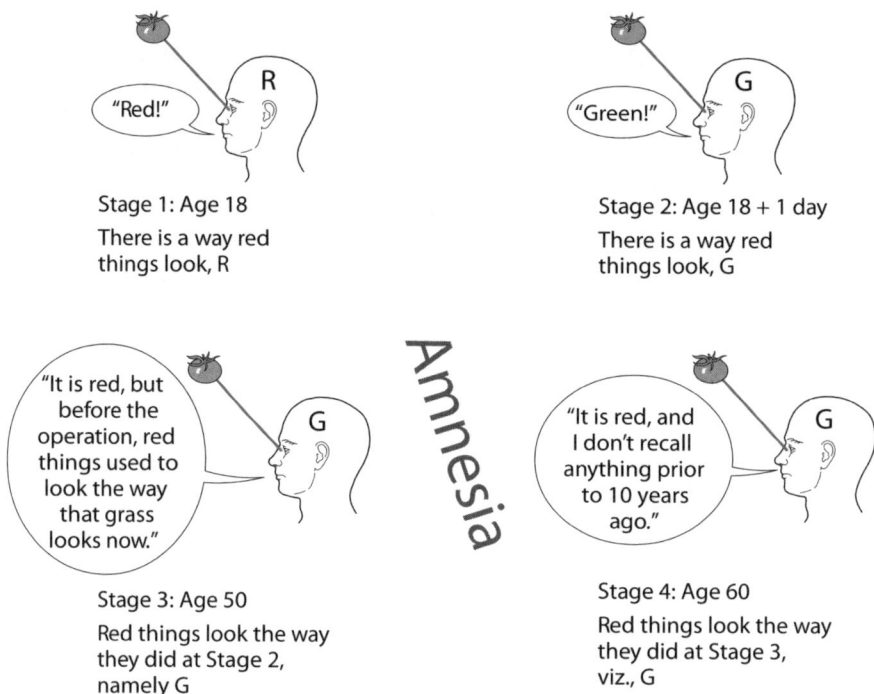

Figure 10.1 Question-begging Inverted spectrum scenario. The captions express the way things look to the subject at each stage in terms of the existence of ways of looking, R and G. R is the way the red tomato looks to the subject at Stage 1. G is the way the red tomato looks to the subject at Stages 2, 3, and 4

question-begging description of the scenario. The point of so doing is to highlight the contrast with another description which is not, I will argue, question-begging. See Figure 10.1.

The captions express the way things look to the subject at each stage in terms of the existence of ways of looking, R and G. R is the way the red tomato looks to the subject at Stage 1. G is the way the red tomato looks to the subject at Stages 2, 3 and 4.

We start at Stage 1 with you at your 18th birthday, at which time you are a normal perceiver. You call red things "red" and red things look red to you. In need of funds, you agree to undergo an experimental color inversion the next day in which a chip is inserted in your optic nerve that changes signals from red things into the signals that would have been produced by green things, and so on for other colors.[23] I have been calling this "crossing the wires in the visual system." If we were relaxed about what counted as a visual "input," we could imagine instead virtual reality goggles that do this trick without any surgery (as mentioned earlier).

The operation is a success: at Stage 2, you are disposed to call red things "green" and they look green to you, and so on: you see colored things as having the complementaries of their actual colors. You become famous to the point where you feel that the paparazzi are ruining your life. You change your name, and your appearance with cosmetic surgery and move to another state, trying to blend in. At first, you have to fight your tendency to call red things "green" and your tendency to stop at green lights, to suppose that red tomatoes are unripe and so forth, but after some years have passed, you naturally and spontaneously react to colors in the normal way. You unthinkingly call stop-lights "red" and stop at them. Even though you unthinkingly call stop-lights "red," at first you think of them as looking green, but your desire to put the operation and its unpleasant sequelae into the past leads you to work to think of stop-lights as looking red. You want to be normal and find it tiresome to be reminded of the operation you had at age 18. By the time you are 30, you spontaneously think of blood as not only being red but also looking red.

How do we know that the colors have not reinverted so that the way things look is the same as at Stage 1? According to the story – which I am claiming is a genuine possibility – you remember very clearly what things used to look like before the operation, and if asked by close relations in private, you say that everything used to look the complementary color of the way it looks now. You can retrieve clear mental images of the look of things at your 18th birthday party, for example. At Stage 3, you are 50, and you haven't thought about your operation in many years. Someone who recognizes you despite the cosmetic surgery says to you: "Aren't you the person who underwent the experimental spectrum inversion?" You say: "Oh yes, I haven't thought about that in many years. But I do clearly recall the look of the ripe tomatoes at my 18th birthday party. They looked to me then the way grass looks to me now, colorwise." If asked to paint a picture of the way things look to you today, you paint the grass green and the sky blue. If asked to paint a picture of the way things looked to you before the operation thirty-two years earlier, you paint the grass red and the sky yellow (Taylor 1966). Another ten years pass, during which time no one asks you about the operation and during which time you don't think of the days before 18 or any of the times someone has questioned you about the inversion. At age 60, you develop amnesia for the period up to age 50 (cf. Putnam 1981). Now, and this is Stage 4, you have no memories for the period before your operation, nor do you have any memories for episodes of remembering that period. However, according to the story, the way red things look to you at Stage 4 is the way green things looked to you at Stage 1. If this example were to be used in an argument against functionalism, Stage 1 and Stage 4 have to be functionally equivalent.[24] However, if the purpose of the argument is to demonstrate qualia – and that is my purpose here – functional and behavioral equivalence is not required. For example, perhaps at Stage 4, red is no more exciting than green.

The way in which this argument is question-begging is summarized in Figure 10.1. The subject at Stage 3 says "I do recall the look of the ripe tomatoes at my 18th birthday party. They looked to me then the way grass looks to me now, colorwise." But what are these ways and why should we countenance them? And if these suspicious ways are coming in at Stage 3, presumably they must have been involved at the outset, in the argument at Stage 1. The relevant bones of the argument diagrammed in Figure 10.1 amount to this:

Stage 1: There is a way red things look to the subject, R.
Stage 2: There is a way red things look to the subject now, G.
Stage 3: The way red things look to the subject remains G.
Stage 4: The way red things look to the subject remains G, even though the function of G is similar to (but not necessarily exactly the same as) the function of R in Stage 1. The subject at Stage 4 is a normal perceiver.

The question-begging aspect is the postulation and naming of the ways things look, even at Stage 1. However, ways need not be brought in at the outset. It may seem that in saying that red things look red, I have sneaked in something illicit, maybe something amounting to "ways" for we would not ordinarily say that red things look red. Isn't that "language going on holiday"? Actually, Wittgenstein is committed to red things looking red at Stage 1 in my view as I will now argue.

Consider Stage 2: red things look green, or as Wittgenstein would put it, at Stage 2, our subject sees red things green. (In Wittgenstein's version, he says "I see everything red blue today and vice versa.") But now if asked how the way he sees things now contrasts with the way he saw things yesterday, it is perfectly natural for him to say. "I see everything red as green today, but yesterday I saw everything red as red." So we are justified in saying that at Stage 1, he sees red things as red. Imagine the subject talking to his doctor where it is better to err on the side of over-explicitness. The doctor is wondering whether there might have been something wrong with the patient even at Stage 1. To be absolutely clear, the patient says that red things look green today but yesterday red things looked red. And that justifies the descriptions given below in Figure 10.2 of Stage 1 and Stage 2.

And once we have gone this far, it is difficult to see how to avoid the descriptions I have given of Stages 3 and 4. If red things look green at Stage 2, then they still look green at Stages 3 and 4. Here is a summary of the essential aspects of the argument.

Stage 1: Red things look red.
Stage 2: Red things look green.
Stage 3: Red things still look green.
Stage 4: Red things still look green even though the subject calls them "red" and is in other respects a normal perceiver.

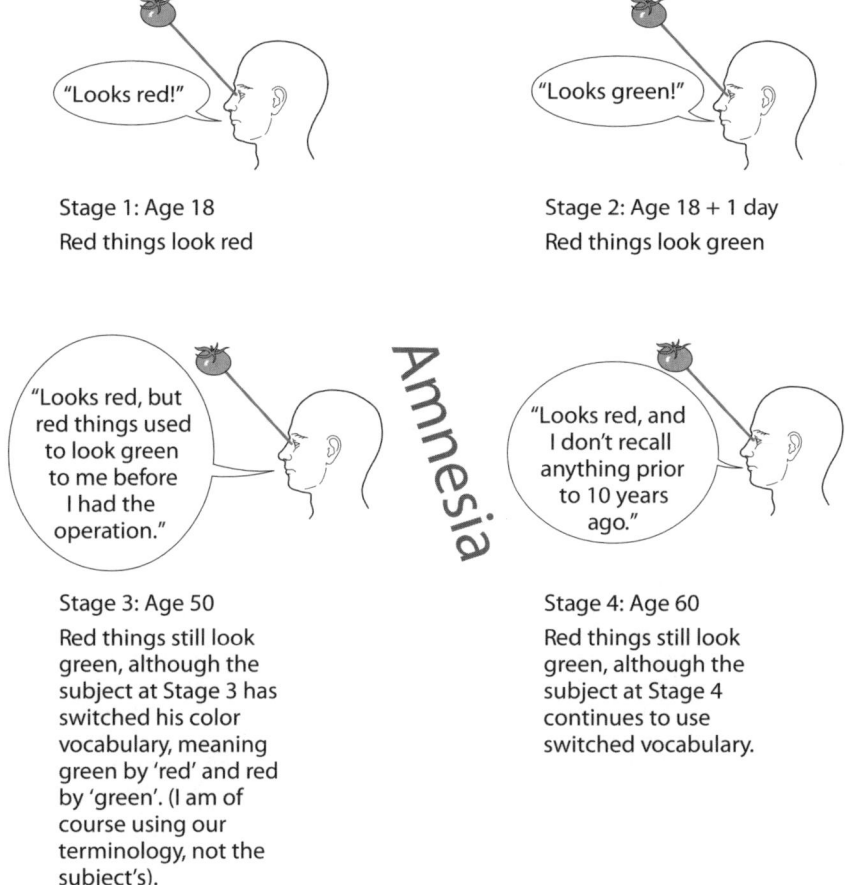

Figure 10.2 Version of the inverted spectrum scenario that is not question-begging, but which violates the Principle of Normality. The same events are depicted as in Figure 10.1, but described without explicit mention of the ways things look or of 'R' and 'G'. The focus is on the colors that things look to have

However, there is a problem with the descriptions in Figure 10.2. At Stage 4, the subject is, I claim, a normal perceiver again. If so, it is false to say that red things look green to him – that would violate the Principle of Normality which says that normal perceivers in normal conditions perceive veridically. And that leads to a further variant of the argument illustrated in Figure 10.3, one that moves back part way to the version given in Figure 10.1.

In this, the final variant, ways are introduced at Stage 4. The idea is that at Stage 4, the subject, who is now a normal perceiver, perceives veridically. White (1986) has suggested that the functionalist should say that once the amnesia hits, the subject's experience instantaneously reinverts. Am I saying

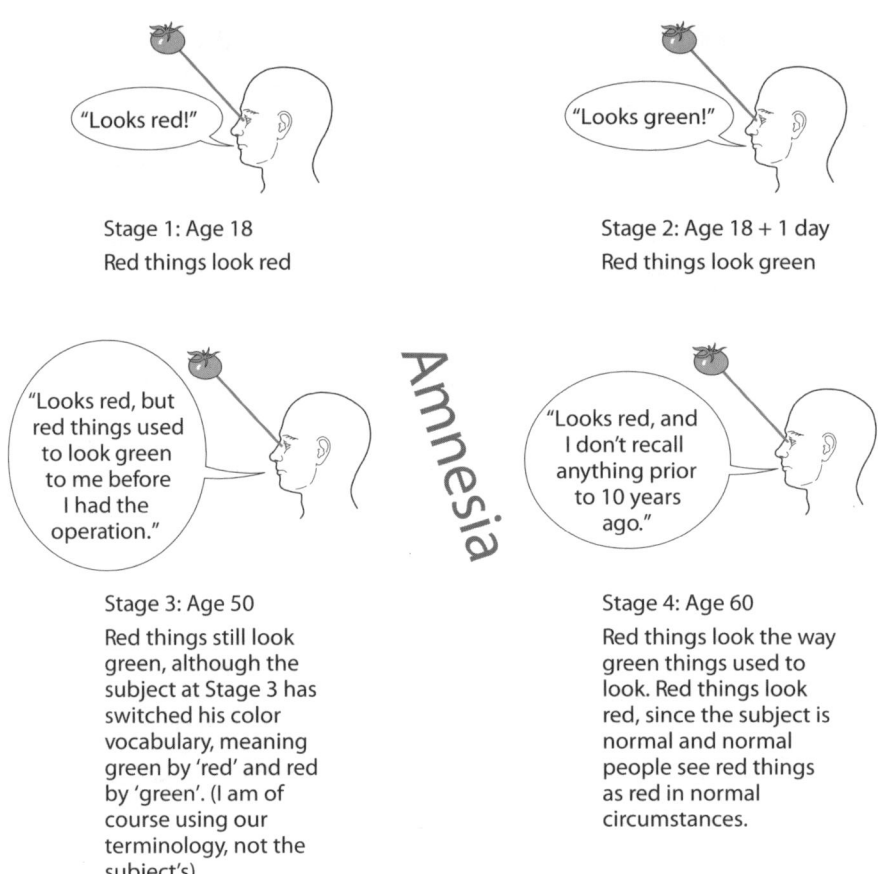

Figure 10.3 Version of the inverted spectrum scenario in which ways are introduced at Stage 4

something similar? Do red things suddenly look red as soon as the subject gets amnesia? No. For an abnormal subject as in Stages 2 and 3, color terms have to be used relative to normality. At Stage 2, the obvious relativity is to Stage 1, just a day earlier, when the subject was normal. But at Stage 3, there is some indeterminacy about how color terms should be used – relative to the normal Stages 1 or 4. Since red things look red at Stages 1 and 4 and since there has been an inversion in between, the most plausible way to accommodate the inversion is in terms of ways. Perhaps ways could be introduced at Stage 3 as well, but in any case Stages 1 and 2 can be described without recourse to ways, so the argument cannot be described as begging the question. The ways at Stage 4 are a conclusion, not a premise. That, in brief, is the argument. In the next section I will elaborate some of the premises.

Premises in the inversion argument for qualia

I have given a way of conceiving of spectrum inversion, but conceiving spectrum inversion does not show that spectrum inversion is possible. It would be agreed by all – even those like Chalmers (2002) who argue that conceivability of the right sort entails possibility – that it is not a straightforward matter to move from conceivability to possibility. (Gendler and Hawthorne 2002; Hill 1991; Stoljar 2006.) My view is that the most significant reasons for thinking that spectrum inversion is not possible are all reasons that involve the asymmetrical nature of the color solid and thus allege that inversion would have to be behaviorally detectable. But since I am not appealing to a behaviorally undetectable inversion, these arguments do not apply here.

David Cole (1990) appeals to experiments using goggles that invert the retinal image, claiming that these subjects adapt in the sense of experiencing a reinversion of experience. A recent study (Linden, Kallenbach, Heinecke, Singer, and Goebel, 1999) suggests previous reports greatly overplayed the extent to which behavioral adaptation to the goggles involves a reinversion of experience. Cole mentions other experiments which I think are irrelevant to the spectrum inversion case but that I do not have the space here to discuss. (See also Hurley 1998.)[25]

I said the subject at Stage 4 is normal. But he has undergone an operation in which the wires in his visual system were "crossed." And what could be more abnormal than that? But wait! "Crossed" is a metaphor. The visual system of the subject at Stage 4 is different from the visual system at Stage 1 as a result of an operation, but why suppose it is Stage 4 that is abnormal rather than Stage 1? An operation can – and often does if successful – restore normality. A hernia is stitched up, a tumor removed, a heart repaired – all cases in which the "after" is more normal than the "before." If we were to discover that all the rest of us were born with the physiological formation of the visual system that obtains in Stage 4 and that it is Stage 1 that is "peculiar," we would regard Stage 1 as "crossed." If we were to find out that our subject at Stage 1 was born with an unusual visual system, we would naturally take the view that the operation "uncrossed" the wires in his visual system, making his visual system normal again. This way of talking makes it look as if the "crossed" visual system must be abnormal, but that is a mistake.

For what would we say if half the population has a visual system like Stage 1 and half like Stage 4? Then we should say that both are normal, that there are two different varieties of normal visual systems. And in that case, both Stage 1 and Stage 4 are normal. The operation has succeeded in changing one normal visual system into another normal visual system. If Stage 1 and 4 are both normal – and possible – there are qualia, since neither our subject at Stage 1 nor our subject at Stage 4 can claim that he uniquely sees red things as red and green things as green.

I think the fact that "crossed" visual systems are normal can be shown by example. The example I have in mind was first advanced by Martine Nida-Rümelin for a somewhat different purpose, as I will now explain. (See Nida-Rümilen 1999.) The three kinds of cones in the retina feed to three "opponent-process channels," as discovered in the nineteenth century by Hering, on the basis of purely behavioral data. The red/green channel operates as follows: If the activation of the R cones is greater than that of the G cones, the red/green channel is excited and the subject sees red (if the other channels are in approximate equilibrium). If the activation of the G cones is greater than the R cones, the red/green channel is inhibited and the subject sees green if the other channels are in approximate equilibrium. The three types of cones send both excitatory and inhibitory signals to three kinds of cells in the structure that is the basis of the next stage of processing beyond the retina (known as the lateral geniculate nucleus). These cells are called "color opponent cells" for obvious reasons.

One form of color blindness occurs when the subject has a genetic defect that substitutes the photo-pigment in the G cones, chlorolabe, for the photo-pigment in the R cones, erythrolabe. With the photo-pigments in the two kinds of cones the same – both chlorolabe – the subject is red/green color blind. It can also happen that another genetic defect substitutes the photo-pigment in the R cones for the photo-pigment in the G cones. In this case, they are both erythrolabe. (See Byrne and Hilbert 2003.) Again, with the photo-pigments in the two cones the same, the subject is red/green color blind. If the two genetic defects occur at once, the subject has the usual G photo-pigment in the R cones and the usual R photo-pigment in the G cones, resulting in normal discrimination. This case – known as pseudo-normal color vision – can be predicted to occur in 14 of 10,000 males, but as far as I know, no such case has ever been noticed. Apparently, the color vision of these people is sufficiently normal so that they do not consult an eye doctor about abnormal color vision.

If the eyes and optic nerves from a pseudo-normal were switched with yours (assuming you are not pseudo-normal), the effect would be – as far as we know – that the red/green opponent cells would be activated in the opposite manner from those in your retina. Red things would look green and green things would look red. The point is that the pseudo-normal is a living example of crossed wires in the visual system.[26] What we do not know is whether the development and history of visual experiences of the pseudo-normal yields something different from the imagined transplant. That is, what is controversial is how hard-wired the connection is between the cones and the color-opponent cells and between the color-opponent cells and the rest of the visual system in the brain. If those connections are hard-wired, then we can expect that in pseudo-normals, the red/green channel would be inhibited in input situations in which it is excited in normals and excited when it is inhibited in normals. Then these subjects are red/green inverted with respect to normals such as you and me.

Byrne and Hilbert give 3 arguments against Nida Rümelin:

> First, even if pseudo-normal vision actually occurs, its frequency will be very low ... ; thus the possibility of pseudo-normal vision does not show that spectrum inversion might be widespread. Second, there is in any case no reason to suppose that pseudo-normal genes would preserve normal visual pathways: the opponent channels might be switched as well, in which case pseudo-normal subjects would not be red–green spectrally inverted. Third, there is evidence that for the M- and L-cones the development of the retinal circuitry for the red–green opponent channel is insensitive to which pigment the cone contains. In other words, pseudo-normal subjects would just be normal subjects.
>
> (Byrne and Hilbert 2003: 19)

The first point is irrelevant to the issue considered here, where normality rather than frequency is what is in question. On the second point: If Byrne and Hilbert are right that we simply don't know whether the genes for pseudo-normal color vision control the brain channels as well as the eye structures, that is enough for the claim that inversion may be actual and at any rate is possible so far as we know. The third point seems to me to count in the opposite direction of what Byrne and Hilbert say. If the development of the visual system did react differently depending on whether the pigment was erythrolabe or chlorolabe, then that would count against the possibility that the cones are hard-wired into the opponent-process channels. The force of the pseudo-normal configuration depends on pigment-insensitive connections between cones and channels.

Nida-Rümelin and others have used this case in an argument for the possibility of intersubjective inversion. I agree with that argument, but I am using pseudo-normals for a less controversial purpose: as an example of crossed wires in the visual system that are normal. It is a case of crossed wires because if a pseudo-normal's eyes were switched with yours, you (and the pseudo-normal) would experience color inversion as in Wittgenstein's original case of the person who wakes up one morning finding that red things look green and conversely. Pseudo-normals who live with their eyes from birth (and before) might not be inverted with respect to the majority, but if their eyes are switched with yours, the effect will be to stimulate the R–G channel in the opposite from normal way.

So pseudo-normals have crossed wires. But are they normal? How can that be when pseudo-normal color vision is the combination of two genetic defects? Chlorolabe and erythrolabe must be more or less equally suited to the two kinds of cones as attested by the fact that none of the more than 4 million pseudo-normals in the world have come to light – as far as I have been able to determine. A pseudo-normal person can equally say that normals are the result of two genetic defects: the cases are symmetrical. Pseudo-normals are less frequent, but I hope no one will take that to be decisive. If pseudo-normals were the more numerous, no doubt they would be in control of the terminology.

The example of pseudo-normals shows I think that intersubjective inversion may be actual and is for all we know possible. But that is not my main point in introducing it. Recall that we are discussing intrasubjective inversion and the issue at hand is whether the visual apparatus of Stage 4 should be regarded as abnormal solely on the ground of difference from Stage 1. I offer the case of pseudo-normals as normal visual systems that differ in a way that could be like the difference that I am hypothesizing exists between Stages 1 and 4, namely "crossed."

The argument for qualia is supposed to be mainly based on the possibility of an intrasubjective inverted spectrum. I did detour through the pseudo-normals as an example of intersubjective inversion but also as an example of a kind of "crossed" visual system that is normal. And the argument can make do with the latter. I talked about others who have visual systems like that in Stage 1 and others who have visual systems like that in Stage 4, but without appealing to intersubjective inverted spectrum. The point is that there is no reason why both visual systems cannot be normal and so no reason why our intrasubjective inversion subject has to be abnormal at either the beginning or end of the process.

Sydney Shoemaker and Daniel Taylor (Byrne and Hilbert 2003; Shoemaker 1982; Taylor 1966) have argued from the possibility of intrasubjective inversion to the possibility of intersubjective inversion. They argue that if Fred undergoes intrasubjective spectrum inversion, then the color experience of others must be radically different from Fred's either before his inversion or after it (or both). My argument is different since my argument does not appeal essentially to intersubjective inversion. An opponent of the Shoemaker–Taylor intra/inter argument[27] might acknowledge that crossed wires in the visual system make for color inversion in the intrasubjective case – as is shown by the testimony of subjects who undergo the procedure – while resisting the claim as applied to the intersubjective case. The idea would be that congenital differences of that sort between different groups of normal perceivers are just alternative realizations of the same phenomenology of experience. I think that this refusal to accept intersubjective inversion can be defeated on its own terms, but that is not my main purpose here.

Objection: "Although the result of the operation is a normal visual system, our subject at Stage 4 is abnormal because of the operation which produced it." Not so, because an operation need not produce anything abnormal. An operation can correct an abnormal defect, yielding normality.

"But the process leading to Stage 4 includes both the operation and the adaptation, and doesn't that make Stage 4 abnormal?" No: adaptation to an operation is often an essential part of the normalizing process. For example, there is a congenital "heart inversion" condition called transposition of the great arteries in which the outputs from the ventricles are reversed. In the normal heart, the pulmonary artery rises from the right ventricle, taking deoxygenated "blue" blood to the lungs (which is then returned to the left side of the heart via pulmonary veins), whereas the aorta rises from the left ventricle pumping "red" blood to oxygenate the body. In the heart inversion condition, the aorta rises from the right ventricle, pumping "blue" blood to the body, whereas the pulmonary artery arises from the left ventricle, circulating "red" blood unnecessarily to the lungs. The effect is that the left ventricle does very little work, quickly losing muscle mass as a result. If an arterial switch operation is done too late (more than about a month after birth), the left ventricle will fail and the child will die, but if the operation is done early enough, the left ventricle can build up mass after the operation via the process of making new heart cells, an ability that the heart loses. The point is that the operation does not immediately restore normality. First, there is a period of adaptation in which the left ventricle regains the lost cells. But the need for a period of adaptation after the arterial switch operation does not make the child's heart forever abnormal.[28]

Memory

Wittgenstein raised the question of how we could distinguish inversion from misremembering, raising the issue of "whether the things stored up may not constantly change their nature" (Shoemaker 1996a: 204). And Dennett (1996a; 1993) has emphasized the issue of the unreliability of memory in arguing against inversion scenarios. Figure 10.4 shows a schematized Stage 1 at the top (that is the topmost of the 4 schematic depictions). Seeing a ripe tomato causes the subject to experience red which causes him to say "Red!," indicating a normally functioning experience as of red. I symbolize a normal experience of red with "R" as in Figure 10.1. I am assuming, contrary to the intervening argument, and purely for mnemonic purposes, that the inverted subject can be seen as abnormal with an experience symbolized with "G." (Less mnemonic symbols that don't make this mistake would be "X" and "Y.") The second portion shows the subject at Stage 2 where seeing the red tomato causes an experience as of green, which causes the subject to say "Green!," indicating the complementary function. The bottom half of the diagram indicates two different versions of the situation at Stages 3 and 4. According to the possibility that I have been emphasizing ("phenomenal realism"), at Stages 3 and 4, red things look green. The subject says "Red!" because there has been a terminological inversion that cancels out the color perception inversion. But memory skeptics such as Dennett wonder how we can rule out the case schematized in the last line in which the compensating inversion occurs earlier than I imagined and the subject misreports his experience, remembering falsely what red used to look like.

Dennett's claim is that the two possibilities represented in the two scenarios at the bottom half of Figure 10.4 cannot be distinguished, concluding that they are not really different. (He is explicit about advocating "first person operationalism.") However, he gives no reason to doubt that they can be distinguished empirically, as indicated in Figure 10.5.

The bottom two hypotheses from Figure 10.4 elaborated present implementations of the bottom two scenarios of Figure 10.4. In the top case in Figure 10.5, the possibility that I have been emphasizing is elaborated. The subject at Stage 3 sees a ripe tomato and contrasts the way it looks color-wise with the way ripe tomatoes used to look. The machinery of this comparison involves a comparator device that compares the neural implementation of the experience with the neural implementation of the memory of previous tomato experiences. Of course, this story is physicalistic, but no more so I think than the science section in the Tuesday *New York Times* (see note 12). A Wittgensteinian who wishes to deny this level of physicalism would have to adopt a revisionary theoretical perspective, something that a Wittgensteinian should not do.

In the skeptical scenario at the bottom of Figure 10.5, the memory is itself inverted, as is the experience, so when the subject compares them, the subject says the current experience is not what he remembers. The report is

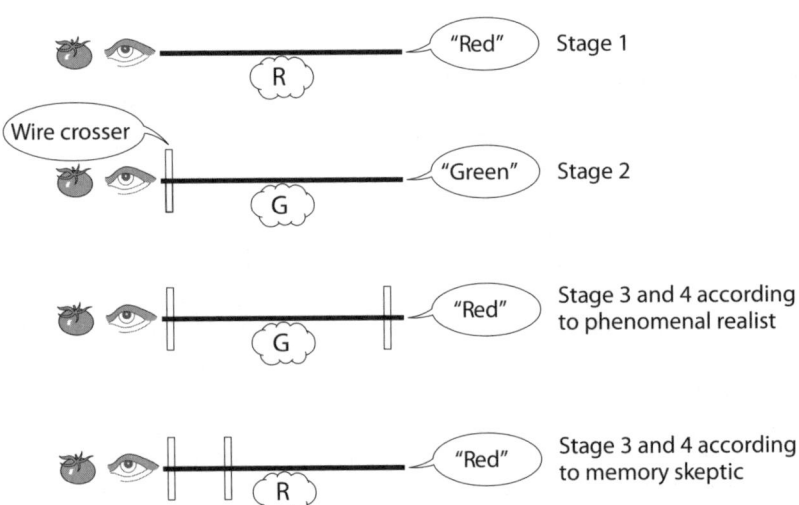

Figure 10.4 The phenomenal realist contrasted with the memory skeptic

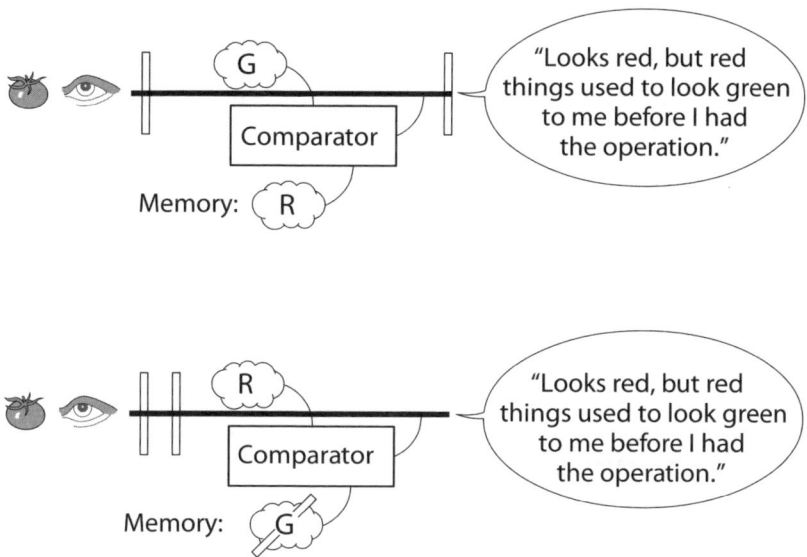

Figure 10.5 The bottom two hypotheses from Figure 10.4 elaborated

the same but the internal reality is not. Dennett wonders how these two hypotheses could possibly be distinguished. Since they cannot be distinguished, he thinks there is no real difference. My response is that there is no reason to doubt that the normal methods of science could distinguish them. For example, perhaps it could be shown that the memory representation does not change in the relevant period. Dennett might object that one can tell whether the memory representation in the brain changes only if one can distinguish the memory representation from the physical basis of the quale itself, whereas his point is that these cannot be distinguished. But since memory and experience are to some extent distinct, they must be distinguishable at the level of the brain. The point of the detail illustrated in Figure 10.5 is that once one makes the hypothesis concrete, the claim that the normal methods of science cannot possibly resolve such issues begins to look like mere skepticism.

The point is further illustrated by a different form of the skeptical hypothesis illustrated at the bottom of Figure 10.6. In this form of the skeptical hypothesis, the memory representation is actually the same as the perceptual representation, but because of an inversion involved in the comparison process, the subject thinks otherwise. Again, why should anyone suppose that the normal methods of science could not find the difference between this case, the one at the bottom of Figure 10.5, and the phenomenal realist hypothesis at the top of both figures?

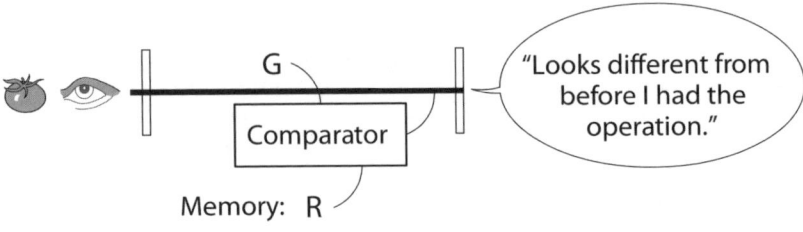

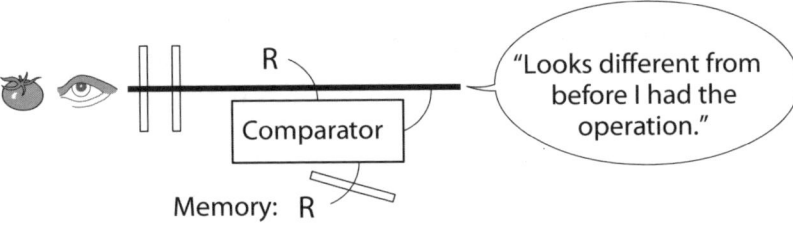

Figure 10.6 The top figure is the same as in Figure 10.5. The bottom figure illustrates a different sort of memory skeptic

Some functionalists hold that the identity of experience and relations among experiences are constitutively tied to memory of those experiences. For example, Sydney Shoemaker (Shoemaker 1966b: 147) says:

> The functional role of a quale must surely include the ways in which the instantiation at one time combines with instantiations of the same or different qualia at later times to produce certain effects ... This means that the total realization of a quale will have to include the memory mechanisms by which qualia have the appropriate "downstream effects".

Functionalists often argue that in crucial cases it is arbitrary whether one says that experiences are qualitatively the same or that there is a memory illusion. Shoemaker and Robert Stalnaker (Dennett 1988; Shoemaker 1996a; Stalnaker 2006) have had an interesting debate in part about this issue, but more generally about whether the kind of combination of functionalism and physicalism endorsed by Shoemaker precludes an inverted spectrum. I am not a functionalist (Block and Fodor 1972; Stalnaker 1999, 2006), and so I don't accept the premise of Shoemaker's argument, but this is not the place to go into that issue.

The Frege–Schlick view

One interesting response to inverted spectrum arguments for qualia involves the doctrine that Shoemaker (1975, 1981; 1982, 1984) calls the "Frege–Schlick" view, and the best defense of that view to date is Robert Stalnaker's (1999, 2006). Shoemaker's version of the Frege–Schlick view is that relations of qualitative similarity and difference only apply intrasubjectively and not intersubjectively. On this view, there can be a genuine issue about whether my experience of red is qualitatively the same or different from my experience of green now or last week but not whether my experience of red is qualitatively the same or different from your experience of red. On that version of the Frege–Schlick view, qualitative relations do not supervene on any conglomeration of naturalistic properties, and not surprisingly, Shoemaker's 1982, 1996a and 2006 discussions of the issue reject it.[29]

I have already given a strong argument for rejecting it, the example of Lefty and Righty mentioned earlier and below.

Stalnaker's version of the Frege–Schlick view is in a way much less radical because what his version rejects "is only a notion of qualia that is both independent of representational content, and also comparable across persons" (2006: 391). He is happy to acknowledge interpersonal qualitative comparisons so long as they can be cashed out in representational/functional terms. In a way though, Stalnaker's version is more radical than Shoemaker's since he rejects intra-personal comparisons of experience over time as well as inter-personal comparisons of experience – if the qualities of the experience cannot be cashed out representationally/functionally.

I said that skepticism about interpersonal comparisons of experience is incompatible with a generally physicalistic world-view. To see this, suppose there are two people who are physical (and functional) duplicates looking at the same object, say the moon, from the same visual angle. Suppose also that they are identical in history of stimulation. Despite identity in everything about them and their environment, current and historical, that could reasonably be supposed to be relevant, the form of skepticism under discussion insists that there is still no issue of fact as to whether their experiences of the moon are the same or totally different. Whether qualia are independent of representational content or not, those duplicates can reasonably be supposed to have highly similar experiences.

Hilary Putnam argued in response to a presentation of this paper at the Putnam at 80 conference (see note 1) that a single sufficient condition – perfect physical identity – does not establish a matter of fact for any other case or give us any reason to think there is any kind of a physically determined metric of similarity. Right, but there is no reason to doubt that normal procedures could not discover the determinants of many comparisons between people.

As I mentioned earlier, Putnam himself has slightly different color vision in his two eyes. Consider Lefty and Righty mentioned earlier, one of whom has copies of Putnam's left eye (inserted at birth), the other of whom has copies of Putnam's right eye. If Putnam sees things yellower through the left eye, we have every reason to think that Lefty will see things yellower than Righty, especially if we can pinpoint whatever it is about the retina or preretinal structures in Putnam's two eyes that very likely are responsible for the difference. Further, examination of your eyes and mine could provide evidence that, other things being equal, your color vision is yellower than mine. One can imagine many cases in which one would be reasonably confident about a comparison between people, independently of any representational or functional theory or any other philosophical theory of the nature of experience. In short, we have mundane reason to believe certain interpersonal comparisons of experience. Wholesale rejection of interpersonal comparisons is incompatible with scientifically informed common sense. Stalnaker's view conjoined with this fact entails that some sort of representationism is true. The possibility of an inverted spectrum is incompatible with leading versions of representationism, so not surprisingly, Stalnaker argues against the inverted spectrum.

Stalnaker's argument is based in large part on two analogies, of which I will discuss only one. It depends on a relational theory of space. Consider an analog of an inverted spectrum for space. We can make sense of the idea that this table is moved 3 feet in the direction defined by the arrow from here towards say the Andromeda Nebula. And that this chair is also moved in that direction. But if everything moved in that direction, would the result be a universe in which everything has moved 3 feet from where those things are now? Of course not. What it is for something to move 3 feet in that direction is for it to move 3 feet relative to everything else. If object A moves 3 feet to the left, then when object B moves 3 feet to the left the "everything else" is slightly different from what it was in the case of A's move, so in the end the relations that define position are the same as when we started. The suggestion is that in the intrasubjective inverted spectrum scenario, there is similarly no fact of change except relative to other color experiences. If they all shift, then there is no change at all.

If one does not believe that the qualitative character of experience is entirely determined by relations to other qualitative characters of other experiences, then the analogy will look wrong. The analogy is certainly at variance with some aspects of common sense. For example, I think common sense leaves it open whether a color-blind person can have exactly the same experience of, say, a black-and-white drawing as non-color-blind people have, despite the fact that the color-blind person's "color space" is different. But the most important point is that this is not an issue to be settled a priori or by common sense. The nature of experience – and I would say the same of the nature of space – is to be settled by the best scientific picture.

Shoemaker (2006) makes another point about the analogy. On the relational theory of space that Shoemaker attributes to Stalnaker, diachronic distance is dependent on synchronic distance. Something at t_2 has moved from where it was at t_1 if its synchronic distances from other things are systematically different in the appropriate ways at t_2 from its synchronic distances from those things at t_1. But there is no comparable dependence of diachronic qualitative relations on synchronic ones. Shoemaker's example (p. 22) is that if two colored lights are flashed, one after the other, I can compare the experiences of them without comparing either of them with the kinesthetic experiences, smells, sounds and aches and pains that accompanied either one of them. Some functionalists might suppose that there is a dependence on synchronic relations even if I don't have to be aware of it in order to judge the relation between the two lights, but if that is the objection to Shoemaker's point, then once again the defense of Stalnaker's analogy appeals to the conclusion.

Stalnaker (2006) replies that the relational view of space that he defends is not the one that Shoemaker attributes to him. On Stalnaker's version of the relational view of space, diachronic distance is not dependent on synchronic distance. Both kinds of distances are a matter of relations in a coordinate system. Actual objects are used to fix the reference of the coordinate system but not to define it in any stronger sense. On Stalnaker's version of the relational theory, distances are real, but locations are conventional. So, once everything has moved 3 feet in the same direction, all relative distances are the same as at the beginning, and there is no overall motion with respect to any location.

Here is a different analogy. Students of Galileo founded the Accademia del Cimento in Florence in the seventeenth century. Members of the Accademia pioneered the study of heat phenomena, making the first thermometers, an example of which is found in Figure 10.7. These thermometers were marked with gradations visible in the picture, but the gradations were not carefully spaced and there was no attempt made to relate the gradations at one end of the scale to those of the other end or of one thermometer with those of another. At the beginning of their investigations, the experimenters did not know whether an intra-thermometer difference of 5 degrees at one end was in any objective way equivalent to an intra-thermometer difference of 5 degrees at the other end or whether there was any inter-thermometer correspondence between 5 degrees as measured by one thermometer and 5 degrees as measured by another. A big advance was made when thermometers and their scales were calibrated to specific freezing and boiling points such as the freezing and boiling point of water. Now there was a meaning to inter-thermometer comparisons, but it was still unknown whether an analog of Stalnaker's theory of space applied. Perhaps there were facts about the temperature difference between the boiling and freezing point of water, but no "locational" facts about either point. That is, perhaps the only facts of temperature were distances between certain temperature points such as freezing and boiling points for

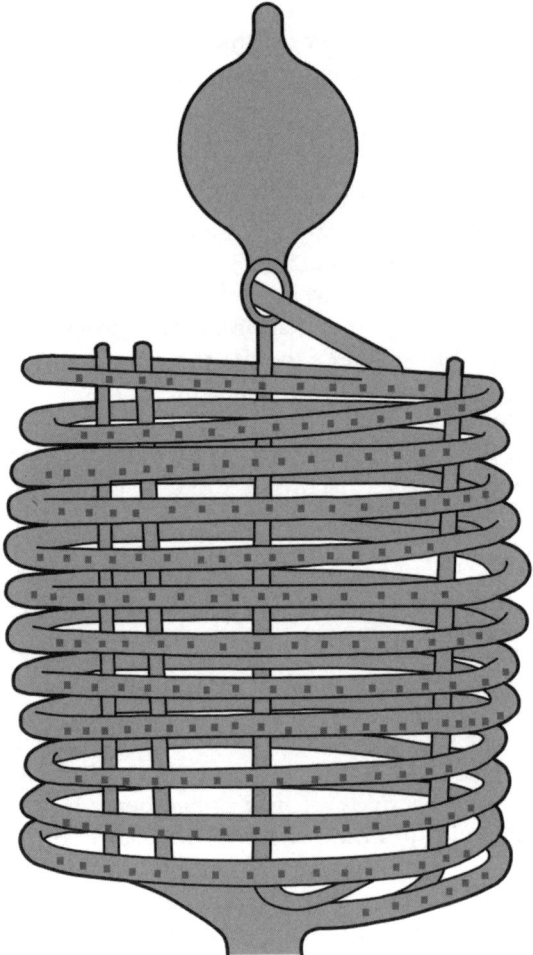

Figure 10.7 Early thermometer

various substances. But as it happened, that turned out false when it was discovered that temperature is mean molecular kinetic energy and hence that there is an absolute zero point at which kinetic energy is zero. That is a "locational" fact that would correspond in the spatial arena to the discovery of a kind of "absolute" space.

Which is the better analogy for phenomenal experience, Stalnaker's space analogy or the temperature analogy? I don't see how anyone could think this is an a priori question. There are two accounts, a functionalist account that roughly fits Stalnaker's view and a physicalist account that roughly fits my view (Stalnaker 2006). I think that there is some preliminary evidence that favors the physicalist view – some of which I have mentioned here – but there is no way to be sure now.

Conclusion

I started with a shifted spectrum argument for qualia and then moved to an inverted spectrum argument. A simple version of the shifted spectrum argument is that there are well-known features of the retina, lens and other parts of the eye that can make color vision in one eye different from the other, say yellower in one eye. And there can be differences between the eyes of two people of the same sort, so we can have reason to think that I see colors as yellower than you do. Human color vision differs markedly from person to person, but people do arrange chips in more or less the same order, differing in where they draw the boundaries. But since training on boundaries and typical examples of colors has some effect, you and I may both see a chip as focal orange, despite the fact that I see it as yellower. So there must be ways of seeing orange, and those ways are qualia. A key feature of that argument and my inverted spectrum argument was that the versions of the shifted and inverted spectrum needed for qualia do not require behavioral indistinguishability of the shifted and inverted pairs – a point that disarms many objections. The upshot is that Wittgenstein is right to say "This is a very serious situation."

Notes

1 This is a somewhat revised version of an article by the same title that appeared in *Philosophical Perspectives* 21, Philosophy of Mind, 2007. An earlier version was delivered at the "Putnam at 80" conference in Dublin, Ireland, March 14–16, 2007. The chapter was written originally for a conference on the work of Paul Horwich in Pécs, Hungary, May 15–16, 2006. I am grateful to Horwich and Putnam for their responses and to Pierre Jacob, the commentator on my paper at the Putnam conference for his comments and to the audiences there, at the University of Oslo in November, 2006, the University of California at Santa Cruz in April, 2007, and at the Ecole Normale Supérieur in May, 2007. I am also grateful to Paul Horwich, John Morrison and Stephen White for comments on an earlier draft.
2 Alex Byrne (2006) and Tim Crane (2000) discuss uses of the term "qualia," and the term's history.
3 Representationism is the view that the phenomenal character of an experience supervenes on its "referential" representational content, where "referential" is meant to abstract from modes of presentation. (The contents assumed by representationists are not object-involving.) In favor: Byrne 2001; Clark 2000; Crane 2001; Dretske 1995; Harman 1990; Lycan 1996; Thau 2002; Tye 1995. Opposed: Block 2003; Burge 2003; Nickel 2007. Harder to classify: Carruthers 2000; Chalmers 2004; Davies 1997; Kriegel 2002; Levine 2003; Pautz 2005; Shoemaker 1994a.
4 Functionalism (Armstrong 1968; Lewis 1970; Putnam 1967) says that pain (for example) can be characterized in terms of its causal relations to sensory inputs, behavioral outputs and to other mental states.

5 Useful discussions of the inverted spectrum that won't be discussed other than in this note are to be found in Chalmers 1996; Cohen 2001; Cole 1990; Kirk 1982; Lycan 1973, 1996; Rey 1992, 1998; Tye 1995, 2000.
6 Wittgenstein's notes have been re-edited by David G. Stern (Wittgenstein 1993) who says that Rush Rhees left out about half the material (pp. 200–201). Since Stern gives the reader much more information about the text, I am using his version. This passage appears on pp. 230–31 of Stern's version and p. 284 of Rhees's version. The square brackets indicate changes in the text by Stern. The bracketed "red" in the first line is accompanied by a footnote saying that the text reads "green" but that this was probably a slip. The 3 dots at the end of the second paragraph are in the text and do not indicate anything left out by me. The "[[284]]" indicates a page number in Wittgenstein's notes themselves.
7 Stern says "The text reads 'green,' but this is because Wittgenstein had changed an earlier use of 'green' to 'blue' but failed to make the change here" (p. 231).
8 In his introductory notes Rhees (1968: 274) notes:

> All that is printed here is a collection of rough notes or memoranda which Wittgenstein made for his own use. He would never have published them – he would not even have had them typed – without revising and rearranging them. Certainly he would have revised the language.

9 Recall that the first passage quoted above seemed to involve a shift from the example of red/green to red/blue inversion. I will treat the first passage as if it concerned red and green.
10 Michael Tye (2002) has responded to me on this point by an account of the difference as one between an experience that ascribes indeterminacy and one that indeterminately ascribes. This distinction certainly makes sense for verbal representations, but bringing it in to solve this problem begs the question by assuming that phenomenal representations are like verbal representations in allowing for this kind of distinction. This issue has been discussed in varying forms in Block 1983; Dennett 1968; Peacocke 1993; Tye 1995.
11 On my view, there are two such epistemic problems. One is the "Hard Problem" (Chalmers 1996): we don't understand why the neural basis of a given experience is the neural basis of that experience rather than another or none. The second problem is the "harder" problem, a version of the problem of other minds. On a naturalistic picture of consciousness, there is no problem about the consciousness of other humans, but when we ask about robots that don't overlap with us in what we take to be the physical basis of our conscious states, there is a problem of how to think about the question of whether they have conscious states (Block 2002).
12 More specifically, I am assuming that the phenomenal character of experience supervenes on physical states of the body and, in a concession that makes the view I am assuming a very weak form of physicalism, the physical environment surrounding the body and even the past physical states of that environment. Of course some will balk at even such a weak form of physicalism, but it would be very interesting if it turned out to be incompatible with a Wittgensteinian point of view that supposedly prescinds from "theorizing," given that this minimal physicalism is deeply engrained in the day-to-day practice (and not just the theology) of the psychology and neuroscience of perception and in my view in common-sense ways of thinking about perception. (See Nida-Rümelin 1999.) I don't think an approach to the mind that stresses "leaving everything as it is" can lightly require giving up such practices.

13 It should also be said that although some kinds of visual experience are localized in the brain, notably experience as of a face or as of motion, the same cannot be said for color. Color appears to be represented at a number of occipital sites, mainly in V4 and V8.
14 Note that it is clear from the first passage I quoted that for the kind of inverted spectrum that Wittgenstein is willing to accept, he accepts *both* intrasubjective and intersubjective versions of the innocuous scenario. The individual he describes sees everything differently today than yesterday – that's the intrasubjective version. And he also endorses the intersubjective version in saying "I think we should under these or similar circumstances be inclined to say that he saw red what we saw blue." So it does not appear to be the intrasubjective/intersubjective difference that is at issue between the innocuous and dangerous scenarios.
15 I have emphasized the importance of normality and expressibility in ordinary language in arguments for qualia in "Sexism, Racism, Ageism and the Nature of Consciousness" (Block 1999), in which it is argued that males and females, although equally normal, see colors that they classify as red slightly differently. Likewise for old/young and races that differ in pigmentation. (Versions of these arguments transformed for the somewhat different purposes of this chapter will be briefly summarized in the section below on shifted spectra.) And, as mentioned earlier, Horwich (forthcoming) also argues that the difference between an innocuous inversion and a dangerous one is expressibility in public language by normal perceivers.
16 In Block (1990) I inadvisedly called violations of the Principle of Normality the fallacy of intentionalizing qualia.
17
> Suppose everyone had a box with something in it: we call it a 'beetle'. No one can look into anyone else's box, and everyone says he knows what a beetle is only by looking at *his* beetle. – Here it would be quite possible for everyone to have something different in his box. One might even imagine such a thing constantly changing. – But suppose the word 'beetle' had a use in these people's language? – If so it would not be used as the name of a thing. The thing in the box has no place in the language game at all; not even as a something: for the box might even be empty. No, one can 'divide through' by the thing in the box; it cancels out, whatever it is.
> (Wittgenstein 1958: §293)

18 The Fregean view has some affinities with that of Paul Churchland. Churchland concedes the conceivability of an inverted spectrum, allowing that different perceivers might have qualitatively different experiences which all have the functional role characteristic of the experience of red.

> Such intrinsic qualia merely serve as salient features that permit the quick introspective identification of sensations, as black-on-orange stripes serve as a salient feature for the quick visual identification of tigers. But specific qualia are not essential to the type-identity of mental states, any more than black-orange stripes are essential to the type-identity of tigers.
> (Churchland 1984: 40; see also Churchland & Churchland 1981; Clark, 1985)

What I don't understand about Churchland's view is how he can maintain functionalism despite allowing that qualia escape the functionalist net. In the end, I suspect that his view is really a mixed functionalist/physicalist view similar to that of Shoemaker (1982): functionalism supplies conditions of similarity and difference of qualia, but physicalism supplies the natures of specific qualia.

19 One complication that I have not mentioned is that the structure of qualia space contains four privileged planes that correspond to the "unique" colors, e.g. reds that are not at all yellowish or bluish. See Pautz (2005).

20 One argument against inverted spectra that is not based on an appeal to asymmetries is given in Byrne & Hilbert (1997). However, that argument is directed towards the conjunction of the possibility of an inverted spectrum together with the thesis that there is a failure of match between the phenomenal character of a sensation and its intentional content. It is not an argument that purports to show that inverted spectra are impossible.

21 For more details see Broakes (2007); Byrne (2006); Churchland (2002); Hardin (1997); Hilbert and Kalderon (2000). A slightly more accurate description of the point about red and green is that desaturated near-red is pink but a desaturated near-green is near-green rather than green.

22 One point on the side of an undetectable inverted spectrum is that the undetectability can be relative to culture and environment. That is, what is required for an undetectable inverted spectrum is that there is an environment – including cultural environment – in which there are two individuals (or stages of a single individual) for whom there is no possibility of detecting an inversion. If those two subjects are undetectably inverted with respect to one another, then they cannot express the difference in public language, even if in a different environment and culture they would have been detectably inverted. For example, consider a people who live underground in circumstances of little light, never seeing the sky and in which there are few stable colors – other than black and white. We would also have to imagine that the culture has a prohibition against seeing the unclothed human body, one's own or that of others. The point is that the environment can be restricted in ways that restrict the application of color asymmetries that would show up in less restricted circumstances.

23 I speak as if there is a single kind of inversion but actually there are many different types of "inversion" in the sense of different ways to systematically map the color solid onto itself without disturbing relations among points in the solid. See Palmer (1999).

24 The spectrum inversion argument against functionalism that I have given in other places is a straightforward extensional argument. The functional state that functionalists must associate with an experience can occur without the experience, and conversely. Of course, it is always open to the functionalist to complicate the functional role so as to avoid the counterexamples. But so doing will in effect bring in physicalist ideas in an ad hoc manner, and so the resulting view will be an ad hoc combination of functionalism and physicalism. Patricia and Paul Churchland (1981) argue that although spectrum inversion is clearly possible, nonetheless functionalism wins. Their reason is that a functionalist natural kind will be more natural than a qualia-centered natural kind, the latter being unnatural from the point of view of neuroscience. However, they do not take on the issue of whether the ad hoc changes I just mentioned will push the functionalist kind below the qualia-centered kind in naturalness.

25 One example: subjects do adapt – experientially – to goggles that are colored with one color on one side and another on the other side. But in that case, there is a line in the middle of the visual field where the colors meet and that is the kind of defect that the visual system is built to adapt to.

26 Let me remind the reader that I am assuming a weak form of physicalism in which phenomenal character is supervenient on the physical body and its surrounding current and past environment. See note 12.
27 Called the "intra-inner" argument in Shoemaker (1975).
28 I am grateful to Dr. Peter Lang, Department of Pediatric Cardiology at Children's Hospital, Boston, for filling me in on this issue. The description in the text concerns "dextro" or "complete" transposition of the great arteries. See the Wikipedia entry at http://en.wikipedia.org/wiki/Dextro-transposition_of_the_great_arteries
29 Shoemaker's 1984 discussion takes it much more seriously.

Bibliography

Armstrong, D. M. (1968) *A Materialist Theory of the Mind*, London: Routledge and Kegan Paul.
Bacon, J., K. Campbell, and L. Reinhardt (eds.) (1993) (eds.) *Ontology, Causality and Mind: Essays in Honour of D. M. Armstrong*, Cambridge: Cambridge University Press.
Block, N. (1978) "Troubles with Functionalism," *Minnesota Studies in the Philosophy of Science* 9, 261–325.
——(1980) "Are Absent Qualia Impossible?," *Philosophical Review* 89, 257–74.
——(1983) "Mental Pictures and Cognitive Science," *Philosophical Review* 93, 499–542.
——(1990) "Inverted Earth," in J. Tomberlin (ed.), *Philosophical Perspectives* 4. Atascadero, CA: Ridgeview, 53–79.
——(1994) "Qualia," in S. Guttenplan (ed.), *A Companion to Philosophy of Mind*, Oxford: Oxford University Press, 514–20.
——(1995) "On a Confusion about a Function of Consciousness," *Behavioral and Brain Sciences* 18(2), 227–47.
——(1996) "Mental Paint and Mental Latex," *Philosophical Issues* 7, 19–49.
——(1999) "Sexism, Racism, Ageism and the Nature of Consciousness," *Philosophical Topics*, 26(1 and 2), 39–70.
——(2002) "The Harder Problem of Consciousness," *Journal of Philosophy* 99(8), 1–35.
——(2003) "Mental Paint," in M. Hahn and B. Ramberg (eds.), *Reflections and Replies: Essays on the Philosophy of Tyler Burge*, Cambridge, MA: MIT Press, 165–200.
Block, N., and J. A. Fodor (1972) "What psychological states are not," *Philosophical Review*, 81, 159–81.
Boghossian, P., and J. D. Velleman (1989) "Color as a Secondary Quality," *Mind* 98, 81–103.
——(1991) "Physicalist Theories of Color," *Philosophical Review*, 100, 67–106.
Broackes, J. (2007) "Black and White and the Inverted Spectrum," *The Philosophical Quarterly*, 57(227), 161–75.
Burge, T. (2003) "Qualia and Intentional Content: Reply to Block," in M. Hahn and B. Ramberg (eds.), *Reflections and Replies: Essays on the Philosophy of Tyler Burge*, Cambridge, MA: MIT Press, 405–16.
Byrne, A. (2001) "Intentionalism Defended," *The Philosophical Review*, 110, 199–240.
——(2006) "Inverted Qualia," in E. N. Zalta (ed.), *Stanford Encyclopedia of Philosophy* (Vol. Winter 2006 Edition). Stanford, CA: The Metaphysics Research Lab of the Center for the Study of Language and Information
Byrne, A., and D. R. Hilbert (1997) "Colors and reflectances," in A. Byrne and D. R. Hilbert (eds.), *Readings on Color*, Volume 1: The Philosophy of Color: MIT Press.
——(2003) "Color realism and Color Science," *Behavioral and Brain Sciences*, 26, 3–21.

Carruthers, P. (2000) *Phenomenal Consciousness: A Naturalistic Theory*, Cambridge: Cambridge University Press.
Chalmers, D. (1996) *The Conscious Mind: In Search of a Fundamental Theory*, Oxford: Oxford University Press.
——(2002) "Does Conceivability Entail Possibility," in T. Gendler and J. Hawthorne (eds.), *Conceivability and Possibility*, Oxford: Oxford University Press, 145–200.
——(2004) "The Representational Character of Experience," in B. Leiter, *The Future for Philosophy*, Oxford: Oxford University Press.
Churchland, P. (2002) "Brain-Wise: Studies in Neurophilosophy," Cambridge, MA: MIT Press.
Churchland, P. M. (1984) *Matter and Consciousness*, Cambridge, MA: MIT Press.
Churchland, P. M., and P. S. Churchland (1981) "Functionalism, Qualia and Intentionality," *Philosophical Topics*, 12, 121–32.
Clark, A. (1985) "Spectrum Inversion and the Color Solid," *Southern Journal of Philosophy*, 23(4), 431–43.
——(2000) *A Theory of Sentience*, Oxford: Oxford University Press.
Cohen, J. (2001) "Color, Content and Fred: On a Proposed Reductio of the Inverted Spectrum Hypothesis," *Philosophical Studies*, 103, 121–44.
Cole, D. (1990) "Functionalism and Inverted Spectra," *Synthese*, 82, 207–22.
Crane, T. (2000) "The origins of Qualia," in T. Crane and S. Patterson (eds.), *History of the Mind–Body Problem*, New York: Routledge, 169–94.
——(2001) *Elements of Mind*, Oxford: Oxford University Press.
Davies, M. (1997) "Externalism and Experience," in N. Block, O. Flanagan and G. Güzeldere, *The Nature of Consciousness: Philosophical Debates*, Cambridge MA: MIT Press, 309–27.
Dennett, D. C. (1968). "The nature of images and the introspective trap," *Content and Consciousness*, London: Routledge.
——(1988) "Quining Qualia" in A. Marcel and E. Bisiach (eds.), *Consciousness in Contemporary Science*, Oxford: Oxford University Press, 381–414.
——(1991) *Consciousness Explained*, Boston: Little Brown.
Dretske, F. (1995) *Naturalizing the Mind*, Cambridge, MA: MIT Press.
Farrell, B. (1950). "Experience," Mind, 59, 170–98.
Field, H. (1973). "Theory Change and the Indeterminacy of Reference," *Journal of Philosophy*, 70(14), 462–81.
Frege, G. (1884/1953) *The Foundations of Arithmetic*, Oxford: Blackwell.
Gendler, T., and J. Hawthorne (2002) *Conceivability and Possibility*, Oxford: Oxford University Press.
Hardin, C. L. (1997). "Reinverting the Spectrum," in A. Byrne and D. R. Hilbert (eds.), *Readings on Color*, Volume 1: *The Philosophy of Color*, Cambridge, MA: MIT Press, 289–301.
Harman, G. (1990) "The Intrinsic Quality of Experience," *Philosophical Perspectives*, 4, 31–52.
Harrison, B. (1973) *Form and Content*, Oxford: Blackwell.
Hilbert, D. R., and M. E. Kalderon (2000) "Color and the Inverted Spectrum," in S. Davis (ed.), *Color Perception: Philosophical, Psychological, Artistic and Computational Perspectives*, Oxford: Oxford University Press, 187–214.
Hill, C. S. (1991) *Sensations: A Defense of Type Materialism*, Cambridge: Cambridge University Press.

Horwich, P. (in progress) "The 'Mystery' of Consciousness," a chapter of an unpublished draft of a book on Wittgenstein.
Hurley, S. (1998) *Consciousness in Action*, Cambridge, MA: Harvard University Press.
Kind, A. (2003) "What's so Transparent about Transparency," *Philosophical Studies*, 115(3), 225–44.
Kirk, R. (1982). "Goodbye to Transposed Qualia," *Proceedings of the Aristotelian Society*, 82, 33–44.
Kriegel, U. (2002) "Phenomenal Content," *Erkentniss*, 57: 175–98.
Levine, J. (1991). "Cool Red," *Philosophical Psychology*, 4, 27–40.
Lewis, D. (1970) "How to Define Theoretical Terms," *Journal of Philosophy*, 67, 427–45.
Linden, D. E. J., U. Kallenbach, A. Heinecke, W. Singer, and R. Goebel (1999) "The myth of Upright Vision. A psychophysical and functional imaging study of adaptation to inverting spectacles," *Perception* 28(4), 469–81.
Lycan, W. G. (1973) "Inverted Spectrum," *Ratio*, 15, 315–19.
——(1996) *Consciousness and Experience*, Cambridge, MA: MIT Press.
Moore, G. E. (1903) "The Refutation of Idealism," in *Philosophical Studies* (pp. 1–30), Totowa, NJ: Littlefield, Adams & Co. (1965), p. 25.
Nagel, T. (1974). "What Is it Like to Be a Bat?" *The Philosophical Review*, 83(4), 435–50.
Neitz, J., and G. Jacobs (1986) "Polymorphisms of long-wavelength cones in normal human color vision," *Nature*, 323, 623–25.
Neitz, M., and J. Neitz (1998) "Molecular genetics and the biological basis of color vision," in W. G. Backhaus and R. Kliegle and J. S. Werner (eds.), *Color Vision: Perspectives from Different Disciplines*, Berlin: De Gruyter, 101–19.
Nickel, B. (2007) "Against Intentionalism," *Philosophical Studies*, 136(3), 279–304.
Nida-Rümelin, M. (1999) "Intrinsic Phenomenal Properties in Color Vision Science: A Reply to Peter Ross," *Consciousness and Cognition*, 8, 571–74.
Palmer, S. (1999) "Color, Consciousness and the Isomorphism Constraint," *Behavioral and Brain Sciences*, 22, 923–43.
Pautz, A. (2005) "Sensory Awareness is not a Wide Physical Relation," *Nous*, 40, 205–40.
Peacocke, C. (1993) "Review of M. Tye, The Imagery Debate," *Philosophy of Science*, 60, 675–77.
Putnam, H. (1967) "The nature of Mental States," in W. Capitan and D. Merrill (eds.), *Art, Mind, and Religion*, Pittsburgh: Pittsburgh University Press, 37–48.
——(1981) *Reason, Truth and History*, New York: Cambridge University Press.
——(1999) *The Threefold Cord: Mind, Body and World*, New York: Columbia University Press.
Rey, G. (1992) "Sensational Sentences Switched," *Philosophical Studies*, 68, 289–319.
——(1998) "A Narrow Representationalist Account of Qualitative Experience," *Philosophical Perspectives*, 12, 435–58.
Rhees, R. (1968). Notes for Lectures on "Private Experience" and "Sense Data": Note on the Text, *The Philosophical Review*, 77(3), 271–75.
Shoemaker, S. (1975) "Functionalism and Qualia," *Philosophical Studies*, 27, 291–315.
——(1981) "Absent Qualia Are Impossible: A Reply to Block," *Philosophical Review*, 90: 581–99.
——(1982) "The Inverted Spectrum," *The Journal of Philosophy*, 79, 357–81.
——(1984) "Postscript to 'The Inverted Spectrum'," in S. Shoemaker (ed.), *Identity, Cause and Mind*, Cambridge: Cambridge University Press, 351–57.
——(1994a) "Phenomenal Character," *Nous*, 28, 21–38.

——(1994b) "Self-knowledge and 'inner sense'," *Philosophy and Phenomenological Research*, 54, 249–314.

——(1996a) "Intrasubjective/intersubjective," in S. Shoemaker (ed.), *The First-person Perspective and other Essays*, Cambridge: Cambridge University Press, 141–54.

——(1996b) *The First-Person Perspective and Other Essays*, Cambridge, UK: Cambridge University Press.

——(2006) "The Frege–Schlick View," in J. Thomson (ed.), *Content and Modality*, Oxford: Oxford University Press, 18–33.

Stalnaker, R. (1999) "Comparing Qualia Across Persons," *Philosophical Topics*, 26, 385–405.

——(2006) Shoemaker, "The Frege–Schlick View," in J. Thomson (ed.), *Content and Modality*, Oxford: Oxford University Press, 254–57.

Stoljar, D. (2006) *Ignorance and Imagination*, Oxford: Oxford University Press.

Taylor, D. (1966) "The Incommunicability of Content," *Mind*, 75, 527–41.

Thau, M. (2002) *Consciousness and Cognition*, Oxford: Oxford University Press.

Tye, M. (1995) *Ten Problems of Consciousness*, Cambridge, MA: MIT Press.

——(2000). *Consciousness, Color, and Content*, Cambridge, MA: MIT Press.

——(2002) "Representationalism and the Transparency of Experience," *Nous*, 36(1), 137–51.

White, S. (1986) "Curse of the Qualia," *Synthese*, 68, 333–68.

Wittgenstein, L. (1958). *Philosophical Investigations*, 2nd edn. Oxford: Blackwell.

——(1968) Notes for Lectures on "Private Experience" and "Sense Data," *The Philosophical Review*, 77(3), 275–320.

——(1993) Notes for Lectures on "Private Experience" and "Sense Data," in J. Klagge and A. Normann (eds.), *Ludwig Wittgenstein: Philosophical Occasions 1912–1951*, Indianapolis: Hackett Publishing Company, 202–89.

COMMENTS ON NED BLOCK'S "WITTGENSTEIN AND QUALIA"

Hilary Putnam

Ned Block writes that "Hilary Putnam mentioned that he sees colors differently in different eyes" (p. 290 in this volume). Actually, I already noticed when I was a college student that when I looked at a sandy beach in bright sunlight, the exact color of the sand looked different if I looked with my right eye shut and if I looked with my left eye shut. Later I discovered that I can get other people to have a similar experience, if I tell them to go outside and find a white wall (or a wall some pale shade of gray or yellow) some distance away and try looking at it with their left eye closed and then with their right eye closed. As Block mentioned, the explanation turns out to be very simple: the maculae of the two eyes are not identical with respect to pigmentation. But that doesn't mean that the macula of one eye is "normal," nor that the macula of the other eye is abnormal. This is not a hypothetical case, and it does not depend on a thought experiment.

As I say, I have experienced it in my own case. And it also doesn't really depend on the names we have for the various colors and shades of colors. First of all, the difference isn't so great that with one eye closed I would say "It's a gray wall" and with the other eye closed I would say, "It's a white wall." In the case of my experience when looking at a beach in bright sunlight, what I might have said is that the beach seemed to be slightly different shades of yellow, depending on which eye was open. But I wouldn't say that it seemed to be yellow when viewed through my left eye alone, and gray when viewed through my right eye alone. The difference was not that extreme. And it wouldn't have affected my "matching" performance on a color chart. No matter which eye is shut, if the beach matches yellow$_{32}$ with the left eye shut, it will match yellow$_{32}$ with the right eye shut. And by the way, our notion of "exactly the same color" has itself been affected by and refined by technology, especially by mass production and the resultant need for standardization.

My own experience thus prepared me to accept one of the points that Block makes: the view (common to "intentionalists" and "disjunctivists" in the philosophy of perception) that the phenomenal quality of a subject's visual experience upon looking at (hearing, feeling, smelling, etc.) a certain portion of her environment is exhausted by the objective appearance-properties (e.g., looking such-and-such a shade from such-and-such a point in space under such-and-such lighting conditions) of that portion of the environment is untenable. This view is, of course, a strong form of "naïve realism," and while I think naïve realists are right to say that what we see (hear, feel, smell, etc.) when we perceive objects and events in our environment are properties of those objects and not properties of our qualia (something Block also thinks is right, as his paper makes clear), it is a mistake to say that describing what we perceive in objective terms also completely describes the phenomenology of the perceptual experience. That phenomenology is determined by a combination of objective and subjective factors, and representationalists err by failing to recognize the contribution of the subjective side. On all this Block and I are in agreement.

In my comments after Block's talk in March 2007 I went on to say:

> The assumption you [Block] need for the full picture you want, and that I cannot go along with, is the assumption that sameness of qualitative character is well-defined both when we consider one person at different times and when we consider different people at the same *or* different times. In other words, you need to assume that there is a fact of the matter, albeit what you call an "ineffable"[1] one, about whether the qualitative character of the experiences of the two subjects, or the one subject at different times, is the same or different. I think that we should give that up. I myself believe that there are no good candidates in present-day neurology for a relation of sameness of qualitative character which is well-defined in that sense.

I also considered the idea (which Block advocates) that the requisite relation of "sameness of qualitative character" could be fixed by finding out *which brain-states* qualia are (assuming that a "mind–brain identity theory" is correct for qualia). And I said, "Now, that certainly suggests that some straightforward identification of qualia with certain brain states is going to be discovered. But if there were such an identification, knowing *which one it is* is a probably unsolvable epistemological problem."[2]

But I no longer agree with this. I now think that my claim that determining which brain-parameters determine qualitative character is "a probably unsolvable epistemological problem" was wrong. This is a claim to which Block devoted an important paper (Block 2007), which had not appeared when I made those remarks. In that paper, Block wrote:

> I will give an empirical argument that we can achieve a better fit between psychology and neuroscience if we assume that the

perspectives just described are wrong. ... The alternative I have in mind is just the familiar default "method" of inference to the best explanation, that is the approach of looking for the framework that makes the most sense of all the data, not just reports.

(ibid.: 486)

Block's argument in that paper (to which I refer the interested reader) convinces me, and I am happy to withdraw the objection to the assumption I could not "go along with" in Dublin.

Notes

1 By "ineffable" Block does not mean "indescribable in principle," but indescribable in ordinary language with the terms used to describe objective appearances, e.g., "such an such a shade of red."
2 I remarked that this is a point I argued for in Putnam (1981: ch. 4).

Bibliography

Block, Ned (2007) "Consciousness, Accessibility, and the Mesh Between Psychology and Neuroscience," *Behavioral and Brain Sciences* 30: 481–548.

Putnam, Hilary (1981) *Reason, Truth and History*, Cambridge: Cambridge University Press.

11

AFFORDING US THE WORLD

Charles Travis

'While I was speaking to him I did not know what was going on in his head.' In saying this one is not thinking of brain-processes, but of thought processes. The picture should be taken seriously. We would really like to see into his head. And yet we only mean what elsewhere we would mean in saying we would like to know what he is thinking.

(*Philosophical Investigations* §427)

In *The Threefold Cord*, in describing the faulty underpinnings of the bad side of internal realism, Putnam says he once thought of

> perceptual inputs [as] the outer limit of our cognitive processing: everything that lies beyond those inputs is connected to our mental processes only causally, not cognitively.
>
> (1969: 16)

In which case there is this problem:

> What my 'model theoretic argument' showed is that interpretations of our language – even ones that make true the very sentences that are 'really true', true from a 'God's eye view' (assuming [this] makes sense) – can agree on what these inputs are while disagreeing wildly on what our terms actually refer to.
>
> (ibid.)

On the idea that there was some sort of problem here he now comments,

> How could the question "How does language hook onto the world?" even appear to pose a difficulty unless the retort: "How can there be a problem about talking about, say, houses and trees when we see them all the time?" had not already been rejected in advance as question-begging or 'hopelessly naïve'?
>
> (ibid.: 12)

This need one can feel to construct our relations to windfall cherries, or bowls of them, or peccaries on our path, out of something inside a boundary of the sort Putnam mentions, with perceptual inputs stationed along them, sentinels looking out at something beyond, is an expression of a difficulty Wittgenstein expresses in another context like this:

> It is so difficult to find the *beginning*. Or, better: it is difficult to begin at the beginning. And not try to go further back.
> (On Certainty: §471)

Here the felt need to start too far back manifests itself as a compulsion to look inside the head for what is to be found in the world around us; specifically, to look there for what it is we (*really*) respond to in – as we call it – seeing some cherries. This *Drang* (henceforth 'The *Drang*') runs very deep through much of philosophy of mind. It has various tributaries. It is easy enough to cut off one or several while leaving the *Drang* in place. What makes for it is not yet well understood.

1. Seeing is a form – visual – of awareness of one's (spatial) surroundings. Sight *affords* awareness of some of what is there, or there happening. Seeing that dirty cup on the counter, just after having started the dishwasher, is enjoying some of what vision places on offer. Seeing it to be a cup, or even an object (an integral piece of dry goods) is a further achievement, tied, as Frege says, to thinking and judging (1897: 149). Following the cup's career is yet another. Seeing places all this in reach. It remains *au courant*, as testimony does not.

The question what it is to see a bowl of cherries thus asks us to fasten on *that* item, and ask how we are privileged with access to how *it* is when, and in, seeing it. *What* we see would then be no more than is in our surroundings, and in view. What sensitivity to *that* would we enjoy in seeing it? That would be the question.

It is thus remarkable that, from about the time Montaigne read Sextus to a bit after VE day – three centuries plus – nearly no one thought that strategy worth a glance. When, for example, in the late 1930s, H. A. Prichard wrote 'Perception', one was entitled to take for granted that this approach was wrong. Prichard begins,

> I assume that 'perception' is a word used for the genus of which what we call seeing, hearing, smelling, tasting, and feeling or touching are the species.
> (1950: 52)

All well so far. He then remarks that in the 'everyday attitude of mind' of both philosophers and non-philosophers, one counts "'chairs and tables, boats going downstream, and so forth" as the sorts of things one sees. But, he announces, and only barely argues, this obviously will not do:

> It need hardly be said that this view, much as we should all like to be able to vindicate it, will not stand examination.
>
> (ibid.: 53)

Argument is sparse and shaky. Prichard was unusual among philosophers of perception in several respects. But not in this one. What we need to do, on the research strategy he is determined to follow, is not to ask, of the cherries before me, how I am sensitive to *them* in seeing *them*, but rather to ask what *else* it is to which visual experience might allow me to be sensitive. To Prichard's credit, he realized that such a something else would have to be available to my awareness only, and hence could not be an object of judgement. Cook Wilson had at least that much good effect.

2. There are various perception-specific roots of Prichard's amazing research strategy – the argument from illusion, in various forms, among them. There is failure to see how *special* the uses of language are on which 'N saw O' does not imply O's presence in the scene. There is also a general attitude towards philosophical good faith expressed in finding it unremarkable that we could all, pre-philosophically, be *that* wrong as to what we *saw*. But The *Drang* is not confined to perception. It surfaces in views of thinking things so. Michael Dummett expresses it. In his 'inadvertent' book on Frege, in a chapter really more about Kripke, he writes:

> The content of a belief appears to depend, not on the mode of presentation as determined by commonly agreed linguistic convention, together with the relevant circumstances, but on the connection which the individual subject makes between the expression and its referent ...
>
> An accurate characterization of a speaker's belief requires an account of his personal understanding of the words by means of which he expresses it ... When we follow our usual procedure of characterizing someone's belief by means of a sentence considered as having the meaning that it does in the language to which it belongs, we are very often giving only an approximate statement of the content of that belief.
>
> (1981: 115–16)

Parallel to the obvious strategy for studying what it is to see a bowl of cherries, the obvious strategy for studying what it is to think something would be first to ask what there *is* to think or not, and then, of some given thinker, which of *these* things he does think. First ask: 'What is it that might *be* so or not?', then, 'Of that, what does N *think* so?' I mention something to be thought, and say someone to think *that*; as a rule there is no issue of approximation. (Frege gives us excellent reasons for thinking of thinking in this way. I leave them unmentioned here.)

Again, though, there is something that makes that obvious strategy seem – and not just to Dummett – hardly worth a second look. Instead, to see what someone thinks, we need to look inside his head. It is not the world he thinks about, but views of it from a vantage point you would have to be him to enjoy, which determines what he 'really' thinks – now not a matter of his answer to the question whether there are cherries.

Jerry Fodor (e.g., 1998, 2008) feels the *Drang*. On his view, for me to think there is a peccary on the path is for me to bear a certain relation to something *literally* in the head. In the (English) sentence 'There is a peccary on the path', there is a string of letters beginning with 'T' and ending with 'h'. (The obvious one.) That string is the string it is independent of any considerations of how it is to be understood. If a given instance of that string is also an instance of the sentence 'There is a peccary on the path', then, as an instance of that sentence (but not just as that string) it is to be understood in a certain way. Similarly, on Fodor's view to think something is to relate to something with an identity entirely independent of anything to do with representing; which thing also, as it happens, is to be taken in a certain way – does, in fact, have some representational properties. That something has whatever representational features that subject's contact with the world has happened to bestow on it. Its having the features it does is very much a part of that subject's particular vicissitudes. At the same time, that something belongs to a language – a systematically structured collection of such somethings – and, as such, represents as it does by virtue of its place in that system. The remarkable thing is now that that system of such somethings just happens to draw just those distinctions which are drawn by the distinctions there are between one Fregean sense and another. Here there really are the problems Putnam pointed to in his development of Skolem's thought.

Fodor is, of course, moved by proprietary factors, notably by a misguided sense of naturalism. That is why I began here with Dummett, who is certainly not in thrall to any *such* compulsion. Though they may understand 'in the head' differently, Dummett and Fodor share a view of the work what is in the head would have to do. There must be deeper roots. My candidate is the idea that there is such a thing as '*the* distinctions there are between one Fregean sense and another'. For the moment I merely point out the parallel.

3. Putnam is sometimes too modest. In *Cord* he records having learned from Austin how to resist one sort of temptation to look inside the head (for what in fact is located outside it). Austin did much, I think, to show us how there is no need to look anywhere but in the environment to find what it is that we see (more generally, encounter, are made aware of, in perception).

But even before discovering Austin, Putnam taught us some very valuable lessons in how to resist temptations to look elsewhere. I will now introduce a particular such temptation, and then say briefly how Putnam defuses it. I will appeal to an idea which, in *Cord*, he presents as 'the face of perception'. But the idea is much deeper, and longer standing, in his thought than that title for it.

One can introduce the temptation by asking how we differ from cats. There is the business of the tails, and so on. But when we are done with that, it seems we may need a look inside. Cats do not see the world as we do. Let us grant, for the moment, that there is a sense in which they are not thinkers (*rational* animals) at all. (As usual in philosophy, 'rational' now takes on a special meaning. You can't reason with my cat. You can't reason with Aunt Ida either. Aunt Ida is just not rational. But not in the sense in which, here, a cat is meant not to be.) The point about cats can be put this way: cats are Pyrrhonian. Things may seem to them certain ways. Feline constitution naturally inclines them to respond to seemings in certain ways. Seemingly something large approaches. The cat dives beneath a hedge. Natural inclinations thus guide the cat. But here 'guide' can only mean *cause* it to do things. For that is all a natural inclination can accomplish. We, by contrast, are thinkers, that is, judgers in Frege's sense: we take truth-evaluable attitudes towards things. To judge is to hold true (or so). It is just when I stand in that way towards something being so that its being so bears, for me, on what to think and do as its being so in fact bears on what is to be done and what it is right to think (insofar as I grasp this bearing). That there is a peccary on the path may be good reason for me to think I am in Oxfordshire, given its bearing on the excess wealth of the local landed. But it is reason for *me* so to think only insofar as I take the fact in.

So we have this situation. In fact there is a peccary on the path. In fact, this means I am in Oxfordshire. I judge there to be a peccary on the path. I know that peccaries about means I am in Oxfordshire. But we need a link between the first fact about the peccary, and the first fact about me. That there is a peccary on the path must make this the thing for me to think. Seeing is to forge that link. I see the peccary; in my seeing it, that there is one becomes the thing for me to think.

The core difference between me and a cat (on present assumptions) is that the cat is Pyrrhonian, I am a judger. But now this can seem to call for a further difference in the nature of our experience. For, in thinking of the link just mentioned, one might think like this. What *really* makes it rational for me to judge there to be a peccary is *the fact* that there is a peccary. If my visual experience is to make that fact bear for me on what to think, then it must provide – make me aware of – something shaped as that fact is for me to respond to with that attitude. For, the thought would be, it is hard to see how anything not so shaped could bear a *rational* relation to whether to think there to be a peccary. So, it may seem, in seeing the scene before me I gain something to respond to that the cat does not – am made aware of something that the cat is not. Such an object of awareness is shaped just as my thoughts are. So, the thought goes, it is shaped by what shapes my thoughts.

So that I am a judger and the cat not now seems to entail a further difference: what I experience in seeing the scene is other than what the cat does – *in experiencing the same scene*. This forces us to look inward for the difference. The difference, we have decided already, is the upshot of conceptual capacities I, but not the cat, enjoy. Now, of course, if the cat and I are watching an approaching game warden, I may experience an uneasiness the cat does not – despite the bird in its mouth. The shiver going up my spine, but not the cat's, would be a difference in what we experience. The cat may thank its lack of conceptual capacities for its aplomb. But if the difference in what we experience is conceived as a difference in what we experience *visually* – how we (thus) experience things *being* visually – my conceptual capacities are responsible for differences in the cat's, and my, objects of *perception* – in this case, sight. And then it seems – there being only one *scene* for the cat and me to gaze at – those differences will have to be found by looking inside. My conceptual capacities certainly do not shape the peccary. If they shape any object of perception, it will have to be one found where no peccary can tread. We are now adrift, cut off from the world.

4. Putnam is, in a number of ways, an antidote to any such drive to look inward to find what is experienced. I begin with what seems most important for the present purpose. Grant that cats are Pyrrhonian, we judgers, and not vice versa. By the preceding line, it is meant to follow that visual experience must provide us different things to respond to than it provides the cat. Putnam shows why it does not.

Cats do not judge, and we do, the thought is, because they lack certain capacities we have: *conceptual* capacities. So it takes conceptual capacities to judge. The idea, in brief, is: to judge is to commit to things being a certain way; to do that one must grasp what it would be for things to be that way – when, that is, they would so count. Putnam shows what is contained in such a grasp; hence what judging requires. Now, one good idea about judging is that we could not *judge* as to how (which ways) our surroundings are – so much as make intelligible *commitments* as to this – unless experience were able to make the way those surroundings are bear, for us, on how to think them; bear for us, that is, according as *what* we experience bears on what is *so*. And the idea, of which Putnam will help disabuse us, is that in order to do that experience must provide us *objects* of experience differing from those feline experience supplies a cat. Any such idea, I have suggested, is disastrous.

In *Cord* Putnam makes the right point with an image borrowed from Cora Diamond (1981). Long before that, though, he made the point without that image. Seeing this will help see how he matters to present matters. The image is of a *face* of a concept (or of a way for things, or for something, to be). Applying that image (before developing it), a conceptual capacity would be one to see the *face* of being such-and-such way there is for things to be – e.g., the face of a thing being a sofa – in its indefinite potential manifestations in things, or some thing, being as they are/it is. Following Wittgenstein, Putnam develops the image, in *Cord*, in terms of games. When would a game be a form of poker? Is there a recipe for this? There need not be. If I invent a game, like central cases of poker in some respects, but which one can play by oneself, to a *Spielkenner's* eye – the eye of someone with a proper sense for what *matters* in poker – my invention might just be recognizable as another form of poker, or as not that. What ways for things to be we have in mind when we ask whether something would count as (being) such-and-such, which particular cases are cases of these things, does not float independent of what the *Kenner* – the person with a proper sense for things – would find. This is one crucial point.

To see how central this idea has always been to Putnam, consider another example. Newtonian mechanics speaks of a physical quantity called kinetic energy. Relativistic mechanics speaks of a quantity called energy. Are both these theories thus speaking of *energy*? We can recognize the face of a concept, *energy*, in what both speak of. That *is* an answer. There is no other. (See Travis, 2011, essay 9.) Which should make the centrality of the idea apparent.

On the points so far Putnam is one with Wittgenstein, though not Wittgenstein as read when Putnam first made them. And, I suppose, he is one with all at this roundtable. In *Cord* Putnam uses the point against Michael Dummett's conception of how a concept stands to its applications. But for technical details which do not matter here (the difference between rules and axioms), he might equally well be making it against Paul Feyerabend, or against any of many other people. On Dummett's account a concept is fixed by (given, identifiable) rules for its introduction and elimination. Any different rules would *ipso facto* govern a different concept. If we think of a concept, as we may, as intrinsically of a given way for things to be – of being round, say – then, equally, a way for things to be is fixed by such rules. It is the way things would be just in case those rules licensed counting things being as they are as things being that way. Again, different rules *ipso facto* speak of a different way for things to be. If this is so, then if Newton spoke of energy, Einstein did not, and vice versa. To which Putnam says in *Cord*,

> The difference between Dummett's Wittgenstein and Diamond's Wittgenstein parallels the difference we saw earlier between Dummett and myself. Dummett wants to say that the rules for the application of expressions such as 'too small to see' change with the invention of the microscope, and therefore the meanings of the expressions change, or rather they are given new meanings in their new contexts

of use. I want to say that the question is not one of distinguishing between the 'rules' of the activity of using words and components of the activity that are not 'rules', and that here too the question is one of our ways of 'seeing the face' of one activity in another.
(Putnam 1999: 64)

A concept is not identified by any given set of principles, or rules, in the way Dummett (along with many others) supposes. It may be that it applies (is satisfied) according to such-and-such principles, given the occasion there in fact will be (or in fact can be) for applying it. But its applications are not bound by any such principles in the sense that whatever applied differently simply would not be that concept, no matter what. Different occasions for applying it are liable to require different principles of application. Or at least the concept being, and being of, what it is always leaves room for that.

I will make Putnam's point in several ways before I am done – just now by asking after how *recognition* capacities relate to conceptual capacities. The image, *face of ...* , appeals to resemblances with the phenomenon of facial recognition. One can recognize a human face, or, again, a similarity between faces within a given family, or between Pia's face and, say, Nicole Kidman's. One can recognize Pia's face across the span of a lifetime, and through a wide range of distortions life, or beauticians, may inflict on it. Just at this point, there is an idea which can spoil the comparison sought for. Facial recognition is a topic for psychologists. It is not obvious what allows us to see right away that that is David Soul at the next table, twenty years after his last appearance. But a psychologist might find out. The idea is precisely to look for features, to which we are sensitive, and which remain constant across the years. It is no mean intellectual achievement to find them. But they can be found. One *might* try to conceive the concepts, to which Putnam applies the image, on this model: what features remain constant across all the cases of what would fit the concept is not evident. It would be a considerable intellectual achievement to find them. But they are there, and may be found.

This would spoil the image, which was to be one of there being, in some sense, *no* features in common to all the cases where a concept applies – except that they are all ones of being that which the concept is a concept of – a way for things, or for something, to be – and are all recognizable as one by a *Kenner* – one with a proper sense for such things. But the image is not spoiled if we attend to what success for the psychologist would be. The psychologist identifies features which *do* allow us to recognize a face, as encountered in the circumstances in which we might encounter it. It would be good enough, perhaps more than that, if he could do that much. Working according to our sensitivity to those features, we can count as having a *capacity* to tell a face. For *most* things there are to recognize, any *such* capacity is liable to stop being that in a hostile environment. Perhaps you can recognize Pia by her face. But perhaps not if everyone has plastic surgery so as to look just like her; or if she has radical enough plastic surgery so as not to. The surgery would not detract from the psychologist's achievement. That the capacity he seeks is one liable to fail is what makes that achievement possible in the first place.

A *conceptual* capacity positions us to do something a recognition capacity, as just conceived, would not. It positions us to recognize when a given recognition capacity – an ability to tell peccaries, say, when you see one – has ceased to be that. It allows us to make sense of the idea that, while it would be a peccary if this were decided by those features to which the some-time recognition capacity is sensitive, for all that it is not one. I have described a cognitive achievement to which a psychologist might aspire, *in re* recognizing someone's face. We need not suppose that a parallel achievement is in the cards when it comes to recognizing when a recognition capacity like that for faces would have failed – what it might be for something to have *those* features, but not be a peccary, or Pia's face. There may be all sorts of things that could make a situation count as one which was that way. And now we have the wanted image. Someone – the *Kenner* – may *have* the capacity to recognize what our *conceptual* capacities position us to see, to make the right sense, on the right occasion, of those situations these capacities allow us to understand; but there need be nothing external to his sense for such things, standing towards *what* he is prepared to recognize as those abstract features of faces, discussed above, stand towards an instance of the face, to which a *Kenner's* sense could be held accountable. This is a form of an idea which, I think, has informed much of what is most exciting in John McDowell's philosophy.

How, if this is right, would a conceptual capacity relate to a recognition capacity, construed, as above, as a proper subject for psychology? Such a recognition capacity would be exhausted by some set of principles governing its operations; the conceptual capacity would not. What this need not mean, though, is that a conceptual capacity is, intrinsically, sensitive to things of a very different shape than a recognition capacity might be. We tell pigs by their looks. We are sensitive to the presence of a certain look. We can thus tell pigs when we see them, at sight. When we tell, of a particular case, that it is what would be, or not, a case of things being such-and-such way, we need not be telling by, or sensitive to, anything very different in kind. Experience – say, visual experience – cannot make the world bear on what we are to think unless it engages with our conceptual capacities. It must provide that to which such capacities are sensitive; that by which we can *see* the reason there is to think that, say, there is a pig before us – perhaps just that there is one. But such capacities need not be different in kind from those which allow us to tell a pig when we see one. And, I will suggest, for that they need not bring any more into view than *might* be in view for a cat too when confronted by a pig. This is *one* way to spell out Putnam's point. Now for another.

5. The above point about conceptual capacities, and their relation to recognition capacities, conceived as subjects for the psychologist, is so important that I am going to put it in another form. Frege found something *intrinsically* general about a thought – a particular way for a posture towards the world to make *its* correctness, independent of any taking of it, turning *entirely* on how things are. Frege expressed the point thus:

> A thought always contains something which reaches out beyond the particular case, by which it presents this to consciousness as falling under a certain generality.
>
> (1882: *Kernsatz* 4)

A thought *demands* something of the particular case for its being as represented. It cannot, the idea is, demand *everything*; that is, that the particular case be *just* the way it is. One can put this by saying that, for principled reasons, it must be so that things *could have* been represented as any given thought represents them without their *being* precisely as they are. Not *everything* in how things are matters to whether one could represent them as any given thought does; not everything, thus, matters to whether they *are* as represented. This is to say that if the particular case *is* as represented, if it is the way it was represented to be, then it instances (realizes) things being that way in only one of an indefinite variety of ways this could be done. If the pig is in the sty while Pia prepares a daube, then there is also a way for the pig to be in the sty while Pia suns herself in the *chaise longue*. There is a *range* of cases in which things being as they were would be their being such that the pig is in the sty. There is a generality – something for a particular case to be – which reaches just to that range. Such is the generality under which the thought that the pig is in the sty brings the particular case. Such is the intrinsic generality of thoughts.

The particular case is that which the thought represents as a certain way. Which is just: things being as they are. Things being as they are, so far as that goes, does not bring anything under any given generality; or present anything to consciousness as so falling. If it presented anything to consciousness, that could only be itself. It cannot be instanced in an indefinite *variety* of ways. If we were to speak of it as instanced at all, that would have to be only by itself. But that would be at best a degenerate use of 'instance'. In fact, it is not *instanced* by anything. For it makes itself hostage to nothing for correctness. It is neither correct nor incorrect (except in the sense that it is just *so* wrong for Bush to be president). All of which is to say: it reaches to no range of cases; it has no reach. The generality of a thought consists of its representing things as some way that might be instanced in an indefinite variety of ways. What does the instancing *has* no such generality. If we call what has this generality *(the) conceptual*, we might call what lacks it *(the) nonconceptual*.

Frege further tells us,

> The fundamental logical relation is that of an object falling under a concept. All relations between concepts are reducible to this.
> (1892–95: 25)

Frege's notion of a concept is of something at the level of reference, not sense (in his sense) – the level at which, for him, a thought belongs. He does not quite manage to invest his notion with that generality which marks a thought. But, as he does insist, a thought, on any decomposition of it, has some element – some proper contribution to the thought's doing what it does – which shares the generality of a thought (in fact, whose generality the thought restricts in some way), which is being about a way there is for *something* to be, so under which those objects which are that way may be said to fall. Such elements identify one thing we might call, and what I here will call, a concept.

If an object is that way for something to be which identifies the concept – the way it, or that element in thoughts which identifies it, represents things – we may speak of that object as falling under the concept. For an object to fall under a concept in this sense is for its being as it is to be it being the way that concept represents a thing; or, equally, for things being as they are to be this object being that way. The object's being as it is thus *instances* what the concept is a concept of, or, in shorthand, simply the concept.

An object's being as it is belongs to the nonconceptual. So the fundamental relation Frege speaks of can be read as, or as mirroring, an at least equally fundamental relation between the conceptual and the nonconceptual. This relation is fundamental, *inter alia*, in this way: if we are to be thinkers on whose thinking the world may bear *rationally* – so if we are to be thinkers at all – then we had better be able to recognize instances of its holding. One could not so much as have the conceptual in view (or in mind) without such competence. Perhaps being a crisp entails being greasy. But one does not grasp *that* fact (or thought) without an adequate grasp on what an instance of a crisp, or being greasy, would be. Absent any grasp of how these concepts reach, what would make it being a *crisp* and *greasy* that one is thinking of? This is another point Putnam has made unmistakable for us. Take any structure of internal relations, such as entailments, between concepts, divorced from any identification of the reach of these concepts to the nonconceptual, and the 'concepts' remain mere tags: *nothing* in such a structure can make the tags reach to some one set of cases – bring things under some one generality – rather than indefinitely many others. Such is the message of 'Models and Reality' (Putnam 1977).

A recognition capacity in the present sense – an ability to recognize a pig at sight, say – would be a capacity to recognize the reach of the conceptual to the nonconceptual. One sees, and recognizes, instances of something being a pig. By the same token, so would a conceptual capacity in the present sense. As it had better be if it is to be a *conceptual* capacity at all. For it is, *inter alia*, an ability to recognize the limits of any given recognition capacity. So if we have recognition capacities, and their corresponding conceptual capacities, we are in shape to be thinkers; to think things of the world we inhabit. And, I think, only if that. I further think we can feel safe here.

Perception's *essential* role in the life of a *thinker* is to allow the world to bear, for him, on what he is to think according to the bearing of what that thinker is aware of on what is so. It thus does such things as allowing the presence of the pig before me to bear, for me, on whether to think *that* there is a pig there. For it to serve this role requires nothing less than for it to bring the nonconceptual – that which the world provides – within reach of our recognition (so conceptual) capacities. Perhaps an easy way to see this is this. Perhaps that a pig is in the sty means that the farmer is home. Perhaps perception – vision, in this case – allows me to see that a pig is in the sty. If it accomplishes this much, then it has brought that fact about the world to bear on what I am to think: if I also see enough of factive meaning, the thing for me to think is that the farmer is home. But if that were *all* perception accomplished, or the only accomplishment to its credit, it would not have fulfilled its appointed role. For (see above discussion), if the pig is in the sty, this is so in just *one* particular way of the indefinitely many ways there are for it to be so – e.g., the pig sleeping in the mud, or standing by the railings. What perception must make available to me, to make the world bear on my thinking as it is perception's job to make it bear, is *the way* in which that general way for things to be, a pig being in the sty, is instanced by things being as they are. This it can only do by bringing the nonconceptual in view; making it available for exercise by me of my recognition, and conceptual capacities.

Such is needed, for one thing, if perception is to allow me to see how *this case* of a pig being in the sty bears on what else is so. Perhaps, often, a pig in the sty is black pudding on the way; but not when it is this prize pig, or the neighbour's pig – the sort of sizing up I must be positioned for if that pig in the sty is to get its full bearing, for me, on what to think and do – e.g., whether to gather apples for the *geitespek*. More crucially, it is the pig's presence in the sty that bears on whether there is a pig before me. If I am to take it, fully rationally, simply on grounds of what I see, that there is a pig before me, seeing must confront me with nothing less than the pig's presence, in its full glory, as it were: things being as they are, at least at that place where the pig is present. I must be able to see, e.g., just what sort of thing it is that is the pig in the sty here; just *how* it is. One reason is this: suppose it is a piglet, or a pot-bellied pig, or a tusked wild boar that is in the sty; or, again, a pig carcass, or just the hind quarters of the pig, the rest of it in that crib of corn, or the baby's crib. *Is* the way things are the pig being in the sty? That depends on what you understand by a pig being in a sty. Such is one sort of question over which it is perception's job to allow me to exercise my savoir-faire, or cultivated sensibility.

So perception makes – and must make – the way things are bear, for me, on how to think things are through positioning me, *inter alia*, to exercise my abilities, such as they are, to recognize instances of (the image of) what Frege calls the fundamental logical relation – that between the nonconceptual and the conceptual where the first instances the last. Now for Putnam's point. Conceptual capacities need not reduce to recipes; to recognition capacities insofar as these are tractable problems for psychology, as conceived above. It need not always be that for a concept to fit is for what it fits to have a certain constellation of (perhaps highly abstract) features. Conceptual capacities are liable to rely, at least for some purposes, on an irreducible sense for how the nonconceptual would connect to some given bit of the conceptual. It will do for the exercise of such capacities to have access, notably perceptual access, to the nonconceptual, which is to be related to one or another bit of the conceptual. Indeed, as we have just seen, often nothing less than such access will do for full exercise of such *irreducible* capacities.

Indeed, as we have seen, conceptual capacities *cannot* always reduce to recipes. Just maybe, a conceptual capacity *in re* being a bachelor reduces to capacities to recognize when something's being as it is would count as its being male, and when it would count as its being married. But then, what of these capacities? If *all* our conceptual capacities were thus reducible, we would be in that position which 'Models and Reality' showed to be impossible: a position in which all there was to bring the conceptual within our view was internal relations between bits of it – a structure identified independent of how anything it structures reaches to the nonconceptual. In that position, thought vanishes entirely from our lives.

If conceptual capacities were all reducible, it might do for perception merely to bring bits of the conceptual to bear on our thought; merely to afford us awareness of them (if we can even really make sense of this idea). But our conceptual capacities do not work like that, which is another reason that perception cannot have done its job if it falls short of bringing the nonconceptual in view. Conversely, it would be fine for it to do just that. Exercising our capacities to recognize what would count as things being one or another given way, we can then supply relevant bits of the conceptual ourselves. This is what Frege had in mind when he wrote:

> Although a law of nature obtains quite independently of whether we think of it or not, it does not emit light or sound waves by which our visual or auditory nerves could be affected. But don't I see that this flower has five petals? One can say that; but then uses the word 'see' not in the sense of mere perception by means of light, but something involving thought and judgement.
>
> (1897: 149)

The pig before me, when I see it, is what allows me to see – recognize, register – that there is a pig before me. Perception need only bring the pig in view. The rest lies in my capacities for knowing what it is I see – when perception has brought a pig in view; when it thus makes that there is a pig before me the thing for me to judge.

6. Which expressions, on which faces, are ones of grief? Which circumstances would be ones in which Newton and Einstein spoke of the same physical quantity (one truly, one falsely) in speaking of 'energy'? Answers to such questions are not provided simply by things being as they are. It takes a *Kenner* to see them. Just for this reason, experience must supply us with something for a *Kenner's* capacities to work on. Just for that reason, perception must do no less, and need do no more, than bring the nonconceptual into view. Some philosophers, such as Gareth Evans and Christopher Peacocke, have missed this point. For them, perception could make the world bear on what we are to think *only* by presenting us with recognizable bits of the conceptual. Peacocke puts it this way:

> By perceiving the world, we frequently learn whether a judgement with a given conceptual content is true or not. This is possible only because a perceptual experience has a correctness condition whose holding may itself exclude, or require, the truth of a conceptual content.
>
> (1992: 66)

It is thus for experience to make something conceptual do the *world's* bearing on what we are to think – a hopeless assignment. For Evans and Peacocke, that assignment is to be carried out in experience representing things as so – for reasons we have seen, again a hopeless project.

Such a view inevitably sends us searching inward looking for the *real*, or first, objects of visual awareness. Why? Suppose that visual experience provided (visual) awareness merely of what was before one's eyes – a scene. Bracketing billboards and the like, scenes do not represent anything as so. For a scene to do that, it, just in being as it is, would have to fix some generality under which it presented things – presumably just itself – as falling. It would have to reach in a particular way to what were to be instances of things being as it represented them. As we saw in setting out the conceptual–nonconceptual distinction, such a thing is just not on. On the other hand, if experience representing things as so is to be the route by which it makes the world (or anything) bear *for me* on what I am to think, then it must be recognizable to me just *what* way my experience represents things to be – in a fairly minimal sense: I must be able to say of the way I find things, and perhaps of ways I might, that, given this, my experience was *right* (*casu quo* wrong) as to how things were. My experiencing, visually, what I do must make this so recognizable. My experiencing, visually, the *scene* will not turn the trick. So I must experience, visually, something else – just what Evans provides, or tries to, in making perceptual experience an *internal state*, whose content we get at by asking ourselves certain questions as to how, in it, things seem to us – answers to which float entirely free (in principle) of how the scene in view *is*, or how *it* seems.

Evans and Peacocke are on a hopeless, though as we have also seen, needless, search. A search for what distinguishes us from cats (more generally, Pyrrhonian creatures) *can* send us on a similar, and, I think, similarly doomed, search. The idea would be: for non-Pyrrhonian creatures like us, conceptual capacities would have to shape *something* in experience. Kant thought they shaped reality itself, taking reality to be just what there is to experience, and to judge of – things being as they are. (Kant thought they shaped only a special tract of reality. But I bracket that.) So, for Kant, they shaped precisely the only objects of (our) perception there are or could be. But suppose that, while holding the general view, you reject the idea that conceptual capacities can shape a peccary. So they do not shape reality in this sense. So, if there *is* any perception, they do not shape its objects – what is perceived, e.g., the scene before you. Now you are on your way inward, I have suggested, looking for what they do shape.

Of course, with Putnam and Frege on board, conceptual capacities are still located *somewhere* in experience. Frege put things rightly. They are located in our responses to what we experience (perceptually): in our recognizing what we do *in* that which we experience, e.g., visually, that of which *sight* affords awareness – such things as a case of a pig in a sty. But now, suppose we do not want to locate conceptual capacities merely there. One insists on their shaping the very things which, by means of our senses, or at least in perceiving perceptually, we experience. Then we are, inevitably, on our way inward. We must end up in something like Evans' position, in which perceptual experiences are internal states.

I want to end, then, by posing a question to John. It is a question, not an accusation: I am not at all confident I understand him on the relevant point. But the question is whether John McDowell is not committed to (a very subtle version, to be sure) of that same gaze inward that I located in Evans. A text which raises this question – and which I think I don't understand – is a response to Hubert Dreyfus, entitled 'What Myth?' (2009) In it, John takes up the question of what distinguishes us from cats. (I take bits of this out of order.) He writes,

> My experience might disclose to me that an opening in a wall is big enough for me to go through. A cat might see that an opening in a wall is big enough for it to go through. My experience would be world-disclosing and so conceptual in form in the sense I have introduced. The cat's perceptual intake would not be world-disclosing and so, in the relevant sense, not conceptual in form. It is irrelevant to

this difference between the cases that there is that match in what the cat and I would be getting to know through the exercise of our perceptual capacities.

(McDowell 2009: 321)

The match between the cat and John is: both would come to know that an opening in the wall is big enough. The difference is that John's experience would be 'world-disclosing', the cat's not. For the moment, let 'world-disclosing' be a place-holder for what distinguishes feline from human experience. Anyway, John tells us, that difference has a consequence. John's perceptual intake is, in a certain sense, 'conceptual in form'. Not the cat's. So John takes in, perceptually, something the cat does not. He thus experiences, *perceptually*, e.g., visually, something the cat does not. I do not think John means something like, the cat experiences things being all bright and shiny, John their being all dull and matte-finished, or that, where John sees a hole in the wall, the cat draws a blank, or sees what looks as though it is bricked-up. I note that if what John takes in, perceptually, is just what he sees, or what is before his eyes, then, since it is the same *scene* John and the cat see, their perceptual intake is so far the same. I note too that that the hole in the wall is big enough for a philosopher to pass through, or just that there is a hole, is not *in* the scene, as the whole itself is. (Cf. Frege on petals.)

It *looks* as if other passages give a clue to what John has in mind. Here are two:

> Granting that belief-formation, on the part of a rational animal, is an exercise of the animal's rationality, why should we suppose rationality must be operative also in the constitution of that to which perceptual belief-formation is rationally responsive? ... Perceptual experiencing, on the part of a rational animal, is not just something that can elicit rational responses in the shape of perceptual beliefs. ... the perceptual experiencing of rational animals is itself rational openness to the world – which includes openness to affordances, as I have been insisting. So capacities that belong to a subject's rationality must be operative in the subject's experiencing itself, not just in responses to it.
>
> (McDowell 2009: 316–17)

> What is important is this: if an experience is world-disclosing ... all its content is present in a form in which ... it is suitable to constitute contents of conceptual capacities.
>
> (ibid.: 319)

So perceptual experiencing of rational animals – us and not cats – is 'rational openness to the world'. This is, presumably, another form of the distinction John is getting at with the term 'world-disclosing'. This requires, he tells us, that a subject's rationality must be operative in his experiencing itself, not just in responses to it. Which means, on the above line of thought, that it is operative in *constituting* 'that to which perceptual belief formation is rationally responsive'. I take it that perceptual belief formation is belief formation on the basis of what is experienced; so that what it is responsive to is that which is perceptually experienced.

Why should one seem to see such connections? Suppose that *what* I experience perceptually – by sight – is just the trail before me, that peccary glaring at me, half turned in my direction. I might respond to that in recognizing what I thus see as a case of a peccary being on the (or a) trail before me. *That* is a rational response to what I see, as I – I claim Putnam and I – insist. It exercises my ability to link up the nonconceptual with the conceptual, to register instances of Frege's fundamental logical relation (or its mirror, as constructed above). So far, my conceptual capacities have no role in constituting *what* I respond to. For them to do that, they would have to constitute, in part, the peccary, or its glare, or something of this sort.

But John thinks – or *seems* to think (this is a question) – that my perceptual intake, what I respond to, what I apply my capacities to in forming beliefs based on it, must be 'conceptual in form', or 'in a form suitable to constitute the content of conceptual capacities'. So it could not just be the peccary, poised as it is, or its pawing of the path, or etc. It is tempting, I confess, to read this as an idea that what I, but not the cat, *perceive*, that of which I am afforded visual awareness, or some of it, belongs to the *conceptual*, rather than the nonconceptual, as if it were such things as *being on a path*, a way there *is* for something to be. Behind which it is also tempting, I confess, to find a picture on which, for my benefit, but not the cat's, the world is presented articulated into those particular ways for *things* in general, or for some thing, to be, which things *are* in being as they are (or the scene before me in being as it is). What would make such an idea attractive (to the extent that it can be) would be the idea that only something of conceptual form could bear *rationally* on questions of what to think (or of what is *so*) – the very idea which moves Evans and Peacocke to their own form of cutting us off irretrievably from the world.

I hope, and expect, that I am reading John wrongly. In any event, there is this to say about the above ideas. First, as Frege saw, the idea of encountering the conceptual *perceptually* makes no sense. This is what Frege is getting at when he observes that, while the sun, or a flower, is a visible thing, emitting rays arriving in our eyes, that the sun has set, or that the flower has five petals is not. It is not before us to be seen. Neither are ways there are for a thing to be. They are something else entirely. Second, there is no one way which is *the* way the world, or that part of it, the scene before me, articulates just in being as it is. Nor does merely its being as it is alone decide just what generalities it instances. Nor does what perception provides for me to respond to commit me to any one particular way of articulating it. This is related to the conceptual not being literally *in* the scene. Third, if the world is ever going to bear for *me* on what to think (more generally, what to do), according as it *does* bear on what the thing to think (or do) would be, then perception had better provide me opportunity for exercising my capacities to link the nonconceptual with the conceptual – to recognize those particular instancings, each in its own way, of those ways for things to be which are in fact instanced. Hence, fourth, if I am equipped with capacities for making the world so bear – capacities which acts may well lack – there is no need for those capacities to shape that which I experience perceptually (visually). That would not just be *de trop*; it would spoil everything.

Finally (see point 1), if we needed to make bits of the *conceptual* objects of perceptual awareness, we would have to look elsewhere than the scene in view, where they are not to be found. We would have to look elsewhere, too, to find things that our conceptual capacities could shape. Where the peccaries are is, as noted, the wrong place to look. So it would be no surprise if here, just as with Evans and Peacocke, though in a different form, the wholly mistaken idea that only the conceptual can bear rationally on what to think *so* – that *rational* relations hold only *inside* the conceptual – drives us to posit inner objects of perceptual awareness, parts of every experience in which – if we are lucky – the world is revealed to us. But I neither know nor expect that John holds that wholly mistaken idea.

7. Putnam speaks of a face of the conceptual. He also speaks of a face of perception. He models both on facial expressions. Here he endorses Diamond, who explains that when we say two faces have the same expression,

> This is not like saying the mouths are the same length, the eyes the same distance apart; it is not that kind of description. But it is not a description of *something else*, the expression, distinct from that curved line, the dots, and so on.
> (Diamond 1981: 249)

And he goes on to say:

> Seeing an expression in a picture face is not just a matter of seeing the lines and dots; rather it is a matter of seeing something *in* the lines and dots – but this is not to say that it is a matter of seeing something *besides* the lines and dots.
> (Putnam 1999: 63)

What I have been trying to bring out above is that to see things which are present in this sort of way, one needs to have the nonconceptual in view; something on which to exercise capacities to link that of a sort to fall under given generalities with the generalities it in fact falls under. With that in view, there is no need for any other sort of experiential intake on which to base, rationally, judgements as to how things are in our environment. The best of John's work stresses the presence, in precisely this way, of a wide range of phenomena which have seemed intractable to philosophers who failed to recognize this form of presence – such things as virtues, or understanding, or personal persistence through time. He, if anyone, should have a hold on what this means for the nature of experience.

A recognition routine might settle whether a peccary is yonder by presence or absence of those distinctive stiff bristles. The routine would work only in amenable environments. If it were the custom to shave peccaries, or some other beast had the same bristles, it would not work. A conceptual capacity addresses the very different question of what it is for something to be a peccary – what would and would not count (when). Is a butchered peccary in the shop window a peccary? Conceptual capacities are engaged in moving from routine to routine; from one way of recognizing something to another. They get us from Newton's account of how to tell how much energy an object has to Einstein's, revealing one thing each would be right about in favourable circumstances. *Such* achievements may be beyond the reach of non-linguistic creatures. For all of which (modulo differences in visual equipment) what they see remains what we do: none other than what may come as well before their, as before our, eyes.

Bibliography

Diamond, Cora (1981) 'Wright's Wittgenstein', *The Philosophical Quarterly*, vol. 31, 1981; reprinted in *The Realistic Spirit*, Cambridge MA: The MIT Press, 205–24.
Dummett, Michael (1981) *The Interpretation of Frege's Philosophy*, London: Duckworth.
Fodor, Jerry (1998) *Concepts*, Oxford: Oxford University Press.
——(2008) *LOT 2*, Oxford: Oxford University Press.
Frege, Gottlob (1882) '17 Kernsätze zur Logik', *Nachgelassene Schriften*, 189–90.
——(1892–95) 'Ausfuhrungen über Sinn under Bedeutung', *Nachgelassene Schriften*, 2nd edn. Hamburg: Felix Meiner, 1983, 128–36.
——(1897) 'Logik', *Nachgelassene Schriften*, 2nd edn. Hamburg: Felix Meiner, 1983, 137–63.
McDowell, John (2009) 'What Myth', in McDowell, *The Engaged Intellect*, Cambridge, MA: Harvard University Press, 308–23.
Peacocke, Christopher (1992) *A Study of Concepts*, Cambridge MA: MIT Press.
Prichard, H. A. (1950) 'Perception', in Prichard, *Knowledge and Perception*, Oxford: Oxford University Press, 52–68.
Putnam, Hilary (1977) 'Models and Reality', Presidential Address to the Association for Symbolic Logic; reprinted in *Realism and Reason: Philosophical Papers*, vol. 3, Cambridge: Cambridge University Press, 1983.
——(1999) *The Threefold Cord*, New York: Columbia University Press.
Travis, Charles (2011) *Objectivity and the Parochial*, Oxford: Oxford University Press.
Wittgenstein, Ludwig (1953) *Philosophical Investigations*, Oxford: Basil Blackwell.
——(1969) *On Certainty*, Oxford: Basil Blackwell.

12

CONCEPTS IN PERCEPTUAL EXPERIENCE

Putnam and Travis

John McDowell

In his Dewey Lectures (published as Putnam 1999), Hilary Putnam argues eloquently against a picture according to which in perception our minds relate to the world outside our skins only at an interface constituted by our sensory receptors. This picture can seem compulsory if we identify our minds with machinery inside us: our nervous systems, or parts of them. But Putnam urges that we should not make that identification. We should understand talk of minds as a way of talking about minded beings *qua* minded. And to be minded – to "have" a mind – is (among other things) to have cognitive capacities that reach beyond our sensory surfaces, all the way to the things we perceive or think about.

Charles Travis thinks he can exploit Putnam's rejection of the interface picture in arguing against the very idea that perceptual experiences have content. He thinks the idea that distinctively rational capacities are operative in the experience of rational animals, in a way that is up to a point analogous to the way conceptual capacities are operative in their judgments, tends in the direction of the interface picture. He thinks it risks forcing us to suppose that what we encounter in perception is not the objects in the environment that we, for instance, see, but instead some items inside the supposed interface.

But a general association between the very idea of content and the interface picture cannot be right. In rejecting the interface picture, Putnam is concerned with conception, as he puts it, just as much as with perception. His point is not just that our perceptual capacities can reach all the way to the worldly things that we, for instance, see. Even when our capacities for thought are directed at a subject matter that is not perceptually present to us, they can reach all the way to the reality in virtue of which, in the best case, our thinking represents things as they are. Modifying a remark of Wittgenstein's that Putnam cites approvingly we can say: "When we think that such-and-such is the case, we – and our thinking – do not stop anywhere short of the fact; but we think: *this – is – so*" (Wittgenstein 1953: §95). And it would be absurd to suppose the claim that thought reaches all the way to its subject matter debars us from crediting acts of thinking with content. The idea of content-involving states or goings-on does not bring the interface picture with it. So far as rejecting the interface picture goes, the idea that experiences have content may be innocuous.

Putnam thinks it is a mistake to follow Kant in working with a restricted notion of experience, one that fits only rational animals, in something like the traditional sense. Putnam insists that if we want to say "No percepts without concepts," we have to accept that animals that are not rational have concepts. And of course that is right if we make "percepts" apply indifferently, as of course it can, to the upshots of perceptual capacities in rational and non-rational animals. But Putnam thinks this rules out supposing that conceptual capacities, in a sense in which only rational animals can have such capacities, might be operative in the perceptual experience of rational animals, even though such capacities are *ex hypothesi* not operative in the perception of non-rational animals. I think this reflects a blind spot for the point of the restrictiveness that characterizes the Kantian notion of experience, and for the possibilities of combining it with common sense about what perception is for non-rational animals.

Travis shares this blind spot. And Travis connects this with resistance to the interface picture. The Kantian conception, with its insistence on seeing the experiences of rational animals as actualizations of capacities that belong to their rationality, figures for Travis as a way to succumb to the pressure to look inward, rather than to the surroundings of perceiving animals, for the objects of their experiences: that is, as a way to lose Putnam's admirable insistence that the interface picture is wrong, that in our experience we are open to the world.

I think Travis is out on a limb of his own here. Putnam's objection to the Kantian conception is not that he thinks, as Travis does, that it pushes us towards the interface picture in our understanding of the perceptual capacities we rational animals have. Putnam's objection to the Kantian conception is that he thinks it cannot do justice to the way perceptual capacities enable non-rational animals to be on to things in their environments.

As I said, I think this is a blind spot on Putnam's part. The Kantian conception does not threaten a sane understanding of what perception is for non-rational animals.

Nothing in the Kantian conception requires its adherents to resist if someone, for instance Putnam, wants to use the word "experience" differently, so that it fits whenever a creature, rational or not, is on to things through the operation of perceptual capacities. If "percept" goes with "experience," and if we use "concept" in such a way that only rational animals can have concepts, that would mean that we cannot say "No percepts without concepts." Alternatively, we could keep "No percepts without concepts" by giving "concepts" a different use. Nothing in the Kantian conception requires its adherents to resist if someone wants to use the word "concept" in such a way that any creature, rational or not, that can discriminate X's from non-X's thereby counts as having the concept of an X. We would just need a different expression to apply to capacities that are distinctive in being operative in rational thought. There are no substantive divergences yet in view; we just have to take care to keep track of the different ways of using these words.

An adherent of the Kantian conception can acknowledge that the perceptual capacities of animals, whether rational or not, enable them to be on to things in their environments. There is no problem about combining that acknowledgment with holding that conceptual capacities, in a sense in which only rational animals can have conceptual capacities, are in play in the experience of rational animals. Putnam thinks the Kantian conception cannot cohere with registering a commonality between the perceptual capacities of rational animals and those of other animals. But that is simply wrong. Insisting on a discontinuity between what perception is for rational animals and what perception is for non-rational animals is perfectly consistent with acknowledging that in both cases capacities for perception put a creature that has them on to objects that are, for instance, in its field of view.

What is the point of insisting on the discontinuity?

Without prejudice to commonalities between rational and non-rational animals, we can say that rational animals are special in being capable of knowledge on a demanding conception: roughly, belief for which a subject has an entitlement that is potentially self-conscious, an entitlement that includes a potential for knowing what it is that entitles one to one's belief. As with "experience" and "concepts", so with "knowledge." We can concern ourselves with knowledge in this demanding sense without needing to deny that there is a perfectly good sense in which the perceptual capacities of non-rational animals equip them with knowledge. But to concern ourselves with the demanding conception is to concern ourselves with a kind of knowledge that draws on capacities possessed only by rational animals.

Now it is obvious that perceptual acquisition of knowledge involves sensibility: that is, a differential responsiveness to features of the environment, made possible by properly functioning sensory systems. But sensibility, so understood, is something we share with non-rational animals. So if perception is to afford us knowledge that conforms to that demanding conception, our having that knowledge available to us must involve not only sensibility but also capacities that belong to our rationality.

It may seem that we can accommodate this thought without needing to accept the Kantian idea that capacities distinctive to us as rational animals are operative in our experiences themselves.

Consider Travis's example of an experience in which he sees an animal in a way that enables him to know that it is a peccary. This knowledge is knowledge in the demanding sense. The concept of a peccary – the content deployed in exercises of a conceptual capacity, in a sense in which only rational animals can have conceptual capacities – figures in what Travis's experience enables him to know. And we can accommodate this without supposing that a conceptual capacity with that content is in play in his experience itself. Travis's possession of the concept of a peccary includes an ability to tell a peccary when he sees one, at least on a good enough sighting. On the occasion he envisages in his example, that ability is triggered into operation by the animal, which his experience anyway makes visually present to him. The force of that "anyway" is this: his having the experience we are considering, in which the animal is visually present to him, does not itself draw on the conceptual capacity that is operative when he thinks of things as peccaries.

So far so good, I think. But Travis thinks the point generalizes, and that is open to question. In Travis's picture, perceptual acquisition of knowledge on the demanding conception draws on distinctively rational capacities only, so to speak, downstream from experiences themselves, in judgments in which one makes what one can of things that experiences anyway make perceptually present to one. And now the force of that "anyway" is quite general: having things present to one in experience does not itself draw on conceptual capacities. In Travis's picture, we do not need to appeal to anything except sensibility, which we share with non-rational animals, in order to say how experience makes things present to us. Capacities that are special to rational animals, not shared with other possessors of sensibility, do not enter into our experiences themselves.

This flies in the face of what I think is a Kantian insight. To have things present to us in experience is to have things given to us for knowing on the demanding conception: that is, given to us as the rational subjects, the potential possessors of knowledge on the demanding conception, that we are. And Kant thinks capacities that are special to rational animals must be operative in our having things given to us in that way. That is, capacities that belong to our rationality must be operative in our experiences themselves, not just in judgments in which we apply concepts to things that our experiences anyway make present to us. As I have conceded, we need not suppose that a capacity whose content is given by "peccary" is operative in Travis's experience of seeing a peccary, even though the experience enables him to know that what he sees is a peccary. But Kant's idea implies that the point does not generalize in the way Travis thinks it does. Some conceptual capacities – perhaps capacities involving concepts of the animal's colour, size, shape, posture, and so forth – must be operative in the peccary's being visually present to Travis, visually given to him for knowing on the demanding conception.

As the way I have expressed the thought indicates, there is nothing wrong with holding that in experience things are given to us for knowing. But we can put the Kantian thought like this: when Travis takes it that sensibility by itself suffices for things to be given to us in experience, he falls into a version of the Myth of the Given. What should be innocuous givenness degenerates into mythical Givenness.

As Travis understands it, the Kantian thought implies that our conceptual capacities shape what perceiving gives us to respond to. That is why he thinks it generates pressure towards the inward look. His conceptual capacities certainly do not shape the peccary he sees in his example. So the idea that his conceptual capacities shape what perceiving gives him to respond to would lead to looking elsewhere than in the environment, where the peccary is, for what his experience gives him to respond to. Where else, then, but inward? And then we lose Putnam's insight that we must reject the interface picture.

But this starts from a misunderstanding of the Kantian thought. The Kantian thought leaves unthreatened what Travis rightly insists on, that it is the peccary itself, not some inner item, that he encounters in his experience. The Kantian thought is not about what is encountered, but about capacities operative in encountering it in the way Travis does, which is its being given to him for knowing on the demanding conception of knowing.

Suppose there is a cat with Travis on the occasion of his peccary sighting. The Kantian conception does not threaten the idea Travis thinks it threatens, the idea that what Travis sees is the very same thing that the cat may also see, that is, the peccary. Travis's seeing is special, according to the Kantian conception, but not in a way that implies a difference in what is there to be seen by him. In Travis's experience the peccary – the same thing, by all means, that is also seen by the cat – is visually present to him. Its visual presence to him is its being visually given to him for knowing of the distinctively rational sort that he, and not the cat, is capable of. When one says the peccary is visually present to Travis, "is visually present to" expresses a relation whose obtaining draws on distinctively rational capacities had by one of the relata, namely, in this case, Travis. A relation of which that is true is not one in which peccaries, or anything, can stand to cats. But this leaves unthreatened what Travis wants to insist on. What stands in that relation to Travis is the peccary itself, the same thing that stands in a different relation, which we can of course express by "is seen by," to the cat.

I think this answers the question Travis puts to me at the end of his remarks. The question reflects his suspicion of the Kantian conception. He thinks the Kantian conception leads to the conclusion that what rational animals encounter in perception is not what non-rational animals encounter in perception. But it does not. In forming an impression to the contrary, Travis ignores the difference between claims about the content of the perceptual experiences of rational animals and claims about their objects, what is encountered in them.

Clarity about this is not helped by Travis's treatment of the idea of things being as they are or something's being as it is. On the ground that items so specifiable do not have the kind of generality he focuses on, Travis thinks such items belong on the other side of a divide from the conceptual, in a sense (harmlessly non-Fregean) in which the paradigm of the conceptual is a Fregean *Gedanke*. He conceives such items as objects for perceptual experience in something like the sense in which, say, peccaries can be objects for perceptual experience: things that are encountered in experience and, in the case of subjects with the requisite capacities, brought under concepts in judgments based on experience. I think this is confused. A peccary's (say) being as it is does not stand to its being some particular way it can be truly said to be (say grunting) in anything like the relation in which the peccary, which is certainly not a conceptual item in that sense, stands to the concept of being that way: the relation we can express by saying the peccary falls under the concept of being engaged in grunting. The peccary's being as it is does not fall under, but rather includes, its being any particular way it can be truly said to be, which is conceptual in the sense Travis uses. The peccary's being as it is belongs on the same side of the divide Travis should be concerned with as its being any particular way it can truly be said to be.

Putnam suggests that philosophers find the question how language (or thought) makes contact with objects puzzling in a way they should not, and would not if they gave due heed to the retort: "How can there be a problem about talking about, say, houses and trees when we see them all the time?" I think Putnam is right about this, and the Kantian conception of experience, freed from Travis's misreading of it, puts the point in just the right light. (Given his blind spot, this is a light that Putnam himself cannot quite contrive to see it in.)

The point Putnam is making should not seem to turn on a one-way explanatory dependence of conception on perception. If there were nothing to our seeing houses and trees apart from their impinging on our sensibility, how could the fact that we see them make our ability to direct our thoughts at them less mysterious? Houses and trees impinge on the sensibility of cats too, but that does not enable cats to direct thoughts at houses and trees in the sense in which we can, the sense that generates the puzzlement. But we can surely alleviate puzzlement about how our powers of thought can reach all the way to houses and trees, if we can see how such powers are in play not just in judging and claim-making, but also in experiences in which houses and trees themselves, not some internal surrogates, are perceptually, for instance visually, present to us.

Bibliography

Putnam, Hilary (1999) *The Threefold Cord: Mind, Body and World*, New York: Columbia University Press.

Wittgenstein, Ludwig (1953) *Philosophical Investigations*, Oxford: Blackwell.

COMMENTS ON TRAVIS AND MCDOWELL

Hilary Putnam

Travis's "Affording Us the World" and McDowell's "Concepts in Perceptual Experience" are fascinating essays. Travis and McDowell are philosophers whose work I admire and have learned from (which does not mean there aren't any disagreements between us). In his essay, McDowell sees me as agreeing with Travis in a denial that "perceptual experiences have content," but I would not put my view that way. And Travis claims that "(visual) awareness of one's spatial surroundings" is the same with me and with *cats*, and that "ways for things to be" aren't among the things that are "there to be seen," and I have problems with both of those claims. So there is plenty for me to discuss in these papers.

Re: "perceptual experiences have content"

When McDowell says that perceptual experiences have content he means *conceptual content*, as he makes clear. But what is conceptual content? That is not so clear. Moreover, McDowell has himself modified his view in an essay published in 2009.[1] In any case, in his great book, *Mind and World*, McDowell wrote:

> *No subject could be understood as having experiences of color* except against a background of understanding that makes it possible for *judgments endorsing such experiences* to fit into her view of the world.
> (McDowell 1994: 30)

He claimed that this applies also to inner experiences such as the experience of "seeing red" produced by a blow on the head, or even the judgment that I have a pain (ibid.). Thus McDowell's claim that the experiences of a "subject" (by which he means, as he also makes clear, a person capable of understanding the question of the *justification* of any one of her judgments) have conceptual content entails that even sense impressions of the most primitive kind are only possible for such a subject if she has the conceptual abilities required to understand such judgments as "that was an experience of red" or "that was an experience of pain."

In the 2000 essay McDowell gives up the claim that the experiences of such a "subject" (which experiences he refers to by the Kantian term "intuitions") presuppose that the subject *already possesses* the concepts (including demonstrative concepts, like "this shade") needed to describe their content, but he takes the ability to *form* such concepts to be "in play" when one has those experiences, and he describes those abilities as "discursive" abilities. Thus it is clear that McDowell *still* takes the learning of a language to be a prerequisite for having experiences in the sense in which rational beings – beings that can understand and respond to requests for justifications for their judgments – have experiences.

According to McDowell, I resist this idea because I have a "blind spot." To reassure me that his discontinuity thesis does not threaten the idea that cats and dogs have experiences, he writes:

> Nothing in the Kantian conception requires its adherents to resist if someone, for instance Putnam, *wants to use the word "experience" differently*, so that it fits whenever a creature, rational or not, is on to things through the operation of perceptual capacities. If "percept" goes with "experience," and if we use "concept" in such a way that only rational animals can have concepts, that would mean that we cannot say "No percepts without concepts." Alternatively, we could keep "No percepts without concepts" by giving "concepts" a different use.
> (McDowell, p. 342 this volume; emphasis added)

But I am not reassured! If McDowell's claims are right, then not only do cats and dogs not have sense impressions of the sort with which we language-users are familiar (in *Mind and World* McDowell seems to me to use "impressions" and "experiences" interchangeably), but neither do small children, until they learn to speak, and not just to speak, but to understand requests for justifications for what they say. And to say, as McDowell, in effect, does say "Well, if you want, you can give the word *experience* a 'different' use; you can decide to say that when a cat or a child learns to respond differentially to the presence or absence of, say, something *hot* by the way it feels to the touch, then it has 'experiences' of heat," does not address my *utter disbelief* in what McDowell claims. I see no reason whatsoever to doubt that a two- or three-year old child (and probably even a neonate) experiences heat and pain much as I do now; or, to be more precise, to doubt that the phenomenal quality of the experience is much the same as it will be when the child grows up.[2]

I have used the expression "phenomenal quality" here, in full knowledge that talk of the "phenomenal quality" of experiences may be a "no-no" to both Travis and McDowell. Indeed, the distinction between an apperception and a mere sense impression goes missing in both of their essays. And it is because it goes missing that I wrote that I would not put my view as a simple *denial* that "perceptual experiences have content." (Most of this essay will be an explanation of this remark.)

McDowell, though not Travis, takes Kant as his philosopher of perception of choice. (Travis' is Frege, obviously (Travis 2008).) And Kant, at one crucial point, makes a mistake that, it seems to me, foreshadows, even if it was not the source for, McDowell's belief that every experience of any (adult language-adept) human is accompanied by a full-fledged conceptualization.[3]

In Kant's language, a fully conceptualized experience of a rational being is accompanied by the *"Ich denke."* It involves, in terminology that Kant also uses, both *apperception* and *apprehension*.[4] And the possibility of an experience that is not accompanied by the *"I think"* is dismissed thus:

> The *I think* ["Ich denke", in German] must be capable of accompanying all my presentations; otherwise something would be presented to me which could not be thought at all, which means no less than: the presentation would be either impossible, or at least nothing to me ... Consequently every manifold of perception has a necessary relation to the I think, in the same subject in which the manifold is found.
>
> (Kant 1998: §15, §16, B 131)

What is right in what Kant writes is that when I have an experience that I do not attend to at all, or apply any predicate to (even the predicate "*my* experience"), I cannot *at the same time* think of it as mine. But it does not follow that it must be "nothing to me," because I may very well be able to *remember* it later – certainly a moment later, and on some occasions, many years later. (I myself have a few memories from the time when I could barely talk, from around age two.)

Try the following simple experiment: walk around a crowded beach, or a busy street, or any other place where the scene is colorful and variegated. Now stop, close your eyes, and try to remember some of the scene that you did *not* particularly attend to, or think about, just before you closed your eyes. If you are like me, you will find that you can remember parts of the visual scene that you did not "conceptualize" in any sense of "conceptualize" I can understand, because you were not attending to them at all, although they were part of the total scene. Your present memory-experience of that part of the visual scene is, obviously, conceptualized, but the experience *of which it is a memory* was not.

Someone might suggest that *all* I now know is what my "conceptualized" memory experience of what I saw at age two, or even of what I saw a moment ago but did not attend to at the moment, is like; that there is no way to talk about the "phenomenal character" of any such experience at the time it was peripherally experienced but not attended to. But to accept this suggestion would amount to total skepticism about something we know, or have every reason to think we know, of our experience from memory, including short-term memory. The total introspectable quality of an experience certainly can be modified by paying attention to it. But my memory tells me something of the immediately past color-appearance of the apple that is on the table as I type these words (I am working in my kitchen). I do not claim that we can recover all the details of any past experience, even an immediately past one, nor that my memory of the details I do remember is completely accurate. But memories are not an interface behind which past experiences are somehow "hidden." They reveal our past experiences, and they do not have to be perfectly accurate to do that.

McDowell's position as of 2009 does not require him to deny this. All he still insists on is that I could not have had those experiences if I had not had the conceptual powers needed for a certain counterfactual to be true. The original experience may indeed not have been conceptualized in the literal sense (brought under a concept), but *it could have been* – could have been even if I did not already possess the appropriate concept and do not, in fact, possess it now. As Hilla Jacobson and I interpret "Avoiding the Myth of the Given" in a joint paper,[5] the counterfactual McDowell is assuming is:

> (AC:) *The attention counterfactual*: For any phenomenal aspect [any "intuition" in McDowell's Kantian terminology], *had* the subject attended to the feature [e.g. the particular shade of color of an object] represented in that intuition, she could have recognized it [brought it under a concept] at the time the experience was had.

Moreover, (AC) itself admits of more than one interpretation. On one interpretation, (AC) requires the *actual possession* of the appropriate concept as a condition for having the particular "intuition" (or "sense impression"). On another interpretation – and this is how Jacobson and I understand "Avoiding the Myth of the Given" – (AC) requires merely the *ability to acquire* the appropriate concept *upon having* the experience, and the attention counterfactual expresses a condition upon having that ability. In our joint paper, Jacobson and I argue, largely for empirical reasons, that on either interpretation (AC) is false. But I shall not repeat those arguments here. Instead, I shall simply say that even if (AC) were true, I do not see how it is supposed to follow that the subject, who is admitted to have had the experience at a time when the appropriate concept was *not* formed (because the "intuition" in question was not attended to), nevertheless was able to have the "intuition" only because the "discursive ability" to form such a concept was "in play." Indeed, since the sense in which that discursive ability was supposed to be "in play" is supposed not to be accessible to empirical science (McDowell 2010), that power, and its mysterious activity, would seem to belong to Kantian transcendental psychology, a project I see no sense in or hope for. (Moreover, I certainly did not have "discursive abilities" McDowell talks about at age two!)

Where McDowell went wrong

In *Mind and World* as well as subsequently, McDowell (rightly, in my view) rejects the "coherentism" that he finds in Donald Davidson's claim (taken, as Davidson acknowledges, from Neurath) that experiences do not (that is, cannot, are not the sort of thing that can) *justify* beliefs, or be evidence for or against them.[6] Nor does Davidson think that our beliefs have determinate semantic relations to objects in the world: on Davidson's account, reference is determinate only to the extent that translation practice is determinate; but translation practice only correlates linguistic expressions with other linguistic expressions, so that (if he is right) language as a whole has no connections to the world other than purely causal ones. As McDowell puts it,

> [F]or Davidson receptivity can impinge on the space of reasons only from outside, which is to say that nothing can be rationally vulnerable to its deliverances. Davidson differs from Quine only in that he is explicit about this and clear-sightedly draws the consequence: we cannot make sense of thought's bearing on the world in terms of an interaction between spontaneity and receptivity. If we go on using the Kantian terms, we have to say that the operations of spontaneity are rationally unconstrained from outside themselves. This is indeed a way of formulating Davidson's coherentism.
> (McDowell 1994: 139)

The alternative to "Davidson's coherentism" that McDowell sees is a "minimal empiricism, which makes out that the very idea of thought's directedness at the empirical world is intelligible only in terms of answerability to the tribunal of experience, conceived in terms of the world impressing itself upon perceiving subjects" (Davidson 2001: xvi). In "The Very Idea of a Conceptual Scheme" (as McDowell reads that famous paper in the first chapter of *Mind and World*) Davidson rejects minimal empiricism because he sees it as involving "The Myth of the Given," that is, the incoherent idea that something totally non-conceptual can rationally justify a belief. McDowell agrees that this *is* an incoherent idea, but he suggests that Davidson has a "blind spot" (ibid. 14); Davidson does not consider the possibility that impressions might themselves be conceptualized, or (as in "Avoiding the Myth of the Given") shaped somehow by our rational powers ("spontaneity") so as to make them fit to stand in justificatory relations to conceptually structured claims and beliefs. In sum, McDowell thinks we have to combine "minimal empiricism" with a Kantian notion of what an "impression" is. But McDowell himself has a blind spot, I believe.

What McDowell's blind spot keeps him from seeing is, in fact, almost in view when McDowell writes, "One option would be to renounce empiricism, at least with experience construed in terms of impressions" (McDowell 1994: 17). What the last nine words imply is that one possible option would be, not to "renounce empiricism," but to *reconceive experience*, by construing it, in its role of justifying beliefs, as something other than "impressions."

This is not what McDowell does, however. What he does is *reconceive impressions*, by adopting his Conceptualism. What I wish to propose is not that *impressions* are themselves (always and necessarily) shaped by our discursive abilities, as Conceptualism requires but rather that *there are more sorts of experiences than just "impressions."* Specifically, there are *apperceptions*.

Apperceptions and impressions

Although both Leibniz[7] and Kant[8] take "apperception" to involve the awareness of one's "inner state" or of one's "self," that is not how I shall use the term here. Instead, I shall use it in the sense, found in many dictionaries, of a "fully conscious perception." That a fully conscious perception is something that takes place "inside" us, is a survival, in both Leibniz and Kant, of Descartes' picture of the mind, but the whole "inner sense/outer sense" distinction is dubious once the interface picture of experience is jettisoned, as McDowell, Travis, and I all agree it should be. And I will take the relevant sense of "fully conscious" to be *conceptualized*. (In this sense, *the recognition by means of the senses of an object or event as the sort of object or event it is* counts as an "apperception," while the mere seeing of it that Travis describes as equally available to a human and an animal as long as the object or event is before the eyes, is not.) What I maintain is that *apperceptions are not beliefs caused by experiences; they are bona fide experiences in their own right.* That they are not simply "inner states," however, follows at once from the fact that apperceiving something in my environment is an activity that involves that something; it is, as I have put it elsewhere (Putnam 2012), the exercise of a capacity to function "with long arms," arms that reach out to the environment. Thus, apperceptions aren't qualia; but qualia are not all there is to experiences. To be sure, the line between an apperception and the accompanying qualia, when there are accompanying qualia (the reason for this "when" will be explained in a moment) is not sharp. As William James puts it, in the case of a "presented and recognized material object ... Sensations and apperceptive ideas fuse here so intimately that you can no more tell where one begins and the other ends, than you can tell, in those cunning circular panoramas that have lately been exhibited, where the real foreground and the painted canvas join together" (James 1976: 16). And I have heard some "disjunctivists" argue that talk of qualia is fatally compromised by just the vagueness of the boundary between qualia and "apperceptive ideas" that James pointed out. But "foliage," "weed," "place to visit," etc., etc., all have vague boundaries, and are still perfectly good notions. The very fact that, as I argued above, I can *remember* some unconceptualized qualia means that qualia are not a grammatical illusion, or a product of "bad philosophy."

Two further points, before I continue: (1) while visual apperception is accompanied by qualia in paradigm cases, not all apperceptions are so accompanied; some apperceptions are "amodal", to use a term I learned from Alva Noë (2004). I see a tomato as something that has another side; I do not *see* the other side, but I *apperceive* the tomato as *having* one. (2) There is a difference between what I would experience were my arm simply to rise of itself (an alarming possibility!) and what I experience when I raise my arm of my own volition (something I can clearly apperceive), but there is no *quale* of "voluntariness." There is *something it is like* to raise one's arm of one's own volition; "what it's like" isn't always *quale*. Apperceptions are experiences even when they are amodal. The reason that my position is not, as McDowell takes it to be, a simple denial that "perceptual experiences have content," is that what I deny is that mere *impressions* (qualia) have conceptual content; but apperceptions do have conceptual content, and they are "perceptual experiences."

I am now ready to say what the upshot of all this is: in brief, all the claims McDowell makes about perceptual experiences in *Mind and World* are true of apperceptions and seeming-apperceptions, including amodal apperceptions: they are conceptualized but non-inferential, and they can be judged as wrong even though they seem right. Justification begins with apperceptions, not with impressions.

Isn't this, however, just the Myth of the Given? Aren't my "apperceptions" just perceptual beliefs? Isn't this just the Neurath–Davidson thesis that beliefs are justified by other beliefs in a different language?

My reply should come as no surprise: to repeat, apperceptions are conceptually shaped and they can justify judgments. But they are not the same as perceptual beliefs. I may have an apperception, or, better, a seeming apperception, that one "shaft" is longer than the other in the Müller–Lyer illusion, but I do not *believe* what I seem to be apperceiving. One can seem to oneself to apperceive when one knows that one does not (successfully) apperceive, but one cannot seem to oneself to *believe* when one does not believe. The distinction between qualia and apperceptions is not the same as the distinction between qualia and perceptual beliefs.

In my view, Neurath and Davidson both operated with too narrow a range of relevant factors in perceptual judgment: they had only unconceptualized experiences (sense impressions) and beliefs (which Davidson identified with linguistic objects, *sentences*) to work with. The picture of unconceptualized impressions acting purely causally to "trigger" beliefs is a picture of the mind that either leaves out *intentionality*, or requires the Myth of the Given to forcibly insert it. And Kant, and, following Kant, McDowell, try to reinsert intentionality, and the possibility of a justificatory relation between experiences and beliefs, by insisting that all impressions (with the possible exception of some that are "nothing to us," in the passage from Kant I quoted earlier) are conceptualized; but Conceptualism turns out to be either bad empirical psychology or a claim about mysterious mental powers being mysteriously "in play." Neurath and Davidson have no unconceptualized experiences in their picture; McDowell (and Kant) have only conceptualized experiences. In reality, there are both sorts of experiences. There are both unconceptualized impressions and apperceptions (and, as James noted, combinations of the two).

The most likely cause of resistance to the picture I advocate, I believe, will be the hold on us of the traditional empiricist idea that knowledge *begins* with qualia, and beliefs are *inferred* from qualia. In fact, we do not even know that qualia (which, with Ned Block, I believe to be brain events) occur *earlier* than the related apperceptions.[9] Apperceptions and seeming-apperceptions are not mysterious "beliefs" floating unsupported in an epistemic void; they are the most primitive cognitive experiences we have. And our beliefs about the world, when justified, are justified, however indirectly, by apperceptions (or, more precisely, by apperceptions plus framework principles).[10]

Re: Travis

In one place, Travis writes that he hopes and expects that he is reading McDowell wrongly. In the same spirit, I hope, and expect, that I am reading Travis wrongly in what follows. But I do have to say that, like McDowell, I too read Travis as claiming that all conceptualization takes place "downstream" from perception. And like McDowell I disagree with Travis about this, although not for all of the same reasons.

In the course of describing what he takes to be wrong with McDowell's claim that perceptual experience is conceptualized, Travis uses the following example:

> Now, of course, if the cat and I are watching an approaching game warden, I may experience an uneasiness the cat does not – despite the bird in its mouth. The shiver going up my spine, but not the cat's, would be a difference in what we experience. The cat may thank its lack of conceptual capacities for its aplomb. But if the difference in what we experience is conceived as a difference in what we experience *visually* – how we (thus) experience things *being* visually – my conceptual capacities are responsible for differences

in the cat's, and my, objects of *perception* – in this case, sight. And then it seems – there being only one *scene* for the cat and me to gaze at – those differences will have to be found by looking inside.

(Travis, p. 327 this volume)

Travis uses the example (and a similar example involving seeing a peccary)[11] to support three claims: (1) that thinking of the cat and the subject (say, oneself) as seeing different things will lead straight to the idealist mistake of putting what we see "inside us," and not where it belongs, out there in front of the cat and oneself; (2) the difference between my experience and the cat's (e.g., the fear I feel and the cat does not), is not due to a difference in what we "experience *visually*," but to the fact that after the visual experience is registered some conceptual activity goes on in me that does not go on in the cat. (3) (the main claim of Travis's chapter – if McDowell and I do not misunderstand him): the fact that these particular properties (being a game warden, being a peccary) are used in the examples, and not, say, shapes or colors, is not essential.

McDowell agrees with Travis that I do not visually experience the person who is approaching as *being a game warden*, but he rejects (3), and thus argues that the example does not support the claim that *all* conceptualization is "downstream" from perception. ("Travis thinks the point generalizes, and that is open to question.") In particular, "[C]oncepts of the animal's color, size, shape, posture, and so forth – must be operative in the peccary's being visually present to Travis, visually given to him for knowing on the demanding conception."

My own response to the "game warden" and "peccary" examples, and the claims based upon them, is as follows:

Re (1): Thinking of the cat and myself (or someone who can visualize distinguish peccaries from, say, pigs, and myself) as literally *seeing different objects* will, obviously, imply that we do not both see the same object when we look at the animal before us (respectively, the approaching person). With some familiar premises added (e.g., Russell's arguments in various books (Russell 1912 and 1940)), this will imply that the object we see is not the physical object we are gazing at, and that the immediate objects of perception lie in each individual's "private space." But it is strange that Travis thinks that McDowell's views commit him to the idea that the cat and I or the peccary-*Kenner* and I literally see different objects.

Travis, however, has a second line of attack. Colors and shapes are "ways for things to be." And (via an argument drawn from Frege) Travis concludes that "ways for things to be" are simply not the sort of thing we can perceptually experience:

> First, as Frege saw, the idea of encountering the conceptual *perceptually* makes no sense. This is what Frege is getting at when he observes

that, while the sun, or a flower, is a visible thing, emitting rays arriving in our eyes, that the sun has set, or that the flower has five petals is not. It is not before us to be seen. Neither are ways there are for a thing to be. They are something else entirely.

(Travis, p. 338 this volume)

Voilà! With a simple appeal to Frege, *universals* are banished from the realm of the perceivable. (Needless to say, none of this is to be found in the form of common-sense realism, as I called it, that I advocated in *The Threefold Cord*, a position on which Travis heaps a great deal of praise – praise that is possibly undeserved, given that he seems to be reading things into it that are not there.) Contrary to Travis, I have always believed that we can see *colors* and *shapes* for example, not to mention relations (such as A's *colliding with* B). (Interestingly, the only things Travis speaks of us as being able to "experience visually" are *objects*; does he think that we cannot experience *events* visually?)

Where I differ from McDowell is, as explained above, in not limiting experience – not even *visual* experience – to "color, shape, size, posture, and so forth." I think I can *visually apperceive* that what is approaching me is a policeman (and someone acquainted with game wardens may be able to visually apperceive that what is approaching is a game warden). I think that I can *visually apperceive* that what is in front of me is a pig (and someone acquainted with peccaries, may be able to visually apperceive that what is in front of her is a peccary).

– But what about the cat? Or the person who can't tell a peccary from a pig? These are two different cases. The cat does not have concepts, to be sure, but it does have what I once called *protoconcepts*.[12] There is a forerunner of human apperception to be found in animals that do not possess the discursive abilities that McDowell speaks of. There is, as John Dewey believed, a *continuity* between our rational abilities and those of "beasts." (So, I believe, did Wittgenstein, but that is, like all Wittgenstein-interpretation, controversial.) On the other hand, the person who mistakes a peccary for a pig, or simply doesn't know what sort of animal is before her, doesn't apperceive the presence of a peccary, but she does apperceive the presence of a largish mammal.

But, coming back to the use Travis makes of Frege, what of the objection that "It is not before us to be seen. Neither are ways there are for a thing to be. They are something else entirely." My response is that seeing the color of, say, a piece of furniture in the sense relevant to this discussion is *apperceiving* it; and apperception involves both seeing, in the sense of using one's eyes, and *seeing that*. And *seeing that* draws on one's conceptual powers as well as one's eyes.

As for Frege, the passage Travis quotes is: "But don't I see that this flower has five petals? One can say that; but then one uses the word 'see' not in the sense of mere perception by means of light, but something involving thought and judgment." I have no disagreement with this in the case of a property that involves counting ("has five petals"). But if Frege means that I can only see that I am looking at a red wall (or a policeman, or a pig) by *reflection* ("thought and judgment"), then I disagree. In my case, it is probably true that I can only see that a person approaching me is a game warden by "thought and judgment," but I can simply *see* that someone is a policeman, at least if he or she is in uniform. Of course, "seeing" in that sense is not just "perception by means of light" in the sense in which optics studies "perception by means of light"; the study of seeing in that sense belongs to psychology, not optics.

In sum, it seems to me that *apperception* (as opposed to "perception by means of light" followed by "thought and judgment") goes missing in Travis's (and Frege's) picture. If McDowell's mistake is assimilating all visual "impressions" to apperception, Travis's mistake is assimilating apperception to reflection (and leaving impressions completely out of consideration). But both assimilations are misguided.

Notes

1 I do not know whether this was written earlier or later than the present essay.
2 The case of color vision in cats and dogs is different from that in humans, because it was long supposed that cats, and possibly dogs as well, are color blind. In the 1960s, however, researchers managed to teach cats to discriminate between colors. But the training took a long time. "Untrained" cats show no color discrimination. That is why I used the experience of heat as an example above, and not the experience of red. Cats do, however, readily discriminate different shades of gray!
3 Strictly speaking, this was McDowell's view in *Mind and World*. I discuss the modified view (as of "Avoiding the Myth of the Given") later in this essay.
4 "If we consciously imagine for ourselves the inner action (spontaneity), whereby a concept (a thought) becomes possible, we engage in reflection; if we consciously imagine for ourselves the susceptibility (receptivity), whereby a perception (*perceptio*), i.e. empirical observation, becomes possible, we engage in apprehension; however, if we consciously imagine both acts, then the consciousness of one's self (*apperceptio*) can be divided into that of reflection and that of apprehension. Reflection is a consciousness of the understanding, whilst apprehension is a consciousness of the inner sense; reflection is pure apperception, but apprehension is empirical apperception." Footnote to Book I, Section 4, of *Kant's Anthropology from a Pragmatic Point of View*.
5 Hilla Jacobson and Hilary Putnam, "Against Perceptual Conceptualism," paper read (by Hilla) at *Philosophy in an Age of Science; A Conference in Honor of Hilary Putnam's 85th Birthday*, Harvard and Brandeis Universities, May 30–June 3, 2011.
6 "Neurath was right in rejecting the intelligibility of comparing sentences or beliefs with reality ... Nor can such events be considered in themselves to be evidence, unless, of course, they cause us to believe something" (Davidson 2001a: 173). That (token) experiences, which Davidson regards as identical with brain events, cannot stand in justificatory relations to beliefs is the gravamen of

his famous "On the Very Idea of a Conceptual Scheme," *Proceedings and Addresses of the American Philosophical Association*, 47, pp. 5–20; reprinted in Davidson (2001).

7 In section 4 of the *Principles of Nature and of Grace* (1714), Leibniz says that apperception is "consciousness, or the reflective knowledge of this internal state." He adds that this is "something not given to all souls, nor at all times to a given soul."

8 In a passage from Kant's *Anthropology from a Pragmatic Point of View* previously quoted, *apperception* is said to involve "consciousness of one's self."

9 A point made, I seem to remember, in Dennett (1991).

10 But aren't framework principles themselves ultimately justified by apperceptions? My view since the 1950s ("It Ain't Necessarily So" and "The Analytic and the Synthetic," both collected in Putnam 1975) has been that the question of justification does not arise for framework principles until and unless someone conceives of a workable alternative to them. But that does not mean that they are unrevisable.

11 Peccaries are a species of mammals found in the Americas, and resembling pigs.

12 For a discussion of the differences between the protoconcepts of, for example, dogs, and the concepts of human language-users, see the second lecture in Putnam (1992: 19–34).

Bibliography

Davidson, Donald (2001) *Inquiries into Truth and Interpretation*, Oxford: Clarendon Press.

——(2001a) "Empirical Content," in Donald Davidson, *Subjective, Intersubjective, Objective*, Oxford: Clarendon Press.

Dennett, Daniel (1991) *Consciousness Explained*, Boston: Little, Brown, and Co.

James, William (1976) *Essays in Radical Empiricism*, ed. Ralph Barton Perry, Cambridge, MA: Harvard University Press.

Kant, I. (1998) *Critique of Pure Reason*, ed. P. Guyer and A. Wood, Cambridge: Cambridge University Press.

McDowell, John (1994) *Mind and World*, Cambridge, MA: Harvard University Press.

——(2009) "Avoiding the Myth of the Given," in *Having the World in View*, Cambridge, MA: Harvard University, 256–72.

——(2010) "Tyler Burge on Disjunctivism," *Philosophical Explorations* 13: 243–55.

Noe, Alva (2004) *Perception in Action*, Cambridge, MA: MIT Press.

Putnam, Hilary (1975) *Philosophical Papers*, vol. 2: *Mind, Language and Reality*, Cambridge: Cambridge University Press.

——(1992) *Renewing Philosophy*, Cambridge, MA: Harvard University Press.

——(2012) "Corresponding with Reality," (Prometheus Prize Lecture), in *Philosophy in the Age of Science*, Cambridge, MA: Harvard University Press.

Russell, Bertrand (1912) *The Problems of Philosophy*, London: Williams and Norgate.

——(1940) *An Inquiry Into Meaning and Truth*, New York: W. W. Norton & Co.

Travis, Charles (2008) "Frege, Father of Disjunctivism," *Philosophical Topics* 33(1): 307–34.

Part IV

EPILOGUE

13

ON NIETZSCHEAN PERFECTIONISM[1]

Stanley Cavell

I feel in accord with and enlightened by what I take as the two principal motivating ideas of Stephen Mulhall's paper (Mulhall 2012), namely that Nietzsche's early text *The Birth of Tragedy* is a central work of Nietzsche's perfectionism and that this work proves itself to exhibit in its working the thing it argues: that philosophy's ancient project of projecting, as in Plato, a world beyond in relation to this world, one that explains the coherence and the aspiration of this world, is to be understood simultaneously as a work that itself partakes of, not merely a work that is about, tragedy, a work showing human comprehension to effect and to require not alone liberation but suffering.[2] This understanding in effect turns Plato on his head, showing that what we take as our world's "imitation" of another world more perfect, guaranteeing our quest for knowledge, is itself the manifestation or flowering of a world otherwise dark to itself, allowing it to become known through our journey of perfection.

I will accordingly assume Mulhall's proposal of Nietzschean Perfectionism[3] and let it prompt my own periodic obsession with Emerson and with my sense of Nietzsche's companion obsession. I have sometimes felt, perhaps at moments of exasperation with my inability to make clear to myself some passage of Nietzsche's, how it is that Nietzsche uses, and perhaps means to surpass or disguise, Emerson. *Birth of Tragedy* (henceforward BT) is a comparatively clear place to begin because it seems on the surface to endorse the separation of worlds that Emerson, according to my reading, denies.

In my chapter on Nietzsche in *Cities of Words* (Cavell 2005), which focuses on his text *Schopenhauer as Educator*, the third of his four *Untimely Meditations* (Nietzsche 1997), I contrast Nietzsche's perfectionism with Emerson's, suggesting that whereas Nietzsche metaphysicalizes – places in separate worlds – the visible Apollonian world in relation to the contrasting Dionysian world that it encodes and interprets, Emerson views something like this relation – I think of Emerson's contrast between Intuition and Tuition – as a perpetual individual process of bringing light to darkness, consciousness to unconsciousness, clarity to confusion, a process that is to inspire, but cannot insure, a comparable communal result. But Mulhall's reading of BT as subjecting itself to its own discoveries, forging itself as an instance of the process it describes, is most congenial to me, prompting and demanding further thought. (Is Nietzsche's publication an individual or a communal project?)

In the immediate background of what I will go on to say now is my sense of Nietzsche's use of the architectural disposition of the Greek theater as an image or allegory of conditions of everyday human existence (conditions I think of as a priori, those in the absence of which there is nothing to call human), a disposition Mulhall describes, in part, as follows:

> [T]he place of the chorus in Greek theaters was the orchestra, a semi-circular area in front of the stage. ... The chorus was Janus-faced – it was capable of engaging with the characters in the drama [on the stage] ... inviting them not only to view but to identify with the chorus, and thereby to overcome their metaphysical distance from the drama in which that chorus is involved. The chorus' function as participant-observer thus allows the audience to experience the drama as if they too were participants in it. The dramatic action on stage is then to be understood as a vision of the chorus, and so of the audience – a vision of their suffering, glorified master, Dionysus ... [who] never ceased to be the [heroic figure underlying] all the tragic figures of the Greek stage, Prometheus, Oedipus ...
> (Mulhall 2012: 3)

I interpret the allegory to say that outside the architecture of theaters (but if I am right, there is, in the sense required, no place outside, it is the world) members of the audience are inescapably both participants and observers, separated and connected by the orchestra, a locale of music, namely the presence of chanted speech.

Nietzsche's insistence of the heightened awareness of another as preparation for the appearance of the gods is a perception I find to make a double contribution to the philosophical understanding of our knowledge of others. First, there is the suggestion that this knowledge begins with the fateful knowledge of a particular other, or of those select few, who are able to reveal to observer/participants the reality of the realm of mind. Whereas with respect to the realm of objects, as detailed, for instance, in the passage from Augustine quoted at the beginning of Wittgenstein's *Investigations*, we are not surprised to find this testimony: "When they (my elders) named some object, and accordingly moved toward something, I saw this and I grasped that the thing was called by the sound they uttered when they meant to point it out" (Wittgenstein 1953: §1). Evidently neither the child nor Augustine singles out an object or kind of object as fateful, so long, presumably, as the instances are convenient, harmless, and apt to capture the child's attention and interest.

A second, companion suggestion in Nietzsche's account of theater is that the ecstatic awareness of the particular "glorified" other over-endows, so to speak, that other, placing it as from the realm of divinity. This from the beginning casts human life as one fated to disappointment and longing.

The clearest difference between BT and, say, Emerson's "Experience" (1884) – another essay understandable as about the birth of human experience (opening in what most readers would consider a world of darkness, explicitly of mourning, grieving, shaded by the death of his young son), is that while Nietzsche presents his sense of the human task, giving birth to oneself, as one of finding others in an ecstasy of seeing them, enabling us to grasp human existence as containing the depth of dreams, Emerson stays with the empirical loss of others and of the meaning of loss, one might say of the loss of meaning, and directly turns us upon ourselves, that is upon the fact of words, the defining gift, or curse, of the human, the unnatural animal, perpetually exiling itself from Eden. The plainest challenge to our language in Emerson's "Experience" is to the philosophical use of the word "experience" itself, as elaborated in the philosophy of experience called Empiricism, where all our ideas are said to result from "impressions" made upon us (impressive or not). When Emerson announces, still shockingly, near the opening of "Experience," the death of his young son, he is in effect challenging, not to say ridiculing, the idea that his knowledge of this event can be understood to derive from his impression of it. So far as it has made an impression, Emerson describes it precisely as "falling off from me" (1884). So either he is saying that impressions cannot be the route to knowledge of the world, or he is confessing that he has not arrived at the knowledge of his son's death, or he is saying he may not recognize knowledge when he has it, or somehow all of these at once. He explicitly speaks of knowledge as a curse, but, unlike the events in Eden, not because of its power but because of its weakness, making no lasting and certain impression upon us. He observes: "Nothing is left us now but death" (1884: 20). It is a thought, however, that produces, in the essay to follow, one of Emerson's greatest outbursts of philosophy.

Other characteristic – I would say unmistakable – instances of Nietzsche's BT virtually announcing Emerson's essay "Experience" on his mind is his joining Emerson's mocking there of various somethings philosophy calls "experiences" left isolated and stranded by us. The sense of Emerson on Nietzsche's mind has been so important to my relation to philosophy, that I pause to add two later, to my mind incontestable, instances in which the sense announces itself. In *Beyond Good and Evil* there is excellent instruction to moral philosophy in reading: "'Good' is no longer good when one's neighbor mouths it" (Nietzsche 1973: 71). This recalls for me, as evidently for Nietzsche, Emerson's observation, in "Self-Reliance": "Every word they say chagrins us, and we know not where to start to set them right" (Emerson 1881: 37). Or again, Nietzsche's rebuke, running "'Become mediocre' is the only morality that still makes sense," virtually rewrites Emerson's "The virtue in most request is conformity" (Emerson 1881: 34).

I have been helped, in thinking about perfectionism, and in philosophy generally, more methodically I would say, by Emerson's interest in language than by Nietzsche's contribution of his images of Dionysus and Apollo and dream. I mean that if to make progress in my thoughts about the origin of my dissatisfactions with myself as I stand I had first to present an unheard-of theory of the origin of Western drama in Greek culture, I would not predict much success in my endeavors. Whereas when Emerson urges me to prepare to regard any and every utterance of mine as an Intuition in quest of Tuition, success can at least come in small steps. I'll give an example of such a step when I turn in the second half of these remarks to a crossing of paths between Nietzsche's *Genealogy* and, of all things, one of J. L. Austin's best, and best known, essays, "Other Minds" (1979).

Nietzsche's extravagant opening in BT in metaphysicalizing the play between the realms of Dionysus and of Apollo (however finally controlled his perception will be in his own perfectionist quest to, let me say, put these realms in conversation with each other and hence of himself with himself) opens to view an issue unarticulated, to my knowledge, among philosophers who work by turning upon their words, any and all words that can in a moment capture their attention, which is to say, who work by confronting themselves in their language. I speak immediately of the unfortunately named ordinary language philosophy, by which I mean to invoke primarily, quite exclusively I believe, the work of J. L. Austin and of the later Wittgenstein. What this mode of analytical philosophy leaves largely out of account, or perhaps counts as just one among many routes of tuition, is explicitly the confrontation of ordinary language by formal logic. In this latter mode, the demons of ordinary language can be taken to be as a whole escaped by listening to its gleanings in logic, the region where Apollo finally escapes Dionysus. Whereas what I cannot give up in the perception of the philosophers of ordinary language is that the power, the only power, strong enough to reveal the dangers, or survive the fires, of ordinary language, its revelations and openness to distortions of myself and my world of experience, my disappointments and my longings, is ordinary language itself. If one asks for the justification of one's choosing to remain in those fires rather than accepting the hope of rescue from them, I could do no better than appeal to Emerson's demand for Tuition, namely for that unending confrontation of myself and my powers of Intuition that constitutes a continuing of my education. I trust I do not need to be told that this begs the question (of whether this procedure of self-confrontation amounts to education at all). Citing this very condition acknowledges that I am without justification, at least none that others may not equally justly claim.

I interrupted myself as I was about to speak of Nietzsche's impulse to metaphysics as opening to view an issue for ordinary language philosophizing that is, I believe, unaddressed and perhaps uninteresting to the work Austin exemplifies (not to that work's credit), and one to which Wittgenstein's work repeatedly alludes but does not see as the unnoticed elephant that I take to reside in the ordinariness of ordinary language philosophy. Perhaps it is only a mouse. It may perhaps be glimpsed as arising from within a sense of Nietzsche's inspiration in taking the massive upsurge in the origin of theater to be caused by a response to, or a contesting of, a particular hitherto unnoticed, or unthematized, condition of human existence, put it as the realization that our everyday human lives of recognizable order and disorder, call them comedy and tragedy, are moved and shaped by forces – as powerful as deities – of which we have until now been able to keep ourselves from seeing and making explicit to ourselves. Nietzsche is everywhere aware that he is the vessel of terrifying news. This terrified ignorance means that humanity still fails to, if perhaps it is destined to, know itself, which means fails to interpret and perceive itself, or rather fails to stop avoiding such knowledge.

This is like, and unlike, Socrates' inspiration in contesting the human failure to examine, say to confront, one's life. With a certain luck and willingness for work, ordinary civilized life (free for a time from eventful catastrophe) is neither as extraordinary as hell or heaven; but what we *accept* as ordinary, acceptable, inevitable, is itself generally fantastic. That we *make* it familiar is uncanny. The elephant I invoked a moment ago, or the mouse, is the paucity of philosophical interest in and description of this incessant struggle of, and with, the ordinary, hence the denial of its costs, of what human life, say civilization, needs, and can intermittently hear, what Austin and Wittgenstein have to reveal, call it our incessant dulling yet craving of reason and sense. How many times must we be recalled to ourselves? Which asks: what is human life that it perpetually requires this reminding – as if a continuing battle between remembering and forgetting is what makes human life possible.

I mentioned that I would want to give an example of a small, but methodical, hence consequential, perhaps endlessly repeatable, step that Emerson proposes from Intuition to Tuition, for which I find Nietzsche's move from Dionysus to Apollo to provide a Nietzschean interpretation, I might even call it a provision of the Myth of the Human. Whether the step is to be thought of as small or large, or neither, what interests me now is that Nietzsche and J. L. Austin may be seen to take the *same* step.[4] The opening two of the three essays constituting Nietzsche's *Genealogy* have signature moral words as their titles – "Good," "Evil," "Bad," "Guilt," "Bad Conscience," to which Nietzsche adds (humorously, I cannot but think) as part of the second title: "And the Like" – and the third essay is a running critique, a moral criticism, of our explicitly moral discourse as a whole. Now my claim is not simply that Nietzsche is not especially interested in describing the specific intricacies of our moral vocabulary (as say Austin is throughout the stretch of his study of "Excuses" (Austin 1956) – thus as it were displaying the global geography of human accountability), but that Nietzsche's featuring of a handful of famous moral terms is an invitation to think about the basis of beleaguered human interaction out of the traumatic, unending inundation of speech as such, that for example the simplest assertion ("You are here"; "You're wearing a hat"; "You're not wearing a hat") will contain the will to power. (I am here attempting to follow Nietzsche's advice and example in asking what it betokens that what he sometimes calls "an organ" exists.) Here the organ in question is language. The idea of "betokening" is Nietzsche's transfiguration of Darwinism. What does the possession of the human hand, of the upright posture, of the gait of walking, of smiling, of singing, of courting, betoken? Some in my hearing, I seem to recall, have spoken of Darwinism as accordingly underlying pragmatism. But I cannot think it captures such human facts as exchanging words, or walking, or greeting by smiling, or courting, to speak of such accomplishments as useful. (Any more than I find Wittgenstein's insistence on studying the use of our words to be emphasizing their usefulness – you might as well emphasize the usefulness of having a human body, not always of course a useless reminder – rather than to remind us of, say, the perpetually astounding capacity of words simultaneously for present precision and for seemingly endless variation with context. Then why does philosophizing require reminding of this astounding commonplace?) I should add, nervously, that not having for a long time tried to keep up adequately with Nietzsche scholarship, I may be proposing things now quite well known.

I introduce the following few remarks linking Nietzsche and Austin in noting perhaps my favorite evidence of a perpetual conversation of Nietzsche with Emerson, namely the opening sentence of Nietzsche's Preface to the *Genealogy*: "We are unknown to ourselves, we men of knowledge – and with good reason. We have never sought ourselves – how should it happen that we should ever *find* ourselves?" (Nietzsche 1967: 15). I take this as an explicit response to the opening of Emerson's essay "Experience": "Where do we find ourselves. ... ?" (1884: 20). The suggestion I pick up here is that the philosophical effort to ground moral authority (rationality) in knowledge and universality, from Plato to Mill and perhaps to the *Tractatus*, has been an effort to avoid, or limit, or stylize, confrontation with ourselves – confrontation with the way we live, with its standing aims and passions and actions and choices and apparent necessities.

The step or insight or crossroads I say Austin and Nietzsche share, hence illuminate in one another, can be noted in juxtaposing a sentence from the *Genealogy* with a sentence and a half from Austin's "Other Minds." Quoting from the Nietzsche (opening sentence of the Second Essay): "To breed an animal *with the right to make promises* – is not this the paradoxical task that nature has set itself in the case of man? Is it not the real problem regarding man?" (Nietzsche 1967: 57). Quoting from Austin's "Other Minds" (the section entitled "If I Know I Can't Be Wrong"):

> It is naturally *always* possible ("humanly" possible) that I may be mistaken or may break my word, but that by itself is no bar against using the expressions "I know" and "I promise" as we do use them. ... The parallel between saying "I know" and "I promise" may be elaborated.
> (Austin 1979: 98)

Both thinkers emphasize and explicitly spell out the sense of promising as *giving others one's word*. Austin's obvious contribution here is to link saying "I know" with making a promise as another way, a central way in as it were another tense, of giving your word; Nietzsche's signal contribution is perceiving the right to make promises as paradoxical. Understanding the formulation "giving one's word" as literally describing sharing one's language, one sees the force of Nietzsche's speaking of the task that nature has set itself in the case of man, setting the real problem regarding man, the problem one might say of defining what man is, as a "paradoxical" task. The force is to focus on the fact that the creation of this creature is *nature's* doing. To make a promise is to say that I assume the freedom or power to say, responsibly, that I will do what I say I will do (come what may, so to speak), or put otherwise, to say that I am not wholly determined by nature's laws. But this is just to say that nature itself is the cause of my freedom from, or in, nature. Declaring the assumption of freedom in promising may be imagined to have caused, over millennia of experimentation, countless mishaps with the giving, or proto-giving, of words, recognizing when this giving, the saying and address of a word, is in order, and how much may be promised, or addressed, to whom, how explicitly, under what constraints of time and place, and running what manner and degree of risks. (Working out freedom – as we are still working it out – has not required an influx, from without, of the breath of God. Not God, but the absence of God, is the paradoxical. This is why Darwin and Herbert Spencer are invited to make appearances in the *Genealogy*. How can we go so far as to imagine that there is no God? To share a language is to share a culture, so that in breeding man, nature has created human culture, the precipitate of unfathomably many promises, as essential to the human as nature itself is. So the step I see Austin to share with Nietzsche's sense of the creation of the human is the step, or perpetual steps, from nature to culture, namely from the non-human animal's subjection to nature, or say to natural law, that is, from the register of instinct, inclination, impulse, innocence, intuition, to the human subjection to human culture and the possibility of freedom, call it autonomy, self-legislation. Or instead of a step, say rather the oscillation or weaving of one realm with the other, a foot in each, an understandably awkward gait of human progression, however ineluctable.

I have increasingly found myself expressing this idea by saying that man is the unnatural animal. Nietzsche does not, I believe (though I have looked for its occurrence a number of times, and continue to keep an eye out), say precisely this, but such a concept would capture his precise drift, and prepare us to look more steadily at what we call ordinary and what extraordinary in human life, what we call normal and what perverse, what is invisible and what eventful. And the connection with Nietzsche allows us to see (or allowed me to stress) that Austin appreciates and responds to the nature of the dividing human animal. Remember his words:

> It is naturally *always* possible ('humanly' possible), that I may be mistaken or may break my word, but that by itself is no bar against using the expressions I 'know' and 'I promise' as we do in fact use them.
>
> (Austin 1979: 98)

Austin does not enclose "naturally" in scare quotes, as he does "humanly," but had he explicitly done so it would have helped convey his sense, plain enough anyway to my ear, that he is identifying the conjunction of the human and the natural, and at the same time signaling that there is something all but interminably suspicious in this identification.

Nor does he go beyond saying that he is speaking simply of how we in fact use these business words instead of standing by his claim, or insight, that how we in fact use them (throughout their tracks across language) shows what we understand these things called humanity and nature in fact to be. Leaving such things insinuated is a cause of Austin's striking certain philosophers of my acquaintance as "cagey." I wish, on the contrary, that Austin had so far let himself out of the cage of propriety as to question why we formulate such a thing, or do such a thing, as breaking a promise. This idea unguardedly or freely announces that the human has it in its power to destroy the thing that makes it human, call it the power to become monstrous, and it confesses that that too is only human.

A million philosophers, and fresh ones every week, most famously I suppose in Plato and Descartes and Kant, see and have seen man as existing in two worlds, a doubled creature. Not often have the two worlds, or doubling, looked as they do in Nietzsche and Austin, as I have sketched certain moments of theirs. One could say that these worlds classically present themselves to such philosophers (not philosophers alone) as separate places, low and high, here and there, but for Nietzsche and Austin they appear instead as past and future, endlessly linked, in strife, in the shifting thing called the present (the thing Thoreau calls "the meeting place of two eternities"). I will bring these remarks to a close by indicating the working of such ideas in a further sentence or two from "Other Minds" and from the *Genealogy*.

In Austin's elaboration of the relation between saying "I promise" and saying "I know," he alludes to his discovery of what will become best known as the performative utterance, one specifically with what he calls illocutionary force.

> To suppose that 'I know' is a descriptive phrase, is only one example of the *descriptive fallacy*, so common in philosophy. ... Utterance of obvious ritual phrases, in the appropriate circumstances, is not *describing* the action we are doing, but *doing it* ('I do' ... 'I warn', 'I ask', 'I define'). Such phrases cannot, strictly, *be* lies, though they can 'imply' lies, as 'I promise' implies that I fully intend, which may be untrue.
>
> (Austin 1979: 103)

Austin clearly recognizes that we feel

> an objection to saying that 'I know' performs the same sort of function in talking as 'I promise'. It is this. Supposing that things turn out badly, then we say, on the one hand 'You're proved wrong, so you *didn't* know', but on the other hand 'You've failed to perform, although you *did* promise'.
>
> (Austin 1979: 102)

The difference is brought out more garishly if, as I was introduced to Austin's idea soon after the time of the publication of "Other Minds," the idea of the performative utterance took the form of claiming, for example, "To say 'I promise' ('I warn,' 'I define' ...) *is* to promise, to warn, to define." Some philosophers were quick and pleased to ridicule the proposed invitation to say "'I know' *is* to know," whatever unknown thing may transpire.

Austin's rich exploration did not exactly leave him routed here, but he left the issue less formidably formulated than the philosophical stakes in play for him will call for, perhaps still, or again, call for. Austin does name the stakes, even if he does not sufficiently well describe them, in the following summary.

> In both cases [namely of knowing and of promising] there is an [a philosophical] obsession: if I know *I can't be wrong*, so I can't have the right to say I know, and if I promise *I can't fail*, so I can't have the right to say I promise. And in both cases this obsession fastens on my inability to make *predictions* as the root of the matter ...
>
> (Austin 1979: 103)

The stakes are that the reigning Anglo-American philosophies of the post-World War II period, positivism and pragmatism, were both of the unshakably obvious opinion that all (empirical) knowledge of the world was based upon, and alone justified by, prediction (the verification theories of meaning and of truth). Unshakably obvious, except sometimes for some of us who, even early on, were restive about saying that even statements about present objects implicitly contained favorable predictions of countless nests of hypotheses, or hypothetical statements, e.g., "If I let hold of it, it will drop (and break, or shatter, or bounce, etc.)," "If I touch it, it will hold its shape (or burn my finger, or come apart, or giggle as if tickled) … " Put bleakly, the stakes I am citing for Austin were to defend philosophical method as something (however akin to) decisively distinct from the method of science, which, however successful and glamorous, is accordingly not philosophically "the root of the matter" of human knowing and responsibility.

Naturally I am struck by Austin's wording in countering the idea that "I can't have the right to say I promise," a formulation that quite perfectly negates Nietzsche's perception of the human animal as one bred "with the right to make promises." Unable, however, to join forces with Nietzsche's Tuition of this Intuition of human possibility, Austin alarms or tricks himself into falling back on an observation so weak and obvious as to give up the heart of his claim to know, namely,

> [T]he conditions which must be satisfied if I am to show that a thing is within my cognizance or within my power are conditions, not about the future, but about *the present and the past*: it is not demanded that I do more than *believe* about the future.
> (Austin 1979: 101)

I can imagine circumstances in which my well-attended brick and stone house will not be standing tomorrow, but do I *believe* it will remain standing, am I of this *opinion*? Would it be so much as coherent of me, let alone cautious, under present unthreatening conditions, to *predict* this? I think of Descartes' describing his project in his *Meditations* as "[applying himself] earnestly and freely to the general overthrow of all my former opinions" (Descartes 2009: 10). The picture of beliefs, opinions, predictions – in Wittgenstein's *Investigations* it will be observing the introduction of hypotheses – as detailing our fundamental access to the existence of the world and of others in it, reaches with one hand for responsibility in claims to know, exactly after the other has knocked it away. (The problem of justifying our knowledge of the world in modern philosophy, taken as a matter of justifying "all my former opinions," is from the beginning bypassed in its consequent treatment of the world as one more object, a very large or extensive one, the largest.) Should it console Othello to be told, on seeming to have proof of Desdemona's faithlessness, that he should not have taken himself to *know* what the future held, hence left himself exposed to tragedy.

But to caution that, with respect to the future, belief is all that is demanded, is terribly to underrate humankind's ineluctable exposure to the future. A claim to know and an offer of promise both suffer this exposure, but differently, and it remains a philosophical task to understand the modes of human exposure. I think of it as the task of describing human finitude.

I add a pair of thoughts about Austin's appeal to his discovery of the performative utterance as an explanation of the force of saying "I know." The appeal plausibly, indeed brilliantly, speaks to the accusation that the claim to know goes beyond human capacity. But Austin's eagerness to protect the claim to know from amounting to a claim protected against coming to grief, seems to be what leads him in effect to turn away from his evident knowledge that human existence is inherently open to grief. Austin is the philosopher, after all, who endowed modern philosophy with the coherent topic of "Excuses," contributing permanent riches to the investigation of the concept of human action and the evaluation of human conduct; but in the present case he seems reluctant to regard the claim to know as a signal and pervasive human crossroads needing and open to excuse (or explanation: "I could have sworn the money was in the safe deposit vault," "Did I dream there was a letter?").

It is true that an unappeasable wish to know and an access to knowledge have from early on in human intellectual or imaginative history been singled out for unique roles in human tragedy and misery, as in Sophocles' *Oedipus Rex* and Moses' story of the expulsion from the Garden of Eden, not to mention Faust. So the issue of failure is not well captured in Austin's proposal that, if grief comes, in the case of a broken promise you can say "but you did promise" (it may actually matter to say so, there may still be time to do some good, to issue a stern reminder), but that in the case of collapsed knowledge you must say "so you did *not* know." This latter reproach can sometimes still be meant as a general reminder (you do, you know, have a tendency to thoughtlessness; try to be more aware, another time the stakes may be much higher), and indeed the reproach may be declared even when there has been no grief: you were lucky on this occasion, you were an hour off about the time of the departure, but the train just happened to be an hour late. But suppose the train had been roughly on time and because of your misinformation it left without your friend, hence without his having the chance to join the last hour of the journey with the love of his life, hoping to talk her out of going through with her conventional marriage. (Do I continue to see too many movies?) In that case even a perfect excuse is nothing; neither is a reasonable apology. The problem is that you cannot forgive yourself; you are *cursed with the knowledge* of your hand in an avoidable collapse (or unavoidable if the gods had determined to curse you this way). It isn't a matter of what you did not know, something perfectly clear to go over and repeat to yourself, something mercilessly, irremediably past. It is a matter of what you, irreversibly, did know – that the question here was of urgent importance; that you checked only your handwritten note to yourself after a phone call two days ago, not the published timetable – how far does responsibility extend, where are its rules?

Why is knowing singled out in this way? What is this sting of knowledge? Austin's linking of knowing and promising brushes each with the power of the other. Promising emphasizes an intimacy that the intellectual register of knowing, perhaps increasingly, wishes to escape. Reciprocally, knowing takes over an aspect of promising that Nietzsche formulates, not without prejudice, moved by a promise's defiance of nature, as "ordain[ing the future]" (Nietzsche 1967: 58). My example of the self-satisfied friend being casual about a time of departure smacks of this trust in the power, or magic, in knowing. I have a suggestion, in parting now, about how this happens, or, as Nietzsche puts things, what it betokens about a human organ or institution.

It is notable that when philosophy refigured itself in the light of the scientific revolution of the seventeenth century, the question of the origin and nature of human knowledge (sometimes spelled understanding, sometimes reason), of its kinds and its limits, became European philosophy's fundamental subject of its modern reign, extending through the eighteenth century. It remains true of the dominant strain of English-speaking philosophy until the present, but not, after Hegel, on the continent of Europe. I note two consequences of this cataclysmic turn to epistemology. One consequence is almost too obvious to mention, I mean the loosening, or souring, of the relation between philosophy and theology. The other consequence is equally obvious but so far as I know has not received much, if any, deliberate study, I mean the fact that epistemology with respect to material things became philosophy's first and founding occupation, rather leaving the knowledge of oneself and of others to take care of themselves. I mean this observation, with whatever supplementary qualifications are necessary to make it sufficiently accurate, to be uncontroversial. (This again will not be true in German philosophy after Hegel.)

What most specifically I wish to call attention to in parting now is a further consequence of this dominance of the knowledge concerning material things, true still of Austin's wonderfully original and inventive essay "Other Minds." I mean the consequence that knowing and knowledge become conceived as projects, for example as the amassing of collections (of things or of facts), or the construction of experiments. (I take Nietzsche to be registering something of the sort just after his opening declaration of the *Genealogy* that we are unknown to ourselves, we men of knowledge, flying away from ourselves, as if uninterested in ourselves, to "the beehives of our knowledge," revealing that "there is one thing alone we really care about from the heart – "bringing something home" (Nietzsche 1967: 15), as if otherwise we live impractically, in emptiness.) It becomes, as it were, only natural, somehow imperative, to take the philosophical problem of knowledge to be "What do I know?," "What do I (we) *really* know?," "How much can I know or actually see?" Questions in the opposite direction, call it passive, are "Am I known?", "To whom and to what extent am I known?," "To what extent, and to whom, can I, or should I, or dare I, make myself known?" These questions are, in such an environment, unnoticed or awkward or impertinent to philosophical inquiry.

Not unnoticed, or impertinent, however, to Montaigne or in a while to Rousseau or to Emerson – or dare I say? – to Augustine or to Luther. On Luther's account of things, in which the Mass is a promise, your acceptance of this promise is transformative of yourself. Does philosophy – ought it or may it responsibly – care about these outliers of confession? Might it have mattered if Austin had suggested a relation, in addition to "I promise," between saying "I know" and saying "I confess"? Here the connection is that each in its way may have to be *extracted*. This piece of Wittgensteinian "grammar" should attract moral attention also to the one *to whom* such words are given. What is the desire to hear – to know by hearing? The will to power at least as readily or eagerly expresses itself passively as well as actively. The necessity for passiveness, with passion, in knowing, is instanced in Nietzsche's Preface to the *Genealogy* where he cautions:

> Regarding my *Zarathustra*, I do not allow that anyone *knows* that book who has not at some time been profoundly *wounded* and at some time profoundly *delighted* by every word in it.
> (Nietzsche 1967: 12, emphases added)

I seem to be suggesting not only that philosophy has unfinished business in working out its relation to science, but as well that this accompanies unfinished business in working out its relation to theology. In the Vintage edition combining Walter Kaufmann's translations of the *Genealogy* and *Ecco Homo*, Kaufmann includes with his translation of the latter an Appendix of variants from earlier drafts. I quote a sentence from each of the two paragraphs of the opening discarded variant. First:

> Emerson with his essays has been a good friend and cheered me up even in black periods: he contains so much skepsis, so many 'possibilities' that even virtue achieves esprit in his writings. A unique case!
> (Nietzsche 1967: 339)

Second:

> In cases in which I find it necessary to recuperate quickly from a base impression – for example, because for the sake of my critique of Christianity I had to breathe all too long the swampy air of the

apostle Paul – a few pages of Petronius suffice me as a *heroic* remedy, and immediately I am well again.

(Nietzsche 1967: 340)

I quote the notice of Emerson mostly for its cheer but also as a reminder to those who know of Nietzsche's regard for Emerson of its explicitness and tenderness. I note the reference to Saint Paul not because one is likely to underrate Nietzsche's sense that the struggle for philosophy continued to demand with every breath the struggle against theology (as well as against metaphysics), but because Paul, unforgettably to my mind, in one of his endlessly quoted passages, acknowledges religion's struggle against the despair of being known, of the capacity to make oneself known. From First Corinthians 13: "For now we see through a glass, darkly, but then face to face: now I know in part; but then shall I know even as also I am known." The second, echoing sentence places first, to my ear, my acknowledging of faith in being known (not merely "in part," prejudicially) as the condition of my acknowledging without stint the existence of another, offering my vulnerability, my exposure to this knowledge.

I want philosophy to be interested in this order of things, able to learn from it. The first sentence – "For now we see through a glass, darkly, but then face to face" – given its crushing over-familiarity to us – should not blind us to the sound of it as seeming merely a hasty, or say literary, summary of Cartesian skepticism, with its knowing air of absolute separation between our state now and our state then. I want theology to be interested in philosophy's willingness to maintain, however transformed, its perplexity over the possibility of skepticism, hence in the possibility that a *finite* face can happen to inspire my undeniable consciousness that I am known (whether in part or as a whole need not arise, it is neither here nor there, neither only now nor just then). Call the life of skepticism the willingness for the unpredictable oscillations of knowledge and ignorance, or say rather the perpetual arising, or wresting, of knowledge out of ignorance, of acknowledgment out of denial. In the absence of such willingness, the destructiveness internal to perfectionism, its confrontation of our present standing, hence the risk that its aspiration will not find its way, remain fatally ignored.

Notes

1 This piece originated in a panel on Nietzschean perfectionism organized by James Conant for the 2008 Christmas meetings of the American Philosophical Association in Philadelphia. I was given the role of commenting on the papers of the two other panelists, Stephen Mulhall and Paul Franks. Because of family medical emergencies, Conant was unable to attend the meetings, and Paul Franks could not complete his contribution in time for me to comment on it, which I hope to do on another occasion. My solution was to use the first half of my time to

comment on Mulhall's text and, learning from Franks that his paper was to be focused on the *Genealogy of Morals*, to use the second half of my time to begin working out a link between the *Genealogy* and J. L. Austin's essay "Other Minds" that has drawn my attention in the past but which I had never tried exploring with what seemed to me sufficiently rewarding results. The resulting text turns out to break certain new ground for me. I dedicate it to Hilary Putnam as a grateful nod to his exploratory and liberating spirit.

2 It was some years ago that I claimed for Emerson that he invented something I there named the "tragic essay."

3 [Editor's note:] Cavell is responding to Mulhall (2012) where, in turn, Mulhall discusses, among other things, Cavell (1994).

4 The clue for me here, on learning from Paul Franks that he would be for our panel considering particularly *On the Genealogy of Morals*, hence on my returning to that text, became my recurring sense of that work as proposing that this genealogy – that which creates or provides the necessary conditions for a moral life, say, for self-confrontation – is the human animal's coming into the possession of language, human speech.

Bibliography

Austin, J. L. (1956) "A Plea for Excuses," *Proceedings of the Aristotelian Society*, New Series, 57: 1–30.

——(1979) "Other Minds," in *Philosophical Papers*, 3rd edn, Oxford: Clarendon Press, 76–116.

Cavell, Stanley (1979) *The Claim of Reason: Wittgenstein, Skepticism, Morality, and Tragedy*, Oxford: Oxford University Press.

——(1990) *Conditions Handsome and Unhandsome: The Constitution of Emersonian Perfectionism*, La Salle, IL: Open Court.

——(1994) *A Pitch of Philosophy: Autobiographical Exercises*, Cambridge, MA: Harvard University Press.

——(2005) *Cities of words: pedagogical letters on a register of the moral life*, Cambridge, MA: Harvard University Press.

Descartes, René (2009) *Meditations on First Philosophy*, New York: Classic Books of America.

Emerson, Ralph Waldo (1884) "Experience," in *Essays: Second Series*, Boston: Munroe.

——(1881) "Self-Reliance," in *Essays: Second Series*, Boston: Munroe.

Mullhall, Stephen (2012) "Orchestral Metaphysics: *The Birth of Tragedy* between Drama, Opera and Philosophy," in Daniel Came (ed.), *Nietzsche and Art*, Cambridge: Cambridge University Press.

Nietzsche, F. (1999) *The Birth of Tragedy*, ed. R. Geuss and R. Speirs, trans. R. Speirs, Cambridge: Cambridge University Press.

——(1967) *On the Genealogy of Morals* and *Ecco Homo*, trans. Walter Kaufmann and R. J. Hollingdale, New York: Random House.

——(1973) *Beyond Good and Evil*, trans. R. J. Hollingdale, London: Penguin Books.

——(1997) *Untimely Mediations*, ed. D. Breazeal, trans. R. J. Hollingdale, Cambridge: Cambridge University Press

Wittgenstein, L. (1953) *Philosophical Investigations*, Oxford: Blackwell.

INDEX

2N2C (no non-causal contribution thesis) 67

abduction 109, 113–14
abstract entities 31, 99n4, 185
acceptance-behavior 173n26
accommodation, as dialectical process 60
accommodation conditions: definition of 58–59; and partial denotation 60; and social practice 72
accommodationism: applicability of 61; and causal structures 67, 79; and efforts at explanation 70; and error 73–74; intentions and purposes in 66; key features of 61–62; natural kinds and reference in 58–60, 63; and reductionism 64; *see also* materialist accomodationism
agent's point of view 250
Allbritton, Rogers 22–23, 95
analytic–synthetic distinction: and evaluation of beliefs 159–60; and fact–value dichotomy 241; methodological relevance of 150, 158, 160–61, 169; Putnam's criticism of 9, 145–47, 162; Quine's rejection of 151, 155; successor definition to 147–49, 179
analyticity: Putnam on 8, 148, 170n3; Quine's attack on 9, 149
anti-individualism 12, 265–66, 268

anti-realism: bivalence 42–43, 53, 74–75, 78; botany, anti-realist approach to 51; epistemic arguments for 109; Putnam's critique of 101–2, 222; and scientific realism 22–23
anti-reductionism 6, 39, 46, 48, 52
apperceptions 14, 349, 352–54, 356–57
apriori–aposteriori distinction 147, 155, 168–69
apriority: contextual 167–68; identification of 145; and justification 164, 174–75n41; necessary choices in 146; Putnam's defense of 148, 155; Quine's deflation of 171n17
attributes, Quine on 185, 187
Austin, J. L.: influence on Putnam 5, 28, 325; and justification 247; and knowledge 372–73; and nature of humanity 364–69; and performative utterance 371; and philosophical method 369–70; and realism 133, 140
auxiliary statements, adjustment of 157, 160

beables 238–39
behaviorism 3, 47, 81
belief: and experience 152, 351–52, 354; formation of 132, 245, 337–38; and prediction 370–71; revisability of 147
belief systems: adjustments of 149, 157, 159; as bases for hypotheses 151
Bell, J. S. 232, 237–38
Benacerraf, Paul 3, 192
broad-spectrum notions 32

INDEX

Carnap, Rudolf: on empirical appraisal 146, 162; on fact 242–43; influence on Putnam 3, 6; on ontology 185; Putnam's disagreements with 9; and analytic–synthetic distinction 155, 170n7, 179–80; and conventionalism 148
Cartesian Theater 279, 281
Cartesianism 11, 25, 110, 114, 281, 374
causation: conceptual access to 70; and non-reductionist materialism 71
cause, total 50, 68–69
Cavell, Stanley: definition of philosophy 14, 30; as pragmatist 35; and external world 132–33; and Putnam's readings 5
Chomsky, Noam 2–3
Churchland, Paul 313n18
Churchman, C. West 33
cognitive capacities 77, 341
cognitivism, relative 242
coherentism 351
color: asymmetry in 292–93, 298; interpersonal comparisons of 282–83; language 284–85, 287–90, 292, 298; properties of 278, 280; realism 275; similarity relations in 290–91
color vision: in animals 357n2; physiology of 289, 299–301, 311; Putnam on 356
common sense: as common belief 131–33; conceptions of 127–28; and judgment 136–38; Moore on 130–31; Putnam's portrayal of 128–29, 198, 208; as quietism 133–34
commonsense realism: and epistemic position 8, 25; and observables 104; Putnam's use of term 20, 127–29; as successor to Naïve Realism 5
concepts: Frege's notion of 332; histories of 208, 210; and images 327–30; limits of 208; and perception 342–43; thick 240–43, 245, 247, 251–52, 254n4; vagueness of 241
conceptual capacities: and experience 336, 342–44; and the non-conceptual 334–35; and recognition capacities 327–31, 333, 340, 345, 347–48
conceptual pluralism 10, 29–30, 206, 244

conceptual relativity: and conceptual pluralism 29–30; denial of 27, 221; in mathematical physics 28; and metaphysical realism 196, 221; Putnam on 8, 10, 23–24, 45–46, 196
conceptual schemes: as interface 26; and objects 40–41, 44–45, 111, 196; representational function of 86; and truth 207, 210, 220–21
Conceptualism 352, 354
confirmation holism 151, 155
confirmation skepticism 149, 159
consensus, and truth 220
consequentialism 78, 85
constructivism: and ontological relativity 7, 10; Putnam on 102, 111–12, 114
conventionalism 146–49, 161, 165, 170n3
correspondence theory of truth: and metaphysical realism 7, 40, 42, 114; and One True Theory 244; pragmatist critiques of 85–86; Putnam's rejection of 97–99; and Realism 104–5, 107, 113; vagueness of 32
counterfactuals 73, 124, 235, 350
cultures, ethical life of 251–52

Davis, Martin 3
de Gaynesford, Maximilian 21, 24
deduction, theory of 185–86
default reasonability 174n35
demanding conception 343–45, 355
denotational refinement 60–61, 80
Descartes, René 30, 352, 368, 370
Descriptivism 4
Devitt, Michael, debate with Putnam 7
Dewey, John: theory of inquiry 253; on truth 96, 219–20; on values 11; and pluralism 205; and rationality of animals 356
dichotomized thinking 1
direct realism 128–32, 135–36, 138
disciplinary matrices: accomodation demands of 58–59, 66; inferential architecture of 79–80; natural kinds and reference in 62
disjunctivism 319, 353
disquotation 97–98, 105, 267
The Drang 323–25
Duhemian holism 155–59, 161–62, 166

377

INDEX

Duhemian impliers 156, 160, 162, 164–69
Dummett, Michael: Devitt's critique of 112–15; influence on Putnam 4; on perception 324–25; Putnam on 101, 328–29

economics 57, 254
Emerson, Ralph Waldo: on Intuition and Tuition 361–62, 364; on meaning of human existence 363; and perfectionism 361–62, 364
emotivism 241, 250
empirical equivalence 158–59, 161, 164, 166, 169
empirical evidence, and beliefs 162
empirical knowledge 146–47, 151–52
empirical sensitivity 149
empirical significance, unit of 151
empiricism: and analytic–synthetic distinction 155; constructive 22; and conventionalism 161; minimal 351–52; Quine's brand of 150, 158
epistemic access condition: definition of 58; and efforts to explain 70; and partial denotation 60; and social practice 72
epistemic evaluation 124, 148
epistemic priorities, distinction of 148–49, 161
epistemic reliability 55, 60, 63, 86
epistemic situation, Cartesian conception of 25
epistemic special status: and holism 155; and linguistic stipulations 146–47; of principles 164–66, 179; in realism 109–10
epistemic value: judgments of 240–41, 245, 247, 249–50; and realism 104, 113, 123
epistemology: naturalizing 155; turn to 372
equivalence thesis 105, 115n9
essentialism 109, 115n1
ethical concepts 240–41, 252
ethical judgements 240–41, 245, 247, 251, 257
ethical terms, semantics of 96
ethics: and human interests 96; objectivity of 240, 250; and ontology 46, 48–49, 78; pluralism in 84–85; Putnam on 8, 19–20, 78; as world-involving practice 245

Ethics without Ontology 9, 11, 190, 240, 243
evaluation, and description 34
evidential indistinguishability 158–59, 161, 164, 166, 169
existence dimension 103–4, 114
existential quantifier 194–95, 197
experience: conceptualization of 27, 330, 344–45, 349–50, 354; epistemic problems with 312n11; intentional contents of 285–86, 288, 296; interpersonal comparisons of 307–8; Kantian notion of 342–43, 345, 348; and language 348; modes of 13; objects of 13, 327; phenomenal character of 286, 291, 310–11, 319–20; qualitative character of 308, 320; unconceptualized 353–54
experiential states 13, 275, 283
explanatory power 70, 111
explanatory value 138, 187
externalism: and mind 264–66; semantic 12, 24, 264, 266; use of term 263

fact: empiricist notion of 242–43; objectivity of 247–48; triple entanglement of 28, 33
fact–value dichotomy: and ethics 240–42; Putnam's argument against 11, 98, 220, 253–54
fallibilism 9, 147, 150, 180–81, 208
falsification, ambiguity of 151, 153, 159
Feigl, Herbert 3
Fig-Leaf Realism 103, 111
Fine, Arthur 70–71, 106, 110
flourishing 78
Fodor, Jerry 325
Foucault, Michel 208
foundationalism 73–74
framework principles 164, 179, 354, 358n1
freedom, kinds of 108
Frege, Gottlob: on thought 331–32, 338; and color language 286–88; and correspondence 32; and objects 193, 355–57
Frege–Schlick view 291, 307
functionalism: and inverted spectrum hypothesis 295, 297, 306, 314n24; in philosophy of mind 22; Putnam on 3, 24–25; and qualia 313–14n18

INDEX

Gifford lectures 5
Gödel's incompleteness theorem 194
God's Eye View: attributed to realism 102, 114; and model theoretic argument 322; Putnam's rejection of 7, 110, 209, 221–22
Goodman, Nelson: Putnam's engagement with 95, 209, 211–13, 219, 222–23; and knowledge 216; and pluralism 10
goodness 48–49, 78–79, 84, 214
Grice, Paul 34

Harrison, Bernard 292
Hempel, C. G. 3
Hilbert's Tenth Problem 3
history: foliation-dependent 11, 237–38; Putnam on 208
Hitler, Adolf 19–20
holism: and analytic–synthetic distinction 147–49, 154–55, 161; and logical knowledge 189; as methodological constraint 9; Quine on 150–54; and underdetermination 174n40
homology 72–73, 82
Horwich, Paul 279, 281–82
HPC (homeostatic property cluster) 53, 59–60, 74–75, 78–81, 84
Hume, David 211, 242
hypersurfaces 229–35
hypotheses: empirical consequences of 160; evaluation of 147, 150–51, 153–54, 159–60; and observation 148, 152, 245; revision of 156–57; theoretical 151, 168, 171n12
hypotheticity, degrees of 169
hypothetico-deductivism 158–59, 163, 172–73n25

idealism: and accomodationism 66; and constructivism 7; and existence dimension 103
idealization, and inductive practices 73–74
ideology 27, 68, 80–84, 221
idiolects 263–64
ignoratio elenchi 101, 112, 114–15
imagination, deanthropomorphization of 211
immunizability 154, 156

impressions: and apperceptions 14, 349, 352–53; and beliefs 353–54; conceptualization of 347–48, 351; and experiences 348; and interface conception 133
independence dimension 103, 113–14, 122–23
indispensability arguments 6, 19, 185
induction: importance to mathematics of 180; and natural kinds 55–57, 74; reliability of 55, 73
inductive inference 55, 73
ineffability 285, 320, 321n1
inference, rules of 163, 193, 175n41
inferential architecture 57–58, 62, 80
inferential connections 152
inferential practices 56–58, 61–62, 80, 85–86
inquiry: democratization of 254; empirical 6, 39; limits of 51, 64, 73–74, 208; theory of 253
insight, representational theory of 86–87
intentional content 285–89
intentionality, in Putnam's work 1, 24–25
interface conception 128, 133, 341–42, 345, 352
internal realism 4; and conditional statements 124; lack of objectivity in 104; Putnam's critique of 5, 7–8, 26, 209, 322; Putnam's support for 4, 7, 10, 20–21, 111; Putnam's use of term 21–23, 99n1, 107; and truth 220–21; and verificationism 25
introspection: and concepts 280–81; observational model of 279–80
inverted spectrum hypothesis: and behavioral indistinguishability 292; dangerous case of 277–82, 285; intersubjective 300–301; intrasubjective 283, 293, 301–2; and memory 303–6; possibility of 288–89, 293–99; undetectable 314n22; Wittgenstein's kinds of 12–13, 276–77, 282–85
irrealism 223

Jacob, Pierre 287
James, William: influence on Putnam 209; on natural realism 26; on truth 207; on values 11; and perception

379

352–53; and pluralism 10, 205–6, 210; and Wittgenstein 214, 216
Judaism 11

Kant, Immanuel: on common sense 135–37; on conceptual capacities 336; metaphysics of 123; on perception 349; Putnam on 96; and nature of humanity 368; and objects 193
Kaplan, Abraham 33
Kaufmann, Walter 373
knowledge: perceptual acquisition of 343–44; philosophical inquiry into 362–63, 370–74
Kuhn, Thomas 66–67, 208

language: abstract entities in 31–33; and causal structures 60; and externalism 263; going on holiday 296; ideal 193; and mind 266; natural 9, 191, 193–94; in Nietszche 366, 375n4; and objects 346; ordinary *see* ordinary language; and perception 325; philosophy of 4, 254; and qualia 12–13, 284, 287, 292, 313n15; reference in 267; successful use of 85–86; theory of 110, 112
language games: differences among 215–16; operational constraints on 26
lebenswelt 206, 216
Lenin, Vladimir 112, 121, 123
life, human form of 215, 365, 367–68
linguistic legislation 54, 62, 146
linguistic reference 52, 263–68, 270
Locke, John, on natural kinds 55
logic: and construction of truth 249, 259–60; demarcation of 190; first-order 175, 188–89, 192–93, 195, 197; formal 87, 197, 364; intuitionist 25, 195; modal 183–84; propositional 185–86, 188–89
logical empiricism 47, 87, 145, 161
logical positivism: conception of science 6; Putnam's opposition to 1–3; Quine's inheritance from 158
logical relation, fundamental 332, 334, 338
Lorentz-invariance 230–32, 235, 237–38
Lorentz-transformations 225, 230, 237
Luther, Martin 373

macrophenomena 69
materialism: compositional approaches to 69–72; nonreductionist *see* non-reductionist materialism; Putnam's critique of 9
materialist accommodationism 61, 64, 66, 68, 74
mathematical knowledge 180, 193
mathematical logic 26, 33, 191, 193–94, 203
mathematical objects: existence of 184, 192–93; indispensability argument for 185; in quantum mechanics 238; vague 43
mathematical propositions, equivalence of 183–84
mathematical realism 6, 9
mathematical truths 3, 145, 172, 241
mathematics: epistemology of 179, 202; and metaphysical realism 184; philosophy of 9, 19, 22
Maxwellian electrodynamics 228, 238
McDowell, John 28, 34, 96
meaning: externalist approach to 12, 263–65; knowledge of 147; and use 131
The Meaning of the Concept of Probability in Application to Finite Sequences 2
measurement-event 231
memory, unreliability of 303–6
mental phenomena 51, 64–66, 71, 87
mental states: and externalism 265, 272; and inverted spectrum hypothesis 282–83; as plastic 3
mereological sums 10, 24, 27–28, 97, 196
meta-ethics 19, 85, 250, 254
meta-theory 189
metaphysical innocence 66–67
metaphysical inquiry 79–81
metaphysical materialism 39, 43, 46, 50, 74
metaphysical realism: and ethics 46, 78; features of 50–51; important doctrines of 40–42; materialist 50, 52–54, 78; and methodology 47–48; non-reductionist 49–50, 63–64, 68, 71, 77; objects in 184; as paradigm 103; Putnam's critique of 45, 75, 87, 102, 107–9; Putnam's use of phrase 21, 27–29, 39, 48, 68; and quantification 200n14; and Quine

194; and reductionism 6, 43, 46, 64–65; and scientific realism 7, 22, 70; and totality of forms 10; traditional formulations of 127; truth in 64, 72, 114
metaphysics: beyond meaning 117n26; empirical 79; empiricist critiques of 71–72; and methodology 46; objects in 197–98; Putnam on 96; and semantics 104, 106, 110, 113; use of term 139n6
methodological monism 155
Mill, John Stuart 55, 205, 366
mind: materialist conceptions of 81–82; philosophy of 3, 22; representational view of 7
mind–brain identity theory 3, 320
mind-dependence 44–45, 66–67, 103, 124
mind-independence (MI): and accomodationism 66; different sorts of 44–45; and mathematical objects 42; and metaphysical innocence 67; in metaphysical realism 40–41, 51, 64–65, 77; and Realism 105, 121–22; and reductionism 43
mind–world relationship: and Cartesianism 11–12; Putnam's slogan on 8, 25–26, 29, 96
minimum mutilation, maxim of 153
modal language 184, 199n4
model theoretic argument: and constructivism 111; critique of 102, 107, 114, 322; and determinateness of reference 53, 75; and metaphysical realism 45
modus tollens 151–52
Moore, G. E. 130, 138–39n3, 205, 216
moral image 216, 251–52, 257
moral judgments 240–41, 246, 248, 250, 252
moral phenomena 46, 78
moral realism 61, 78–79, 84
moral relativism 84–85, 242
moral skepticism 248–49
moral values 11, 245, 250, 252
morality, reflective 251
Morgenbesser, Sidney 225
Myth of the Given 345, 350, 353–54
Myth of the Human 365

Nagel, Ernest 3
Naïve Realism 5, 13, 320

naïveté, second 134
names, reference of 267
narratability 227–28, 231–32, 235, 237–38
natural kind terms: epistemic access condition of 76; and externalism 264, 272–73; ideological function of 83; lack of epistemic success 80–81; partial denotation of 60–61; and perception 267; vagueness of 59
natural kinds: definition of 53; accommodationist conception of 54–55, 62; and determinate reference 75–76; mind-independence of 65–66; naturalness of 55–58, 64–65, 67, 74; slogans for 54–55; as social constructions 52, 61–62, 77
natural realism, Putnam's work in 5, 8, 26
naturalism: Putnam on 244, 259; and realism 110–11
necessity: epistemic 170n2; logical 146, 169; objective 148
neo-Kantianism 66, 68
neo-rationalism 171n9
Newtonian mechanics 66, 227–28, 328
Nida-Rümelin, Martine 300–301
Nietzsche, Friedrich: on Emerson 363–64, 366, 373–74; on Greek theater 362–63, 365; on moral vocabulary 365–66; on promises 366–68, 370, 372
noetic pluralism 206
nominal essences 54–55, 116n17
nominalism: Putnam's attack on 185, 188; Quinean 186–90
non-cognitivism 85, 96, 241–43, 247–48, 250
non-reductionist materialism: defence against Putnam 52; as metaphysical 71; objects in 44; Putnam's critique of 40, 43, 46, 49–50, 68–69
Normality Principle 286–88, 297
norms, in Putnam's work 1

object language 188
objectivity: essential role of 1; without objects 249
objects: access to external 25–26; and beliefs 351; and concepts 332, 346; constitution of 123–25; intangible 99, 191, 202; knowledge of 192–93;

non-natural 249; nonexistent 197; Putnam's conception of 195–98; and quantifiers 195; and understanding 264
observation sentences: Carnap on 9, 243, 247; and justification 259; Quine on 152, 172n19, 173–74n32
occasionalism 51
ontological commitment 8–9, 96, 182–84, 186, 193, 199n12
ontological pluralism 45–46, 52
ontological relativity, Putnam on 7, 184, 195–96
ontology: Putnam's suspicion of 9, 53–54, 97; Quine on 182–83, 185, 191–92, 194; and representation 23; and scientific language 186–87
Oppenheim, Paul 3
ordinary language: experiential content of 279, 283–84, 287; and formal logic 364; and interpersonal comparison 290–91
ordinary language philosophy 364–65
OTT (One True Theory): in metaphysical realism 40, 43; as reductionist 45, 49, 68; science as converging towards 244

pain: non-conceptual understanding of 347–48; as physical process 3; reference of 279–80
paradigmatic judgements 241
paradigms, Kuhn on 66–67
paradoxes 258
partial denotation: and inferential architecture 80; in metaphysical realism 51, 63; and reference 53, 59
Peirce, Charles Sanders 207, 219–20
perception: and cognitive processing 322–25, 333–34, 338; conceptualization of 14, 351–52, 355; contents of 287; and judgment 326–27; and language 266–67; and morality 252–53; and the non-conceptual 335; objects of 12, 26, 280, 327, 346, 355; organs of 280; in philosophy 128–29, 136, 266, 320; Putnam on 12–13, 267–68, 325–26, 341; theory of 5, 138, 279
perceptual experiences: centrality of 12; conceptual content of 338–39, 341–42, 346, 351–55; correctness condition of 335–37; as internal states 336; of non-rational animals 342–43, 345; phenomenal quality of 13, 320, 348–50; and rationality 337
perfectionism 361, 364, 374
persuasion, irrational 34
philosophy: definitions of 14, 30; end of 30; Enlightenment reconfiguring of 372; and pluralism 216–17; practical import of 31, 34–35
philosophy of science: and fact–value dichotomy 254; logical positivism in 6; and methodology 46–47
physicalism: and qualia 281, 283, 312n12; and reductionism 87, 213
physics: best future 244; language of 29; natural kinds in 57; philosophy of 2–3, 19; prestige of 70; reductionism in 50, 87
Plato 216, 249, 361, 366, 368
pluralism: characteristics of 208, 216; history of 10, 205, 209; horizontal 207; and monism 212; Putnam on 206–7, 219; and science 213; vertical 207, 215; Wahl's definitions of 205–6
post-modernism, as hostile to science 88
pragmatism: American 10, 20, 28; and Darwinism 366; and fact–value dichotomy 246; life of 205; and pluralism 206, 208–9; and prediction 369–70; Putnam on 5, 33–34, 208–9, 219
predication 62–63, 75, 185–87
predictions, Austin on 369–70
presupposition, mutual 34
Prichard, H. A. 323–24
principles: as evidence 168; revision of 161–67
private arena model 279, 281
properties: phenomenal 282, 286–87; Quine on 185, 187
propositions, Quine on 185
protoconcepts 356
psychology: folk 174n37; methodology in 47; non-reductionism in 81–82
Putnam, Hilary: Boyd on 88; color vision of 290, 307–8, 319; criticism of Devitt 112; divisions of life 20; engagement with others' work 4; happiness in writing of 217; influence on Devitt 101–2; life of 2–3; political

activism of 11; prevailing themes of 1; publications of 3–4
Putnam, Samuel 2, 14n3
Putnam–Boyd argument 6
Pyrrhonian creatures 326–27, 336

qualia: acceptance of concept 26; and apperceptions 352–54; color spectrum arguments for 278, 281, 284, 288–89, 301, 311; functional role of 306; interpersonal comparison of 285, 288–93, 295, 307; observational model of 282; and perception 287, 353; Putnam on 141n2; and representationism 286; use of term 275–76
qualitative character, sameness of 320
qualitative contents 285–89
quantification: over mathematical and physical objects 193; and propositional logic 186–87, 190; theory of 188
quantum logic 22
quantum mechanics: and beables 238; and conceptual relativity 10–11; narratability in 228–29, 231–34; particles in 198; representations in 28–29; 'unromantic' interpretation of 237
Quine, Willard Van Orman: on analytic–synthetic distinction 145; on natural kinds 72, 77; Putnam's engagement with 2, 8–9, 182, 202; revisability passage 150, 180; symmetry-thesis of *see* symmetry-thesis; and ontological commitment 96–97; and quantification over sets 31

race, metaphysics of 80–83
rationality, Putnam on 208
real essences 55, 116n17
realism: anti-reductionist 45; committments of 65; and conceptual relativity 28, 33; as empirical 21; indirect 128–29, 132, 138; and knowledge of unobservables 47; mind-independence in 66–67; and paradigms 67; and pluralism 208; in Putnam's work 1, 5–8, 102, 106–7, 136–37; and reductionism 87–88; and semantics 102–3

Realism (as metaphysical doctrine): definition of 7, 105, 122; dimensions of 103–4, 114; and freedom 109; and One True Theory 107–8; Putnam's rejection of 136; and semantics 109–10, 112–13
Realism with a Human Face 207, 215
realist materialism 6
reality, aspects of 30–31
recognition capacities 329–34, 340
recurrent statements 166
reductionism: and ethics 48–49; James countering 209; rejection of 6, 46
reductionist physicalism 43–45
reference: accomodationist conception of 59–61, 63, 66, 73, 78, 85; causal theory of 42, 45, 49–50, 53, 63, 73–75; demonstrative 263, 266; determinateness of 53, 61, 75–77, 351; determiners of 264; inscrutability of 194–95, 198; and kinds 62; and meaning 270, 273; in metaphysical realism 63, 75; mind-independence of 66; objective 197–98; and perception 266–67; Putnam on 268
referential situations 60, 76
regulative ideas 208
relativity, understandings of 235
religion: James on 210–11, 222; philosophy and 14; philosophy and *see also* theology
representation: objective 268; theory of 107
representationism 286, 291, 308, 311n3, 320
research, moral judgments in 245–46
revisability: empirically induced 151; general 147–49, 151–52, 161, 165; symmetry of 156–57
Rorty, Richard 26, 30, 33, 110, 125n3, 248
RPC (reference is purely causal) 41–43

Saint Paul 373–74
science: epistemic values in 240–41, 245; epistemology of 87; and ethics 19–20; experimental 162, 259; impersonality of 211; language of 121, 193–94, 243; mature 35, 95; method of 63, 215, 370; morality in 245–46; and philosophy 373 (*see also*

philosophy of science); Realism on 5–6, 104; reference relation in 63; 'special' 50–51, 70–71; vague definitions in 59
scientific image 196
scientific judgments, and fact–value dichotomy 243
scientific justification 148
scientific realism: as empirical 22–23; metaphysical versions of 71; and methodology 47–48; and natural kinds 55; 'no miracle' argument for 6–7; Putnam's use of term 21–22, 95; and unobservables 104
scientism 102
Scriven, Michael 3
Sellars, Wilfrid 3, 30, 196, 222
semantics: context-sensitive 258; and metaphysics 106; and realism 7, 110, 123; referential 83
Sen, Amartya 254
sense-data 25–26, 266
sense-making 137
sensibility 334, 343–44, 346
sentences: and logic 185–86, 188, 191; necessary 9; *see also* observation sentences
set theory 43, 184, 194, 202
Shoemaker, Sydney 279, 285–86, 302, 306–9
similarity, intentional and qualitative 285, 307
simultaneity, hypersurfaces of 234–35
skepticism: and accomodationism 74; Cavell on 206–7; and common sense 132; countering 248, 250, 257–59; and justification 247–48; and metaphysical realism 72
social constructions 52, 61, 67–68, 77, 80–82, 89n5
social practices: criticism of 84; metaphysical innocence of 66–67
sociobiology 82
Socrates 242, 254, 365
space, relational theory of 308–9
spins 29, 226, 233–35, 239
Stalnaker, Robert 292, 306–10
states of affairs 31–33
stereotypes 82, 268–69, 273
Strassler, Matt 23
subjectivity, affectation of 130
substitutional quantifier 195

symmetry-thesis 156–61, 169, 180
sympathy 253, 264
synonymy 187

Tamulka, Roderich 232, 238
Tarski, Alfred, T-schema of 41
tautology 98, 191
temporality 205, 208
theology 312, 372–74
theory: evaluation of 163–64; ideal 7, 107, 221; and ontological commitment 183
theory/observation distinction 163, 173–74n32
'third enlightenment' 254
thoughts, generality of 331–32
The Threefold Cord: common sense in 127–28, 133, 140–41; and commonsense realism 356; disquotation in 97; and internal realism 322
translation practice 97, 351
TRNE (truth is radically non-epistemic) 41–43
truth: accomodationist conception of 61, 86; analytic 148; conceptual 9, 180; correspondence theory of *see* correspondence theory of truth; disquotational view of 32; epistemic accounts of 41, 45, 52, 72, 113; and goodness 214; Pragmatist theories of 96, 207, 219–20; and realism 65–66, 104–5; scientific 71; semantical conception of 203; Tarski's theory of 115n9, 199n6, 203; in virtue of language 147; in virtue of meaning 145
truth values: in metaphysical realism 42; of thick ethical concepts 243
twin-earth methodology 269–70, 274

underdetermination 159, 161, 163, 169
understanding 264, 273
univocality 96, 99n4, 194–95, 197
unobservables, knowledge of 47, 71
utilitarianism 48, 216, 254n6
utterance, performative 369, 371

validity 188–91, 203, 260
value judgments: cross-cultural 242; and factual claims 246–47; naturalist opposition to 245; objectivity of 11, 248–49, 253

values: non-ethical 241; in Putnam's work 1, 241; 'queerness' of 248–49
verifiability 220
verificationism 27, 47, 109, 221, 223n3, 260
vision, and awareness 323, 334
visual experience: and cognitive processing 324, 326–27, 335–36; and inverted spectrum hypothesis 300; localization of 313n13; phenomenal quality of 320
visual system, 'crossed' 299, 301

Wahl, Jean 205–6, 216
wave-functions: as beables 238; collapse of 230–32; evolution of 233–34, 239; and possible worlds 228–30; under Lorentz-transformations 225–27

White, Morton 2, 34
Williams, Bernard 243–44
Wittgenstein, Ludwig: beetle in a box passage 287, 313n17; Cavell's reading of 14; on common sense 128–31, 133–35, 140–41; on inverted spectrum hypothesis 276–78, 301–2; on language 28, 364, 366; on mathematics 191–92; Putnam's readings of 4, 223; on qualia 12–13; and end of philosophy 30; and pluralism 10, 214–16
words, ethical uses of 241
world-involving abilities 25, 32
world-involving practices 244–45
worlds: absolute conception of 244; external 132; multiple 212–13; narratable *see* narratability